JOSÉ FERRER

HOLLYWOOD LEGENDS SERIES
CARL ROLLYSON, GENERAL EDITOR

JOSÉ FERRER

SUCCESS AND SURVIVAL

MIKE PEROS

University Press of Mississippi • Jackson

The University Press of Mississippi is the scholarly publishing agency of the
Mississippi Institutions of Higher Learning: Alcorn State University,
Delta State University, Jackson State University, Mississippi State University,
Mississippi University for Women, Mississippi Valley State University,
University of Mississippi, and University of Southern Mississippi.

Designed by Peter D. Halverson

www.upress.state.ms.us

The University Press of Mississippi is a member of
the Association of University Presses.

Photographs courtesy of Mike Peros unless otherwise noted
Frontis photograph: TCD/Prod.DB / Alamy Stock Photo

First printing 2020

∞

Library of Congress Cataloging-in-Publication Data available
LCCN 2020014476
Hardback ISBN 978-1-4968-1662-7
Epub single ISBN 978-1-4968-3016-6
Epub institutional ISBN 978-1-4968-3015-9
PDF single ISBN 978-1-4968-3017-3
PDF institutional ISBN 978-1-4968-3018-0

British Library Cataloging-in-Publication Data available

For my parents, George and Tessie Peros

CONTENTS

Why José Ferrer?

HOW DID JOSÉ FERRER GO FROM WINNING THE 1950 BEST ACTOR OSCAR for *Cyrano de Bergerac* to headlining the 1978 release *Dracula's Dog*? I grant you the question isn't as lyrical as "Do you know the way to San José?" but I remember pondering this in the summer of 1978. I asked myself: were parts befitting Ferrer's stature not available? Did he need the money? Would I read in the tabloids that he was reduced to accepting any part he could get (like a latter-day Bela Lugosi)? Soon after I had seen Ferrer's name headlining *Dracula's Dog* (a film I did not see on its initial release), I remember paying good money (three dollars) to see the newest Irwin Allen disaster film. It was 1978's *The Swarm*, and I had seen Ferrer's name among the many stars on the very populated poster. Alas, not only was the movie pretty poor, but Ferrer's appearance amounted to a virtual "die-on"—soon after he appears, spouting some inane and hyperbolic dialogue, he falls victim to the killer bees.

At age eighteen, I was already an admirer of José Ferrer's work, having seen several of his films, among them *The Caine Mutiny*, *Nine Hours to Rama*, and *Enter Laughing*. Prior to the advent of Turner Classic Movies, these films could be regularly seen on the many commercial stations that New York had as I was growing up in the 1970s. One indelible memory was that of seeing *Cyrano* on WOR-TV (Channel Nine), especially since that channel would occasionally present films unedited, with only one commercial break. *Cyrano* was one such film, and Ferrer's depiction of Cyrano's wit, heroism, integrity, and self-sacrifice moved me then, and continues to impress. Even now, when I show the film to my English classes at Bishop Loughlin High School, my wary students—who admittedly are not receptive to films that are not in color—will allow the romance and heroism of *Cyrano* to melt their hearts.

Back in 1978, when I was contemplating what I perceived was the plight of José Ferrer, I was not yet ready to write a book (or, for that matter, even an article). Years later, after I completed my first book *Dan Duryea: Heel with a Heart*, I was considering what my next project would be. It occurred to me (after scouring various book and publishing sites) that there had never been a biography about José Ferrer. To my eyes, this seemed like a grievous oversight, since the most cursory research revealed that Ferrer not only had a lengthy career on film but, preceding that, he had established himself as an actor/producer/director on the Broadway stage. In fact, the 1946 Broadway revival of *Cyrano de Bergerac* was the result of his convincing various skeptics that the classic play could—and should be done. The success of *Cyrano* resulted in his being offered roles and contracts with the major movie studios; throughout the 1950s, Ferrer would effectively shuttle between Broadway and films. In the early 1960s, when major film roles were in short supply, he would turn more and more to the stage and television—Ferrer would work in all three mediums up until his death in 1992.

Even so, there was no book about Ferrer. When I told friends and colleagues that my next project was a biography of Ferrer, they were dutifully impressed—but not in the way I had hoped. Many reactions were along the lines of: "He played Cyrano . . . wasn't he married to somebody famous . . . that's right, *Audrey Hepburn*!" Yes, people were confusing José Ferrer with Mel Ferrer—and strangely enough, although they were not related, they did have one major thing (among others) in common: Mel (going under the name Melchor) Ferrer directed José Ferrer in the stage production of *Cyrano*, and their lives professionally intersected occasionally throughout the years.

Oddly enough, the fact that people were misremembering or wrongly associating the two Ferrers strengthened my resolve to write this biography. In addition, as opposed to the stable and successful life of my first subject, Dan Duryea, José Ferrer led a much more colorful professional and personal existence. He was married five times (twice to singer Rosemary Clooney); he ran afoul of the House Un-American Activities Committee as a suspected communist in the early 1950s (at the height of his success); he was an eminently quotable presence, although in his early years he took no prisoners, exhibiting youthful arrogance and a disdain for any art form that wasn't the theater—which made it awkward when Ferrer later pursued film roles.

Finally, there was the slow, inexorable decline of his career—something that Ferrer frequently pointed out to interviewers as early as the mid-1960s. He would say often that he had his successes in the 1950s and then entered a freefall. Fueled by Ferrer's personal recollections, my book was originally going to be much more doom-laden—the original title was to have been *José Ferrer: Master of All but His Fate*. Rest assured, the book still contains plenty of conflict and darkness. However, as I would discover, during Ferrer's fallow periods he was rarely idle; quite often he would support new playwrights by starring in their plays (for little money) or directing and promoting the works of others. Ferrer would also try to be as much a father as he could to his six children (one by first wife, actress/acting teacher Uta Hagen; the other five with singer Rosemary Clooney), supporting them in their interests—even when these included the theater.

It also became clear that there are various reasons why actors take on parts that the viewers deem unworthy of their talents. Some (like the aforementioned Lugosi) might very well need the money and accept any role they can get. There are others who take on roles to finance more creative projects that they presumably control (such as John Cassavetes and Orson Welles). And then there are others who simply *need* to work. (How else does one explain the presence of Anthony Hopkins and Al Pacino in the lamentable 2015 *Misconduct*?) I include Ferrer in this category, and his multifaceted career, with its occasionally questionable choices, reflects all that—as you will no doubt see when you read further.

At the beginning of the research process, I visited several of the institutions that a biographer of any theatrical figure would consult. Of course, the University of Southern California's Cinema Arts Library was of immeasurable help, with the inestimable Ned Comstock guiding me in my research there, while also forwarding several helpful items (unsolicited, mind you) after my visit. The Margaret Herrick Library also contained several articles and clippings that were helpful in my research. The UCLA Film & Television Archive also proved to be of assistance, particularly with hard-to-find television and film titles (notably the *Hallmark Hall of Fame* broadcast of "Truman at Potsdam"). There was also a great deal of archival material to be found at the Katharine Cornell-Guthrie McLintic Special Collections Reading Room at the New York Public Library for the Performing Arts. Among these were not only an array of José Ferrer clippings and interviews, but also the Uta Hagen-Herbert Berghof Papers. These papers contained correspondence and interviews with valuable insights into Hagen's union with Ferrer.

I also discovered that, as with my previous subject, Dan Duryea, many of Ferrer's papers and personal memorabilia resided in one institution. In this case, the José Ferrer Collection could be found at the Howard Gottlieb Archival Research Center at Boston University. Laura Russo proved very helpful in furnishing both the collection and the time for me to peruse it.

While all these resources were extremely useful, I did want "the personal touch"—insights from people who knew Ferrer, worked with him, and were perhaps even related to him. I reached out to his son, the actor Miguel Ferrer, and while his representatives were kind enough to quickly get back to me, they also conveyed that Miguel probably would not cooperate. (It was later that I realized that I had probably contacted Ferrer while he was suffering from the cancer that would eventually take his life.) I did manage to locate Ferrer's widow, Stella, and his first daughter, Letitia (by first wife Uta Hagen), but they respectfully declined to be interviewed for this project. Needless to say, I was very close to giving up hope on contacting Ferrer's relations.

And then I sent a "private message" via Facebook to Terry Botwick, a film producer who is also the husband of Monsita Ferrer (one of José's daughters with Rosemary Clooney). Mr. Botwick, whom I did not previously know, was gracious enough to send me Monsita's contact information. This led to a happy correspondence which resulted in a delightful afternoon at Monsita's Southern California home, talking to her and her visiting sister, Maria. They are both intelligent, lovely ladies who adore their parents. They are also are not shy about discussing either their parents' strengths or shortcomings. Monsita and Maria put me in touch with their brother, Rafael Ferrer. Rafael regaled me with several stories of working with his father onstage (like his father, Rafael has an expressive, resonant voice—he is presently much in demand for voiceovers), providing me with many valuable insights into his father's character and convictions. (When I later spoke with their brother Gabriel, he encouraged me with the project but felt there was little he could add to what his siblings had already provided.)

In addition to Ferrer's immediate family, I am also grateful to the contributions from some of Ferrer's other relatives. I spoke to his (much younger) cousin, tennis champion Gigi Fernandez, and while she couldn't provide print-worthy stories, she did refer me to her uncle Charles Ferrer, who still lives in Puerto Rico and was happy to share how proud he was of his cousin José. Another of Ferrer's nephews, Carlos Campo, currently the president of Ashland University, wrote me a beautiful letter about his uncle, with many incisive observations about Ferrer, along with some poignant reflections about how important Ferrer was to him, both personally and professionally.

It was also satisfying to gather some reflections from some of Ferrer's colleagues such as Sean Young, Richard Thomas (who would refer to me as "the Ferrer guy"), Carol Lynley, Lee Harcourt Montgomery, Christopher Lloyd, and television producer Stuart Goodman. I was also fortunate to speak with director Jeff Kanew, who directed Ferrer in one film (*Natural Enemies*) and elicited one of the actor's better, more understated later performances. Author Luis Reyes provided thoughts about Ferrer's importance to the Latino community. Veteran actor (and friend) H. M. Wynant also provided an interesting anecdote about the young, brash Ferrer. Finally, I interviewed two performers who had worked with Ferrer on the 1966 national tour of *Man of La Mancha*. I am truly grateful to singer/producer Jana Robbins, who spoke to me after some initial reluctance (you'll see why later in the book) and turned out to be very insightful into Ferrer's professional and private personas. It was Jana who put me in touch with Tim Jerome, who understudied Ferrer during his run in *Man of La Mancha*. Tim spoke at great length about Ferrer's dedication, professionalism, and value as a mentor. Milly Barranger, author of a fine biography of director Margaret Webster, also provided some useful observations, while historian/raconteur David Del Valle was good enough to share his thoughts about collaborating with Mr. Ferrer on a documentary.

In addition to the aforementioned individuals, I would like to thank my friends and colleagues at Bishop Loughlin High School for their encouragement, including Assistant Principal Cecilia Gottsegen, Principal Edward Bolan, Brother Dennis Cronin, William Mason (historian par excellence and a darned good photographer), Ted Frank, Desta Moe, and the delightful members of the English Department, especially retired Chairperson Regina Bratichak. I must also thank Luis Montes, who is not only a fine Dean of Discipline, but possesses a technical expertise that helped me maximize my own middling computer competence.

Craig Gill, director of the University Press of Mississippi, has my undying gratitude, providing an abundance of support during the research and writing process. I'm also grateful to his assistant, Emily Bandy, and project manager Shane Gong Stewart. I would also like to extend my thanks to writer/editor Carl Rollyson and the other readers who contributed valuable input on how to improve my initial manuscript. I am indebted to both Pete Halverson and Jordan Nettles for all their work on the book design and photos. I also owe a great deal to my copyeditor, the very perceptive Peter Tonguette, who also brought his expertise to my earlier book.

Leila Salisbury, former director of the University Press of Mississippi, also proved extremely supportive in the early stages. I'd also like to acknowledge my former professor from Stony Brook University, Dr. Krin Gabbard. He may not remember this (many students have come and gone since), but he provided many encouraging words when I first became interested in writing about actors and film.

I would also like to acknowledge friends and family who supported me during the process. There are too many to name, but I hope you know how grateful I am. A few were particularly helpful including Dennis Bartok from the American Cinematheque; Vinny and Elizabeth Visco, for their insights into the Latino male; Dan "the Man" Madigan, who supplied a place to stay during some much-needed research. Of course, I owe a great deal of thanks to my supremely talented brothers, Steve and John, as well as John's partner, the versatile Jim Braswell, and my wonderful parents, George and Tessie Peros. They all provided both unconditional love and lodgings, whenever these were required. Finally, there's my wife, Barbara, who provided endless support, patience, and research assistance throughout the entire project. You have my eternal gratitude and love.

JOSÉ FERRER

CHAPTER 1

The Many Sides of José Ferrer

ONE OF ACADEMY AWARD-WINNER JOSÉ FERRER'S REGRETS WAS THAT he never appeared in burlesque or vaudeville. Those might have been the only theatrical feats that the prodigiously talented Ferrer didn't accomplish, since he began in the arts as a gifted young pianist, then became the leader of his college jazz band, and later, in both stage and subsequently film, found success as an actor, director, producer, and writer. Ferrer also loved to sing, and he achieved limited success as an opera singer in the early 1960s. The versatile Ferrer even appeared onstage in a ballet, dancing the role of the doctor in a 1963 production of *Coppelia* for the Royal Poinciana Playhouse. He also realized his dream of being a Broadway *musical* star as the lead in Noël Coward's *The Girl Who Came to Supper* (1963), and as a temporary replacement for Richard Kiley in the Broadway hit *Man of La Mancha* (1966), followed by a lengthy tour.

In his prime, from the mid-1940s to the late 1950s, José Ferrer was everywhere—he possessed energy enough for three men. Ferrer reached an artistic peak in 1952: he was simultaneously represented on Broadway by three plays that he had produced and directed, *Stalag 17*, *The Fourposter*, and *The Shrike* (the last of which he also starred in), while his movies from that year, *Moulin Rouge and Anything Can Happen*, were playing in neighborhood cinemas. At any given point in the early 1950s, Ferrer might be acting in a Broadway play, directing a play, preparing to direct a play, working on an adaptation, securing the rights to a play— and when Hollywood beckoned, he would add film roles to his already crowded theatrical output.

Ferrer was also the first actor to receive the US National Medal of Arts and the first Puerto Rican actor to be honored with his own commemorative stamp by the US Postal Service. It might be surprising to learn that Ferrer was born in Puerto Rico, especially since some of his most widely known roles were as French historical figures, including the poet/swordsman Cyrano de Bergerac, the artist Henri de Toulouse-Lautrec in *Moulin Rouge*, the Dauphin in *Joan of Arc*, and the unjustly persecuted Captain Dreyfus in *I Accuse!* Yet Ferrer was proud of his Puerto Rican heritage and conscious of his influence on his fellow Puerto Ricans. He was equally proud of being an American. Even so, Ferrer has never been the subject of a major work that encompassed both his celebrated career and turbulent life—until now.

It might be that in spite of (or maybe because of) his early success, many found it hard to warm to Ferrer. Although his friends knew him as "Joe," the public and several of his peers believed Ferrer was a little cold and arrogant, with an expertise that some felt was all show and little heart. Lyricist and future collaborator Alan Jay Lerner (Ferrer would direct Lerner's 1979 Broadway musical *Carmelina!*) wrote that while he admired Ferrer's talent, he felt that the actor "had the soul of a pistachio nut." Veteran character actor H. M. Wynant recalled Ferrer attending a 1949 Chicago production of *High Button Shoes* (Wynant was in the chorus) and after the performance, Ferrer summoned the cast and admonished them: "Don't get into the business unless you get in as a *star*—otherwise you'll be treated like shit!" These were not particularly encouraging words for then-chorus member Wynant, who had aspirations beyond the chorus which have since been more than realized.

Yet there were those who admired Ferrer both personally and professionally and believed him to be a prodigiously talented and magnanimous figure. Actress and producer Jean Dalrymple, who was one of the founding members of New York City Center, remembered how Ferrer volunteered to commit to a season of revivals in the early 1950s to help the struggling City Center overcome mounting financial pressures. Writer and director Garson Kanin thought "there was no limit to what he could do as an actor." Kanin's wife, Marian Seldes, who knew Ferrer as both actor and director, felt that "as a director, he made you believe he could do anything." Even Wynant said: "I consider him one of the major American actors and have the utmost respect for him and his work."

Ferrer is perhaps best known for *Cyrano de Bergerac*, in which he appeared as the flamboyant yet insecure swordsman and poet who is all nobility and self-sacrifice when it comes to satisfying his true love, Roxane, even supplying his handsome rival Christian with the words and voice needed to capture her affections. Delivering Rostand's lines in his expressive baritone, it was a career-defining performance for Ferrer, both in 1946, when he starred in the revival on Broadway (eclipsing Walter Hampden's fondly remembered earlier incarnation as Cyrano) and won the Tony Award, and in 1950, when he starred in the film version and won the Oscar for Best Actor. He also revisited the role in 1955 for a live television broadcast, and this performance garnered him an Emmy nomination, making Ferrer the first actor to be nominated for all three major acting awards for the same role.

Yet there is a great deal more to José Ferrer, both in theater and film, and away from the spotlight, too. Early in his career, he had been mentored by such theatrical luminaries as Jed Harris, Guthrie McClintic, and Joshua Logan, the last of whom was a schoolmate of Ferrer's at Princeton University. It was Logan who cast Ferrer in the 1940 revival of the low-comedy hit, *Charley's Aunt*, gaining both of them praise and making Ferrer a bona fide star. He might have continued as a comedy actor, but he was not content to do so. Ferrer always felt the need to stretch himself and his talents; his later wife Rosemary Clooney would say he didn't know how to tell himself "no." (As it turned out, that would apply to Ferrer in areas outside of professional life as well.) He co-directed an unsuccessful play called *Vickie*, and in 1943, succeeded Danny Kaye in Cole Porter's *Let's Face It*. His biggest theatrical triumph of that year would be as Iago in director Margaret Webster's production of *Othello*, a success both on Broadway and in its subsequent tour. He would also attract the attention of Hollywood, particularly from writer/director Billy Wilder, who was interested in hiring Ferrer to play the alcoholic writer in *The Lost Weekend*. Although Wilder wanted Ferrer, he didn't get the role, as Paramount and Wilder settled on actor Ray Milland, who was under contract to the studio at that time.

Ferrer's next stage triumph would be in *Cyrano*, which resulted in Hollywood courting *him*, and in 1948 he made his film debut as the Dauphin in *Joan of Arc* under the direction of Victor Fleming. He was nominated for an Oscar as Best Supporting Actor for his theatrical and entertaining performance, providing much-needed spark to the mostly lumbering proceedings. At this point, Ferrer's predominant passion was the theater, as he was either directing, adapting, or performing in classics by Chekhov and O'Neill. Ferrer would acquire a reputation as a theatrical dynamo—and it didn't hurt that many of his early ventures achieved success, including his turn as a philosophical older gentleman in *The Silver Whistle*.

Ferrer's theatrical career alone merits attention, particularly his fertile period from the mid-1940s through the late 1950s. In 1950, Ferrer directed and starred in a successful revival of *Twentieth Century* and immediately followed that with the hit *Stalag 17* (which he prepared while starring in *Twentieth Century*). His well-received staging of *The Fourposter* in 1952 segued into a darker exploration of marriage with *The Shrike*. Horton Foote's *The Chase*, directed by Ferrer, proved to be a commercial and artistic failure, but it reflected Ferrer's willingness to take on serious, socially relevant material, as he had done with his direction of the 1946 drama *Strange Fruit*, which addressed the topic of race relations through the story of a doomed interracial romance.

Although money was essential to Ferrer—as soon as he became rich and famous, he cultivated a lavish lifestyle complete with multiple residences and an appetite for the finer things—he was still capable of magnanimous gestures (a la *Cyrano*). Ferrer might turn down a role because it didn't come with the right price tag, but on two separate occasions, in 1948 and 1953, he would commit himself—for roughly $85 per week—to staging and starring in a series of shows for the then-struggling New York City Center. Ferrer's involvement in the 1953 season, which included revivals of *Cyrano* and *The Shrike*, assured the theater of its first profitable season.

Throughout this period of Ferrer's career, the critics were effusive in their praise of Ferrer, both as director and actor. As a director, reviewers praised his choice of material, his excellence with the actors, and the occasional innovative staging; as an actor, the critics generally focused on his rich, resonant baritone, which could be quite a flexible instrument, as he could utilize it to move you, amuse you, or even arouse you. If Ferrer and Cyrano are identified as one, it is because they both possessed sheer bravado and a willingness to test themselves. These passions could also lead them astray. In Cyrano's case, his loyalty to Roxane and his uncompromising nature come at a great personal cost. For Ferrer, his passions might lead him to alienate those who might otherwise employ him or cause emotional damage to those who had counted on his fidelity, both personally and professionally. It is this dichotomy, which I will return to later, that also makes Ferrer an ideal, if occasionally troubling, biographical subject.

As a director, Ferrer was primarily identified with his staging of dramas, but he could be quite adept (if sometimes a little heavy-handed) with his handling of comedy. In addition to his successful staging of *Twentieth Century*, Ferrer directed *My 3 Angels*, a Broadway hit in 1953 starring

Walter Slezak, in which three Devil's Island convicts, a hapless family, rapacious relations, and a helpful snake elicited gales of laughter from appreciative Broadway audiences. In 1958, Ferrer would direct (and co-write the libretto for) skilled farceur Tony Randall in *Oh, Captain!*, a musical remake of *The Captain's Paradise*.

During this prolific period, Ferrer would alternate between the stage and the more financially rewarding film work. He would be—with one notable exception—in fairly high demand for either acting or directing chores during most of the 1950s. Ferrer would win his one and only Oscar for reprising *Cyrano* for the screen, and would receive another nomination for his portrayal of the tormented artist Toulouse-Lautrec (as well as portraying the artist's demanding father) in John Huston's sumptuous 1952 production of *Moulin Rouge*. Ferrer impressed as the hopeful Georgian immigrant Giorgi Papashvily in *Anything Can Happen* (1952), the reluctant defense counsel Barney Greenwald in *The Caine Mutiny* (1954), and the composer Sigmund Romberg in the all-star 1954 musical biography *Deep in My Heart* (fulfilling another dream to sing—and dance somewhat—on screen).

Perhaps his only cinematic misstep in the early 1950s was when Ferrer bellowed and pontificated his way as a judgmental, intolerant would-be savior opposite party girl Rita Hayworth's *Miss Sadie Thompson*. Yet Ferrer's participation in this 1953 Columbia release was essential to his maintaining his status in Hollywood. Prior to this film, Ferrer had been called before the House Un-American Activities Committee, as he had been named as a suspected communist in the publication *Red Channels*. In May 1951, Ferrer testified twice before the committee. He chose not to plead the Fifth Amendment, instead electing to explain the causes he supported, the speeches he made, the meetings he attended—all while praising the work of HUAC. It was neither a triumphant nor disastrous appearance, but the fact that Ferrer was not "cleared" immediately would lead some producers to reconsider casting him and cause many on both sides of the political fence to picket him. This will be explored at length, as well as how Ferrer's involvement in *Miss Sadie Thompson* helped restore him to Hollywood's good graces.

Ferrer made his film directorial debut with the 1955 screen version of *The Shrike*, earning favorable notices both for his performance as well as his choice of June Allyson in an atypical role as the shrewish wife. (He also took some heat for softening the play's bleak ending.) His only commercially successful directorial effort in the 1950s was the 1955 fact-based World War II drama *The Cockleshell Heroes*. While the film received praise, especially for its suspenseful second half, Ferrer the director became involved in some post-production one-upmanship with the producers and departed abruptly. Ferrer would be granted a degree of autonomy for his 1950s films, but he was still at the producers' mercy when it came to final cut—a development that he would continually lament in interviews through the years. In 1956, director Ferrer and writer Al Morgan would adapt Morgan's novel *The Great Man*, making it an intelligent exploration of the darker side of both celebrity and the media. Ferrer would be applauded for enticing Ed Wynn into making his first dramatic appearance. In 1958, Ferrer directed and starred in the comedy *The High Cost of Loving* for Metro-Goldwyn-Mayer, then journeyed to England to make a film version of the Dreyfus scandal, *I Accuse!*, having been denied permission from the French government to shoot in France, where the events depicted in the film had actually taken place.

Although Ferrer was still enjoying some success in films, his stage fortunes took a gradual turn for the worse. In 1958, *Oh Captain!* did not become the long-running success its creators and investors (including Ferrer) had anticipated. Ferrer immediately followed that with *Edwin Booth*, but despite his performance, direction, as well as his showmanship in attempting to attract the public, the expected audiences failed to materialize. *The Andersonville Trial* was a qualified success on Broadway in 1959, despite the harsh subject matter regarding offenses and conditions at a Civil War prison camp. His 1959 production of *Juno* received middling notices and closed soon after its opening. Ferrer would say on numerous occasions that his career went into freefall after the 1950s. Although he still found employment as an actor, and even sporadically as a director, Ferrer would never again reach the heights of sustained excellence and activity he enjoyed in the 1950s.

Yet Ferrer persevered, trying to remain employable by always being the consummate professional; however, in interviews, he would unceasingly point out that he was mainly an actor for hire, without the creative freedom he had previously enjoyed. The 1950s and '60s were also a time when he tried to get his own projects underway, including an adaptation of *Death in Venice*. Ferrer's career would center mainly on film and television, both in low-to-medium budget efforts and in prestigious works from top-rank directors, including David Lean's *Lawrence of Arabia*, Stanley Kramer's *Ship of Fools*, and Billy Wilder's *Fedora*; he also acquitted himself nicely in Woody Allen's *A Midsummer Night's Sex Comedy*, both amusingly pontificating and gently moving as the aging scholar. Here Ferrer also was allowed to indulge his love of singing (although many would tell him it's an area where he could use improvement, he studied voice for many years). Projects like these did not come often enough, and his resume of the late 1960s through the 1990s consists of the occasional worthy effort offset by plenty of B-grade dramas, thrillers, and horror movies (of all kinds).

Ferrer did make time to return to the stage, but the results were variable. He finally landed a lead musical role on Broadway with 1963's *The Girl Who Came to Supper*, with music and lyrics by Noël Coward, but in spite of their efforts (and Florence Henderson as the Girl), the show did not become a hit nor the annuity that Coward was anticipating. His desire to be a Broadway musical star was better served when he took over the role of Cervantes/Don Quixote in *Man of La Mancha*, replacing Richard Kiley for two weeks on Broadway in 1966, before embarking on a successful tour and followed by another limited run on Broadway as Don Quixote.

There were also several directorial endeavors, but only a few of these were for Broadway or off-Broadway engagements. Ferrer directed an adaptation of Thomas Wolfe's work *The Web and the Rock* and the play *White Pelicans*, both for the Theater de Lys (to be renamed the Lucille Lortel Theater) and both critical and commercial failures. He also scored an off-Broadway triumph succeeding Elias Rabb in *A Life in the Theater*. Ferrer's final foray on Broadway was in 1979 as the director of *Carmelina*, a troubled Alan Jay Lerner musical adaptation of the 1968 movie *Buona Sera, Mrs. Campbell* that closed after a few performances. Toward the end of his life, Ferrer was cast as the lead in *Conversations with My Father* but had to withdraw because of illness. While his theatrical career had fallen from the heights he scaled in the 1950s, Ferrer rarely stopped working.

José Ferrer: Success and Survival not only addresses the meteoric rise and gradual descent of Ferrer's career but also the conflicting desires that led to several failed unions before his fifth and final marriage. His first marriage was in 1938 to the actress (and subsequent teacher and author) Uta Hagen. They met while onstage in summer stock, gave married life a chance, and produced a daughter. Ferrer and Hagen would also attempt to become a theatrical couple, not unlike Alfred Lunt and Lynn Fontanne, but a subsequent theatrical engagement would lead to their undoing. A very successful Broadway production of *Othello*, starring Paul Robeson (Othello), Ferrer (Iago), and Hagen (Desdemona), resulted in a national tour—and also sparked an affair between the married Robeson and Hagen. Seemingly unfazed by this, Ferrer, who had been seeing other women, began a relationship with the actress and dancer Phyllis

Hill. After Ferrer and Hagen divorced in 1948 (partly the result of Ferrer and his private detectives surprising Hagen and Robeson on Christmas Eve), Ferrer married Hill.

That marriage was also doomed, since Ferrer made no apologies for his time-consuming passions—even if these were only for creative fulfillment, they still led to constant separations from wife Phyllis, who was ensconced in their house in upstate New York (aside from taking the occasional small role in a Ferrer-directed play). It was during this period that he began alternating between Hollywood and Broadway, with little time to build, let alone maintain, a relationship. Not long after Hill and Ferrer separated in 1951, Ferrer was seeing the singer Rosemary Clooney; what began as a casual affair deepened, so that when Ferrer finally divorced Phyllis in 1953, he married Clooney a few days later.

Ferrer and Clooney clicked on several levels—at first. Both had achieved success in their respective fields; he was a natural teacher and she wanted to learn. Clooney and Ferrer both wanted to have a large family. They were also in the midst of successful careers, but Clooney put hers on hold and devoted much of her time to raising the ever-expanding brood. (Clooney and Ferrer would have five children between 1955 and 1961.) Ferrer also made few apologies for desiring the occasional companion outside the homestead, which led to confrontations, compromises, and eventual reconciliations, at least for a time. Clooney and Ferrer separated in 1961, but after their initial divorce became final in 1962, they began to see each other again; Clooney was there for moral support when Ferrer took on the musical *The Girl Who Came to Supper*. They reconciled and eventually remarried in 1965, but personal and professional difficulties, including their respective affairs, exacerbated an already tenuous relationship and they divorced (for good) in 1967.

Ferrer would again find some contentment in the mid-1970s with his fifth and final wife, Stella Magee, who had been Ferrer's personal secretary when he was filming in Europe in the early 1960s—and, as one will see later, had also been acquainted with Rosemary Clooney. Up until his death in 1992, Ferrer would shuttle between films and television, while also performing and directing onstage, usually far from Broadway; he would also later make his permanent residence in Florida. Ferrer received several honors during his lifetime, including an honorary doctorate from the University of Puerto Rico (1947) and his induction into the Theater Hall of Fame (1981). He also was the recipient of more honors posthumously, including becoming the first Puerto Rican actor to be honored on a postage stamp.

Ferrer was fearlessly versatile. Rosemary Clooney, as well as their daughter Monsita and son Rafael, would all say that he couldn't accept the word "no," so he would attempt to be the best in anything he tried, whether it was acting, directing, producing, or writing. Ferrer believed anyone could master anything so long as there was time to learn. For Ferrer, that included playing the piano, tennis, dancing, fencing, drawing, cooking, windsurfing, golf, and singing (including operatic stints in the 1960s).

Ferrer could be incredibly neglectful when it came to both his finances (which he professed to have little "feel" for) and relationships. He also fretted constantly that his current job would be the last, so that he could become intolerable during his bouts with unemployment—even if these periods were for a very short time. Ferrer could also be very generous, both with his time and talent. When Ferrer was in his seventies, he assumed creative control for the Coconut Grove Playhouse in Florida, accepting a token salary of $1 per year. He also never stopped being a champion of new authors, agreeing to star in promising works for minimal financial compensation.

Several current actors would remember Ferrer with affection. Christopher Lloyd viewed Ferrer as a mentor from their time in the play *White Pelicans*, while Richard Thomas, who worked with Ferrer and got to know him through the Players Club, believed that Ferrer was "one of the funniest men I've ever known" and an incredible storyteller. Maria, one of the five children Ferrer had with Rosemary Clooney, remembered her father as being "stupidly funny. He would do *anything* to make us laugh. We were in London at a white-tie dinner. There are dignitaries . . . he's conversing in French. And while all this is going on, he takes his napkin and makes little rabbit ears jumping across the table—just enough so *I* could see it! Because of his exterior, people don't understand how down to earth he was." *José Ferrer: Success and Survival* explores the many facets of Mr. Ferrer, an artist whose resilience enabled him to persevere through a lifetime's worth of triumphs and disappointments—and then some.

CHAPTER 2

From Puerto Rico to Princeton and Performance

IT WAS A GREAT SOURCE OF PRIDE THAT JOSÉ FERRER CAME FROM Puerto Rico—San Juan, to be precise. He was born José Vicente Ferrer de Otero y Cintron on January 8, 1912, in Santurce, a district in San Juan. The future actor/director was the son of wealthy, prominent parents. His father, Don Rafael Ferrer y Otero, was a lawyer, while his mother, Maria Providencia Cintron y Cintron, came from a family of plantation owners. The Ferrers were an aristocratic family, originally from Spain; this is indicated by Ferrer's full name reflecting the Spanish tradition of adding the name of the mother to that of the child. Don Rafael and Maria lived in Puerto Rico because of their widespread financial interests there, and later became naturalized citizens of the United States. José would try to downplay his family's wealth, saying, "I suppose there was money in the family . . . my father had a good law practice and there were plantations on my mother's side, but we weren't rolling in wealth." This would be disputed by his own daughter Monsita, who assured me, "They had enormous wealth . . . sugar cane, tons of property." When José was seven months old, he was taken to New York for an operation as he had been born with a soft palate. Had this been left untreated, José might have developed a speech impediment or experienced severe breathing difficulties.

When José was six years old, the family returned to New York. His father had been a graduate of St. John's College and later received his law degree from Syracuse University, while his mother Maria was an alumna of Sacred Heart College in Manhattanville, New York. Don Rafael and Maria felt that their children, including José and sisters Elvira and Leticia, should be educated in the United States. José attended Loyola High School; all three children were taught French, English, and Spanish. A voracious learner from an early age, José also enjoyed music and learned the piano. Their Aunt Monserrate lived with them for a time; she was Don Rafael's sister and an accomplished composer and pianist in her own right. Monserrate would help José develop his talent, and his exceptional abilities suggested a possible career as a concert pianist. (Ferrer's daughter would be named Monsita in honor of Monserrate).

José graduated from Loyola High School at the age of fourteen and applied to Princeton University when he was fifteen. Ferrer easily passed the entrance exams. He also told the dean that he spoke three languages and could compose symphony scores by ear. In response, Princeton recommended that he complete another year of preparation to acquire some seasoning (some might call it a "cooling-off" period). Ferrer spent that time in Switzerland at a fashionable, elite private school known as the Institut Le Rosey. It was one of the world's most expensive boarding schools, with the main campus in Rolle and the winter campus in Gstaad. Le Rosey would pride itself on its academic and athletic program; it also was known for its exemplary bilingual and bicultural education. Ferrer would later say that he learned some things at the school that proper young gentlemen weren't supposed to know. The young José also added to his linguistic abilities, picking up German and Italian, in addition to Spanish, English, and French.

For the sixteen-year-old José, 1928 would prove to be an important year. He would finally be admitted to Princeton—and his mother Maria would unexpectedly pass away. José's mother was an intelligent, adventurous woman, and she wanted her children to have these same attributes. As an affluent woman, it wouldn't have been unusual for Maria to walk into José's room (he was the oldest) and say, "I've always wanted to go to Rome for Easter," and then leave with young José at her side. Although they had a governess, Maria would travel without her husband, with only the children by her side—as well as her personal physician, as she had a heart condition and did not want to be too far from medical assistance.

It was Maria who wanted the children to speak French, so she hired a governess who was French. While the older José would give his father much of the credit for his subsequent love for learning, his mother's importance cannot be underestimated. Her passing left a void that José hoped his father could fill. José would attribute his energy and curiosity to his parents: "It comes from having a mother and father who gave me a tremendous education . . . they inculcated a thirst for knowledge, inquisitiveness . . . to be as good as you can be." Don Rafael would remarry three years later, to Carolina Garcia Fuya, with whom he had another child, Rafael, who became José's stepbrother, and would later attain fame as an artist himself.

At Princeton, Ferrer originally planned to focus on architecture. Although this was his intended course of study, the sixteen-year-old Ferrer, with his musical background and burgeoning flair for self-promotion, soon explored other avenues of academia—notably extracurricular. Borne of a desire to earn some money to supplement a small allowance, Ferrer formed a college band called José Ferrer and his Pied Pipers. Initially Ferrer's combo was a six-piece dance band, with Ferrer himself playing the piano. According to Ferrer, "I didn't know what I was doing . . . it was during the Depression when big orchestras weren't in demand. No one could afford them. We usually ended up playing at coming-out parties." None other than tall, accordion-playing classmate James Stewart was one of his vocalists (though anyone who has heard Stewart warble "Easy to Love" to a grimacing Eleanor Powell in 1938's *Born to Dance* would know singing was hardly his forte). There is at least one extant recording of José Ferrer and the Pied Pipers, done in 1931 in New York City at the Standard Sound Recording Corporation. It was a 78 rpm record of the song "Love Comes but Once," co-written by Ferrer and his bandmate Syd Wise, with a "vocal chorus by James Stewart."

The Pipers would vary in size over the years with as many as eighteen members at one point. "When the Depression hit," Ferrer would explain, "rich papas who couldn't afford Paul Whiteman hired us. We made a lot more dough than college boys should have in their pants." Ferrer led the band throughout his stay at Princeton, and his Pied Pipers would not only have engagements in New York, Philadelphia, and Washington, but internationally as well. In 1930, the band toured France, Italy, and Switzerland, and the following year, the Pipers were hired for a seven-day cruise. "I was very good with the stick. Leading the band was the best thing I did." Ferrer may well have been too good at it—ultimately at the expense of his studies. While his other classmates, such as Stewart, graduated in 1932, Ferrer had to remain another year to make up for classes lost to excessive musical merriment.

This extra year could well have been a blessing in disguise. Ferrer's flair for performing had caught the attention of the members of the

Princeton Triangle Club, which was the oldest collegiate musical comedy theater troupe in the United States. It also included among its members, such future theatrical mainstays as the aforementioned Stewart, Myron McCormick, as well as stage (and film) directors Joshua Logan and Bretaigne Windust. In his last year at Princeton, Bert Brush, president of the Triangle Club, asked Ferrer if he would play the lead in their annual student musical. According to Ferrer, "The head of the dramatic society tapped me on the shoulder and said, 'I think you're a born actor and I want you to play the lead in my new comedy show.'" After some mild protests along the line of "I can't act," Ferrer gave in: "Once I was in, I was hooked."

Though this was the story Ferrer gave to interviewers, it wasn't as simple as that. While he had been approached by Brush, Ferrer still had to audition, and he was granted this opportunity because Bert Brush was the president—and Ferrer's roommate. After his audition, Ferrer had gone to a movie and while in line, he heard some upperclassmen talking about him, specifically that they didn't like him and were just giving him a chance because of Bert. Ferrer would later tell his son Rafael: "I got so angry that when I did the callback, I full out 'let it go.' This was anger driven. Nothing to do with acting chops." Ferrer would be cast in the play, and son Rafael would feel this was essential to understanding his father: "The minute you tell him *no*, he's gonna do it." Classmate Logan was close to Ferrer in college and would later collaborate with him professionally; he recalled Ferrer as "far above most Princeton men in charm, talent, and cultivation. They resisted him like they would resist any exotic element. He never bowed down before the golden calves of Princeton and because of that he was an outstanding Princeton man."

Ferrer not only accepted the lead role of the valet—he also rewrote the book. The plot of *It's the Valet* consisted of a number of mistaken-identity elements that were mainstays of farce. When the show opened on December 14, 1932, audiences approved both of the show and the performance space, which was none other than the Metropolitan Opera House. Reviewers at the *New York Times* also caught the opening, with Ferrer earning special mention for playing the lead role "in the style of the Marx Brothers." There was one potential audience member that Ferrer could not persuade to attend. His father, Don Rafael, refused to see his son's theatrical debut, since he had a rather dim view of farce as a mode of artistic expression. Despite Ferrer's discomfort with his father's stance, the show's critical and popular success instilled in the young man the notion that architecture might not be his pathway to success.

Instead, maybe theater was the career path he should have pursued all along.

For the time being, Ferrer would continue his academic career. He graduated from Princeton in 1933 with a degree in architecture, but elected to alter his course of study when he began attending Columbia University: "I thought I'd be no good as an architect so I went to Columbia to study modern languages and become a college professor." Staying in New York City only confirmed Ferrer's feeling that the theatrical life was for him: "In New York I began to hang around with some theater people . . . the only thing that made any sense to me was to be an actor . . . architects were starving in 1933. Honors students were making $25 as draftsmen *if* they could get a job." Ferrer studied languages and even began his dissertation, but he never completed it. As Ferrer would later recall, in 1935, he was in a Greek restaurant in Greenwich Village with his friend and fellow Princeton alumnus Jimmy Stewart, where he told Stewart: "You're witnessing a great moment in a man's life, the moment of decision. I've just decided—I'm going to be an actor." That night he moved into the furnished room that Stewart was sharing with another Princeton alum, Myron McCormick.

Ferrer made his professional acting debut for the Periwinkle Players on Long Island, performing on their Long Island Sound showboat, the good ship *Periwinkle*. He then headed for Suffern, New York, to join a theatrical company that was run by Logan. Ferrer assumed a number of duties under Logan's direction, for minimal monetary compensation. He said, "They paid me $10 a week to kill myself. I was lucky to get three hours sleep a night. I drove a station wagon, picked up actors, delivered press releases." Although lacking remuneration, there were rewards of another kind; one of the stars Ferrer chauffeured was the actress Ruth Gordon, who would recommend him to Broadway legend-in-the-making, producer/director Jed Harris. In August 1935, Ferrer played a small role as a Roman sentinel in a production of *Caesar and Cleopatra*, starring Helen Hayes as Cleopatra. Hayes, a respected actress on both stage (*The Good Fairy, Mary of Scotland*) and screen (*A Farewell to Arms*), thought highly of Ferrer and subsequently recommended him to the esteemed Mr. Harris.

After a road company tour of the successful madcap Hollywood farce *Boy Meets Girl*, Ferrer made his Broadway debut in September 1935 as the Second Policeman in *A Slight Case of Murder*. Ferrer's onstage contribution consisted of one line: "What's going on here?" He also doubled as stage manager and chauffeur. (One can only speculate what today's theater unions would say about that.) The play reads as a fast-moving farce about a reforming racketeer dealing with a bevy of bodies, live and otherwise. It is also widely known today because of a successful 1938 film adaptation starring Edward G. Robinson lampooning his iconic gangster persona. Yet this Howard Lindsay and Russel Crouse concoction, populated by amusing Damon Runyon-esque characters, only managed to eke out a run of sixty-nine performances after it opened on September 9, 1935. Ferrer's Broadway debut did entice his father into attending a performance. After the show, Ferrer asked his father what he thought. According to Ferrer, "He looked at me sadly and sighed."

Ferrer then appeared onstage as a chauffeur (a welcome respite from being one) in a whimsical comedy called *Stick-in-the-Mud*. Thomas Mitchell starred as a presumably lovable codger in a play by Frederick Hazlitt Brennan that won more praise for its riverboat setting than for the onstage theatrics. Mitchell also directed, but even his abilities could not redeem the play in the critics' eyes, as many of them viewed this vehicle as leisurely, derivative, and mild—at best.

Even though these fleeting appearances in misbegotten shows didn't do much artistically for Ferrer, Jed Harris had taken notice, and, thanks to Helen Hayes's continued support, Ferrer was cast in his first lead role on Broadway. It was the light comedy *Spring Dance* by Philip Barry, then best known for *Holiday*, his sophisticated exploration of life amongst the upper classes and the discontented, somewhat radical notions of some of its members. *Spring Dance* would revolve around two girls from Smith College, but the story did not originate with Barry; he was originally engaged to rewrite the original work by Eleanor Golden and Eloise Barrangon, but he did such an extensive revision that the play's writing credit reads "*Spring Dance* by Philip Barry, adapted from an idea by Eleanor Golden and Eloise Barrangon."

Spring Dance had its out-of-town tryouts in Cape Cod in July 1936 prior to an August opening, and while the notices in Cape Cod seemed to herald another hit for Barry and Harris, some backstage drama threatened to overshadow the light fare in front of the curtain. Specifically, a young Imogene Coca was playing the female lead (a college girl who may well lose her beau), having been handpicked by the director, Jed Harris. The reviewers fell in love with Coca, applauding Harris for his casting acumen, but Barry did not share Harris's enthusiasm and exerted pressure on Harris to let her go. The actress Louise Platt would replace Coca when the show reached Broadway; in addition to being Harris's onstage star, she would later become Mrs. Jed Harris.

Despite all the backstage drama, Ferrer had the chance to observe the dynamic Harris in action, dealing with playwrights, last-minute replacements, and all the technical elements involved in making the rhythms of light comedy reverberate onstage. Even though Ferrer was being paid as an actor, he concentrated on learning all he could about the artistic and practical aspects of staging a production. He was also happily left out of the well-publicized theatrical warfare between Barry and Harris, so that when the play opened on Broadway in August 1936, audiences and critics were able to view the young actor as a genuinely talented surprise. The *New York Times*, one of the few publications to give a positive notice, commented on a young impressive male in the cast: "Save special mention for José Ferrer, who disappears with many honors of the evening."

The *Times* notice was an anomaly, as the *New York Evening Post* critic wrote that the play was Barry and Harris's Waterloo, although the critic did add that "fortunately it takes more than one Waterloo to turn such a dynamic figure as Harris into the Bonaparte of the Longwood days." *Spring Dance* would only run for twenty-four performances, closing that September and leaving Ferrer again among the ranks of the unemployed.

During the brief run, Ferrer was able to demonstrate his skills as an able farceur, which caught the attention of the director George Abbott, and a few weeks after the final performance, Ferrer landed one of the leads in Abbott's production of *Brother Rat*. Once again, Ferrer was fortunate enough to be in the company of a nascent theatrical legend; Abbott would not only stage this energetic farce, but (unofficially) take a hand in the scripting. Ferrer would absorb this hands-on approach and utilize it after he realized his own ambition of becoming a director. This effervescent comedy centered on three upperclassmen at the Virginia Military Institute, with Ferrer, Eddie Albert, and Frank Albertson as the three leads. Albertson was the cadet constantly getting his friends into scrapes, while Ferrer and Albert played his loyal but befuddled buddies. In the context of the play, "Brother Rat" is a term of comradeship, and Ferrer's character served as the anchorman of the trio and the steadfast balance for Albertson's antics.

Brother Rat opened on December 16, 1936 and became the first critical and commercial success for star Ferrer. The majority of the raves went to Abbott's deft handling of the material. Reviewers felt that Abbott propelled the farce into a sure-fired frenzy, taking well-worn incidents (like "necking and hazing") and turning them into "chucklesome moments." Ferrer was also praised for his straightforward, zestful acting. While the play enjoyed tremendous success with both critics and audiences—*Brother Rat* would run for 577 performances at the Biltmore Theater, closing in May 1938—Ferrer would exit the production long before the finish. (A movie of *Brother Rat* would be released by Warner Bros. on October 1938, but only Eddie Albert recreated his stage role—Ferrer's role went to Ronald Reagan.) Throughout his career, Ferrer would not be receptive to lengthy runs, saying that he would get stale and become bored with the repetition, and this feeling only intensified as he got older.

Ferrer's next three Broadway appearances were in shows that posed no danger of possible long runs; his first Broadway appearance post-*Brother Rat* was in an original comedy called *In Clover* by Allan Scott, starring Myron McCormick and directed by Bretaigne Windust, his old friend from Princeton. Alas, this Windust/Ferrer teaming was no guarantee for success; the *New York Times* felt the play to be "a disorderly spree, getting progressively worse as it grows frantic." *In Clover* opened on October 13, 1937 and folded after only three performances.

Next was another comedy called *How to Get Tough About It*, directed by the formidable Guthrie McClintic, who would go on to direct Ferrer's next three Broadway appearances. Written by Robert Ardley, the play would again star Myron McCormick, this time paired with Katherine Locke as a boatbuilder and a waitress, respectively, with Ferrer in a featured role as Vergez, a racketeer whose presence threatens the happiness of the young would-be couple. Critics found the play likable but haphazard and formless, but the actors did receive some praise; this Broadway outing would only enjoy slightly more success than *In Clover*, opening on February 8 and lasting a grand total of twenty-three performances.

Before his next Broadway appearance (and his third under the direction of McClintic), Ferrer accepted a role with a theatrical company in Ridgefield, Connecticut. The play was called *Latitude of Love*, and its focus was on a young lady whose fiancé supposes is innocent and chaste, but in reality, is anything but. Ferrer's leading lady was to be Uta Hagen. She was born on June 12, 1919, in Germany, and her family moved to Madison, Wisconsin, where her father, Oskar, would become a professor at the University of Wisconsin and start one of the first Art History departments in the United States. Her mother, Thyra Amalie Hagen, was also a native of Germany and a renowned soprano who was able to continue her career in Madison. They had brought Uta to visit Germany when the girl was nine; there she saw the famed actress Elisabeth Bergner play Joan of Arc and fantasized about becoming an actress herself. Later, Uta would attend the University of Wisconsin High School (an alternative high school) and subsequently register at the University of Wisconsin.

She remained there for one unfulfilling semester before departing to satisfy her desire to become an actress.

At nineteen, Hagen had already achieved a measure of theatrical success by 1938, as well as the support of some theatrical powerhouses, prior to her role in *Latitude*. While tolerating school in Wisconsin—her real interests were acting and dancing—she wrote to the renowned theater actress Eva Le Gallienne to ask for an audition. Le Gallienne was impressed by Hagen's phrasing: "Forthright and honesty . . . one felt a personality there." She would offer Hagen the part of Ophelia in her 1937 production of *Hamlet*; the production (and Hagen's performance) earned glowing notices. Le Gallienne then recommended Hagen to Alfred Lunt and Lynn Fontanne for their version of *The Sea Gull* in 1938. Hagen's interpretation of Nina received good reviews, with the *New York Times* critic Brooks Atkinson referring to her as "grace incarnate." After this success, she was supposed to join a new summer theater company in Falmouth, but the company folded before the season even began, which is why Hagen found herself in Ridgefield, Connecticut, for the comparatively lightweight *Latitude of Love*.

In both her autobiography and in later interviews, Hagen would recall that while she took an instant dislike to Ferrer in that first week of rehearsals, "once we started playing we fell in love." If one scene stood out for both Ferrer and Hagen, it was the scene where Ferrer was supposed to give boxing lessons to Hagen, who would then proceed to knock his socks off. On closing night, Hagen put some real power behind her swing and by all accounts, scored a clean knockdown.

Anyone who has been involved in the theater is aware that during the rehearsal period and subsequent run of the show, many romances develop that never last beyond the final curtain, but for the young Uta and José, their desire for each other, fed in large part by a mutual love for acting and art, allowed their relationship to deepen after the professional engagement ended. After *Latitude of Love*, Hagen proceeded to do a few short-range stints in *Arms and the Man* and *Mr. Pim Passes By*; during these engagements, Ferrer continued his courtship of her, impressing Hagen with his seemingly unquenchable thirst for knowledge and his love for the arts. Hagen then decided to do *Suzanna and the Elders* for the Westport Country Playhouse in Connecticut, partly because of its relatively close proximity to Suffern, New York, where Ferrer was performing in *Stage Door*. In a letter to her parents, Hagen would say that "José is a serious artist in the best sense, with a deep conviction that theater is the most beautiful thing on earth."

After completing her run in *Suzanna and the Elders*, Hagen traveled to Wisconsin to see her parents, particularly her mother, Thyra, who had been ill. Thyra passed away soon after, and Ferrer found himself missing Uta terribly during what turned out to be an extended stay in Wisconsin. He would write to her to offer some solace after her mother's loss, and one can see in this excerpt that he saw his future as being inextricably linked with hers: "People have been leaving the world since the beginning of creation—we are born to die. I said these things to myself after the loss of my mother and they were no consolation. But darling, we still have each other and though no one can take the place of your mother, you can still have a life with me."

When Uta returned from Wisconsin, Ferrer hoped they would have time for each other, but their respective ambitions threatened to derail their romance. Uta had signed to tour with the Lunts in a tour of *The Sea Gull*, while Ferrer had just landed a role in the forthcoming production of *Mamba's Daughters*, starring Ethel Waters. Uta did not want to remain away from José, since her absence only solidified her desire to be with him. When Uta was offered a role in Marc Connelly's new play, the Lunts would not release her from her contract. Even downing a bottle of sleeping pills didn't elicit any sympathy from the Lunts; instead, a compromise was reached wherein Hagen would only perform in *The Sea Gull* and not the other small roles she was assigned, thus providing her the opportunity to periodically return to New York and see José on a more frequent basis.

Ferrer would write Uta regularly when she was away. In one of these letters, one can see that the couple had no less a champion than the famed producer/director Jed Harris, who had done much already to advance Ferrer and Hagen in their professional lives. In a letter from August 1938, Ferrer tells Uta, "I went to the fight last night with Jed . . . for no good reason he started to tell me that I should marry you, and that we should have a continuity in our lives together . . . and then he said if we had a good reason, we should have a baby and that would settle everything. I guess we can't avoid it. I'm sorry but I don't see how you can get out of becoming Mrs. F."

One person who might have expressed some reservations was José's father, but in another letter to Uta from September 1938, he discusses a long talk he had with his father, on a night where he didn't have to rehearse the upcoming *Missouri Legend*. According to José, the conversation lasted a good four hours, during which "he told me about his affairs, and I told him mine—I don't mean love affairs—I mean what we had on our minds. And did I give him a dose of Uta! I showed him your baby pictures and everything—and he loved them. I told him about you and your family—I'm just getting him ready, you know." He also goes on to relay some good news on the professional front—namely, a shot at directing: "I had a temperature last night at rehearsal. McClintic arrived a little high and said that Dorothy Gish [Lillian Gish's sister and an actress in her own right] had gotten him tight. There is a fight scene between Dan Duryea and me which hadn't been staged yet. McC just threw himself on the bed and said you boys go ahead and stage that scene. So I directed it—the first thing I directed in New York. And people say it looks very real."

José and Uta's mutual desire to add some permanence and a veneer of normalcy to their lives led to their setting a wedding date, after what was seen by many as a whirlwind courtship. In a letter to Uta in November 1938, the twenty-six-year-old Ferrer expresses a mix of joy and self-confidence, as well as an understanding of how his notions may be perceived: "I'm so happy . . . we're going to get married. Thursday December 8! What a day! It'll probably rain-snow-mist-thunder all over the joint. Isn't that awful? You must always trust and have confidence in me, as everything I do is with your good in mind." Ferrer also alludes to previous disagreements in the letter when he reminds her that "when I don't do things as hurriedly as you might wish, it's because I know the slow way is the better way. Sometimes you can get a lot more done by taking your time than by getting it done fast."

Their wedding did indeed take place on December 8, 1938, at the Holy Trinity Roman Catholic Church in New York City. José's best man was his father, who had traveled from Puerto Rico for the occasion; a second ceremony would be held on December 18 for Professor Hagen's benefit. Shortly after their wedding, the demands of work would force them apart, since Ferrer was to begin rehearsing *Mamba's Daughters* and Hagen had to tour with *The Sea Gull*. Hagen would later reflect that she held high hopes for their marriage, both in romantic and in creative terms: "We fantasized a perfect life . . . we made our home in Greenwich Village, played on Broadway, toured, and when it was clear I was pregnant, it seemed as if our dreams came true. But our first few years exploded daily in melodrama, with childish egos jockeying for position."

While Hagen was touring with *The Sea Gull*, Ferrer found himself associated with a minor success with *Mamba's Daughters*. Based on a 1929 book by Dubose Heyward that explored racial boundaries in the early part of the century, the book was adapted by Heyward and his wife, Dorothy, expressly as a showcase for the formidable Ethel Waters, who had achieved renown as a powerful singer. This was her first dramatic role, and Waters played Hagar, one of the daughters in the title, who gives birth to a daughter herself (later to be played by Fredi Washington), without knowing who the father is. Waters would please audiences with her magnetism, if not totally win over the critics, while Ferrer in a supporting role (in the major white part among a mostly black cast) was noted to act with "remarkable skill and feeling." The play, under Guthrie McClintic's direction, opened in January 1939 and ran for a total of 162 performances.

It was almost inevitable that Hagen and Ferrer would attract the attention of Hollywood, but neither anticipated the attention would come so quickly, as they were both committed to "a life in the theater." As artists, they were also wary of Hollywood in terms of both its overtly commercial nature and what they felt was the crassness of the overall product. In two letters written to Uta in January 1939 (she was still on tour with *The Sea Gull*), Ferrer describes meeting with various Hollywood "types" and his overall dissatisfaction. In early January, he tells Uta about his trip to MGM's New York office to speak with the head of MGM's New York talent division, Al Altman: "I had a nice talk, telling him I didn't want to leave you, and he said he thought a picture contract for the two of us would be terrific So I said it was up to you, and that you didn't want to do pictures, that I only wanted them for the money and the publicity and I didn't care whether I went out there or not." Ferrer would publicly repeat this refrain on numerous occasions, specifically that if he "went Hollywood," it would only be in search of some fast, relatively easy money, as well as the publicity being a Hollywood star might generate (thus benefitting his theater work).

Ferrer did not pull his punches when it came to dealing with Hollywood insiders, either in his letters or in person. In another January letter to Uta, Ferrer writes about going to Jed Harris's Manhattan apartment after a performance: "Lewis Milestone, the movie director and two other people came in, like celebrities and friends of celebrities, they had that cold hard indifference toward anyone else. They'd been there two minutes when I got up and said loudly, 'I think I better get the hell home.' Jed said, 'I think you should too.' So I said, 'Yes, I find your friends too impressive.' He said, 'You shouldn't say that. They're sweet darling people.' I said, 'I know it, only they don't feel that way about me.' I said goodnight all around and I waltzed out. Isn't that slick?" In these letters, and in other comments he made at the time, one can see Ferrer's acrimony toward these celebrities and even Hollywood itself—yet had they demonstrated some kindness and respect toward him, might his feelings have changed? If one is to believe Ferrer, all it took was two short minutes for him to solidify his antipathy toward Milestone and his cronies in the cinematic community.

In 1939, however, both Hagen and Ferrer began receiving film offers. They met with RKO (not MGM, despite the New York meeting), a studio known for both its lightweight fare, such as its many screwball comedies and the Astaire-Rogers series, and more prestigious films like *King Kong* (1933), *The Age of Innocence* (1934), *The Last Days of Pompeii* (1935), and *Alice Adams* (1935). Hagen and Ferrer were not content to be mere contract players at RKO; they had some conditions of their own. One of them was the right to turn down scripts, which was a luxury afforded to only a few major stars. The other was their desire to be considered a team and be paired on a regular basis. RKO did not say no to this request, and Ferrer and Hagen both made screen tests. Both Ferrer and Hagen thought they were terrible; RKO liked the tests and wanted to cast Hagen and Ferrer with some specific projects in mind. Hagen was offered the plum role of Esmeralda in the big-budget production of *The Hunchback of Notre Dame*. At this stage, British actor Robert Morley, who had scored a success in MGM's *Marie Antoinette* (1938), was also being wooed by RKO to play a prominent role. There was little doubt that this *Hunchback* was to be an important production.

Almost simultaneously, Lewis Milestone, known for his masterful adaptation of *All Quiet on the Western Front*, was preparing to direct the film version of John Steinbeck's *Of Mice and Men*, which had already won acclaim as a novel and on Broadway (starring Wallace Ford and Broderick Crawford as the itinerant, ill-fated ranch hands George and Lennie). Milestone wanted to test Ferrer for the part of George, while Uta was being offered the role of the belligerent Curley's young, flirtatious wife. She declined, with the part eventually played by Betty Field. Ferrer also passed on the role of George, which would be masterfully portrayed by Burgess Meredith in the classic 1939 film (opposite Lon Chaney's equally indelible Lennie). By the summer of 1939, Hagen and Ferrer went back to New York, frustrated with what they perceived as intransigence on the part of Hollywood, and what they took to be the crassly commercial nature of the cinema (as opposed to the artistic possibilities they believed were inherent to a life in the theater).

They were not idle long; both did summer stock in 1939. In Mount Kisco, they performed *Seventh Heaven*; at the Paper Mill Playhouse in

Milburn, New Jersey, they were both in the ensemble of Sidney Kingsley's *Men in White*. Ferrer then directed Hagen for the first time in *Pursuit of Happiness*. This collaboration seems to have proven beneficial not only for their working relationship but also for Ferrer's directorial aspirations, since their mutual mentor Guthrie McClintic gave them the chance to be in the same cast in a Broadway-bound play; Maxwell Anderson, who had achieved acclaim for his distinctive blank verse plays such as *Winterset*, was now ready with his latest effort, *Key Largo*. It would star Paul Muni as a disillusioned Spanish Civil War deserter who redeems himself defending a family against bandits in Key Largo, Florida. (The 1948 John Huston/Humphrey Bogart movie would have Bogie as a World War II veteran facing mobster Edward G. Robinson, as Huston altered the play considerably, especially its reliance on blank verse.) Ferrer was cast as Victor D'Alcala, a heroic but doomed soldier, with his participation limited to the play's prologue set in Spain, during which Ferrer's courage would stand in stark contrast to Muni's cowardice. Uta Hagen was to portray Ferrer's surviving sister, who helps Muni to confront his shortcomings when the action shifts to Key Largo, Florida.

Key Largo opened on November 27, 1939, at the Ethel Barrymore Theater. The reviews were mixed but respectful. The *New York Times* critic Brooks Atkinson felt that the prologue was the most powerful section, in terms of both the staging and in Anderson's writing. He also singled out Ferrer for his acting choices, noting that though he "underplays the decisive-mindedness of the hero in the prologue, his modest sincerity makes the great decision a natural one." Hagen was also cited as being "admirably cast," and Muni was found to have "redeemed a part that might be personally contemptible . . . he plays the part with a simple, masculine force." Although its creators hoped for more critical acclaim, *Key Largo*, thanks to film star Paul Muni's ability to attract audiences, managed a run of 105 performances.

Even though Hagen and Ferrer didn't share any substantial scenes together (and this was really Muni's show—his first Broadway appearance in seven years, during which he became one of Hollywood's biggest and most demanding stars), Hagen and Ferrer were united in their feelings about Muni. They both felt Muni was rather self-indulgent and lacked discipline during the six-month run. According to Hagen, "In the whole six months, he [Muni] played fully twice . . . he was dazzling— but twice in a six-month run." Her feeling about her husband's work was altogether different: "I thought Joe was sensational . . . this was the beginning of his real flowering as an actor." (Ferrer was known as "Joe" to his close friends and would frequently sign correspondence, formal or otherwise, as "Joe.")

Hagen, who would become of the theater's foremost acting teachers, also noted her and Ferrer's different approaches to their craft: "I worked very formalistically: literally line-reading, setting every shape and sound—Joe had worked on a Stanislavski-improvisation approach. Joe worked internally. I thought I did too, but my aim was for the set shape." For the moment, they were living the actors' dream (slightly modified to fit the married acting couple): working together on quality plays, honing their craft, and developing a mutual respect for each other's developing talents.

CHAPTER 3

Othello: Paul, Uta, and José

AFTER *KEY LARGO* COMPLETED ITS RUN IN FEBRUARY 1940, FERRER AND Hagen took further steps to settle down. They purchased a white stucco house in Ossining, New York. Adding to their outward bliss, Uta's father remarried—and Uta became pregnant and was due to give birth in September 1940. During the eventful summer of 1940, Ferrer had suggested to his old Princeton classmate Joshua Logan that they shake the mothballs out of the classic farce *Charley's Aunt*. The play had originally been staged at London's Royalty Theater in 1892, moving to the Globe Theater in 1893. It had since been revived onstage, with three film adaptations, the most recent starring Charles Ruggles in 1930. Logan thought a revival would do well, and together they mounted a production at the Mount Kisco summer theater. Hagen noted the unflagging energy he brought to the production, not only as a farceur but as a director: "Joe has a tremendous burning enthusiasm, and he has the faculty of instilling that enthusiasm into the players in the cast."

Charley's Aunt proved to be such a smash that Logan and Ferrer, with the encouragement of the backers of the show, decided to move the production to Broadway, this time under Logan's direction. Ferrer didn't hesitate to add to his own imprint to the show, whether penciling in some new lines or borrowing bits of business that worked in previous productions (as well as the film version released in 1923). An element of irony that was noted by certain reporters was that while many of the gags centered around the fact that Ferrer's character, Lord Fancourt Babberly, can't understand Portuguese, Ferrer himself knew Portuguese rather well.

When *Charley's Aunt* opened in October 1940, both director Logan and actor/creative force Ferrer were enthusiastically received, partly because of the bright ideas grafted onto what was felt to be a hoary script, and partly because of the sheer zaniness and inventiveness that they brought to the production. One reviewer marveled at how Ferrer "screamed about the stage, swinging from trees, getting out and then into his clothes again, and successfully eluding the clutches of two deluded gentlemen who thought him a fair dish." Brooks Atkinson of the *New York Times* praised Logan's inventive direction (though much of it resembled the earlier Ferrer-directed version at Mt. Kisco) and felt that Ferrer blazes through the farce "at a hop, skip and jump, which seems to be the right way to plunge through it." Ferrer himself would attribute the revival's success to "two of the best low-comedy minds of the century's—mine and Logan's."

By the time *Charley's Aunt* opened, Ferrer was not just the toast of the town but he was a new father as well. Daughter Leticia Thyra Ferrer was born October 15, 1940; labor had to be induced because Uta had been pregnant for ten months. Uta would say in her memoir that she was named "Leticia," since it meant happiness, and "Thyra," in honor of her mother. Having bought their home in Ossining the previous spring, Uta spent her time there with Leticia. Ferrer managed to get there most days, unless he had both a matinee and evening performance. In interviews from the period, Ferrer and Hagen appeared to be relishing their new roles as parents, with Ferrer conveying that "we work in shifts . . . Uta stays up with the child for a while and then I take over. But it's hard to sleep under any circumstances when a youngster's crying in the house." He also noted, with some pride, that "would you believe it, Uta stayed up with the child for two hours last night and when I came on my shift, she went to sleep in five minutes!"

Because of *Charley's Aunt* and its astounding success, Ferrer was both the busy (and tired) parent and actor, as it continued for 233 performances at the Cort Theater, followed by a short tour. After that, Ferrer and Hagen spent some together with Leticia at their Ossining retreat, and it was here that Hagen was able to observe her husband's difficulty with relative inactivity. According to Hagen, there was a period of doing nothing, and she saw that "Joe's already getting restless." Ferrer also was trying, none too successfully, to present a brave front when the film version of *Charley's Aunt* was released by Twentieth Century-Fox in 1941. It starred Jack Benny in a well-received performance that nonetheless did not approach Ferrer's high-energy approach.

While Ferrer would claim to be at peace with the decision to cast Benny, it rankled him privately that he was not even considered. In public, Ferrer would make a big show of proclaiming he didn't care, but his statements betray a little bitterness—and not just toward the film's producers: "Hollywood is the Black Hole of Calcutta. I hate the place . . . as soon as they make a name for themselves, playwrights go to Hollywood, where the money is quick and easy." He was further incensed when he saw the movie version: "It was a damn dull movie . . . it's an old-fashioned, damn, dull play anyway. It needs to be set up just right. On Broadway it was set up just right . . . beautifully cast, setting was good, everyone worked continuously to get every last laugh out of that old wheeze."

To ease what was becoming an uncomfortable period of inactivity, Hagen and Ferrer decided to do another play in Suffern, New York. It was *The Guardsman*, which had been a Broadway success for the Lunts. They also began looking for plays that they could do together. As if on cue, Jed Harris directed Ferrer's attention to a light comedy about military men and their wives called *The Admiral Had a Wife*. Ferrer liked the script, especially since it had a solid part for Uta, and would provide another opportunity to collaborate in front of the footlights, with Ferrer himself directing. As Ferrer would later recall, this was his first time trying his hand at producing: "I found this play by Lowell Barrington, which took place in Pearl Harbor and deals with ranking officers going to cocktail parties, having a good time and not minding the store. I raised the money, we played in Baltimore for a week."

The Admiral Had a Wife received some good reviews on the road. Critics described the comedy—which had Pearl Harbor as its setting and focused on a naval wife, played by Uta, trying to get her husband promoted—as good entertainment. Many felt the play was packed with funny situations and had a cast that handled light comedy gracefully. There were a few dissenters though, and much of the criticism centered on Hagen's role as the well-meaning but dim wife; several reviewers felt her character lacked sympathy and that Hagen, for all her acting skill, was unable to overcome it.

With the feeling among cast and reviewers that the play was headed for success, *The Admiral Had a Wife* was supposed to begin Broadway previews in early December 1941. As Ferrer recalled in September 1991, on what would have been the show's fiftieth anniversary, "We were to open in New York on December 10, 1941. On December 7, God reached down, put a finger in all our lives and changed all our plans. The Japanese bombed Pearl Harbor and we couldn't very well do a funny show on Pearl Harbor."

There were some attempts to save what turned out to be a seriously ill-timed production. Ferrer and the author tried to do a rewrite, enlisting John Patrick and Johnny Monks (from *Brother Rat*). They tried to change the setting, but according to Hagen, "There was nothing to be salvaged when the premise of the play was that admirals were morons and a lieutenant's wife could run them ragged." Despite Ferrer's persistence in believing that *The Admiral* still had some life in it, the producers felt they had to close the play. In a press release, Fred Spooner stated that, after considering the possibility of rewriting, they decided to withdraw the play: "What we intended as a simple comedy approach to manners concerning the United States Navy might now be misinterpreted as a dis-respectful and trivial treatment of a serious situation in the present war." The total loss for Ferrer and the producers amounted to about $20,000 (the equivalent of $356,000 in 2019). Although this would cause Ferrer to seriously reconsider investing in one of his own productions (recall Max Bialystock's immortal advice in Mel Brooks's *The Producers*: "Never put your money in a show!"), it was a practice he would repeat time and again.

The play's unscheduled closing left Ferrer and Hagen free to do a ben-efit performance of *The Threepenny Opera* to raise money for the Soviet Union, which was an ally of the United States in 1941. (It would be activities like this that would come back to haunt Ferrer in the early 1950s.) The performance was co-directed by Ferrer and Margaret Web-ster, who would later become an important part of both their lives as she had them in mind for a certain Shakespearean play. Before they commit-ted, Hagen and Ferrer went to Ann Arbor, Michigan, to perform *Charley's Aunt*, after which Ferrer went to the St. Louis Muny Opera House to do a revival of *No, No, Nanette* before audiences that approximated 11,000 people (including the hundreds of free seats that were allocated to service members and their families). The shows at the Muny had a customary rehearsal period of about one week; performers such as Eddie Cantor marveled at how professional the shows were in the limited time pro-vided. From today's perspective, it might seem unusual to associate an actor like Ferrer with lighthearted fluff like *No, No, Nanette*, but the actor always maintained that, despite the highbrow image that he believed had been unjustly thrust upon him, he cultivated a great appreciation for such "lowbrow fare" as musicals, comedies, and vaudeville.

After Ferrer's engagement in *No, No, Nanette*, director Webster reached out to him again since they had a congenial working relationship when they co-directed *The Threepenny Opera*. By 1942, Webster, who was the daughter of actors Ben Webster and Dame May Whitty, had established herself in the theater, first with various theatrical companies in England, including the Old Vic from 1929 to 1930. Upon her return to the United States, Webster found herself in great demand as a director, particularly after a series of Shakespearean productions starring the renowned Maurice Evans. Although Evans is perhaps best-known today as Dr. Zaius in *Planet of the Apes* or as Samantha's puckish father on the hit 1960s television show *Bewitched*, in the 1930s and '40s, he was a revered classical actor. Under Webster's direction, Evans had triumphed on Broadway in *Hamlet*, *Twelfth Night*, *Henry IV, Part 1*, and finally *Macbeth* during the 1941–42 season, costarring with Judith Anderson. After Evans joined the army following their production of *Macbeth*, she had to turn to other potential tragedians for her *Othello*.

Webster then thought of acclaimed singer/actor Paul Robeson, who had already captivated American audiences with his riveting portrayal of *The Emperor Jones*, as well as his stirring rendition of "Ol' Man River" in the 1936 film version of *Show Boat*. Robeson's powerful singing voice and commanding screen presence enabled the black performer to be regularly cast in leading roles, especially in England, where race did not play as much of a factor for minorities seeking major parts in medium-to-high-budget films. (In the United States, this wasn't the case—witness the number of black actors such as Hattie McDaniel and Canada Lee who had to endure years of playing sidekicks or servants.) Robeson was extremely busy in the 1940s with his films, recordings, and concert tours.

It was to Webster's great relief that Robeson was available for a proposed production of *Othello* for the summer of 1942. Robeson had already done the part before, in a 1930 London production that Webster had seen. She remembered that his performance as Othello was seriously flawed, and the critics agreed (though they approved of Peggy Ashcroft's Desdemona and Maurice Brown's Iago). The *Times* reviewer felt Robeson played "thrillingly upon the nerves" with "a tranquil dignity and a melancholy infinitely sad." A dissenting critic felt that Robeson delivered his speeches with "sonorous monotony." Robeson concurred with the more critical views, but he had studied and restudied the role, and felt ready to revisit it. Robeson also believed the time was right for a black actor to do the part on Broadway, and that Broadway audiences, in turn, would accept a black actor in the role.

In the recent past, the part of Othello had generally been played by white actors using "soot" black to play Shakespeare's naïve, noble Moor. While there were several black actors who had played the part, even in professional productions in and around New York City, none had been done on Broadway. Perhaps the most prominent black actor to take on the role was Ira Aldridge, a celebrated actor who had portrayed Othello in the mid-1800s in London and Belfast, but even Alridge never played the role in the United States. Producers and financial backers, in the 1800s and in 1942, were hesitant to trust American audiences to tolerate a story that required a black man to love, marry, and murder a white woman, even though Shakespeare's play was a 400-year-old classic. Webster would recall, "Everybody was scared . . . a few fell back on scholastic arguments, that Othello was a Moor, not a Negro, or expressed doubts as to Robeson's technical equipment as an actor. But mostly they were scared of the issues the production would raise." Webster and Robeson were undaunted, but they had to wait two years to mount a production, mainly because of Webster's directorial commitments, including *Macbeth*, starring Maurice Evans. When they were finally able to move forward, Robeson and Webster decided to finance the production themselves, since the usual backers had made themselves scarce.

While Robeson was set for Othello, being the production's *raison d'etre*, it was believed that Webster's creative muse, Evans, would be an ideal Iago, Othello's gleefully unapologetic, malevolent lieutenant and willful manipulator of the honorable, anguished, and increasingly jealous Othello. Evans was consulted early on and he refused, believing that audiences wouldn't accept him in a supporting role. There were those that felt Webster and Robeson would have a difficult time finding a suitable Iago and Desdemona, as some might refuse to play opposite a black actor or be wary of potential audience response. Even though Peggy Ashcroft had done Desdemona, she was English, and the production had been in London.

It's a small world, though, as far as theater is considered; in 1942, Webster was almost four years into a romantic relationship with Eva Le Gallienne. When Webster was contemplating who should portray Iago and Desdemona (Othello's innocent bride and, along with Othello, the major victims of Iago's villainy), Le Gallienne suggested both Ferrer and Hagen to Webster for these two iconic roles. After meeting with both actors, Webster agreed to hire the pair; Webster herself would assume the role of Emilia. Ferrer didn't know *Othello* very well, but he willingly took direction from Webster. One early criticism concerned Ferrer's tendency to stand with his hands in his pockets; Webster suggested he keep his hands free for gestures. Hagen found Webster to be a brilliant woman who was a less-than-brilliant director. She felt Webster belonged in a university and was ill-equipped to deal with the temperament and technical limitations of someone like Robeson.

The company would have a two-week rehearsal in Cambridge before opening at the Brattle Theater in August 10, 1942. The production then moved to Princeton (Robeson's birthplace) for a week beginning August 17. *Othello* received mixed reviews, with Robeson coming off rather well but Hagen and Ferrer a little less so. John Russell Brown's critique in *New York World Telegram* stated that "so far Ferrer is the body but not the mind of Iago . . . he hides his thoughts so well that he does not seem to be thinking at all." Despite the lackluster reviews, Robeson's star wattage was enough to convince the backers that this *Othello* should come to Broadway. However, Robeson's many commitments, particularly concerts and personal appearances, would mean that this would have to be delayed for about a year.

Not to be dissuaded from performing together, Ferrer and Hagen were cast in a slight farce called *Vickie*. Written by S. M. Herzog, there were similarities to the late, lamented *Admiral Had a Wife* since Hagen was again cast as a well-meaning, if dimwitted wife (this time opposite Ferrer's inventor husband). In addition to performing, Ferrer was also co-director with Frank Mandel. The show had its initial previews in Washington in September 1942, and while the Ferrers received good notices as a team, the play itself was almost universally disliked.

Certain onstage mishaps didn't help to make *Vickie* any more bearable, though they provided fodder for Ferrer for years to come. One notable instance was when Hagen was supposed to make a comic exit but instead took an unscripted fall). Ferrer rushed backstage, and an unaware actor (who was sharing the stage with Ferrer but had not seen him exit) made an entrance and directed his lines to an absent Ferrer, prompting another actor to say, "Who the hell are you talking to?" In the interim, Ferrer was at Hagen's side, got her some brandy, and then went in front of the audience and declared: "My wife has met with a major disaster." A few minutes after that, Hagen emerged onstage with a strapped ankle, receiving cheers from the audience. This resounding applause could not save *Vickie* from the onslaught of negative reviews, and the play wound up closing in late October, after a run of only forty-eight performances.

After *Vickie* closed, Ferrer tried to produce Howard Richardson and William Berney's play called *Dark of the Moon* but couldn't raise enough money. Ferrer found himself on Broadway again in February 1943, starring as Danny Kaye's replacement in the hit musical *Let's Face It!*, with music by Cole Porter and a book by Herbert and Dorothy Fields. Kaye's manic performance, as well as his facility with both the comedic and musical elements, had captivated both audiences and critics. By the time Ferrer joined the cast, the show had been running for over a year, and Ferrer did not possess enough star power (or critical approbation, for that matter) to offset the drop in box-office returns, once the magnetic Kaye departed. It was not a happy experience for Ferrer, noting, "I was lousy with Kaye's material." *Let's Face It* would post its closing notice two weeks into Ferrer's run, ending in March 1943.

In early summer 1943, talks would begin about finally taking *Othello* to Broadway as the opening production of the Theater Guild's thirty-sixth season. The show would have the financial backing of Lawrence Langner, Robeson's friend since the 1920s and a founder of the Guild. Robeson would be available in August, and Ferrer and Hagen were under the assumption that they too would reprise their roles. However, producers Langner and Theresa Helburn wanted to replace both Ferrer and Hagen, citing weak reviews and their relative unfamiliarity to audiences. There was another factor: Ferrer was insisting on costar billing for him and Hagen—both said they won't do the play without the other. Robeson wanted both Hagen and Ferrer, fearing their onstage magic would be lost if any of them were not involved. By June, both Hagen and Ferrer were hired and they believed that was the end of any contract squabbles and life continued, for better or worse; they bought a townhouse on East Fifty-ninth Street, but in July, Hagen had to undergo an emergency operation for both a swollen gallbladder and the removal of her appendix.

And then there was the not wholly resolved matter of who would be playing Iago and Desdemona. The producers were still unconvinced about Ferrer and Hagen—primarily Ferrer, since they (including Webster) thought his Iago needed improvement—and because he had held up negotiations because of his insistence on star billing. (Webster was also furious with Robeson for jeopardizing the production.) Actors Stephen Schnabel and Virginia Gilmore were then signed to play Iago and Desdemona, much to the chagrin of Hagen, Ferrer, and, most important of all, Robeson. Robeson insisted that he would absolutely not do the show without the Ferrers. Webster would later write: "No Ferrers, no Robeson, no Robeson, no show, and I, as usual, left to straighten it out." This meant buying out the contracts of Schnabel and Gilmore (which Robeson helped financially). She also wanted to toss the Ferrers "off the balcony into 52nd Street," but instead persuaded them to forego equal billing with Robeson and be prominently featured in all display advertising. In addition, all of Ferrer's salary demands were met. Robeson had the contractual clout to do this, since his contract clearly stated that "the final decision as to all matters pertaining to the selection of the cast . . . shall be solely and exclusively with Paul Robeson."

A six-week period of rehearsals began in August 1943, and previews would begin in New Haven in September 1943. Hagen particularly impressed the director as "deeply moving"; while Robeson had continued to improve, he didn't have the technique to work internally, and was seemingly content to work on surface effects, and Webster felt she was not the ideal director to address Robeson's limitations. On October 4, the production moved to Philadelphia, opening at the Shubert Theater on October 19, 1943; it would be the first major production of *Othello* to have a black actor in the leading role on Broadway in an otherwise all-white cast. The reviews were favorable; many noted the play's importance both as an exemplary production, but also in terms of its timing and historical significance. Others praised the sheer force of Robeson's portrayal, as well as the delicate, sensitive portrayal by Hagen.

Ultimately, Ferrer's dynamic portrayal of Iago earned the majority of critical encomiums. Burton Rascoe of the *New York World Telegram* was effusive in his praise: "It is historically commonplace that Iago steals the show, but Ferrer's interpretation goes far beyond the prodigal opportunities of the part. It is a character creation of the first magnitude, played in a manner I dare say you never saw it played before." Howard Barnes of the *New York Herald Tribune* would add that "José Ferrer, playing Iago with an authority which none of us, I think, has seen on stage . . . gives the role a truly demoniacal quality." Ferrer would comment on certain technical aspects of the production, such as acting with a sword as his constant companion: "I learned to keep my sword out of the way, to keep it from standing when I sit, and how to sheath it without looking."

In a departure from his crafting a part "externally," Ferrer decided to build up a case history for his Iago, visualizing him "as a boy of the slums, trying to succeed by getting promotions in the army; when he doesn't, he gets bitter. He turns on Othello. If he can't create, then he'll destroy. He becomes an anti-Christ, like Hitler. A guy who fights only for himself. He never helps anybody; when he does, it's only as a move for subsequent villainy." As for the challenges in playing such a character, Ferrer would say, "Well, Iago isn't too difficult, you know. The toughest thing is its length . . . there are only two things to worry about when you're playing Iago. First of all, you've got to concentrate on variety . . . then you've got to find the strength to play it eight times a week."

In author Martin Duberman's biography of Paul Robeson, Hagen would later recall that she found Ferrer to be at his best during the initial phase of the Broadway run: "I think in the first six weeks as Iago . . . that he was probably the finest Iago that ever was. He cannot sustain a performance. Even to this day, he will go after three, four, five weeks—he hates long runs." Hagen's view was that the longer the run, the more opportunities to find variations and shadings. For Hagen, "the longer I play, the better I like it, because the deeper my performance gets and the richer it is. He will find it boring and go only for outer shape . . . in the beginning the audiences were knocked out. He was the only actor on stage. And then it got more and more tricks, and outer gimmicks and vocalizations."

The early period in what promised to be a lengthy run was a happy one, as *Othello* was playing to sold-out audiences; Robeson, Webster, and the entire company were in good spirits. Plans for a lengthy tour were being made, subject to everyone's availability (especially Robeson's). The Ferrers hosted a Christmas party at which Robeson presented Ferrer with a magnum of Mums champagne; for his part, Ferrer presented Robeson with an eighteenth-century edition of *Don Quixote*.

These seemingly infinite feelings of joy and goodwill would subside in 1944. The Ferrers found themselves $5,000 in debt due to back taxes; Hagen herself was battling depression and found herself dependent on sedatives—she would take some time off from the production to recover. After she returned, the issue of billing interfered with the relationship among Robeson, the Ferrers, and the Theater Guild, with Webster on the side of the Guild. Robeson was insisting on the Ferrers receiving costar billing in smaller type, this time above the title. Director/producer Webster was enraged, and not only at the disruptive tactics of Ferrer and Robeson; since she was playing the part of Emilia, she was also outraged at having been asked to accept billing beneath the Ferrers. Webster didn't believe that either Hagen or Ferrer should be considered "stars" worthy of such billing, while she was still relegated to "support" as far as theatrical standing was concerned. The Theater Guild initially took Webster's side, until Robeson stated that he would cancel the tour unless they agreed to the Ferrers' new billing. Not able to hold sway over the Guild (or Robeson), Webster decided to give up her role as Emilia; the Guild would grant the Ferrers star billing, especially since they had already scheduled the tour, which would have become a nonevent without Robeson's participation.

To further whet the public's appetite for the show, Robeson and the Ferrer decided to make an audio recording of the show for posterity.

It would be performed with the same text as had been adapted for the Broadway production, with only some minor cuts. Webster and the Theater Guild were not consulted about the matter, and Webster was further dismayed to learn that, even though the recording would supposedly feature the original cast, she did not make the cut in her "original" performance as Emilia; instead, her replacement, the actress Edith King (who had been playing Bianca in the production), participated in the record. In hindsight, Ferrer and Hagen would feel the recording was a mistake because it did not capture the vitality of the production. Hagen would be especially displeased with the record, and Ferrer's participation in it: "I think he's embarrassing on that record, but that record has nothing to do with his initial performance." A few critics weighed in on the Columbia Records release in early 1945, saying that while it did not retain the power of the live stage, the vocal power and facility with the text of Robeson, Hagen, and Ferrer were fairly apparent.

Ferrer's resonant baritone could also be occasionally heard in the popular medium of radio. He didn't do as much as one might think, given his vocal reputation, but Ferrer did appear on a few programs and even had his own series for a short time. Besides making guest appearances on variety programs like *The Big Show* and *The Prudential Family Hour* (the latter starring mezzo soprano Gladys Swarthout), Ferrer starred as S. S. Van Dyne's cultivated, intelligent sleuth Philo Vance in a radio series for NBC from July 1945 through September 1945. These episodes would include "The Girl Who Came Back" and "The Case of the Strange Music"; several programs are quite entertaining and can be found online by intrepid listeners. Although Ferrer's involvement with Vance would end with these shows, the series would continue in syndication with Jackson Beck in the part.

For the popular series *Suspense*, Ferrer would star in an adaptation of Edgar Allan Poe's "The Pit and the Pendulum." Ferrer would also be featured in two episodes of *Cavalcade of America*, an anthology series dramatizing events from American history. The episodes, "My Friend McNair" from 1945 and "Sound the Great Bell" from 1951, are both professionally made radio dramas. Ferrer would also appear on a few programs which celebrated both the written word and the actors who interpret them. On *Biography in Sound*, Ferrer and others, including Ethel Barrymore and Helen Hayes, addressed the notion of what is an actor in "The Actor," while the *Anthology* program "Poetry of the Theater, By Theater, and For the Theater" included Ferrer among actors and singers reading the works of poets, past and present. To be sure, his was not a lengthy radio resume, but then again, Ferrer had no shortage of professional commitments.

Apart from Ferrer's continuing participation in *Othello*, another tantalizing offer came his way from none other than the writer/director Billy Wilder. Wilder, fresh from his success with the 1944 classic film noir *Double Indemnity*, was about to film *The Lost Weekend*. The director was so taken with Ferrer's power that he offered him the role of the alcoholic failed writer Don Birnam. If Ferrer had truly been looking for an entry into the Hollywood elite, this would quite possibly be the path. Ferrer never did get the role, and the reasons given are varied, depending on which version of the story one hears. According to Wilder, he pursued Ferrer in defiance of Paramount Pictures, who had originally wanted Wilder to cast a "name" for the part. Thus, the signing of Ray Milland (a likable leading man for Paramount who had previously starred in Wilder's directorial debut, *The Major and the Minor*) occurred mainly because of undue pressure from Paramount.

To hear Ferrer tell it, it was he who had turned down Wilder, maintaining that he was already committed to a lengthy road tour of *Othello*. This is corroborated in the journals of Wilder's collaborator, Charles Brackett, who writes of Ferrer breezing into the office, saying no, and breezing out. Ferrer continued to cultivate an outwardly cavalier attitude toward Hollywood, viewing it as a place for prospective financial gain: "Sure I regret the loss of publicity the picture would have brought me, like I regret every relative who dies who doesn't leave me one million bucks. I never saw the picture, but I may as well say it was great and Milland was superb. I may have to go to Hollywood someday for eating money, God forbid."

When the Broadway production of *Othello* closed, it had set a record with its run of 296 performances. The company was then given a two-month break, after which it embarked on a thirty-six-week coast-to-coast tour. This tour would begin in Trenton, New Jersey, in September 1944 and take the company to forty-five different cities comprising seventeen states, as well as three Canadian provinces. There would be no performances in Washington, DC, or indeed in any cities that had laws on the books discriminating against African Americans in theaters. According to author Milly Barranger in her superb study *Margaret Webster, A Life in the Theater*, Webster had hoped that President Roosevelt would invite the cast to the White House for a command performance, but this did not materialize.

In terms of discrimination, just because the *Othello* tour had been scheduled for cities with a seemingly greater tolerance toward African Americans did not mean that the players would not encounter prejudice along the way. Ferrer would be told by a friend of his that the prejudice in a seemingly welcoming city like Boston could be more covert, as simple as a four-star restaurant telling Robeson that there were no tables available (even if the restaurant was empty), thus encouraging the party to seek other suitable dining accommodations. It might also be displayed with overt racism, as Hagen and Robeson were to discover when they were seen in a Boston hotel elevator arm in arm and were spat on by an angry woman. It could also take the form of a seemingly welcoming city like Indianapolis suddenly registering complaints about desegregating the theater. There were also certain hotels unwilling to give Robeson a hotel room, and when one accommodation was finally found, the Ferrers and Robeson discovered that the room was just a vacant office. Hagen would later recall that the Ferrers had friends in Indianapolis who would allow both Robeson and the Ferrers to stay there. However, before they left the hotel, the Ferrers announced they were leaving and that Robeson could stay in *their* room. Robeson (who had no intention of remaining) then made a ceremonial gesture of going in to use the bathroom before departing with the Ferrers.

This also brings up another matter that would complicate the tour and have lasting repercussions on the Robeson/Ferrer/Hagen dynamic: the married Robeson and Hagen had begun to discreetly see each other when they were not in front of the curtain. As Hagen recalled, the attraction developed during the initial Broadway run. At first, Hagen had not thought of Robeson as a prospective lover, but rather as a "fabulous older friend." Then one night when they were in the wings waiting to make an entrance, Robeson had taken his hand "and put it between my legs . . . I thought what the hell and I got unbelievably excited . . . afterward I looked at him with totally different eyes. He suddenly became a sex object." Hagen would allude to affairs on both her and Ferrer's part in her memoir *Sources* (though she mentions no names in this slim volume, not even Ferrer's or Robeson's). Hagen and Robeson would begin spending more time together, a decision that would not go unnoticed by either Ferrer or Robeson's wife, Essie.

As the rumors spread about their involvement, Hagen believed Ferrer was indifferent, since he was carrying on an affair of his own with a member of the touring company. Hagen believed that her straying spouse was "unbelievably happy to pass me off onto Paul." When the company was in New York, the Ferrers would remain in their townhouse (they closed the Ossining home when they were on tour), with daughter Leticia being cared for at the New York City residence by their black maid Frances. Frances didn't want to wait on Robeson when he came to the house, feeling that blacks "don't wait on each other." However, Robeson eventually won Frances over (before a trip to Boston) when he took her bag and Letty's toys, and carried them down to the platform.

Where the Robeson/Hagen relationship would ultimately go was a matter of some concern to Hagen; Robeson was not only trying to maintain his marriage to Essie but was also carrying on affairs of his own outside Hagen and his marriage. Like Ferrer, he could be temperamental and narcissistic; unlike Ferrer, he could be cruel and violent, especially when drunk. Hagen recalled that while she was on the road, she had missed Lettie and wanted another child. When she reunited with Ferrer and became pregnant, Robeson "went insane" and got very drunk, hitting her—something that Hagen believed helped lead to an eventual miscarriage. Although Robeson shared many traits with Ferrer, including an insatiable curiosity and a scholar's passion for knowledge, outbursts like these would lead Hagen to pull away from her volatile costar.

The tour continued, however, as daughter Leticia joined her parents in Pittsburgh; after their stay in Indianapolis, the company moved to Columbus, then onto Milwaukee and Madison. Hagen and Ferrer stayed with Hagen's parents in Wisconsin, and Hagen was treated to a major homecoming when she arrived in Madison. Afterwards, the company would make stops in Minnesota and Winnipeg in December, then play on the West Coast, including Tacoma, Vancouver, Victoria, and Sacramento, prior to a three week stay in Los Angeles. By February, the cast was in San Francisco, where Ferrer was ordered by the draft board to work on a defense housing project. Ferrer's draft status during the war is uncertain. He certainly didn't serve, even though other Princeton colleagues (like Jimmy Stewart) went to war. Ferrer's son Rafael told me that when the subject came up at home, his father would say he had received an exemption of some kind (because of "the serious work his father was doing on behalf of the theater"), but he also had to participate in certain projects when summoned.

Besides San Francisco, other stops would include San José, Boulder, and Denver; the last stop of the tour would be in Chicago at the Erlanger Theater in May 1945. This would be followed with a three-week revival of the play at City Center, complete with a restaging by Margaret Webster.

The revival drew raves from the critics, who thought that Robeson's portrayal deepened, while Ferrer's Iago was seen as "a more sinister schemer" than he had been. Hagen was still seen "as a beautiful Desdemona, if a somewhat cool one." By the time *Othello* finished its run in June 1945, it had played 587 performances. There was supposed to be a European tour, but that fell apart—there were concerns about Robeson's political views, especially since his outspokenness against racial discrimination led him to embrace leftist causes. Robeson's communist sympathies would also win him no friends in an increasingly tense postwar climate, so for now the *Othello* saga would come to a close. Although their affair was now over, Hagen and Robeson did maintain their friendship, especially in light of Ferrer's continued extramarital affairs.

CHAPTER 4

Strange Fruit—Then Cyrano

AFTER THEIR TRIUMPHANT TOUR OF *OTHELLO* ENDED IN JUNE 1945, FERRER and Hagen had decided against any attempts to find a suitable theatrical follow-up. It was apparent that the marriage had deteriorated beyond repair, and the thought of working together on a stage endeavor (or any endeavor for that matter) was not under consideration. Hagen was devoting her time to raising Leticia (or Letty as she was called), while Ferrer was venturing into the realm of producing and directing. In countless interviews, Ferrer stated that while he was relatively unsatisfied when it came to acting he enjoyed the challenges and rigors involved in mounting a stage production. He also liked the fact that producing and directing was a finite affair that you could hand off to a competent stage manager (and financial advisor) once the play opened.

Ferrer was also interested in doing a play with some social relevance; he found such a play in *Strange Fruit*. The play was adapted by Lillian Smith from her own famous and controversial novel, as it was a hard-hitting work that dealt with intolerance and segregation in the South. At the center of the play is Nonnie, a black girl who is going to have a child with her childhood sweetheart, Tracy. Tracy is white, shiftless, and a bit of a weakling but she is from a good family. When Tracy hears of Nonnie's pregnancy, he deserts her and gets his black servant Henry to marry Nonnie, while he proceeds to marry someone of his own race. This sets in motion a chain of events, including Tracy's murder at the hands of Tracy's enraged brother Ed—with the eventual blame pinned on Henry, who is ultimately lynched.

Originally Orson Welles had expressed interest in producing *Strange Fruit*, but author Lillian Smith accepted an offer from Ferrer and his partner, the theatrical lawyer Arthur Friend. It would be an ambitious production, with fifteen scenes comprising ten sets, and a cast of thirty-five actors. For a show of this scope (not to mention the incendiary content), Ferrer, Friend, and Smith were able to quickly assemble a team of approximately one hundred backers. Approximately one-third of the backing came from prominent white citizens of Clayton, Georgia (where Smith resided); the largest investment came courtesy of the Hollywood agent Charles K. Feldman, who invested $10,000. Ferrer himself put up $3,500 and would rarely refrain from offering his own money to help subsidize a production as long as he believed enough in either the material or the possibility of recouping some dividends along the way. There were many other contributors, including the actor Myron McCormick (who had performed with Ferrer in some of Ferrer's earliest Broadway outings), Smith herself, as well as friends and relatives of both Smith and Ferrer.

Ferrer spent most of the summer of 1945 in Clayton (sans Hagen, who remained in New York with daughter Letty) working with playwright Smith (and her sister, who had assisted in the adaptation). As producer/director, Ferrer would make it a practice to serve as an unofficial collaborator on any property he was bringing to the stage and later, the screen. Whenever he worked on a play, the credit remained with the original authors, although in films he would not withhold his participation from the public, either in interviews or in terms of screen credit.

Before casting was even completed, *Strange Fruit* came under fire from various fronts, with some saying the play should not be performed at all. Smith had defied the board of Theater Control in terms of the play's morality, and Dr. Melvin Forney declared the play to be an attack on the evangelical Christian church. To Forney, one particularly galling scene concerned a minister advising Tracy (who had impregnated Nonnie) to give the girl money so she could marry an African American man. Smith said that, among other things, her play attacks the hypocrisy of the church, especially in terms of racial intolerance.

Ferrer made some notable casting decisions for *Strange Fruit*; for the role of the middle-of-the-road, sensible doctor, he selected Juano Hernandez, while the part of Tracy was taken by the young actor Melchor (Mel) Ferrer, whose career (and identity) would occasionally be intertwined with José Ferrer's—they were of no relation, except what would develop in the future. His most interesting choice was for Nonnie. Many black (and white) readers considered Nonnie to be an offensive character, as she was college-educated but in love with "white trash." Both sides felt this was a distorted portrayal of black life. Ferrer would cast Jane White in the pivotal role of Nonnie; her real-life father was Walter White, who was executive director of the National Association for the Advancement of Colored People (NAACP).

Walter White would not hold back his reservations regarding other shows with predominantly black casts; he had previously denounced the musical *St. Louis Woman*, and had heretofore been silent about *Strange Fruit*. Many observers accused Ferrer of casting Jane White to prevent White Sr. from being critical of the play. White himself was also criticized for allowing his daughter to take the role. Ferrer insisted that Jane White read for the part and declared she was sensational. The young actress was honored to be given the difficult role of Nonnie: "I feel Nonnie is a very complex part. . . . I think in the theater, as in all the arts, we have got to reach a point where we have the ability to see a given character as representative of himself alone and not representative of a race, sex, or class."

Strange Fruit rehearsed for two weeks in Georgia, then proceeded to Montreal for its world premiere, followed by stops in Toronto, Boston, and Philadelphia prior to its opening on Broadway. In addition to the large cast, Ferrer had to cope with the overtly theatrical nature of the production, namely, its ten sets and a jackknife stage that supported a turntable stage and a constantly changing panorama. Out-of-town reviews would cite the play's excessive (three hours) length; the play would go from two acts to three acts to accompany scene shifting. Ferrer's reviews note that he does fine, sensitive work on the uncluttered scenes. In spite of Ferrer's entreaties to make certain edits, Smith was intransigent, refusing to make cuts. When the play arrived in Boston (where the source novel had been banned), Smith and Ferrer had to excise certain "profane uses of the name of God" in order for the show to be performed at all.

Ferrer's direction continued to be seen as "careful," with some reviewers believing this "care" contributed to the length. He delayed the show's opening to November 29 so that he and Smith could work on reducing the unwieldy running time. They managed to shave thirty minutes in advance of its new opening date, but the reviews were mixed. Critic Ward Morehouse felt "the play comes to life only occasionally . . . too long, too jumbled, too straggling. . . . Melchor Ferrer gives Tracy a proper feeling of weakness." Ferrer was seen as doing exceptional work on the occasional simple, heartfelt scene, but the *Times* noted that "as it has been staged by José Ferrer, the play sometimes takes on the aspect of a pageant, with people coming on from the wings, saying a few words and then going off again." The performances of the principals received praise, with particular acclaim being given to Jane White's Nonnie and Juano Hernandez's sensible doctor. The vast majority of criticism was leveled at Smith's (and Ferrer's) inability to successfully adapt what had been a dramatic novel into a dramatic work of theater. The consensus was *Strange Fruit* was sprawling, too verbose, and too busy—but there were moments of great power, especially a discussion of racial inequality between Hernandez's doctor and a liberal white mill owner, and in some of the passages between Nonnie and Tracy.

Despite the mixed notices, Ferrer the director had taken on a play that took on such hot-button topics as lynching, interracial romance, segregation, hypocrisy, and intolerance, as well as one that addressed the question of whether true love can pass the color line in the South—or, indeed, elsewhere. (Many states still viewed interracial marriage as something to be discouraged, and still others found such a union to be against the law—a law that would be in the books until the Supreme Court struck down any such statutes in 1966.) Ferrer, in his capacity as a producer, tried to keep the show running despite these notices, by keeping the play itself in the news. He invited Mississippi senator Theodore Bilbo to attend the play, but Bilbo dramatically refused, calling the play "a puny effort to glorify a love affair between a prostitute Negro woman and a profligate white . . . it does not tell the truth about the South, it is pleasing to the small segment of the white race that believes in social equality with the Negro. Of course, I am in favor of segregation of the races." Despite the attempts to use the play's controversy to its advantage and attract theatergoers who demand intellectual stimulation for their dramatic fare, *Strange Fruit* could not find its audience and closed on January 5, 1946, after forty-four performances.

The closing of the play elicited its own share of mixed reactions. There were the expected displays of jubilation from certain publications, with the *Amsterdam News* viewing the closing as "good riddance to bad rubbish." However, Paul Robeson, an outspoken advocate of racial inequality, felt the play was a deeply moving experience. Fredi Washington, a biracial actress who had delivered a powerful performance in the 1934 *Imitation of Life* as a light-skinned black woman who tries to pass for white, authored an eloquent article in the *People's Voice* attesting to the play's intrinsic value: "Listen to what Paul Robeson said . . . for me, it is a prophetic play; here colored people of high quality suffer the terrible frustrations of a prejudice-laden society. Sam's last speech [Juano

Hernandez's doctor] is a clear warning we can't take it anymore. America should heed this."

Despite the short-lived run of *Strange Fruit*, Ferrer himself emerged as a major player, a producer/director willing to take risks with modern, complex material. And so it was with some surprise that he announced what his next venture would be: a revival of Edmund Rostand's classic play about the famous French poet/swordsman with the pesky protuberant proboscis, *Cyrano de Bergerac*. Ferrer wanted to maintain his standing as a theatrical powerhouse, and only a surefire success would allow him to do that. For *Cyrano*, Ferrer would not only produce and possibly direct but would also undertake the star role himself. This is in spite of his view that, "in my book, I'm just a fair actor, but a wonderful producer and director. It may be one of my conceits but I think I'm too sensitive and observant t ogive all my time to posturing and declaiming lines. Shaping the details of a show is a helluva kick. It's almost as creative as writing the play."

Ferrer very nearly did not get the chance to perform what would become his signature role; originally, the producer Jed Harris was prepping the actor Louis Calhern to play the part. Observers wondered why Ferrer would accept the role, given that the actor Walter Hampden was a fairly big man and had been so firmly identified with the part (the last time in 1936). As Ferrer pointed out, Cyrano had already been played successfully by a variety of notable actors of varying physical stature (Ferrer was 5 foot, 10 inches tall) and that the author Rostand "wrote the part for Coquelin, and he was a little fellow. Richard Masefield was no giant. The height and the weight doesn't matter. He didn't fight with his fists . . . he fought with his sword, and you can fight just as dangerously with a sword at five feet-five as you can at six or more. . . . Cyrano's courage was within him. His size doesn't matter a bit. Except of course, the size of his nose."

While Ferrer had been reading scripts, he did come across the famous Brian Hooker version of *Cyrano*, and after Harris had dispensed with the notion of using Calhern, Ferrer believed it was the right time to do not only a classic play which he felt was "an answer to every actor's dream" but also one which practically guaranteed commercial success. Rostand's play was loosely based on the real Cyrano de Bergerac, who was a poet, soldier, and playwright in 1600-era France. While his nose was rather large, it was not the oversized appendage that would later be a major factor in the dramatic conflict in the play. In real life, the heroic Cyrano fought with the Gascons and was wounded in battle, and in 1655, he died of a serious head wound. Rostand would embroider Cyrano's story, adding a love triangle between Cyrano's cousin Roxane (whom he secretly loves) and a young, handsome musketeer named Christian.

The blend of self-sacrifice, braggadocio, romance, and heroism (not to mention the opportunity to compose poetry while engaging in fencing—and the opportunity to enact one of the longest, most moving death scenes in theatrical history) would offer a tour de force for any willing actor. Rostand had written it for Benoit-Constant Coquelin, who played it more than 400 times in Europe and America. Brian Hooker's English translation followed, starring Richard Masefield. Perhaps the most famous twentieth-century version up until 1946 had been performed by Walter Hampden. The venerable Hampden was still active on stage and screen in 1946, with supporting roles in films such as *Reap the Wild Wind* and *The Adventures of Mark Twain*; in his prime, Hampden portrayed Cyrano in five New York productions between 1923 and 1936. His performance had been hailed as the definitive Cyrano of his era, and many reasoned that it would be foolish to try a revival while Hampden's Cyrano was conceivably still etched in people's consciousness.

Many of these objections came from those in Ferrer's inner circle, but the actor proved to be dauntless. Ferrer saw Cyrano as the juiciest role in the theater, one that would provide unparalleled opportunities for the actor; furthermore, as a producer it would give him the chance to dazzle theatergoers with the extravagance of the piece. It also helped that Ferrer had sought out Hampden, who bestowed his blessing on Ferrer, along with the rights to use Hooker's translation. As a side note, Hooker's translation sometimes does not receive the credit it deserves (quite often in productions of *Cyrano*, the praise usually goes to the actor's portrayal or Rostand), which is regrettable, especially if one has encountered other translations. Some are too literal, preserving Rostand's verse and even providing further embroidery; Hooker's translation makes Rostand's verse accessible and preserves Rostand's beauty and wit.

Ferrer not only took an active part in raising capital, he invested some of his own. The original budget was $80,000, a figure that would eventually grow to $135,000, by which time Ferrer mortgaged his Ossining home to raise additional funds. Although the plan was to come to Broadway, Ferrer, along with his creative team and partner Arthur Friend, planned a short tour to begin in New Haven. Ferrer might have surprised a few people when he elected not to officially take on the role of director. Instead, Ferrer hired his lead from *Strange Fruit*, Melchor Ferrer. When asked whether they were brothers, Ferrer would say they were not—although both did actually attend Princeton, only at different times. "Ferrer is a common name among Latin Americans. It means iron worker and compares to being a Smith in the United States. I come from Puerto Rico and Mel is from New York City. Also, Mel's the one with the looks." Their association reaches back before *Strange Fruit*, however, as they knew each other casually when both were on Broadway (José in *Charley's Aunt*, Mel in *Kind Lady*). Melchor was a fledgling director himself and had persuaded José to act in some radio plays. (Later, he would do an unbilled bit in Melchor Ferrer's 1950 film, *The Secret Fury*.) Furthermore, Melchor had a brother named José, who attended Princeton with Ferrer (although Mel's brother would go on to become a surgeon).

Casting the pivotal roles of Roxane and Christian did not proceed as smoothly. On May 4, 1946, Lillian Gish was announced to be Roxane, though to this observer, while she might have brought some star power, the fifty-two-year-old Gish appeared too old for the part. (To see Lillian Gish at this juncture, one might view her in the film *Duel in the Sun* in order to appreciate the author's skepticism.) It might have been a publicity stunt, since on May 22, it was announced that Roxane would instead be played by Ruth Ford, a former cover girl who had made a number of Hollywood films, including *Dragonwyck* and *Wilson*. The part of Christian went to Leif Erickson, a movie actor with such credits as *The Fleet's In* and *Pardon My Sarong*, and who was perhaps better known for having been the husband of troubled actress Frances Farmer (later Erickson would become best known for his lead role as the rancher in television's *The High Chaparral*). Cyrano's nose, which would figure prominently, was designed by the famed mask maker Remo Bufano, and was a permanent rubber nose, designed to be easy on, easy off—with the aid of spirit gum.

The production premiered in New Haven in late May. Although they were now living separate lives, Hagen came up to New Haven to dispense both moral support and acting advice. The early reviews from the local critics were not especially kind. A few offered praise for Ferrer's Cyrano, especially for his work in the dying scene, with critics noting "the open mouth, the halting words, the memory reading of the last letter." However, more critics wrote along the lines of the Boston critics. One such reviewer, L. A. Sloper, would write that "Ferrer has neither the stature nor the presence of the braggart poet." Critic Elliot Norton found that Ferrer was "unable to project the proper eloquence and heroism" and would refer to his Cyrano as "a mumbling shadow." As with his acting audition at Princeton, the criticism and condescension from the Boston critics only motivated Ferrer to prove these critics wrong—later, after the show's success, he would shut down the New York run and return to Boston for a two-week special engagement. According to his son Rafael, "They *still* didn't give him a good review!"

Clearly adjustments had to be made if the play were to succeed under the harsh glare of the New York critics. The revival was granted a summer hiatus, in part so that Ferrer might have the opportunity to do some summer stock at the Suffern Theater (in the midst of all this activity, he had offered his services for a revival of *Design for Living*). While this might seem a little careless, given the pressure Ferrer faced, it also provided him with the opportunity to earn some money to further fund *Cyrano*.

According to Hagen, who was cast opposite Ferrer in *Design for Living*, the production had its share of problems. First among them was Ferrer's insistence on having Phyllis Hill in the cast. Hill was in *Cyrano* as Sister Claire—and she was also Ferrer's current girlfriend. Phyllis Hill was the daughter of Henley Hill, the assistant managing editor of the *Herald Tribune*. She was also a New Yorker, born and bred. At the age of twelve, when she was a student at Friends Seminary, she studied dancing with Mikhail Mordkin. Although she wasn't very good, she still pursued her dream of becoming a ballerina and went to the Ballet Russe de Monte-Carlo, where they soon fired her. She returned to America to work on her technique at the School of American Ballet. She remembered first meeting Ferrer at his brownstone on Fifty-eighth Street: "Joe was giving a party and a friend of mine brought me to see if Joe would give me a part in Cyrano. He did . . . of course I'd seen him before on the stage. If you want to know whether I fell in love or planned to marry him—no."

No doubt that Ferrer believed *Design for Living* would thrive, and his performance would not suffer—that it would be business as usual. However, on the last night of the run, Ferrer used real liquor for his prop bottle, got drunk, and slurred his lines. Hagen was furious. Ferrer would spend the night in their Ossining home, while Hagen returned to their Fifty-eighth Street residence. She also told Ferrer that his presence was no longer welcome there.

Ferrer was never shy about soliciting help on creative matters. He admitted taking the advice of technicians, carpenters, and fellow actors, his rationale being if they have a good idea, he'll take it—and probably get all the credit. Guthrie McClintic, Ferrer's directorial mentor, is rumored to have dispensed some directorial advice, but the real director of the production upon its Broadway arrival would be José Ferrer, not Melchor (though the Broadway program would give credit to Melchor Ferrer). Joshua Logan had come to see a preview and felt that certain lines and gestures were being thrown away. When Logan told director Mel Ferrer about his concerns, Mel brushed him off by saying the play was just an old chestnut. José began assuming the direction, whereupon he incorporated Logan's suggestions.

Out-of-town reviews also found fault with both Ruth Ford and Leif Erickson. The sentiment was that, while Ford was pretty, she was also too casual. For his part, Erickson's Christian was said to display too little passion. When rehearsals resumed in late August, Christian would be played by Ernest Graves, while Frances Reid would be playing Roxane. Reid was known to theatergoers particularly for her performance as Ophelia opposite Maurice Evans's Hamlet. (Prior to her hiring, Lillian Gish's name was floated again in various press releases.) Phyllis Hill remained in her part as Sister Claire; Ferrer and Hill would continue to see each other during the play, which remained an open secret—and which did not escape Hagen's notice. Even though she had long stopped seeing Paul Robeson on a romantic basis, she and Robeson were still close, with Hagen advising Robeson and providing occasional comfort (since he was still very married).

Ferrer's casting decisions and revisions improved the production, for when *Cyrano* opened in October 1946, the reviewers were almost competing to see who could offer the most praise. Howard Barnes of the *New York Herald Tribune* said *Cyrano* "is infused with joy." Brooks Atkinson enthused that "amid all the excitement, swashbuckling and old-fashioned ham that swept across the stage of the Alvin last evening, the theater again seemed to be something worth cherishing and enjoying . . . the Ferrer *Cyrano* is rattling good theater." Though Barnes took note of Ferrer's relatively slight stature in "a part that could do with a little more physical domination, he went on to praise Ferrer as "an actor of keen intelligence . . . his Cyrano has a sardonic wit, a strutting style, a bombastic manner of speech and withal a shyness and modesty. Ferrer has preserved a trace of ordinary human feeling that redeems Cyrano from complete artificiality." Ferrer was also noted for his role in making some wise cuts, and Melchor (the director of record) received praise for the direction.

While *Cyrano* would be a critical success for Ferrer, there were some obstacles to what he had hoped would be a financial windfall. As an actor, Ferrer was taking home $500 per week, mainly because he was waiving his $2,000 a week producer's fee in order to reimburse the backers in a quicker manner. Once the production recouped its $135,000 investment, then he would receive somewhere between $3,000 to $4,000 per week. Ferrer had hoped that the play would run a few years—although this ran counter to his strictly limited-engagement mentality. However, he found much to enjoy in the role, and was well aware that financial rewards would only come through if he continued to play the part.

For the most part, the run—and his private life—were running smoothly. Ferrer was continuing to see Phyllis Hill, and if anything, the affair seemed to gather some steam. On the professional front, he was still on the lookout for more contemporary plays by younger playwrights. However, Ferrer viewed modern playwrights as lacking complete dedication—not just to writing but to a life in the theater: "A young writer who wants to write for the theater should begin in the theater. He should start out as a third assistant stage manager and absorb the theater . . . take O'Neill, or Philip Barry . . . Saroyan and Odets . . . they all, in their way, went through the mill . . . most young playwrights don't want to work that hard." He also viewed Hollywood as a poacher of young talent, believing that many writers only aimed for a quick theatrical hit as a means of heading west for more lucrative opportunities.

When the Christmas season approached, the Ferrers seemed to be maintaining an amicable truce; they were still in their separate residences, with Ferrer in Ossining and Hagen in the New York City townhouse. On Christmas Eve, Hagen surprised Ferrer by decorating his dressing room, complete with a German Christmas tree and a music box. She had also left presents from Letty and herself. Paul Robeson was in New York City, and he and Hagen were to see each other on Christmas night at Hagen and Ferrer's East Fifty-eighth Street brownstone. She had not been seeing much of Robeson in the fall as he was touring the country fulfilling political and concert engagements. According to Hagen (as she recounted to the author Martin Duberman), it was a cozy evening, with Robeson arriving around 9 o'clock, and Hagen herself in some pain because of a bladder attack. They had dinner, and later they were in the living room when Hagen felt some kind of breeze and the door blew open: "And I said, 'you know, there's some man's feet standing there.' It was Joe. And I said, 'you came to wish me a Merry Christmas?' And I'm hugging him, and I look over his shoulders and there's two strangers. A detective and a lawyer, and they're going to "raid" the house. Then Joe came into the room, and I'll never forget. Joe looked so little and Paul so big. And he looked up at Paul and said, 'you son of a bitch,' and Paul just said, 'oh Joe . . .' The lawyer was saying something, the detective never came into the living room . . . it was the most ludicrous scene, then they just walked out. The detective claimed that 'we'd been together,' and we weren't. There were no cameras. No one took pictures or anything. . . . I was fully clothed."

The immediate aftermath of the incident was that Robeson and Hagen's on again, off again affair was over, since Robeson panicked and became very paranoid, perhaps at the prospect of what might emerge from being seen in a white woman's home. Robeson was very much in the news, having met with President Truman to demand an anti-lynching law—an incident like the Christmas affair could have conceivably been blown out of proportion, with all kinds of accusations leveled—including those of rape—by parties not even present.

As for Hagen, any hesitation she might have had about ending her marriage with Ferrer vanished immediately, although the divorce would not be finalized until 1948. Ferrer's "performance," that of the surprised, outraged spouse rang hollow for Hagen, since not only did Hagen believe that Ferrer knew about her liaison with Robeson, he even encouraged it. During the run of *Othello*, he would even warn them if anyone was approaching; Ferrer was busy with flings of his own, so he was almost relieved when Hagen had the attentions of another man. She also felt utter disgust toward Ferrer: "How could I live with that man for ten years and have him do that to me . . . how could any human being, then the whole notion of 'how long we'd been followed . . . how did they know that night he was there. I felt really shat on . . . and then the cowardice of Paul that night . . . racing out that night, going to friends."

If Ferrer had known about the affair, and there was every reason to believe he did, the motivating factor for the "raid" would be to gather some leverage in terms of a later divorce settlement—namely, custody for Letty and a favorable financial agreement. Positioning himself as the aggrieved husband would provide a much better chance of obtaining a legal advantage than as a husband who, along with his wife, was carrying on mutually exclusive, relatively satisfying affairs. Hagen continued to believe that Ferrer only wanted to avoid paying alimony; prior to that fateful evening, he had said nothing about the affair, and never treated Robeson with anything less than genuine affection. As Hagen would later say, between her husband's raid and Robeson's disengagement, she "was mad at men for a long time." However, stranger still was that not only did the marriage continue to sputter on, with periodic attempts at reconciliation, but Hagen and Ferrer would even occasionally work together.

This wouldn't occur until after *Cyrano* finished its run, and Ferrer was still busy making the news for the show. Ferrer announced that for one evening, he and all the principals should "sit the play out" and let the understudies go on in their place. (However, the principals would indeed perform in minor roles—Ferrer would be the Porter, while Ernest Graves would be seen not as Christian but as a lackey). This was not the first time such a theatrical stunt had been attempted, but it was the only one in recent memory and it also attracted attention from the critics. They found that the show still held up, even with the replacements going on instead of the stars. An immediate consequence came for Ernest Graves's understudy, Stewart Long, who was signed for the Australian company of *Born Yesterday*.

Another highlight of the *Cyrano* Broadway run came via the participation of Walter Hampden. Ferrer had made several overtures to Hampden to attend the production, and he was quite impressed with the results, including Ferrer's performance. Ferrer suggested that Hampden himself might take part in the show, perhaps splitting the role of Cyrano for one night only. The result was a special benefit performance in which Ferrer played Cyrano for the first four acts, and Hampden donned the nose for the last act, in which the aging Cyrano expires after at last professing his love for Roxane. What might have been the crowning achievement for Ferrer was that he and Fredric March (for *Years Ago*) were honored with the Best Actor award at the first-ever Antoinette Perry Awards in April 1947. These Perry Awards would soon be known as the Tony Awards, in honor of the late Perry, who was known to her friends by her nickname "Tony."

CHAPTER 5

Screen and Stage

CYRANO DE BERGERAC ENDED ITS RUN ON MARCH 22, 1947, AFTER 193 performances. While there would indeed be a film version in the future, none was planned at this time, and the expensive production did not provide its backers with the anticipated financial windfall. Ferrer himself took the hardest hit, having sacrificed most of his salary—and mortgaging his home—in the hopes that *Cyrano* would be a commercial success. He needed a cash infusion, much more than a few weeks doing theater in Suffern would supply, what with the houses in Ossining and Manhattan, and expensive (and imminent) divorce proceedings.

Thus, when producer Walter Wanger and director Victor Fleming offered Ferrer the opportunity to make his long-awaited movie debut, the actor seized the opportunity. Ferrer would play the role of the Dauphin in the forthcoming film version of *Joan of Arc*. The movie had quite a long gestation period, as film producer David O. Selznick had originally planned to do a version with Ingrid Bergman in the early 1940s, and Jennifer Jones was once announced to play the role (although some might have thought the story of a martyr would have come too soon for Jones after starring in *The Song of Bernadette*). In 1946, Bergman had played the role of Joan on Broadway in Maxwell Anderson's *Joan of Lorraine*. Anderson's play was about a group of actors who were staging a play about Joan of Arc. All the actors in the cast played at least two roles, that of the actors they were portraying *and* the characters in the play within the play. The central character was Ingrid Bergman's Mary Gray, who was also playing the role of Joan. The play would be both a critical and commercial success, earning both Bergman and Anderson accolades for their work. Bergman was at an early career peak, having starred in a string of hits including *Dr. Jekyll and Mr. Hyde* (under the direction of Fleming), *Casablanca*, *For Whom the Bell Tolls*, and *The Bells of St. Mary's*. She was also eager to reprise her role of Joan on the Hollywood sound-stages. (There would be no location filming in France.) Bergman, director Fleming, and producer Wanger would form Sierra Pictures to mount this production, entering into a tentative agreement with Metro-Goldwyn-Mayer to release the film, with Bergman, Fleming, and Wagner getting the biggest share of the potential profits. (Prior to filming, MGM bowed out, as it could not submit to the financial demands of Sierra, and the film would be released by RKO Pictures instead.)

Joan of Lorraine (as the film was still called during the production period) would not be a completely faithful adaptation of the play, since the producers decided to dispense with the original's play-within-the-play structure. The play's author, Maxwell Anderson, was hired to do the screenplay, working alongside Andrew Solt, which gave Anderson hope that the film would retain much of the content, despite the sacrificing of the structure.

This ambitious production provided its share of headaches, most of them falling on the shoulders of its veteran director Victor Fleming. He was no stranger to huge, roadshow productions, having taken much of the credit for the 1939 classic *Gone with the Wind*.

More than 4,000 extras were put to good use, especially during the battle scenes and the scenes where the hordes are storming the palace. However, the logistics were not the major factors in Fleming's worsening outlook toward the film. More often they had to do with the demands of star Bergman, who felt protective of both the role and the property. In the Broadway production, she had convinced playwright Anderson to add transcripts from Joan's trial at Rouen to the finished play. For the film version, she wanted to incorporate more changes. Solt was a willing collaborator, but Anderson was not as cooperative. This set the stage for several arguments between Bergman, Fleming, and Anderson over whose movie this really was. Anderson would say that he was the wronged party, and as the least important member of this triptych (at least as far as studio hierarchy was concerned), he was reduced to being a helpless bystander as Bergman and Fleming grappled for creative control.

Ferrer was able to witness the exchanges firsthand, since some pertained to his character the Dauphin, who would be portrayed as being an early supporter of Joan's until events compelled him to repudiate her. Ferrer's presence on the set was one of the few sources of joy for the director. Fleming had cast Ferrer on the basis of his performances as both Iago and Cyrano, and his physical stature matched how Fleming saw the Dauphin: small in every sense of the word. Fleming would be pleased with Ferrer's enthusiastic participation and his layered portrayal of the Dauphin: "I chose him, not only because he approximated a physical resemblance to the character, but because I knew he would attack the part with more enthusiasm than some actor who wished to return home to his swimming pool." According to Fleming's biographer, the director was probably alluding to the actor Lee Bowman, who had acted opposite Susan Hayward in *Smash-Up* and had recently tested for the Dauphin.

Ferrer certainly did portray the Dauphin with relish; it's not his fault that the film would suffer both from being too talky and overlong. Ferrer had invested the Dauphin with not only simplicity and childlike wonder but even an occasional hint of humility. His early scene with Joan, where he is testing her, also turns out to be a test for himself. It's a remarkably assured performance of what is, in many ways, a weak and even despicable character. Regardless of his ease in front of the camera and the attention he was getting, Ferrer certainly still retained his misgivings about Hollywood. He would tell one of the film's (many) technical advisers, Father Paul Doncoeur, that he took the role only to earn some money and that he would not come back to Hollywood. It also didn't hurt his morale that Phyllis Hill was able to get a small role in the movie.

Because Ferrer had almost limitless energy, he was not content to be in Los Angeles to merely film a movie; he also was playing Prince Hal in the evenings onstage at the Coronet Theater in Los Angeles. In addition, despite Hill's presence, he was still calling Hagen every day. Some of the calling had to do with daughter Letty, but he was also showing his support for Uta's independent theatrical endeavors. Hagen was performing the classic melodrama *Angel Street* (perhaps better-known today as the basis for the film *Gaslight*) at the Variety Playhouse in Bridgehampton. He would even fly in to see the performance and subsequently send flowers, claiming to be "one of her followers."

At least Ferrer could be fairly confident that the increasing difficulties on the production had nothing to do with him—and there were plenty, with escalating and unforeseen costs due to the constant script changes, as well as the costly demands for historical accuracy. This included the white armor that Bergman's Joan wore (which required 500 hours of construction time) and the shipping of horses from Iowa as the horses in the Southern California area were deemed to be too small. Fleming himself came down with the flu, and the production had to be shut down for over a week while he recuperated. After shooting ended in late 1947, some members of the cast were summoned to shoot more scenes. At the initial previews, test audiences were a little cool to the title *Joan of Lorraine*, so RKO decided to change the title to *Joan of Arc*. The studio was then made aware that the title had already been claimed by other studios, including Paramount and Twentieth Century-Fox (not to mention Selznick), and these studios would not part with the title unless remuneration was involved.

This post-filming intrigue didn't concern Ferrer, since he had already returned to New York, intent on parlaying his artistic success with *Cyrano* into something more critically and commercially satisfying. In many ways, his life in the theater would be split in different directions. The pragmatic side of Ferrer believed that art and commercial success needn't be mutually exclusive; he always hoped his more artistic endeavors would be greeted both with public acclaim and a favorable critical consensus. By the same token, he did not believe that something done merely for the sake of escapism was a comedown. He directed and performed in a blend of what one might call "important" works along with plays designed merely to entertain, believing there was intrinsic value in both.

While Ferrer would direct new works by rising (or even established) playwrights, as had been the case with *Strange Fruit*, he quite often turned to the classics, trying to figure out ways to revitalize old chestnuts or provide a new slant on timeworn material. He would also strive to find ways to demonstrate why a particular show would have relevance in the modern day. The other striking element of Ferrer's commitment to the stage is a seeming disregard as far as money was concerned—lest anyone be deceived, even though he professed indifference to financial matters, they were very much on his mind (and a key reason for his "midnight raid" on Hagen and Robeson, as one tabloid would dub it). Yet this same José Ferrer would also enter into an agreement with the then-struggling New York City Center to help organize its upcoming 1948–49 winter season, for a nominal salary.

Ferrer's involvement originated when he and actor/director Richard Whorf were in Hollywood in late 1947; they were both being lobbied by a mutual friend to do a production of Ben Jonson's *Volpone* in Los Angeles. When that collapsed, Ferrer was contacted by one of the directors of City Center, Jean Dalrymple, at the behest of influential co-director Richard Aldrich. She asked Ferrer if he would be interested in starting a permanent theater company for New York's City Center, which had previously presented occasional music performances, dance recitals, and revivals, the most recent being a not warmly received version of *Rip Van Winkle*. Ferrer was intrigued by the possibility of doing high-quality theater for a top ticket price of $2.00 (as opposed to the $6.00 ticket price currently in fashion). He and Whorf agreed to work for $100 per week and would set about finding name actors to also work for similarly modest salaries, the hope being that the combination of star actors and modestly priced shows would enable City Center to turn a profit. It was not an unreasonable expectation, as City Center had a capacity of two thousand people; if even half the seats were filled, the shows would break even if they took in $12,000 per week. Add to that, the number of patrons on the City Center mailing list, and hopes were high that this might lead to a permanent theater company being established at City Center.

Ferrer and Whorf's inaugural production would be *Volpone*, adapted by Richard Barr, with some assistance from Ferrer and Whorf. Barr had already staged a version of *Volpone*, and both Ferrer and Whorf were impressed with the tightness of the piece, as well as the opportunities it supplied the actors. Ferrer also impressed Barr and the City Center board as a fine administrator, persuading the cast to accept an Actors Equity stock contract instead of the Broadway minimum wage. Originally Martin Ritt was supposed to direct, but after some disagreements with Ferrer and Whorf over "artistic vision," Ritt stepped down and Barr was given the chance to direct *Volpone*, starring not only Ferrer and Whorf, but John Carradine and the ever-present Phyllis Hill. The revival would have a two-week run, beginning January 8, 1948. The production received good notices for all involved from most of the leading New York papers. Theater critic George Jean Nathan would proclaim "the show is as free from scholastic reverence as a subsidized college football player and even more athletic." Brooks Atkinson of the *New York Times* was a notable dissenter, feeling that Whorf and Ferrer were "ringmasters of a broad and noisy circus." (Ferrer's paramour, Hill, gained some notice for her supporting role). Ferrer's comic vigor reminded those of his comedic flair that he hadn't exhibited since *Charley's Aunt*.

The second production was to be Patrick Hamilton's *Angel Street*. Ferrer hoped he could engage his estranged wife Uta to star, having been impressed by her work in the play's revival at Bridgehampton. Ferrer said he would only act and direct *Angel Street* if Hagen consented to act opposite him (which must have been difficult for Hagen since Hill was also to be in the cast). However, Hagen must have been in a conciliatory mood and agreed, in spite of ongoing friction between Hagen and Ferrer, as well as their respective lawyers. In January 1947, Ferrer's lawyer, Arthur Friend, intended for Ferrer to have custody of Letty but allow her to remain with Uta, "provided that her manner and method of life warranted . . . her interest and future is all he is concerned with." Hagen's lawyer's reaction to this letter was "amazed. I thought we had clearly understood the agreement was to permit Uta to continue in her custody of Letty . . . that Joe would continue his support of Uta and Letty. If Uta gets a play, Joe's obligation would cease except for such provision for Letty that may be reasonable." With her $100 per week salary, Hagen's finances would not be fully restored by *Angel Street*, but Ferrer strongly felt her performance would lead to more lucrative offers.

After her experience in *Othello*, Hagen had begun to dislike acting. However, she recently felt reinvigorated in terms of her acting skills, after appearing in director Harold Clurman's production of *The Whole World Over* in 1947. In later years, she credited Clurman with helping her get rid of acting tricks. She also met Herbert Berghof when he replaced Stephen Bekassy as Hagen's love interest, an arrangement that extended offstage, too. Berghof was an established stage actor and acting teacher, having been one of the founding members of the Actors Studio, and one of the two people (Clurman being the other) who helped restore Hagen's joy in acting.

Ferrer directed (with Barr's assistance) and cast himself in the meaty role of the evil, manipulative husband who is trying to "gaslight" his wife while trying to find some hidden jewels. The rehearsal period would prove fraught with tension, as co-director Barr was instructed to clear a wide path for Hagen; she had already done the play, and according to Ferrer, knew it much better than Barr did. In addition, the presence of mistress Phyllis Hill, cast as the other woman Nancy (the part played by Angela Lansbury in the MGM Ingrid Bergman/Charles Boyer film version), and known to many as the probable next Mrs. Ferrer, would help to blur the line between reality and theatrical artifice. In the last scene, the tormented wife gets to tell off her husband, who has been subdued and tied up by a Scotland Yard detective. Hagen would say later that the applause she received was in part from a theater community who had understood how much she had suffered during her ordeal with husband Ferrer. Critic Howard Barnes would write that it is Hagen "who gives a scintillating quality to the revival, adding accents of humanity and credibility to what might have been a burlesque." There were some dissenters who remarked that Hagen was almost playing a caricature of a damsel in distress. Nevertheless, emboldened by her work in *Angel Street*, Hagen was no longer professionally affiliated with Ferrer or his agent; she even made plans to make pictures and signed with the powerful Jaffe Agency.

Ferrer and Whorf continued their City Center collaboration in February with a production of Anton Chekhov's *Four One-Act Comedies*. This production received mixed notices, with Brooks Atkinson writing that some of the subtleties in Chekhov's original works have been buried under much comic confusion. Ferrer derived some satisfaction that his girlfriend and protégé Phyllis Hill was noted by several critics for her quiet, low-key acting. The success of the three initial productions was encouraging for the City Center investors, and for Ferrer and Whorf. In terms of the box office, *Volpone* and the Chekhov plays were quite profitable, with *Angel Street* a little less so, despite a favorable critical reception. The enthusiasm from the audiences, particularly younger ones who were attracted by the low-price ceiling, allowed City Center to announce that this inaugural winter season would be followed by a spring season, with Ferrer running the show.

Ferrer was able to attract actors to work at a fraction of what they were worth in Hollywood or on Broadway for a season that would open in April with a revival of another Ben Jonson farce, *The Alchemist*, followed by Eugene O'Neill's *S.S. Glencairn*, consisting of four short plays (including *The Long Voyage Home*, the source for the 1940 John Wayne/John Ford film), and, finally in June, concluding with *The Insect Comedy*. Some notable newcomers to the company included George Coulouris, an actor well known for his continental heavies, notably as Paul Lukas's nemesis in *Watch on the Rhine*, and Ray Walston, who was in the early stages of a career that would take him to *South Pacific*, *Damn Yankees*, and to television fame in *My Favorite Martian*.

Richard Whorf wasn't present for this new series of plays, and though Ferrer made his creative presence felt, the directorial chores were handled officially by others. Morton da Costa would direct *The Alchemist*; he would become best-known for guiding Robert Preston to theatrical glory in both the stage and screen versions of *The Music Man*. Phyllis Hill would also continue to be part of the company. The official dissolution of the Ferrer/Hagen union was imminent, and Ferrer was planning to marry Hill as soon as the divorce was final. When *The Alchemist* opened in early May for a two-week engagement, the acting came in for its share of praise (Brooks Atkinson said, "Ferrer . . . is playing Face with a nice, droll touch"), but some questioned whether the property itself was worthy of revival. Ferrer himself staged *S.S. Glencairn*, and while the director was lauded for a realistic production, many thought the intimate atmosphere of the piece was lost in the giant confines of City Center.

Joséf and Karel Caprek's *The Insect Comedy* concluded Ferrer's second season, eliciting some of the most discouraging notices. An offbeat allegory wherein the insects are seen as a reflection of life among humans, the production was noted for its technical aspects, but whatever Ferrer and company thought was profound about the source material seemed to escape the notice of the critics. *The Insect Comedy* proved to be a disappointing end to the series of revivals. The end of the run would also prove to be the end for the permanent theater company that had been envisioned; actors were getting more lucrative offers and the company was unable to stay afloat.

Ferrer did not remain idle for long, especially since his divorce with Uta became finalized toward the end of *The Insect Comedy*. He married Phyllis Hill in Westport, Connecticut, on June 19, 1948, four days after he signed the final papers, and the day after attending a screening of Carl Dreyer's silent classic *The Passion of Joan of Arc*, which Ingrid Bergman had arranged for the Museum of Modern Art. Since Hagen was retaining the New York City townhouse for herself and Letty, he and Hill would make their home in Ossining. After his divorce from Hagen, he did maintain some kind of presence in Letty's life, even from a distance. In the Uta Hagen Papers at New York Public Library for the Performing Arts, there are several letters in which Letty is referring to gifts that she had received from her father, such as a typewriter that she received a month early because she had told her father she needed it for school. There were also occasions when his plan to have Letty spend the summer in Beverly Hills with him and Phyllis was at odds with Uta's plan to have Letty attend camp in New England. He would write Uta that this was the result of his "natural desire to have her with me as much as possible and Letty's desire to stay where she was enjoying herself."

In June, Ferrer reunited with City Center confederate Richard Barr and headed to the John Drew Theater in East Hampton to appear in a production of *Romeo and Juliet* under Barr's direction. Ferrer had always wanted to play Romeo, and at thirty-six, he felt this was the only venue (and director) that would allow him to perform the role. He would play opposite Mary Anderson's Juliet, and Ray Walston would appear as Friar Lawrence. Although Barr would be the credited director, Ferrer assisted by rehearsing privately with Anderson, while Barr directed the rest of the company.

After he completed his short run in *Romeo and Juliet*, Ferrer came across a script by Robert McEnroe called *The Silver Whistle*. The chief role was that of Oliver Erwenter, a philosophical, aging tramp (as those rogues were referred to then) who brings hope to an old folks' home by supplying them with phony rejuvenation pills. The character represents everything that the residents lack: hope, courage, and optimism—and he even wins the affections of a lovely custodian. McEnroe would say that he created Erwenter out of a composite of windy, unprincipled vagrants that he encountered in a barroom in Hartford, Connecticut; he believed that people, like those in the play's setting, do not use their senses enough to be involved in the world around them. Erwenter, flawed as he is (he is later revealed to be a hobo of merely forty-seven years of age, as opposed to the seventy-seven-year-old he has pretended to be), encouraged his fellow old-timers to become more engaged. Fittingly for a play that had its basis in a Connecticut barroom, *The Silver Whistle* began a successful out-of-town tryout in Westport, Connecticut, at the Westport Country Playhouse prior to its anticipated opening on Broadway. Phyllis Hill had a role in the Westport version of the play, but the producers didn't deem her Broadway-ready, so she did not get to accompany the show when it reached Broadway in December.

Before the play opened, Ferrer and his new wife were able to enjoy the long-awaited premiere of *Joan of Arc*. A star-studded opening in Los Angeles was followed by a publicity tour for star Bergman that included stops in France following Joan of Arc's journey. The film did not receive the critical acclaim that the producers were anticipating. Many thought the film was too long, tedious, with excessive pageantry, and not enough character study. A few thought Anderson's source material was present in name only, even though many of Anderson's exchanges made it directly into the screen version. Some lamented the loss of the frame of Anderson's *Joan of Lorraine*, finding the presentation of the material as a straight historical spectacle to be lacking. As for Joan herself, Bergman was found by some reviewers, including Bosley Crowther of the *New York Times*, to lack the spiritual quality needed to make it credible that so many would be in her thrall. However, Ferrer's Dauphin generally avoided any critical brickbats; Crowther found Ferrer to be "electric" as the weak and vacillating Dauphin, and his scenes with Bergman's Joan have the most vitality in the film. And this counts for any released version of *Joan of Arc*, whether it was the initial roadshow version or the edited version (running 108 minutes) that was later in circulation.

Director Victor Fleming (also a former lover of Bergman's) had found the filming to be extremely taxing. Fleming would attend the premiere, but he died about a month later; *Joan of Arc* was fated to be his last film. While the critical response had been mixed at best, *Joan of Arc* would subsequently be nominated for a number of Academy Awards, including Best Actress, Best Art Direction, and Best Musical Score. In addition, Ferrer himself would be nominated for Best Supporting Actor; he lost to Walter Huston in *The Treasure of the Sierra Madre*, but the movie would win Oscars for Best Cinematography and Best Costume Design. Producer Walter Wanger was awarded a special Oscar for distinguished service and "adding to its moral stature" through his production of *Joan of Arc*, but he refused to accept; he was still angered that the movie itself did not receive a Best Picture nomination.

For Ferrer, the acclaim was surely providing him with second thoughts about inwardly (and outwardly) rebuffing Hollywood's overtures. However, he was preoccupied in November with the imminent Broadway opening of *The Silver Whistle* under the auspices of the Theater Guild, which, quite frankly, could use a hit, as its first two offerings were not commercial successes. There was plenty of positive word of mouth about the forthcoming play, since it had received good notices in Westport and on the accompanying tour. In addition, both McEnroe (who had a day job as a research worker at a Hartford aircraft plant) and Ferrer spent a great deal of time honing and perfecting the material. There was also anticipation on the part of theatergoers regarding Ferrer's first major sustained role since *Cyrano*.

While *The Silver Whistle* was only found to be middling as a play when it opened on November 24, 1948, at the Biltmore Theater (several reviewers found the supporting characters to be either sketches or buffoons), there was no shortage of praise for Ferrer's performance. Howard Barnes of the *New York Herald Tribune* wrote that Ferrer "played the role with complete assurance . . . in awkward moments, he declaims with good humor and dramatic effect." Ward Morehouse enjoyed Ferrer's "rollicking performance as the glib, philosophical wanderer," while *New York Times* critic Brooks Atkinson called Ferrer "the most able, the most stimulating and the most versatile actor of his generation in America. Cast in the part of a beloved vagabond in a dryly entertaining play, he gives a wonderful comic performance and deserves a little raucous cheering from the hustings of Broadway." Atkinson went on to extol Ferrer's thespian merits and how he has enhanced his stature since *Cyrano*: "What he learned in his gutsy performance of 'Cyrano' has helped to give him the latitude and ironic eloquence he brings to the disarming rogue. Mr. Ferrer is a magnetic actor with an excellent voice an alert intelligence . . . he plays with a sense of rich enjoyment."

After the play's successful opening night and with the promise of a long run, Ferrer was in the spotlight once again. He tried to take all this attention in stride, telling reporter Hal Boyle, "I don't particularly like the life I lead. For the simple reason I don't know whether I'm going to eat next year." Ferrer was still on the fringes of financial insolvency, having worked for a nominal salary at City Center following his inability to recoup his financial stake in the critically successful *Cyrano*. Ferrer commented on the vagaries of fame to reporter George Tucker: "I have been through this before. I was a 'great' actor in *Cyrano*. They said I was trying on the mantle of Booth, Barrymore . . . now when I read I'm a 'great' actor, I remember it was only six short months since I reached the absolute bottom. . . . I was rundown in health and didn't have any money." As always was the case with Ferrer, the prospect of a long run—even though it might provide some semblance of financial security—was enough for him to have misgivings, not only about the run itself but about the life of an actor: "It means I'll have to say the same lines, over and over, eight times a week, for perhaps two to three years. That's no way to live."

The Silver Whistle, largely on the basis of Ferrer's box-office appeal, proved to be the first hit for the Theater Guild, with strong grosses continuing into the spring of 1949. However, given Ferrer's difficulty of enduring the monotony of a long run, it should have come as no surprise when he signed to do a film with Twentieth Century-Fox. It would be directed by Otto Preminger under the working title *Methinks the Lady* and would reunite Preminger with his leading lady from *Laura*, Gene Tierney (who had just taken a year off following the birth of her daughter). Preminger himself came to New York to court Ferrer, with Ferrer's contract calling for a salary of $75,000. *Methinks the Lady* would begin filming in Hollywood in late May, which meant the actor would have to depart *The Silver Whistle*, Although there were some attempts to find a replacement for the star, the producers couldn't come up with a suitable one, so *The Silver Whistle* had to close on May 28, 1949. Ferrer originally was supposed to depart on May 1 but convinced the producers of *Whirlpool* (as *Methinks the Lady* was now called) to delay his departure as long as they could. However, he had to be in Hollywood no later than June 2.

Having tried as hard as he could to deflect any ill will from the Theater Guild producers, Ferrer departed immediately after his last performance.

However, Hollywood would not be his first stop. Instead he went to his native Puerto Rico for commencement exercises at the University of Puerto Rico. His arrival at the San Juan airport was greeted by over 1,000 people, and later, at the university, in front of an audience of 3,000 spectators, Chancellor Jaime Benitez presented an honorary degree of Doctor of Fine Arts to a very grateful Ferrer. The citation read that the degree was conferred not just because of Ferrer's place in theater, but because he possessed the artist's unceasing urge for finer achievement. It was his first return to Puerto Rico in sixteen years, but he pledged he would help open the renovated San Juan Municipal Theater; he would also be the first actor to receive an honorary degree from the university.

From there, it was on to Hollywood to begin filming *Whirlpool*. His role was that of Korvo, a smooth astrologer and hypnotist who spends his time trying to convince wealthy gullible women to part with their money. Not that he appears that way from the start—at first, he appears to be solicitous toward Ann, the troubled, privileged housewife (Gene Tierney) of a renowned psychoanalyst (Richard Conte). When she is caught shoplifting, Ferrer's Korvo persuades the store to let her go, and after assuaging her concerns that he might be a blackmailer, persuades her to allow him to help. What Ann doesn't know, however, is that Korvo's concern is a mere mask for his plot to frame her for the murder of his ex-mistress. (A pivotal cocktail party scene includes Ferrer's wife, Phyllis Hill, among the guests.)

There were several talented craftsmen involved with the making of *Whirlpool*, with writers Ben Hecht and Andrew Solt laboring to make a somewhat convoluted plot work, David Raksin composing the score (as had done the Preminger's *Laura*), and Preminger continuing his association with the genre that would become known as film noir, through *Laura*, *Fallen Angel*, *Whirlpool*, and the following year, with *Where the Sidewalk Ends* (reuniting him with both *Laura* stars, Tierney and Dana Andrews). Tierney was excited to be working again with Preminger, and she was also pleased to be acting opposite Ferrer, having admired his work in *Cyrano*. Their scenes together provide the real moments of interest in *Whirlpool*, as Tierney's fragile housewife (the actress had already begun to exhibit signs of mental illness that would lead to her breakdown and withdrawal from films) contrasts effectively with Ferrer's confident, fraudulent charlatan. While Preminger biographer Foster Hirsch viewed this portrayal as "the enticing spectacle of a phony actor playing a phony actor," there is actually a lot more skill and subtlety involved—especially for those unfamiliar with Ferrer's oeuvre, as many filmgoers in the 1940s were. He displays admirable restraint in the early scenes, and his rich baritone is used for all the sensitive shadings he could employ to simulate compassion toward his eventual target. Later, the demands of the plot would force Ferrer's Korvo to abandon these subtleties, as his character would become almost demonic in his desire to frame Ann and humiliate her unsuspecting husband. Even there, however, Ferrer is always smoothly entertaining, with a command of cinematic technique that belied his standing as a screen newcomer.

There is another good performance in *Whirlpool*: that of veteran actor Charles Bickford as the dedicated, crusty cop on the case. (He had previously played a policeman of more murderous intent in Preminger's *Fallen Angel*.) Nevertheless, it's hard for the film to overcome the miscast Richard Conte in the role of the high-society therapist; Preminger, who was known for his heretofore astute casting, seemed to have been bereft of his senses when it came to choosing Conte for the role. Conte was under contract to Twentieth Century-Fox and could be very good, especially in war films and gangster dramas. He had just garnered rave notices as the imprisoned convict in *Call Northside 777*. In *Whirlpool*, however, Conte the actor seems more bemused than his character and stubbornly fails to convince. Ferrer would recall that "Conte was a big mistake. We all felt it while shooting the film. He suggested a New York street type rather than a well-educated psychiatrist."

Critics enjoyed Ferrer's performance when *Whirlpool* was released in late 1949, with Howard Barnes finding Ferrer to be "superb," while Bosley Crowther felt that Ferrer "mouths Hecht's silken phrases with acid savor." In this, Ferrer's second film, many critics recognized the insinuating power of Ferrer's distinctive baritone; as Leo Mishkin of the *Daily Telegraph* wrote, "His velvety voice, solemn poise and assurance lend the role more impact than another actor might have brought it."

With Ferrer's growing stature among critics and producers, it would be difficult for him to resist the lure of the good role—or the good money that would accompany it. He planned to celebrate his good fortune by returning to Puerto Rico for a pleasure trip and then head to Europe. There had been talk about Ferrer reviving his role of Cyrano for a movie, but the financing had not come together yet. Producer/director Robert Rossen had already spoken to Ferrer about playing the lead of a bullfighter in *The Brave Bulls* (when the film was finally made, it was with another Ferrer— Mel.) Gabriel Pascal (*Caesar and Cleopatra*, *Pygmalion*) had also approached Ferrer with offers to appear in two films. One was *St. Francis of Assisi*, while the other would be *Androcles and the Lion*. Pascal wanted Ferrer for the title roles in each, but as Ferrer noted, "It's only in the discussion stages." While in Europe, Ferrer met with French filmmaker Marcel Pagnol about an English version of Pagnol's famed *The Baker's Wife*.

There were two concrete offers that came his way, even before the release of *Whirlpool*. Twentieth Century-Fox announced that it had signed Ferrer to a five-year contract, beginning in March 15, 1950, with at least one picture a year for two years. The studio held an option for two more pictures. The other offer, from MGM, would begin shooting in January 1950, and would cast Ferrer as a Latin American dictator opposite Cary Grant (as a brain surgeon) in the melodrama *Crisis*. (This project had originally been titled *Ferguson*, the name of Grant's character in the film, but it was changed shortly before Ferrer signed on.)

The writer of *Crisis*, Richard Brooks, who had some exceptional credits on his resume, including the 1948 film of *Key Largo*, would make his directorial debut on the film. This came about because Grant owed MGM a film and was lured by producer Arthur Freed (normally a producer of musicals like *Meet Me in St. Louis*) with the promise that it would only be a thirty-six-day shooting schedule. Grant did not know that the writer Brooks had also intended to direct, and as Brooks later recalled, Grant said, "Well if you can write it, you can direct it too." Also, among the cast were fellow Latino powerhouses like Antonio Moreno and Gilbert Roland, along with Signe Hasso and Paula Raymond (a theater friend of both Ferrer and Hagen, she was cast as Grant's wife in the movie).

Ferrer was excited about the chance to play a Latin American (named Farrago), even if the character was the ruthless dictator of a fictitious country—and even if it was another villainous portrayal: "I'm always noted among my friends for my sunny disposition. I'm afraid audiences will think I am the way I appear on screen." He was even more enthused to be working for MGM, seeing the role as a step forward in his career. Working with a first-time director didn't concern Ferrer; to the contrary, he would recall that "we were all a little excited because it was Brooks's first directing job and we were all rooting for him."

Acting opposite Grant, who plays a reluctant surgeon on holiday forced to operate on the ill Ferrer, seemed to be favorable for both actors as they seemed to form a mutual admiration society. Ferrer observed that "Grant had a keen sense of the comic and the ridiculous, and it made working easy and pleasant, and I also remember that he had a very clear idea of what he wanted to do and how he wanted to do it, and on at least one or two occasions quietly made his wishes known and imposed his will." Ferrer was well aware that he had nowhere near the clout to impose that kind of will, at least not in Hollywood. He also did not view this as a repudiation of either Grant or Brooks, since Ferrer had always allowed others to make their views known because of his feeling that collaboration led to a stronger finished product. For his part, Grant enjoyed playing opposite Ferrer: "He makes each scene come alive. The sense of realism when Ferrer plays a scene is almost eerie."

While *Crisis* concerned a brewing revolution in a Latin American country ruled with an iron hand by a failing but still ruthless dictator, the locations would be strictly Hollywood soundstage. There are some interesting moments of moral ambiguity in the movie, as Grant's doctor is unwilling to operate on the malevolent Farrago and is even more unwilling to kill him during surgery to appease rebels who have kidnapped his wife. Ferrer's Farrago is another intelligent, outwardly confident creation of the actor. The character is subject to self-doubt concerning his illness and his capacity to rule. The performance effortlessly combines a modicum of charm with a degree of malevolence and almost childlike need. Grant manages to be an effective contrast, with his stern underplaying and quietly sarcastic demeanor.

Crisis did not emerge as the anticipated artistic and commercial triumph, as several factors stood in its way. For one thing, Frank Launder's British-made *State Secret* (released in the US under the title of *The Great Manhunt*) was released earlier in 1950 and told a similar tale about an unwilling doctor (Douglas Fairbanks Jr.) being pressured to operate on a dying dictator; for another, the publicists at MGM weren't sure how to handle this atypical effort from Grant and Freed. The advertising promised audiences that they would enjoy "Devil-May-Cary in a Hotbed of Adventure!" instead of the grim melodrama that was in store. The movie would register a loss of a few hundred thousand dollars and cause Freed and Grant to reconsider their forays into serious filmmaking; Brooks would proceed to have a successful writing/directing career.

For Ferrer, *Crisis* was mainly a winning proposition. Critics who might have been lukewarm about the film itself praised his performance. *Variety* noted that "dictatorship versus the right of man to freedom is the theme, and the script and direction get up on the soapbox too frequently. The mood is grim where some lightness would have helped. . . . Grant and Ferrer shape their characters with some assurance." Howard Barnes said, "Ferrer plays the dictator with such venomous impact that his comeuppance is something to see." And Bosley Crowther of the *New York Times* felt that "with such a penny dreadful story, it's remarkable that Brooks has been able to get any substance on the screen . . . most of the bitter exchanges between Ferrer and Grant are intriguingly sharp."

CHAPTER 6

Cyrano—the Movie

JOSÉ FERRER WAS ENCOURAGED BY THE FAVORABLE NOTICES FOR HIS performance in his 1950 film *Crisis*, and his marriage to Phyllis appeared to be successful, but there were disturbing similarities to his earlier union with Uta. One was his tendency toward straying outside the bounds of holy matrimony. There were also Ferrer's extended absences from their Ossining home, as Hollywood began to play a bigger role in his life. Phyllis maintained that she would be content spending her time painting the furniture that she and husband José picked up in shops around Ossining, but as a former ballet dancer and aspiring actress, she had hoped for a career apart from his, and this hadn't materialized.

An even more pressing factor concerned Ferrer's name, as it had recently been included in the notorious *Red Channels*, the anti-communist pamphlet published in June 1950. Throughout the late 1940s into the '50s, anyone who had displayed sympathies toward the Communist Party or had contributed to various causes that were seen to be left-leaning would have been fair game for this list. If one's name were found among those listed in *Red Channels*, that person's ability to earn a living would be endangered, especially in the entertainment industry where participation depends in large part on audience goodwill. Based on the extent of the damning information available to investigators (and the public), it might prove difficult for those named, especially in the foreseeable future. In addition to Ferrer, the list included other actors such as Edward G. Robinson, John Garfield, Luther Adler, Stella Adler, Judy Holliday, and Orson Welles. Ferrer's ex-wife, Uta Hagen, was also on the list, and her prospective film career had to be put on hold (although she did continue her work in the theater). As for Ferrer, one possible casualty of his being named to *Red Channels* was the termination of his Twentieth Century-Fox contract, by mutual agreement—or so it was reported.

Despite the potential political pitfalls swirling around him, Ferrer was consumed with the preparation of his next project, the long-awaited film adaptation of *Cyrano de Bergerac*. Since the play and Ferrer had enjoyed critical success on stage, he hoped that the property would attract a buyer—and that he would be naturally part of the package. Producer Stanley Kramer, then with United Artists, had been assuring Ferrer that he wanted to film *Cyrano*, based on Ferrer's production, but others were interested, too. Famed producer Alexander Korda had already purchased the rights to the play, with Laurence Olivier and Vivien Leigh in mind for Cyrano and Roxane; this was to be their first screen teaming since 1941's *That Hamilton Woman*. Screenwriter Ben Hecht had been hired to work on an adaptation. However, Hecht's participation ended after he had made public comments critical of Britain's involvement in the battle over Palestine in the 1940s. Hecht's version was abandoned in 1948, and Korda then made overtures to Orson Welles. While Welles was intrigued, for reasons never made clear he and Korda did not proceed with this collaboration. Moreover, since Korda was in need of ready capital to complete his film version of *Anna Karenina*, starring Leigh and Ralph Richardson, he sold the rights to Kramer and United Artists in 1948.

Writer Carl Foreman, under contract to Stanley Kramer Productions, took what had been a roughly three-hour stage production and labored to reduce the running time to about two hours. It would not be easy; as Foreman would say around the time of the film's release, "here was the problem of words, thousands and thousands of words. Most of them were beautiful, some archaic and obscure, a great many repetitious and expository . . . surgery and suture were necessary for space, tempo and cinematic movement."

By the time United Artists was ready to finance the production, their own resources had become limited, partly due to the lack of commercial success of Kramer's previous films. Nevertheless, United Artists did agree to finance the black-and-white film to the tune of about $800,000 (although Ferrer has maintained for years that it was closer to $400,000). Whatever figure one chooses to believe, the final number was not inordinately generous, especially for a costume drama with many speaking roles, period sets, and battle scenes. Still, Ferrer would forever cite the importance of the film in his life: "Stanley Kramer came to see it. I didn't know him, but he said, 'Someday I'll make a movie of that,' and he did.

I was available and he wanted me. My life was changed by that. We did with very little money in four six-day weeks. Michael Gordon directed it."

Michael Gordon was a rising young director, having just completed *Another Part of the Forest*, starring Fredric March in Lillian Hellman's prequel to her *Little Foxes*, and *The Lady Gambles*, starring Barbara Stanwyck. Gordon and Kramer allowed Ferrer to take part in the preparation process, which included casting the principals. Probably the best-known member of the cast, apart from Ferrer, would be veteran Morris Carnovsky. (Classic film noir fans might remember Carnovsky's villainy opposite Humphrey Bogart in the 1947 *Dead Reckoning*.) William Prince, who had been in films since 1943 (he had also appeared in *Dead Reckoning*), won the role of Christian, while theater actor Ralph Clanton, in his film debut, reprised his role of Cyrano's nemesis, the Comte de Guiche. Several actresses were tested for the beautiful Roxane, including Arlene Dahl and Debra Paget, but the creative team (including Ferrer) decided on Mala Powers, who had just received some attention for her work as a rape victim in Ida Lupino's directorial debut, *Outrage*.

Elena Verdugo, who had appeared in Universal horror films like *House of Frankenstein*, was pleased to be cast in the small but important part of the "Orange Girl." For those unfamiliar with the play or film, the scene with the Orange Girl allows Cyrano to be seen sympathetically by a female character other than Roxane, giving lie to his belief that because of his nose he is unattractive to members of the opposite sex. Verdugo was eager for the opportunity to break out of a "horror rut" and playing native girls: she hoped this small part in a more prestigious film would provide opportunities for more substantial roles. While this may not have immediately materialized, Verdugo would become well-known to audiences as Consuelo Lopez, the able assistant to Robert Young's Dr. Marcus Welby and James Brolin's Dr. Steven Kiley in the long-running television series *Marcus Welby, M.D.*

Kramer and Gordon also proved to be busy with the film's logistics, given the barely adequate funding and the expansive nature of Foreman's adaptation, which presented on screen the battle scenes that were only discussed in the stage version. Although Kramer had managed to get the film in production, he would remember that he "ran into the die-hards and the howlers of gloom who told me that I was going off the deep end. 'José Ferrer in *Cyrano de Bergerac*?' they said. 'How foreign can you get?'" Production designer Rudolph Sternad devised a series of "waltzing sets," the nickname given to sets on wheels, giving the filmmakers more flexibility to meet the needs of mobility, controlled shooting locations, as well as extra compositional opportunities. Sternad and his team were able to recreate seventeenth-century Paris, with its winding streets, alleys, and courtyards, entirely indoors, thus eliminating the need for the company to spend ten days on location. It also eliminated any need for exterior construction; one double soundstage handled most of the shooting. Director Michael Gordon operated on Sternad's eight major sets, which were able to be broken down into thirty-six sets, with each building put in rollers, allowing them to be shifted easily. All this ingenuity behind the scenes provides some insight into how Kramer was generally able to contain costs on what might have been a prohibitively expensive production.

There were other illusions that had to be created and maintained for *Cyrano de Bergerac* to become believable on screen. One of these was Cyrano's nose itself. Joséf Norin, who was in charge of the nose, would work in conjunction with Sternad and his artists to come up with the perfect nose for the cinematic Cyrano. Ferrer showed the team the nose that had been used onstage, and the rudimentary mechanics involved in attaching it—namely, tape and putty. For the screen nose, the Norins decided to make a core of sponge rubber, which would also absorb perspiration. Over two hundred sketches were produced, with the artists providing the distinctive nose with every conceivable shape. After examining the sketches, the Norins made a life mask of Ferrer's face; from that, they made five plaster casts. Once a style was finally chosen, it was tested and photographed with Ferrer in full costume. Approximately $5,000 was spent on the nose, but the nose was seen to be of the utmost importance to creating a plausible cinematic illusion. (As mentioned earlier, the real-life Cyrano's nose was oversize but nowhere near the protuberance some versions would have you believe.) A total of fifty-two noses would be worn by Ferrer throughout the production. The nose, besides being an essential part of Cyrano's character onscreen, also served as a useful instrument between the scenes for Ferrer. According to producer Kramer, when not filming, Ferrer would "exploit every comic possibility he could derive from his nose. He especially loved to tell the ladies on the set fanciful stories about what he called its real significance."

Besides the nose, there was Cyrano's fencing ability, and even though the actor had previously excelled onstage in this regard (he had taken lessons on his own before the play and spent three months practicing immediately before the production), there were more opportunities for swordplay in the film, among them the inclusion of a fight scene against "100 men" that is only referred to in the play and conducted decidedly offstage. Ferrer threw himself into the lessons, alongside the director Gordon, who participated "so I would know what could be done and what could not be done. But while I was fencing with one hand, he was fencing both right and left-handed." Gordon added, "He's no megalomaniac. He simply has a good, objective awareness of his own high value."

In casting Ferrer's opponents, a search was made for those who were both expert swordsmen and versed in making the fights look as though they were to the death—without actually getting injured. Veteran Fred Cavens, who had coached duels in just about every important swashbuckler from the silent era, was engaged as the fencing master, while Albert Cavens, Fred's son (and an expert fencer in his own right), played the role of Valvert, a rival of Cyrano's (and a nemesis later on in Foreman's adaptation). Ferrer would later recall the fencing sequences as "hard work. The whole duel scene [with Cavens's Valvert] was done in one day. We started at nine in the morning and finished at ten at night. The next morning I woke up and I couldn't move, I just lay there. My whole body ached. It was such an important step in my career, such a turning point." The effort paid off, as the dueling sequences are among the most memorable in the film, partly because it is clearly Ferrer doing the thrusting, parrying, and occasional leaping—not to mention composing lyrical poetry in the duel with the aforementioned Cavens/Valvert.

In order for the film to come in at under two hours (Kramer had been requested by the studio not to exceed a two-hour running time), Foreman made a number of significant changes in terms of characters and events. The opening section in *Cyrano* the play, which includes several minor characters, each providing some expository information about Cyrano, was excised in favor of Cyrano making his entrance almost immediately in the film, with the exposition supplied by Roxane (Mala Powers). The character of the renegade poet Ligniere was absorbed into the baker/Cyrano idolizer Ragueneau (Lloyd Corrigan), so that it is a distressed Ragueneau who seeks Cyrano's help against the "hundred men" who threaten him because of the insulting verses he had written about De Guiche. The powerful Cardinal Richelieu, who is only referred to in the original play (and is De Guiche's powerful uncle), is present briefly (even though he goes unnamed in the movie).

Furthermore, the roles of Le Bret and Carbon Castel De Jaloux have been combined (Le Bret's Carnovsky)—and Valvert (Albert Cavens), a De Guiche lackey and presumed Roxane rival who is dispatched early on, is resurrected later to suggest he may be a more insidious threat to Cyrano. There are other differences that directly concern Ferrer's Cyrano, and these will be considered as Ferrer's characterization is explored in detail. Since many who know Ferrer know him from this single performance, it is worth examining what made Ferrer's performance prove to be so indelible for those who saw it then (it was not a huge popular success, although it proved to be a critical one) as well as those who have discovered it since in movie revivals, on television, and on home video.

The film's opening, with its fanfare by the film's composer Dimitri Tiomkin, clearly establishes the theatrical milieu of the piece, both in its initial setting and the subsequent events. Cyrano is introduced early on, sitting in a box, challenging the play within a play's ham actor Montfleury to leave the stage. First, the distinctive Ferrer baritone is heard, after which the audience gets a glimpse of Cyrano, along with his famous nose, seated in his box at the theater, at a slight remove from the action onstage (as well as the viewer). After Cyrano harangues both Montfleury and the theatergoers, causing the frightened ham actor to flee the stage (and in a grand gesture, Cyrano offers the annoyed patrons their money back, in the form of his military pay), he launches into the famous "nose speech," where he belittles an insulting Valvert by suggesting the clever insults he might have hurled at Cyrano, instead of the meager "your nose is, um, rather large." Ferrer makes the most of the imagery inherent in both Hooker and Foreman's adaptation, as well as the opportunities for humor. (Observe Ferrer's pause during "And when it bleeds . . . the Red Sea!") Likewise, the dueling scene opposite Valvert is no minor skirmish but a protracted battle, which Ferrer's Cyrano punctuates with the occasional, extemporaneous composing of poetic verse. This scene, along with several others depicting Cyrano's sword-fighting prowess, aroused the ire of Joseph Breen, the head of Hollywood's Production Code office (often referred to as the Breen Office). Breen told the associate producer Joseph Glass that the scene made Cyrano appear "dangerously close to being little less than a murderer." Glass would assure Breen that Valvert was only wounded (this is made even more clear in the final section of the movie).

Although Ferrer excels in his scenes of bravado, it is Cyrano's quieter, more reflective moments that have greater impact. When Carnovsky's Le Bret asks Cyrano why he does not romantically pursue his childhood friend Roxane, Cyrano softly allows for his admiration of young lovers, then laments he can never be one of them when he views that "enormous shadow on the wall" cast by his nose. Immediately after, when Verdugo's Orange Girl tentatively approaches him with the offer of food (she has overheard Cyrano admit he has given away all his salary), he proudly but tenderly refuses. In an effort to placate her, however, he does accept one drink (water), one grape, one-half of a macaroon, and the gift of her hand to kiss. This is an exquisitely played scene, and Verdugo is so sympathetic that one wishes that Cyrano would stop and "smell the roses" and be done with his pursuit of the beautiful but presumably unattainable Roxane.

When Roxane's chaperone arrives to say that Roxane wants to meet her at 7 in the morning in Ragueneau's pastry shop, the joy Ferrer's Cyrano radiates is infectious, especially since he had just dismissed his own chances to the gently chiding Le Bret. Accompanied by Dimitri Tiomkin's rousing score, Ferrer's Cyrano is no less than ten feet tall, so that when Ragueneau arrives and needs Cyrano's protection against the "hundred" men, Cyrano is only too happy to help. All this braggadocio might prove tiresome (and indeed it sometimes reads that way) were it not for the bits of business that serve to humanize Cyrano. In Foreman's adaptation, after he proclaims that he would like to take on more than mere men ("I need giants!"), theater manager Bellerose (Percy Helton) gently admonishes him, and Cyrano puts his finger over his lips, as if assuring Bellerose he'll keep the noise down. When a concerned Le Bret asks why he could risk his life for a "pastry cook," Cyrano reminds Le Bret that if Ragueneau were to be killed, "then at 7:00, his shop would be closed," thus dashing his hopes for meeting Roxane. Again, it's the little touches that humanize this Cyrano, as when Ferrer gives Carnovsky's Le Bret a friendly, encouraging tap of the sword to assure Le Bret that all will be well.

Of course, when Roxane arrives, she takes her time to reveal what savvy filmgoers know to be the case—that she indeed loves someone else. As in both the film and the play, Roxane is unaware of Cyrano's love for her; she has come to view him as a dear friend, having grown up together in the same region, cousins, if not in blood, then in terms of affection. When Roxane begins to describe the man she loves, Ferrer expertly portrays Cyrano's rising fervor in line with his expectations, especially since the man Roxane is describing seems to be him—until she describes the gentleman as "handsome." It is here the director and composer let Ferrer down. What should have been a poignant moment is turned into a comic one, complete with minor double take and nose wrinkling—and Tiomkin's music more befitting a farcical mishap than a dramatic high point. However, both Cyrano (and Ferrer) soon recover as he simultaneously hides his disappointment from Roxane and allows the audience to read between the lines to see the complex emotional state that Roxane remains resolutely ignorant of. This Cyrano isn't as quickly accepting of

Roxane's request that he protect his rival, the young, handsome new Gascon cadet, Christian. One can see Cyrano's resentment only gradually giving way to a grudging accommodation—and that is only for the sake of a grateful, unknowing Roxane.

Roxane's beauty is coupled with both intelligence and naivete; Mala Powers brings this out somewhat, although certain directorial (and script) choices deny her the opportunity to fully develop her character. For example, after shattering (unwittingly) Cyrano's hopes, Roxane requests that at some point Cyrano must describe how he fought "one hundred men." He replies, "I've done much better since," referring to his preference to taking on "hundreds" instead of facing up to the difficulty of hearing his beloved say she loves another; however, the film has Roxane depart before Ferrer's Cyrano movingly utters the line.

Following a scene that Foreman (or possibly an uncredited Orson Welles) added, depicting the cardinal (who was not seen in the play) advising De Guiche that it would be better to have Cyrano "live by the pen than die by the sword," the movie cuts back to a crestfallen Cyrano among a group of admiring Gascon cadets. After Cyrano rebuffs De Guiche's offer to write some works to "honor" the cardinal, Cyrano launches into one of the most stirring proclamations of individual integrity: the "no, thank you" speech, in which he denounces those who would curry favor and mindlessly follow the crowd as he prefers to think and behave as he chooses, free to march to a different drummer.

What makes Ferrer's delivery so effective, here and in his earlier "nose" speech, is the way he mines the speech for as many variations in terms of intonation and cadence. It builds in power without tiring the listener; he even manages to suggest what Le Bret points out—that all his pontificating is to hide his pain over "losing" Roxane. The scene that follows introduces Christian (sad to say, William Prince plays Christian much like a deer caught in the headlights) to both Cyrano and the audience. In the section in which Christian demonstrates his valor by interrupting Cyrano's tales of his heroic exploits with interjections about his nose, Ferrer has to get his mounting fury across in spite of Tiomkin's jaunty musical interpolations. And when Christian admits he loves Roxane yet lacks the wit to speak to her, which Cyrano follows with the realization that while he lacks looks, he does possess the words, Ferrer makes it believable that he would arrive at the idea of offering Christian the opportunity to use his words in order to win Roxane. In Ferrer's handling of the role, the desire is to ensure Roxane's happiness, vicariously winning her through his own poetry. Others have had different notions on how to interpret

Cyrano; Orson Welles, for one, had hoped to produce a stage version wherein Cyrano is there to help but secretly hopes that Christian will fail so that he can look good by comparison.

In another of Foreman's additions, the viewer sees a montage of Cyrano coaching Christian by role playing Roxane and honing Christian's delivery. The fact that Christian does not appear to be an apt pupil does make it implausible that the charade should continue as long as it does. (In the play, we see none of this rehearsing; we only hear about Christian/Cyrano's effect on Roxane.) In the scene in which Roxane declares that Christian's poetry is superior to Cyrano's, Ferrer conveys Cyrano's covert pleasure while presuming to question Roxane's claims. In a well-played scene, Christian attempts to show Cyrano (and Roxane) that he can handle the courtship all by himself, only to become both tongue-tied and repetitive; for once, Prince's helpless demeanor suits him well, as Christian is unable to live up to the image that Roxane has created.

What follows is the scene that defines *Cyrano* and the power of the actor who portrays him. In any adaptation of *Cyrano*—whether it is the *Cyrano* of Ferrer, or later Gerard Depardieu and even Steve Martin (in his comic modern riff, *Roxanne*)—the staging and the acting have to convince the audience to suspend their disbelief and embrace the unbelievable: namely, that Cyrano can substitute for Christian mid-speech and convince her both of his affections, and that he is indeed Christian. *Cyrano de Bergerac*, in any of its incarnations, is far from realistic; instead, it encourages the audience to embrace the power of imagination in the service of romance, and to ignore trivial aspects of reality, such as that, in this case, Ferrer and Prince do not sound alike. Powers's Roxane—indeed, any Roxane—does remark that "Christian" does not sound like himself (indeed, since Christian's words are by now, coming directly from Cyrano), but the play and the film depend on both Cyrano's fervor and Roxane's belief that it is an impassioned Christian that is speaking beneath her balcony in the moonlight, slightly obscured under the branches of a tree.

Foreman's adaptation preserves the poetry of Rostand's speech (and Hooker's translation), applying some judicious editing, and Ferrer handles this scene and its poetry as if his entire life, like Cyrano's, was a mere prelude to this moment. The audience feels not only the passion of the character, but of the actor. It is as if performer and part have merged, especially when we see the intoxication of Ferrer's Cyrano when he informs Roxane she is finally seeing and hearing the "real him." (Tiomkin's tender underscoring suits the scene and the actor—finally.) After Cyrano succeeds in melting Roxane's remaining defenses, he pushes a now-reluctant Christian (who, implausibly, has misgivings even as he is pressuring Cyrano to ask Roxane for a kiss) up the balcony. Again, it is in these quiet moments that Ferrer's Cyrano is at his most powerful, as in his poignant display of emotional ambivalence upon his realization that it was his words that indeed allowed his rival to win the fair Roxane. Cyrano's satisfaction can only be vicarious, as Christian is the one who enjoys the fruits of Cyrano's efforts.

The scene that follows is almost as implausible, but in a more comic vein, as Cyrano disguises his voice (and hides that distinctive nose) in order to prevent a determined De Guiche from interrupting the hasty wedding of Roxane and Christian (arranged by Roxane, as evidence of both her beauty and intelligence). Cyrano disguises his voice (at least a little more than he did for Roxane) and pretends to have fallen from the moon, and his demeanor so intrigues De Guiche that he pauses to hear this traveler's plan to return. Ferrer merges comic bits of business (hiding his nose, playing with De Guiche's costume) with his energetic, varied delivery, so as to prolong his deception of De Guiche and allow the wedding to continue.

After a surprised and vengeful De Guiche orders Christian and Cyrano to the battlefront in the war against Spain, Cyrano parries Roxane's requests ("Keep him safe!" "I'll do what I can") until she implores him to have Christian write to her every day—which, as the real author, he can promise her. Foreman's adaptation does add significantly more onscreen derring-do for the hero—instead of Le Bret chastising Cyrano for his daily excursions across enemy lines to deliver his letters to Roxane, we are shown Cyrano stealthily traversing the battlefield and "thrusting home" to an unfortunate Spanish soldier, as well as some scenes of skirmishes on the field.

While the play takes pains to dramatize the cadets' plight with an extended (and tedious) dialogue scene marked by constant whining unencumbered by wit, the film almost immediately ushers in Roxane by way of a coach (driven by Ragueneau). Roxane has risked life and limb to bring food to the cadets and see her beloved Christian, from whom Roxane seeks forgiveness for only having initially loved him only for his looks; because of his eloquent, transcendent letters, she now loves him for his soul alone—and declares she would love him "even if he were ugly." This heartfelt sentiment, meant to comfort Christian, only causes Christian more grief, since he is well aware that the soul is Cyrano's. The scene between Christian and Cyrano, in which Christian demands that Cyrano tell Roxane the truth and let her decide between them, is well played by both actors. (For once, Prince summons up some power to be a worthy foil to Ferrer's Cyrano.)

Here is where Foreman makes another change for the better (indeed, many of Foreman's adjustments work quite well, providing more coherence and clarity), as Christian leaves Cyrano to speak with Roxane while he undertakes a dangerous solo mission to determine the size of the incoming Spanish force. (In the play, Christian is shot when he takes a walk to the end of the camp, with the enemy just on the other side.) Ferrer's Cyrano tentatively questions Roxane, seeking assurance that she could love someone who was "ugly" and then, just when happiness is within his reach, the gravely wounded Christian is brought in. After Cyrano assures the dying Christian it is indeed Christian whom Roxane loves, he knows he can never reveal the deception to Roxane, and instead seeks to avenge "two deaths, Christian and his own" on the advancing Spaniards. This sets in motion a lengthy battle scene, complete with explosions and hundreds of extras. The scene was filmed at night for reasons of both historical accuracy and the necessity for disguising the threadbare nature of the sets and costumes.

The onscreen heroics fade into what would have been Act Five in the play, set a number of years after Christian's death, during which an older, poverty-stricken Cyrano (with receding hairline to match) spends his time regaling others about his wartime exploits while still writing articles critical of corruption in high places. In a scene created for the film, after he finishes his boasting, the still-alive Valvert acknowledges that Cyrano is still dangerous with a sword, but casually remarks that Cyrano still "might have an accident." In the play, Cyrano's character does suffer an offstage accident in the form of a log dropped on his head by some unknown lackey. Kramer even filmed a scene with Cyrano being hit on the head by a falling beam, but audiences found it unintentionally amusing, so he had to change it. In the film, Cyrano is seen walking home and is lured into an ambush, suffering severe injuries when he is run over by a speeding horse and carriage. A doctor summoned to Cyrano's room makes it clear that should Cyrano leave his bed, he will die.

Knowing Cyrano and his love for Roxane, nothing will deter him from his regular visit to the convent, where she has been residing since Christian's death. (She has basically withdrawn from life, yet she still welcomes weekly visits from Cyrano.) It is this last scene that reviewers took special notice of when Ferrer first played the role, and the film does preserve the power of his interpretation. After some byplay between Roxane and Cyrano, he asks if he might read Christian's final letter. She registers some surprise, but as he begins the letter, she hears "a voice she had heard once before," and as darkness moves in (along with the ever-present autumn leaves), it slowly dawns on Roxane that it was indeed Cyrano who spoke to her that fateful night and wrote all the letters that she had assumed to have been Christian's. While the play has her discover this after she realizes that Cyrano would not be able to read the letter in the dark—unless he had written it himself—the movie lingers on Cyrano reciting the contents without looking at the letter, until finally Roxane notices it. (As one can see, Roxane, for a supposedly intelligent character, takes a long time to notice practically anything.) Ferrer effectively delivers Cyrano's protestations, as well as his ultimate admission of love; he also requests that she not forget Christian—only that some of her tears might also be for himself.

Since Cyrano does not want to meet death sitting down, he struggles to his feet to rail, almost deliriously, against all his unseen enemies, including vanity (which, he rightly believes, will get him in the end). Again, with Tiomkin's music providing firm support, Ferrer delivers this final speech with notable intensity, with a slight hesitancy that betrays that his character is dying. When Cyrano finally expires, it is only after he declares that while material goods may be taken from him, his character has never lost his honor—or, in this case, his "white plume." It is a moving finish, slightly marred by the fairly obvious Christ symbolism in the form of the final image of Cyrano lying on a cross-like tableau.

When *Cyrano de Bergerac* was released in the fall of 1950, the critics took note of the low-budget, somewhat stagy feel of the production, as well as the perceived inadequacies of the supporting cast, although in all fairness, Mala Powers (referred to as a "lovely, but lifeless girl" by Bosley Crowther) acquits herself well in some of her scenes, and Morris Carnovsky makes a sympathetic sounding board as Le Bret. Director Michael Gordon was given some credit for trying to take advantage of the dramatic, romantic, and tragic possibilities of the material.

However, the critics were not reserved in their praise of Ferrer's performance as Cyrano. C. A. DeJeune of the *Observer* said that Ferrer's portrayal was "one of the most superb performances I have ever watched on the motion picture screen. A performance exactly calculated for the medium in which it appears . . . in order to be moving without descending to pathos, quixotic without braggadocio, tender without weakness, it is necessary for the actor to be filled with passion about his character and to know all the tricks of the trade. This is the sort of actor Ferrer is . . . he uses both heart and mind." Crowther, despite his lack of regard for the supporting cast, felt that "Ferrer speaks the poetry of Rostand with richness and clarity such as few actors have managed on the screen." In spite of the glowing reviews for Ferrer's performance, United Artists did little to help *Cyrano de Bergerac* upon its release; it played some limited engagements at roadshow prices, which attracted some discerning audiences but definitely not the masses. After the film was completed, Ferrer embarked on a three-month tour to publicize the picture and remarked on Cyrano's appeal to the filmgoer: "When audiences see the nose, they realize how Cyrano must have felt. They all have a secret worry somewhere: big ears, flat feet, expanding waistline. So they worry along with Cyrano, and when you get that, you've got a success." He would also tell interviewers that, in contrast to his earlier stated intention of steering clear of Hollywood, he now preferred a constant blend: "Serious acting on the stage is just slavery. Whenever you want to be doing something else, you have to be at the theater. I prefer mixing films with plays. You get more time outside that way—and a better-known name."

CHAPTER 7

Left, Right, Oscar, and Clooney

JOSÉ FERRER'S NEXT MAJOR COMMITMENT WAS YET AGAIN ON THE STAGE—
this time, in the 1950 revival of *Twentieth Century*, with a script by Ben
Hecht and Charles MacArthur based on Bruce Milholland's farce (which
had been already adapted for a successful 1934 film starring John Barrymore and Carole Lombard). *Twentieth Century* presents the strenuous
(and barely legal) efforts of bankrupt Hollywood producer Oscar Jaffe
to get his former leading lady (and lover) Lily Garland to sign a contract with him, amidst an array of characters and complications on an
event-filled ride aboard the locomotive known as the Twentieth Century
Limited.

Twentieth Century would be performed at the American National Theater and Academy (ANTA), and Ferrer wanted to revive it because he felt
it would be "too much darn fun," especially after having spent the previous months filming or publicizing *Cyrano*. Ferrer would not only play the
lead role of desperate producer Jaffe, but he would also direct. He was
familiar with the play, having already directed it in Mount Kisco in 1940
and performed it in 1948 in summer stock.

For the part of Lily Garland, the former stage actress who had previously fled Jaffe's clutches and is now enjoying a successful Hollywood
career, Ferrer thought of asking Gloria Swanson to return to the stage.
He had called her from Beverly Hills in late November (she was in New
York), and after a twenty-minute conversation, talked her into doing a
play with him. (Apparently the conversation did not include the mention
of the play's title, since she had asked just before hanging up, "By the
way, Joe, what's the title of the play?") Swanson, a former silent screen
star who had some middling success in the early 1930s, was enjoying

a career renaissance herself, enjoying the raves for her performance as faded actress Norma Desmond in Billy Wilder's *Sunset Boulevard*. Swanson was at first reluctant to take on the role of Lily (especially since it was slated to open in a month), but Ferrer's powers of persuasion soon swayed her. While both Ferrer and Swanson were hearing "Oscar talk" around this time for their respective performances in *Cyrano* and *Sunset Boulevard*, they were probably unaware of how strongly identified they would eventually become with these iconic roles. For now, they were respected colleagues working together on a breakneck farce filled with flamboyant gestures, extravagant schemes, mistaken identities, and outrageous physical business.

A four-week rehearsal period would begin in late November, with the play opening just before Christmas 1950. Ferrer would praise Swanson as a congenial, hardworking actress who gladly accepted direction. He was happy with rehearsals and thought that *Twentieth Century* as a play still had something to say, especially in its observations about actors. It was also a relief to be directing and performing in something noticeably lighter than *Cyrano*. The critics found Swanson to be both "amazing and sparkling," while Ferrer earned praise both for his direction and acting. Critics and audiences enjoyed the shrewd, spirited performance and his handling of the actors who were found, in the words of *New York Times* critic Brooks Atkinson, "to be entirely authentic after the manner of breathless lampoons of the theater." Atkinson's deepest praise would be offered to Ferrer the actor, as he would say that "as the grandiloquently eccentric producer, Ferrer gives further evidence of his genius as an actor. . . . Ferrer is an actor in the grand manner who also has a sense of humor. You can nearly find everything we all love in his forceful, fluid swagger and in his impetuously funny performance."

As powerful a draw as Ferrer was, he was outshone by the luminous Swanson, who was also relishing her return to the stage. Having been out of the limelight for several years during her career eclipse (in real life, she was far from the recluse that Norma Desmond had been), the success of both *Sunset Boulevard* and *Twentieth Century* afforded her every opportunity to enjoy the renewed attention. She was also prepared to give the veteran Ferrer a few reminders (some unintended) about the nature of fame. After one performance, Swanson lectured him briefly about his responsibilities toward the public and urged him to show himself at the stage door. Ferrer went to the alley of the Fulton, hung around for a few minutes, and then was carried backward by a flood of Swanson fans who had just seen the star emerge from the theater.

While Ferrer was enjoying *Twentieth Century* and its resounding success with both the critics and the public, he still had to contend with the growing "shadows on his wall." The first was the death of his father, Rafael Ferrer, who had passed away from a heart attack in February 1951. Even though the elder Ferrer had initially objected to his son's career, preferring that he become an architect instead (or even a professor), he later enjoyed relating how he had sent his son to Princeton and was "outraged when an American drama critic suggested José become an actor instead." Ferrer had long since reconciled with his son's choice of vocation, and as noted elsewhere, had seen him perform both on the stage and the screen. There was also the matter of his slowly disintegrating marriage, since as much as Phyllis had professed to enjoy painting and antique shopping, she really wanted to resume her career. She had temporarily filled in for Gloria Swanson in *Twentieth Century* and proved to be an able farceur, but her success did little to curb the downward trajectory of their marriage. Ferrer, it appeared, gave little attention to trying to save it; by early 1951, they would be staying in separate residences.

The other pressing matter was the renewed pressure on Ferrer to testify before the House Un-American Activities Committee (HUAC). In March, he had been subpoenaed, along with John Garfield, Abe Burrows, and Anne Revere, to testify about possible communism in Hollywood. When he first received the subpoena, Ferrer stated that he had never been a member of the Communist Party nor was he a sympathizer in any way. There would likely be questions about his association with Paul Robeson, who had made himself a prime target with his outspoken stance on behalf of civil rights and his own appearance of being sympathetic to the communist cause, and his own inclination toward lending his own name to groups that were seen as dangerous by the committee. (While Robeson was presumably a target of HUAC, he was not called to testify before the committee until June 1956.)

Helping to stoke the fires against Ferrer was self-proclaimed proud patriot and right-wing actor Ward Bond. Years before his television stardom on *Wagon Train*, Bond was a member of director John Ford's stock company, a good friend of John Wayne's, and the treasurer for the Motion Picture Alliance for the Preservation of American Ideals. Bond viewed it as his sworn duty to rid Hollywood of its left-leaning celebrities, regardless of whether they were communists or not. In an interview with *Daily Variety* in March 1951, Bond called out Ferrer and other suspected "Reds," including Judy Holliday, Sam Jaffe, and Edward G. Robinson. Bond boasted that Ferrer's award from the California teachers' association had been rescinded because of the Motion Picture Alliance. Bond also felt the tainted actors would have to do much more in front of the committee than just say "I'm not guilty."

The controversy had not prevented Ferrer from getting work; indeed, he had a film role for director George Seaton (of *Miracle on 34th Street* fame) lined up after he completed his commitment to *Twentieth Century*. The threat of career implosion also hadn't seemed to deter RKO and producer Gabriel Pascal, who were still pursuing the busy Ferrer for their adaptation of George Bernard Shaw's *Androcles and the Lion*. Ferrer had initially been offered roughly $75,000 to do the film before the offer was increased to $100,000. The actor, who was reeling in $2,350 with his work onstage in *Twentieth Century*, was astounded to see a further, practically unheard-of offer that promised him a percentage of the gross (as opposed to the net receipts).

This was all very tempting for Ferrer, considering that producing the stage version of *Cyrano* had left him $75,000 in debt, and even after he had made some financial gains, he still had difficulty saving money. Reporter Gilbert Millstein, who had access to Ferrer in the days preceding the Academy Awards, would disclose that while Ferrer had earned $116,000 in 1950, he could only manage to save $3,100. Ferrer would ultimately not accept the role (nor the financial windfall it would have meant), but many in the theatrical community had assumed he would. He was accused of "garroting the living theater," and there were hints that he might be sued by the *Twentieth Century* producers if he departed early. Part of Ferrer's decision to stay with the show was that he had been unable to find a suitable replacement, which might have meant a premature end of the line for *Twentieth Century*. (Although Gloria Swanson was indeed drawing the crowds on her name, the show needed a dynamic, magnetic male costar if it was to be successful.)

Despite his somewhat tainted status in Hollywood, Ferrer still received an Oscar nomination for his performance as Cyrano, and Gloria Swanson, to the surprise of no one, was nominated for Best Actress; many believed that she was indeed the favorite. Bette Davis had also been nominated for her work as the brittle Margo Channing in *All About Eve*, and while this was hailed as Bette's comeback by some, costar Anne Baxter had also been nominated for Best Actress, leading many to think that the vote might be split. As for Ferrer's chances for receiving the golden statuette, insiders believed that Ferrer could not win given his imminent participation in the HUAC hearings and a prevailing sentiment that he was condescending, overly ambitious, arrogant, and egomaniacal. As one theatrical manager put it, "Nobody likes Joe Ferrer but the audience." His acting abilities were also called into question. Ferrer's style was seen to be lapsing more and more into a growing "externalization." A fellow actor observed that "his sense of values has changed. Now I'm more aware of the brilliant technical skill of his performance than in the universal life of the character he is portraying."

Since Ferrer and Swanson were both currently the toasts of Broadway and would not be attending the Hollywood-based Academy Awards ceremony, Ferrer decided to host an Oscar party in New York. Ferrer had chosen the restaurant La Zambra, since he knew the owners and wanted to provide them the business and national exposure. After the evening performance of *Twentieth Century*, not only he and Swanson would be attending but also Judy Holliday, who had been nominated for her role as the big-hearted, presumably dumb blonde Billie Dawn in *Born Yesterday*, and was viewed as a dark horse.

In her autobiography, Swanson remembered the performance on Oscar night as proceeding exceptionally well, and it was a special experience for those in the audience. As Swanson recalled in her memoir, "When I brandished the fake Oscar in Joe's face, they sent up a prolonged cheer, as if they wanted Norma Desmond, my *Sunset Boulevard* character, to step out of Lily Garland, my character in *Twentieth Century*, and take a bow or do a turn." The party at La Zambra tuned out to be a well-attended affair; among the attendees were Holliday, her *Born Yesterday* director George Cukor, *All About Eve* nominee Celeste Holm, and *Asphalt Jungle* nominee Sam Jaffe. All were dining and drinking, with a radio being turned up and a broadcasting crew present so that winners could make their speeches by special hookup with the Coast. Ferrer was seated between Swanson and Holliday, and they were later joined by Cukor. Swanson recalled having mixed emotions as to who the Best Actor winner should be; she thought Best Actor nominee William Holden, her jaded gigolo/screenwriter costar in *Sunset Boulevard*, was "brilliant in our picture and I adored him. But Joe was brilliant in *Cyrano* too, and I adored *him*. Neither could have played each other's part. That was what was so stupid about awards and contests." Swanson also believed that many Academy members might vote against him solely on the basis of his imminent appearance before the House Un-American Activities Committee.

Longtime friend and supporter Helen Hayes read off the list of nominees from Hollywood, and when she announced Ferrer as the winner, all of La Zambra erupted in applause and cheers. When the announcers asked Ferrer if he would like to make a speech, he said he most certainly did. As Swanson would remember, "He said he accepted the award as an act of faith and a vote of confidence, and Joe was too good an actor not to ring all the overtones out of the statement." Still, one reporter did ask Ferrer if he was making a political statement. "You're god-damned right I am! I meant it as a rebuke to all the people who tried to affect the voting by referring to things that are a) beside the point and b) untrue." No doubt a target of Ferrer's rebuke was Ward Bond, who along with columnist Hedda Hopper, would continue a smear campaign against him long after the Oscar was given.

Despite Bond's threats, Ferrer had done strenuous lobbying for *Cyrano*, not only to get nominated but to help ensure his Oscar victory; he had made numerous personal appearances on countless radio and television shows. While preparing to appear on Robert Q. Lewis's television variety show (Lewis was a popular radio personality who had made the early leap to television), Ferrer met an attractive young singer, Rosemary Clooney, who was on the same program. By 1951, Clooney had achieved a fair amount of success in the recording industry, mainly due to her association with Columbia Records and Mitch Miller. She was born in Kentucky in June 1928, with her sister Betty (also a singer) coming along three years later, and her brother Nick, two years after that. Rosemary and Betty developed a sister act called the Clooney Sisters, with Rosemary getting many of the solos because of her wider range. Tony Pastor heard the sisters and hired them to sing with his band. In 1946, Rosemary made her first professional solo recording, "I'm Sorry I Didn't Say I'm Sorry When I Made You Cry Last Night." Although the song isn't remembered now, it so impressed Pastor's band managers, Joe Scribman and Charlie Trotta ("You could feel her heart in that record"), that they became her personal managers. By 1949, Rosemary, now comfortably on her own, appeared on the then-popular television show, *Songs for Sale*. This would lead to other television and nightclub appearances, until in 1950, she had received a contract offer from Columbia Records.

When they first met, Ferrer thought, "She didn't like me. She seemed very aloof. It was just hello and goodbye." Clooney was very interested though: "I matched Joe's curiosity. That was the attraction between us." She was concerned about dating a married man, but Ferrer assured her that he and Phyllis were separated. Clooney would later say that host Lewis warned her against seeing Ferrer; Lewis told her that "he plays fast and loose with the ladies." Ferrer was sixteen years older than Clooney, but that wasn't a deterrent to her. She recalled in her autobiography *Girl Singer* that "he loved to teach, and I loved to learn." Since Ferrer was still technically married to Hill, and since Clooney was very much under contract to Mitch Miller (as well as the morals clause that was in her Columbia contract), they initially tried to avoid being seen together as a couple. Clooney would recall that friends Merv Griffin and Judy Balaban would frequently go out with them; as Griffin said, "We'll be the beards." For a while, the romance and deception were both thrilling and satisfying, but Ferrer certainly did not have the time (or the freedom) to make the relationship more permanent.

One month after Ferrer won his Academy Award, he made a return trip to San Juan, Puerto Rico, for a special one-day visit. As the first Puerto Rican actor ever to win the coveted statuette, Ferrer was feted by both houses of the Puerto Rican legislature, after which he was driven past thousands of admirers to La Fortaleza, the governor's residence, where he would receive his Oscar from Puerto Rico's Governor Luis Munoz Martin. Governor Martin would say of the proud Ferrer, perhaps alluding to Ferrer's homeland difficulties: "My regard for him is the same that I have felt all my life for the humble, generous and unselfish men, like our soldiers fighting against Communism in North Korea and our peasants fighting against poverty in the ridges of the soil of Puerto Rico." Ferrer was humbled by all the attention and accepted the award with a grace befitting *Cyrano* himself: "I want to express my pride as a Puerto Rican and as a man for the effort that the Puerto Ricans are making in the face of the most adverse circumstances, determined not to be defeated either by scarcity or illness nor to be dominated by hatred or envy." He concluded with a reference to *Cyrano*: no matter what failed him, he "held high and unsullied, *my plume.*" Five hours after the ceremony, Ferrer presented the Oscar to Chancellor Jaime Benitez of the University of Puerto Rico to be displayed as a permanent trophy.

While this particular trip was brief, the importance of the Academy Award, and of Ferrer's well-publicized visit to Puerto Rico, cannot be underestimated. Ferrer had many relatives in Puerto Rico, where he would maintain a residence for many years. José's cousin Charles Ferrer would recall Ferrer's visits to the island and his devotion to his sisters, particularly Elvira, with whom he remained close all his life. He also remembers being introduced to Phyllis, José's wife at the time whom Charles found to be "a very nice, enchanting lady." Charles also recalled how accessible his cousin José was to both friends and strangers. On more than one occasion, José visited Charles's home, where "he looked at my rooster, picked it up—and kissed it!" Seeing the rooster's agitated reaction, José then said, "That's pollo loco!" Years later, when Ferrer brought *Man of La*

Mancha to Old San Juan, Charlie would see the show twice and remember that "we went to the dressing room with mother, dad, and my sister. He was always very nice to me and my family." Despite Ferrer's stardom, Charles saw in his cousin both humility and graciousness, qualities he finds inherent in many of his fellow Puerto Ricans.

It's also worth noting how important Ferrer was becoming for the Latino community. While other prominent Latino actors were already known to moviegoers, many of the roles these actors portrayed were somewhat stereotypical ethnic characters. Anthony Quinn was a Mexican actor who began his career at Paramount in the 1930s and climbed the ladder playing a variety of ethnic roles, including Native Americans, Arabs, and Mexicans; in 1952, he would win the Best Supporting Actor Oscar playing Eufemio Zapata opposite Marlon Brando's doomed Emiliano Zapata in *Viva Zapata!* Gilbert Roland, another Mexican-born actor active since the silent era (in Latin lover roles), had recently completed *We Were Strangers* (1949) and *Crisis* (1950), two films where he played passionate Latino rebels (the latter also featuring Ferrer).

In addition to these veteran actors, there were those Latinos who were gaining stardom in both film and television. Ricardo Montalban and Fernando Lamas, both under contract to MGM, were among the younger Latino actors who were also largely called upon to play characters who adhered to the "passionate Latin lover" stereotype. In 1949, Montalban had strong roles in the noir *Border Incident* and the World War II drama *Battleground*; in both, he played a character named Rodriguez (no relation to each other). The following year, he would romance Jane Powell in *Two Weeks With Love*. Lamas, an Argentinian actor who began appearing in Spanish-speaking films in the 1940s, would also find himself romancing Powell in 1951's *Rich, Young and Pretty*. Cuban-born bandleader/actor Desi Arnaz had some good roles in the early 1940s in *Too Many Girls* (1940), costarring wife Lucille Ball, and *Bataan* (1943). On television, the savvy Desi embraced the stereotypical Latin male opposite wife Lucille in the 1950s sitcom *I Love Lucy*, whether it was banging his bongo drums or unleashing his exasperation with Lucy in periodic foreign-language streams of consciousness. (Arnaz also had displayed fine comic timing onscreen and sound business sense offscreen, the latter attribute exemplified by the formation of Desilu Productions.)

Ferrer was different from his fellow Latino actors in that he did not adhere to the stereotyped Latino; in fact, his classical training, his sonorous voice, his elocution all led many to perceive Ferrer as an American. Yet the fact that Ferrer was able to shatter this stereotype helped not only to legitimize Latino actors in American film, but also demonstrate to his fellow Puerto Rican Americans that they might have the same chance to succeed. His daughter Monsita would maintain that for all Ferrer's life that he was a proud Puerto Rican but an equally proud American, grateful for his success and hoping to inspire others to similar levels of achievement. For scholar (and nephew of Ferrer) Carlos Campo, "Before him, it was a rare occurrence to see a Latino who was not stereotyped or even ridiculed . . . of course he was the first Hispanic to win an Academy Award, but the way he broke through into American cinema as a Hispanic and shattered stereotypes about them was perhaps his most profound contribution." (Rita Moreno would be the next Puerto Rican actor to win an Academy Award, a Best Supporting Actress Oscar for her role as the fiery Anita in the 1961 musical *West Side Story*. Costar George Chakiris also won a Best Supporting Actor Oscar for his role as Bernardo, the leader of the Sharks—but Chakiris was an American of Greek descent playing a Puerto Rican.)

Although Ferrer would have preferred to remain longer in Puerto Rico, his theatrical obligations as the busiest man on Broadway precluded that possibility. Not only was Ferrer still acting and directing *Twentieth Century* (which showed no signs of declining receipts, especially because of the Oscar attention), he was in the process of preparing for his appearance before HUAC—and busy directing yet another play that was due to open in May: a grim comedy set in a German POW camp, *Stalag 17*. The play, which would become more widely known because of a subsequent film adaptation by Billy Wilder starring an Oscar-winning William Holden, was written by Donald Bevan and Edmund Trzcinski, both of whom had spent two years in a German POW camp. Ferrer's association with the play began long before 1951; as Ferrer would later recall, "The authors brought me the play. I thought it was funny and exciting but it seemed unrealized. . . . I had been doing some directing at the New York City Center for nothing . . . and I thought it was time to look after my acting career, so I said to the *Stalag 17* authors, 'Fellas, I like your play—but . . .'" Three years later, the writers invited Ferrer, still performing nightly in *Twentieth Century*, to the Lambs Club to see a production of their reworked play. After Ferrer saw the performance, he asked the writers to his house in Ossining, where he told them his concerns and "we kicked around possible solutions." The following Monday he told them he would direct the show on Broadway.

The authors of *Stalag 17* brought a wealth of personal experience that lent some verisimilitude to their endeavor. Donald Bevan was a gunner who had been shot down during an aerial mission, while Edmund Trczinski was a radioman who had bailed out. Both spent two years in the real Stalag 17, a German prison camp in Krems, Austria, not far from Vienna. They also operated a camp theater during their interment there. Two cast members from *Twentieth Century* left that production to join *Stalag 17*. Edward Platt, later known as the long-suffering Chief in *Get Smart*, became a fixture in many of Ferrer's plays, occasionally repeating his roles in the film versions (as he would later in Ferrer's production of *The Shrike*).

In addition, Robert Strauss would transfer from *Twentieth Century* to play the role of Slosh; he would make such an impression that he, along with Harvey Lembeck, would reprise their roles on film for director Billy Wilder. (Ferrer wanted to adapt it for the screen, but he had not yet directed on film, and after Wilder expressed an interest, it was his to make.) For the part of Sefton, the wheeler-dealer who looks at war as a profit-making enterprise, even within the confines of a prison camp, Ferrer chose John Ericson. The young, handsome actor, later to appear among veterans like Spencer Tracy and Robert Ryan in *Bad Day at Black Rock*, had just starred in MGM's *Teresa*, under the direction of Fred Zinnemann.

Since Ferrer was still appearing nightly in *Twentieth Century*, he was able to have the opening for *Stalag 17* held during the afternoon so that he could attend that night's performance. The play would receive a glowing notice from Brooks Atkinson of the *Times*. He felt that Bevan and Trczinski's play excelled with its blend of tense melodrama and clowning, though he felt the humor occasionally padded the play while the real action, involving the search for a planted traitor in the barracks, was "a taut and harrowing business." Atkinson also noted that the play was "staged with theatrical expertness." Many of Ferrer's cast members also garnered praise, especially Strauss, Lembeck, and Ericson; under Ferrer's direction, Ericson was found to have given "a vivid and honest performance." *Stalag 17* would also prove to be a success with audiences, as it remained at the Forty-eighth Street Theater for a run of 472 performances.

A few weeks after *Stalag 17* wowed the critics and the public, Ferrer would not only have to prepare for his imminent departure from *Twentieth Century*, but as its producer, keep the play running (as he had to leave to fulfill a commitment to film *Anything Can Happen*). There was also the matter of his impending appearance before HUAC weighing heavily on his mind. As far as *Twentieth Century*, Ferrer had located two veterans with the star power to keep the show running: Robert Preston and Binnie Barnes. Although Preston was a few years away from his dynamic turn as Harold Hill in *The Music Man*, both he and Barnes were seen as having the requisite glamour and flamboyance to inhabit the characters of Oscar and Lily. When they assumed the roles in late May 1951, there was some audience drop-off, but box-office receipts slowly rebounded as Preston and Barnes were able to sustain the show through the summer months. It also helped that they, along with the rest of the company, agreed to lower their salaries in order to reduce the running costs.

On May 22, 1951, Ferrer finally made his first appearance before the House Un-American Activities Committee, which included Frank Tavenner, Donald Jackson, and Bernard Kearney. The presiding judge was Francis E. Walter. Ferrer would be represented by his lawyer, Arthur Friend, and Washington attorney Abe Fortas (Ferrer would later portray Fortas in the television movie *Gideon's Trumpet*). He presented himself to the committee as someone who had "always been opposed to communism." Ferrer also questioned why he was not allowed to appear voluntarily, since being "subpoenaed has caused considerable damage to my wife and me in our professions and has resulted in some personal unpleasantness." Ferrer had been tainted not only because of his association with Paul Robeson, but by his association with various politicians, causes, and meetings that were now deemed as communist-leaning and a potential threat to national security. He tried to impress upon the investigators that he was not a communist sympathizer but allowed that he had "casually and freely" permitted the use of his name by various organizations. Like many actors who appeared before HUAC, Ferrer had certainly lent his name to certain causes, especially if there were other names connected. In the aftermath of World War II, these causes had been labeled as communist fronts, including the Joint Anti-Fascist Refugee Committee, the Independent Citizens Committee of the Arts, Sciences, and Professions, and a group which had backed Benjamin Davis for election to the New York City Council.

The committee queried Ferrer about all these and more during two lengthy sessions in May 1951. He was accused of having lent support to groups wanting to abolish the Wood-Rankin Committee (a major part of the HUAC in the 1940s), the methods of which were equated with medieval torture or Nazi Germany by its critics. Ferrer had earlier expressed disapproval of how Parnell Thomas had conducted the hearings of the infamous Hollywood Ten, the group composed of ten Hollywood writers and directors who had gone to jail for contempt after having challenged the legitimacy of the HUAC. These included writer Dalton Trumbo and director Edward Dmytryk. Their cause had been taken up among many in the Hollywood elite, but the Ten disillusioned their supporters with their behavior in the courtroom, leading many to disavow their association with them or their cause. When asked point-blank by Kearney whether the present committee should be abolished, Ferrer replied "no," to which Kearney added, "Was this after the subpoena was issued?" While Ferrer admitted that he had opposed some of the things the committee used to do, he said he thought differently about it now.

Reading over Ferrer's testimony, one can see the actor doing his best to walk a tightrope. There were many occasions when he blamed his own carelessness or ignorance. Ferrer would tell the committee that in many ways he was a soft touch, and when asked to appear at a benefit, he would frequently do so without knowing what he was getting into. When queried about something that was presumably outside the scope of his memory, he was ready to assume "the charges against me are true" or default to "I can't recall." One also sees throughout the two days of testimony that many of these questionable activities were revisited; perhaps the committee was looking to fill in gaps or catch Ferrer in some kind of contradiction. Several times during the course of the two days, Ferrer found it necessary to reiterate that he was never a member of the Communist Party nor did he sympathize with their aims, and that the party itself should be outlawed.

One by one, Ferrer took pains to explain or disavow any alleged communist connections. Regarding the Citizens Committee of the Arts, Sciences, and Professions, Ferrer said he joined in 1944 because it was supporting the fourth term election of Franklin D. Roosevelt. Ferrer said he joined the Joint Anti-Fascist Refugee Committee in 1945 because, as he was a person of Spanish descent, he supported its declared purpose of "relief for refugees from the Spanish dictatorship." He was reluctant to admit that he attended certain meetings, and said that if he had, it was only to act as a master of ceremonies. He was also questioned about his participation at a meeting of writers at the Hotel Astor, which was to begin a national campaign against the HUAC. Ferrer declared he was against censorship, and that reason, along with his fondness for director Moss Hart, caused him to appear and introduce speakers. He would remind the committee that "like a great many people in the arts, I am opposed to censorship."

Among other actions that Ferrer was forced to either answer for or defend included his letter of greeting to the Moscow Arts Theater. Ferrer felt the theater to be a growing symbol of something positive in the art world and thus divorced from any political implications. He also had to discuss his invitation to a peace conference at the Waldorf, which it turns out he didn't attend (since he had a prior dinner engagement with columnist and future host Ed Sullivan). Ferrer did not repudiate the conference, but he told the committee that he wished he had. Ferrer would add that it does present a problem to repudiate a cause or a conference: "If you write a letter to the people involved with your name on the letterhead, your name has been used. The damage has been done."

Ferrer also had to answer at length for his association with the American Committee for the Protection of Foreign Born, as Tavenner had determined that there had been some communist infiltration of that group. At first Ferrer sought to minimize his involvement, saying he had only lent his name and that he had done so only because First Lady Eleanor Roosevelt's name was used to solicit sponsors. Tavenner would say her name was not used, but existing documents clearly show that Tavenner was either mistaken or lying. Besides which, Ferrer freely admitted that he would be predisposed to help the foreign-born in any legitimate cause. He told the committee this was "because of the fact that I am a Puerto Rican, that I was born in Puerto Rico, that I was born an American citizen as all Puerto Ricans are, and I am deeply aware of the fact that although I myself have always been treated admirably in this country, I have many Puerto Rican friends, and many I don't know, who are treated as foreigners in this country, and as people who are unwanted. I am extremely sympathetic to their problems and do all I can to alleviate them." But then when Tavenner states that the organization has been cited as subversive, Ferrer can only reply "I know that now."

There were other items that emerged during Ferrer's two days of testimony before HUAC. He admitted to never having voted, claiming his failure to do so was due to logistics; this willful neglect of his civic duty did not endear him to his interrogators. Ferrer discussed his honorary degree from the University of Puerto Rico and how people had urged him not to accept because they felt the University was "a tool of American imperialism." When it was brought up that the left-wing newspaper the *Daily Worker* had praised many of his performances, he took the time to remind the committee that he had also received some pans from that particular communist-based publication.

Ferrer's associations with Paul Robeson and the politician Benjamin Davis proved to be problematic for the actor. When asked about Robeson, he admitted to having some political discussions with Robeson, but only regarding Roosevelt's re-election and the importance of Wendell Willkie, but said he had no reason at the time to believe that Robeson was a communist sympathizer. In his testimony, Ferrer said he now believed that Robeson has attempted to aid the Soviet Union. He also admitted to not having seen Robeson since 1946 (presumably the night he and detectives interrupted Robeson and Hagen's Christmas night). As for Benjamin Davis, he said that he had met Davis at a birthday party given for Robeson in 1944, when the two were then starring in *Othello*. Ferrer would subsequently endorse Davis for the New York City Council, believing that Davis was a Democrat, and claiming not to know that Davis was a communist. At first, Ferrer said that he did not recall (he would use "I do not recall" as a refrain quite often) either meeting or supporting Davis, but said he probably had. Committee member Donald Jackson would say that while he did not believe Ferrer to be a communist, he also believed that Ferrer had given aid and comfort to the Communist Party. In the end, Ferrer reiterated that he had never been a member of the party and had never knowingly supported any kind of organization sympathetic to the party. That the committee did not immediately provide a clean bill of health for Ferrer seemed to imply that he did "aid the enemy," however unwittingly, which did not endear him to the far-right. For their part, those on the left believed Ferrer too willingly caved under questioning, and writers for certain publications in question, like the *Daily Worker*, would not easily forget.

On his second day of testimony, Ferrer was compelled to revisit his actions regarding the Moscow Arts Theater, specifically his congratulatory letter. Ferrer presented a letter from Lawrence Langner, a powerful director of the Theater Guild as well as a prominent patent attorney. It was akin to a letter of reference, attesting to Ferrer's patriotism and opposition to all things communist. Ferrer would maintain that his telegram was meant to show support for the Moscow Art Theater's artistic achievement and was thoroughly devoid of any political significance. He also told the committee that his *Othello* director Margaret Webster was the one who had asked him to send the telegram; later in that day's session, Ferrer admitted that it was Edward Choate who had called him to attend a meeting entitled "Stop Censorship." Ferrer would claim that the meeting had nothing to do with abolishing HUAC, but it was rather only a meeting to take a stand against censorship.

Here again the investigators would hand Ferrer a list of names and ask him to read the list and admit whether he knew the names. This particular list included artists like Moss Hart, John Hersey, and Margaret Webster. Ferrer could do nothing but admit to knowing them, since these associations were well-known; to say anything else would constitute perjury, and to not answer would mean contempt. (Under the law, if one didn't invoke the Fifth Amendment, one had to answer the questions.) This tactic would be somewhat akin to asking Ward Bond (hypothetically, of course, as Bond was on the "right" side of HUAC) to testify whether he knew John Ford and John Wayne. Bond would have to answer "yes," but any affirmative answer would serve to help legitimize the mission of HUAC. Mr. Velde would suggest to the chairman that "no unusual significance should attach to these names," and that Ferrer did not name them to be communists.

Ferrer would claim not to have "named any names," and in the sense of not naming anyone to be a communist, he may have been accurate, but it did not lessen the impact of what he had done. He had mentioned Webster and Choate, admitted to discussing politics with Robeson, and grudgingly admitted to knowing Davis—but insisted that he did not know they had been communists. Ferrer also pledged, time and again, to lend his name and presence to arresting the scourge of communism, promising to do whatever it takes. He also reminded the committee that he felt it was performing a service for the American public, and they could rely on him to further their cause. (Contrast this to Paul Robeson's appearance before HUAC in 1956, wherein he denounced the committee, proclaiming, "You're the un-Americans, and you ought to be ashamed of yourselves.") Raphael Nixon, one of the investigators for the committee, would say that "we never had any evidence that José Ferrer, Edward G. Robinson, or John Garfield were Communists." One who was not convinced was the powerful columnist Hedda Hopper, who had earlier published a list of Ferrer's so-called transgressions against democracy. There were also those like the reporters for the *Daily Worker* and other left-leaning organizations who felt betrayed by what they perceived as Ferrer's groveling before the committee.

Ferrer still had his professional commitments in place, which contrasted with other actors whose careers and contracts were terminated soon after their involvement with HUAC—especially if they had failed to provide any names. Ferrer would find himself among those who were "graylisted" and had to claw their way back after they first proclaimed themselves dupes and now claimed to be committed to fighting, first and foremost, for America. Edward G. Robinson was but a prominent example, but Ferrer must be included in this category, too; both were free in the past to lend their names and support to now-dubious causes, and both would have to make some sort of reckoning, either public or private, to stay in the committee's good graces and continue in their chosen careers. Ferrer's choice of action was to declare himself wholly in favor of HUAC's mission and state that "it was performing an important function." As Ferrer would recall later to author Lee Pfeiffer, "Just the innuendo that you might be a Communist was enough to put you on a blacklist. Well, not a blacklist, but a graylist. The fact is I was and am politically left-wing, but I was never a Communist. Neither was Eddie Robinson, but the same thing happened to him. He had it worse than I. He was a Jew, and there were prominent people in the HUAC who were anti-Semitic. To be a Jew to these people was almost as bad as being a Communist." Ferrer would later say of Robinson, who had appeared before the HUAC in 1950 with scores of documents, that "Robinson felt humiliated and he thought he was vindicated." Ferrer might have well been feeling the same way about his own appearance.

It would certainly appear that way whenever people would ask Ferrer about his testimony before HUAC. Actress Sean Young would say that when she asked him about his appearance before the committee, Ferrer became very uncomfortable and did not wish to discuss it. His ardent support for HUAC's mission was seen as a betrayal and lost him some admirers and friends, at least for a time. Ferrer's nephew Carlos Campo, currently the president of Ashland University, recalled the time he reached out to his uncle when he was doing his dissertation in the 1980s. Campo asked his uncle if he would be willing to connect him with Arthur Miller, who had taken a public stand against the HUAC, especially with the publication of *The Crucible*. Campo said Ferrer contacted Miller, which led to years of correspondence between Miller and Campo. "Now my uncle and Miller were both impacted by the hearings and there was more than a bit of tension between them, but they reconciled and were good friends by the time I began my work in the late 1980s. As you might imagine the fact that my uncle connected me to Mr. Miller and played such a pivotal role in my development as an educational professional, I have perhaps idealized him even further than I would have otherwise." As Campo suggested, the healing would not be immediate; for now, Ferrer was fortunate to still have his career, though he was still not sure who his friends were.

CHAPTER 8

He's Everywhere

WITH THE HUAC HEARINGS BEHIND HIM, IT IS IRONIC THAT FERRER'S next assignment was to star in George Seaton's *Anything Can Happen*, since the lead character is a Georgian immigrant (at a time when Georgia was still part of Russia) who finds his way in his adopted homeland, the United States. The film was based on a bestseller by George Papashvily and his wife, Helen, who described their work as an autobiographical novel. Seaton (who directed and shared the screenplay credit with George Oppenheimer) was best known for his charming soon-to-be Christmas classic, *Miracle on 34th Street*, but he had also either written or directed such warmhearted comedies as *Junior Miss*, *Apartment for Peggy*, and *Mister 880*.

The movie, embellished with incidents from the pen of Seaton and Oppenheimer, tells the story of Giorgi Papashvili, a Georgian immigrant who arrives in the US without knowing a word of English. He locates (with the help of his friend Nuri, played by Kurt Kasznar) other Georgian emigres, including his Uncle John (seventy-six-year-old newcomer to film, the Hungarian actor Oscar Beregi Sr.). The gregarious Giorgi is a good-hearted, eager-to-learn fellow with a love for playing and singing folk music—a talent that endears him to future American bride Helen, played by Kim Hunter, fresh from her performance as Stella in *A Streetcar Named Desire* (indeed, producer William Perlberg cast Hunter after seeing her in a preview for the film). The plot follows Giorgi's efforts to assimilate while retaining aspects of his own culture and finally trying to make a success of himself in America so that he can win over the smitten but still hesitant Helen.

A substantial part of location filming took place in New York, as well as New Mexico and such California locales as Pasadena and West Covina. The opening shots of the film were captured aboard an incoming Italian Line ship, the SS *Saturnia* (with the author George Papashvily appearing as an extra). As he had with the locations, Seaton applied the same care with the supporting actors. Besides Oscar Beregi Sr. (who was reputed to be Czechoslovakia's leading actor before the postwar communist government came to power), others making their film debuts included Kurt Kasznar, who had achieved some success as a playwright; George Voskovec, who was known as the Czech Charlie Chaplin; and stage actors Oscar Karlweis and Gloria Marlowe (known for her appearances in Broadway musicals). In addition, *Anything Can Happen* marked the return of Eugenie Leontovich to the screen after a hiatus of ten years. In order to assure that his cast members displayed proper accents, Seaton hired Vladimir Babashvily, a new American citizen, to tutor the cast in the proper Balkan intonations.

Ferrer, who throughout his life would maintain an undaunted love for singing (it was not utilized onstage or onscreen to the extent he would have liked—and some, notably future spouse Rosemary Clooney, would always question that aspect of his talent), was finally able to make his vocal debut in this film. In addition, Ferrer also was to play the guitar, and though the playing would be dubbed, Tiny Timbrell, a guitarist from the Harry James Orchestra, came in to coach Ferrer on the proper ways of playing the five-stringed guitar that Ferrer strums at various points.

According to the *Hollywood Reporter*, singer Robert Merrill was originally going to play Giorgi (along with Nancy Olson, who would be replaced by Hunter). Perlberg and Seaton had also contacted Ferrer, but according to Seaton, they had doubts that Ferrer would be able to fit the film into his crowded schedule. Furthermore, even if Ferrer had been available, would he commit to a script without any kind of creative input? Or would he demand to look over the screenplay and make changes? When they initially contacted Ferrer, Perlberg and Seaton did not even have a finished script. Ferrer allayed these fears by assuring them he trusted their work, and only had one question: "When do we start?" When Ferrer finally received the completed script, according to Seaton, he put forward only one request: "Please don't change it."

Seaton praised not only the actor's performance but his demeanor on the set; as Seaton had heard stories of Ferrer being difficult or overbearing, he was relieved to find that none of this was in evidence. As Seaton recalled: "Engaged as an actor, Ferrer used his many other talents only as contributing factors to his performance. His experience as a theatrical manager gave him comprehension of Perlberg's problems as producer; his directorial background made him appreciate my difficulties behind the camera, and his overall knowledge of the entertainment field lightened the load of all the other departments." As Seaton also pointed out, Giorgi was a difficult role, not because "it ran the gamut of standard theatrical emotions but simply because it didn't." Ferrer's Giorgi was a simple, average human being, but great artistry is essential to playing someone average—otherwise, one might produce an average performance.

Ferrer's performance in *Anything Can Happen* is likable, occasionally broad, sometimes subtle, and all of a piece. There is very little showiness on display; instead, he imbues the part with a delicacy, even in its more overtly comic moments. It is an assured performance of a character who is gradually overcoming his insecurities: being in a new country, finding a sense of belonging, finding love. On a technical note, Ferrer's accent, far from being too exaggerated, is fairly credible, as the actor sounds believably Georgian (and not with a Chinese accent, as a *New Yorker* critic suggested).

Giorgi's relationship with Hunter's Helen (who is reluctant to commit because her heart has been broken before) develops along slightly familiar lines, distinguished somewhat by the characters' respective love of folk music. The two actors have a pleasing rapport with each other, so that it seems a contrivance on the writers' part to separate them. Throughout *Anything Can Happen*, Ferrer displays qualities that are not as evident in other films: tenderness, vulnerability, and on occasion, sheer goofiness (without becoming clownish). There is a restraint to Ferrer's playing, whether in his tentative courtship of Helen, or his inability to navigate a sore spot concerning his uncle (namely, the uncle's inability to become a US citizen). Even when Ferrer sings and plays the guitar, he communicates not only the character's joy but the actor's. Ferrer's Papashvili is perhaps the closest Ferrer came to giving a relaxed, even romantic performance. Under Seaton's direction, Ferrer succeeds in providing some artistry in his depiction of the average man.

As Seaton would further recall, besides his artistry onscreen, Ferrer certainly knew how to channel his other talents. Between scenes, Ferrer would spend his time reading other play submissions, approving advertising copy for *Stalag 17* (still playing to capacity audiences on Broadway), planning speaking engagements and radio appearances, and taking singing and dancing lessons. One of the scripts that Ferrer had been considering was a two-character piece that came his way from Hume Cronyn, along with an invitation to see it performed.

The Fourposter, as Jan de Hartog's play was called, had originally come to Cronyn's attention when he was hunting for a property he could perform onstage with his actress wife, Jessica Tandy. While Cronyn and Tandy had acted together in film (notably as husband and wife in the Fred Zinnemann/Spencer Tracy film *The Seventh Cross*), they had yet to find a suitable theater piece. De Hartog had written the play during the Nazi occupation of Holland, and it covered thirty years in the life of a married couple. The play's action was all on one set, which incorporated the bedroom and the four-poster bed of the title. However, when Cronyn discovered the existence of the play, it was in the context of an article that announced a forthcoming film version, to be directed by Joseph Losey. Cronyn wondered why he hadn't heard of it. When he called his friend Losey, he told Cronyn that the play was not a hit when it was performed in London.

However, Losey believed in the property and sent a copy of the screenplay to Cronyn. Cronyn read both the screenplay and the play, and thought the play was a little better, "except for one scene at the end, which I felt didn't belong." This last scene moved the play closer to the realm of tragedy (as opposed to the character comedy it had been previously), but Cronyn wanted to try out the play—ending and all—with wife Jessica on the summer theater circuit. However, she did not care for the script and was reluctant to do it until Cronyn had reminded her that her last theatrical triumph (*Portrait of a Madonna*) owed a great deal to Cronyn's faith in that material. Once Tandy was involved, Cronyn found the bookings hard to come by—some objected to the one-bedroom set, while others thought a two-character play would be box-office poison. The bookings they did get were in various parts of Ontario, and later, the Lakewood Theater in Maine and Bucks County, Pennsylvania.

Cronyn was convinced that, despite the gloomy ending (which would have to be rewritten), he and Tandy had a potential Broadway hit on their hands, and by now he had secured the American rights to the play. He hoped to get the playwright Jan de Hartog to come to America to work on revisions, but the playwright proved to be quite elusive and evasive; he also had passport problems, since he was officially an alien who had been a resident in an occupied country during the war and needed to have proof that he was neither a Nazi nor a collaborator. (De Hartog had written a book called *Holland's Glory*, which had been a rallying point for the Dutch Resistance.)

Besides Cronyn's problems in securing the services of the original author, the director of *The Fourposter* (whom Cronyn would refer to as "a sweet and talented man, but lacked experience") departed the production, leaving Cronyn to assume the director's mantle—and, as Cronyn would recall, this was "an arrangement that had domestic drawbacks." The play's last engagement was at the Lakewood Theater in Maine, and Cronyn asked Ferrer to come and take a look, hoping that Ferrer would direct it himself. Happily, de Hartog's visa difficulties were resolved around the same time, and both the author and the prospective new director would be in attendance for the final performance.

Ferrer agreed to direct *The Fourposter*, with the production bound for Broadway under the aegis of the Playwrights Company, but all involved, including de Hartog, knew the play needed work. Cronyn was also able to extend the engagement at Lakewood, so they would rehearse during the day and perform at night, inserting and learning new lines and bits of business. De Hartog did come up with a new ending, as well as several other ideas which, according to Cronyn, "were sparked by Joe." Cronyn recalls only one blowup, when Ferrer, who felt that there were perhaps too many opinions coming from too many sources, threatened to withdraw. Cronyn calmly persuaded Ferrer to remain, and he would recall, "Thank God he decided to stay with it, because without him I don't think we would have had the success to which he so richly contributed. Mr. Ferrer is a superb director."

Despite the fine job Ferrer was doing, the play still came under the scrutiny of the members of the Playwrights Company, which consisted of Maxwell Anderson (*Winterset, Key Largo*), Elmer Rice (*The Adding Machine*), Robert Sherwood (*The Petrified Forest*), theatrical producer Roger Stevens, and lawyer (and theater aficionado) John Wharton. The company attended the production in Wilmington and listed a number of concerns; Ferrer himself boycotted the meeting, since their arrival had been announced, and he believed that in this case "there were too many cooks." Some of their criticisms had to do with the material itself, others had to do with Cronyn's portrayal of Michael, which Sherwood, in particular, thought should be portrayed with more charm.

Also weighing heavily on both Ferrer and Cronyn was the possibility that a film version of *The Fourposter* might be in circulation when the play was on Broadway. When Cronyn purchased the rights to the play, he did not secure the film rights, even though he had been given the opportunity. Producer Irving Allen (who would later work with Ferrer on the 1955 war film *The Cockleshell Heroes*) had the rights but was having trouble with the financing; he offered to sell the rights to Cronyn, but Cronyn declined. Then producer Stanley Kramer acquired the rights, and his intended film would star Rex Harrison and Lilli Palmer. Cronyn and Ferrer were rightly concerned that audiences might prefer to see the glamorous Rex and Lilli as opposed to Hume and Jessica. Luckily, Cronyn was able to discover that during the journey of *The Fourposter* from London stage to American cinema, with its myriad versions, that de Hartog had written a new, funny scene that Cronyn referred to as "the bottle scene." This scene was in the movie, but the producers did not have the rights to it. Armed with this knowledge, Cronyn persuaded Kramer and Columbia Pictures to delay the release of the film.

With the outside complications having abated, Ferrer was able to help modulate the performances of Cronyn and Tandy, add even more bits of business, and *The Fourposter* was able to open on Broadway in October 1951 at the Barrymore Theater. It was an immediate hit; Cronyn recalled that the backers were able to recoup their investment in six weeks. The reviews were glowing; Brooks Atkinson of the *New York Times* wrote, "*The Fourposter* is the most civilized play we have had on marriage for years . . . it is beautifully staged, set, and acted. Mr. Ferrer's direction is relaxed, pointed and amusing; and it is not afraid of a broad joke now and then." Cronyn and Tandy stayed with the play for over 600 performances, both in New York and on tour. When they departed, Burgess Meredith and Betty Field took over. Besides all the critical approval, Ferrer and Cronyn were perhaps even more honored to receive this missive from Oscar and Dorothy Hammerstein, who admitted they viewed the play through "a film of tears, the most satisfying kind of tears because they were inspired not by sadness or solemnity, but by the recognition of the beauty that lies in all the married lives of all the stumbling, bumbling human beings who try to do their best with each other."

At this juncture of Ferrer's career, he barely had the time to bask in the reviews or audience response; privately, he was still seeing Rosemary Clooney and trying as hard as he could to keep their relationship a secret from the press. He was also about to begin directing and acting in another, more corrosive view of marriage, Joseph Kramm's *The Shrike*, one in which the leading male character is confined to a psychiatric ward— and very much at the mercy of his wife. The journey for this particular play began in 1948, when Kramm was directing Ferrer in a Maryland production of *Twentieth Century*. Ferrer and Kramm, a former actor and copyeditor, would remain friends after the production, and Kramm spent time between 1948 and 1950 making the rounds of psychiatric wards and eventually writing his play. He showed it to Ferrer in May 1950; Ferrer immediately optioned *The Shrike*, realized he would be far too busy with the film of *Cyrano*, and allowed the option to lapse. After that film was completed, Ferrer optioned *The Shrike* again; this time he had to relinquish the rights when he became committed to both *Anything Can Happen* and *The Fourposter*. Producer and mentor Jed Harris had also expressed interest in producing the play, but luckily for Ferrer, after he was finished bringing *The Fourposter* to Broadway, he saw that the rights were still available. This time he secured them with every intention of following through.

The Shrike is a devastating psychological melodrama about Jim Downs, a downcast stage director who is having some trouble finding employment (that part might have appealed to Ferrer's sense of irony). He tries to commit suicide, and after he recovers, expects to be allowed to go home, but the audience discovers his wife, Ann, has been plotting against him. As becomes clear, the wife is indeed the shrike of the title; just as the shrike itself is a seemingly harmless bird that is really a predatory creature that impales its prey, so is wife Ann. Outwardly concerned, cooperative with the doctors, claiming to want only the best for husband Jim, she is seen undermining him at every turn (usually more apparent to the audience than the unfortunate Jim). Her resolve is only strengthened when she discovers Jim wants to break it off and begins seeing another woman.

Ferrer believed the play was a complex, significant work, challenging to him both as actor and director. He explained why he stuck with the play through his seemingly never-ending series of options: "The play always fascinated me. It's deceptively simple. It deals in grays, rather than blacks and whites. Jim Downs is repelled by his wife but is also attracted to her . . . the suicide pattern is his. I think he's destined for a life of torment."

While director Ferrer was not overly concerned about the choice of actor Ferrer assuming the role of Jim, he would have to take care to find the right Ann. He ultimately decided on the actress Judith Evelyn, who had some formidable Broadway credits on her resume, including the lead roles in both *Angel Street* and a revival of *Craig's Wife*. She was skilled at playing both the victim and the victimizer. Ferrer had little doubt that Evelyn would excel in the role of Ann, saying before the opening: "I think Judith Evelyn is so right as the wife; it's right in the key of the play, which doesn't point a finger of accusation at anybody."

Ferrer, who was also still seeing Rosemary Clooney, especially when he was in Hollywood either filming or meeting with Hollywood producers, was also able to include Phyllis in the Broadway cast of *The Shrike*.

She had a small role, and even though they had not yet officially split, Ferrer had informed Clooney they were indeed separated (lest Clooney be known as seeing a married man and damaging her own reputation). Ferrer was trying to be particularly careful, as he was already somewhat tainted by his appearances before HUAC. That he had been publicly "exonerated" didn't assuage the suspicions of those both on the left and the right; at one point, Ferrer was considered for the role of the theatrical impresario Jeffrey Cordova in the MGM musical *The Band Wagon*. The role was seemingly based on Ferrer, as Cordova in the film has two plays on Broadway while starring in a third, yet Ferrer did not get the part. (British star Jack Buchanan would play it—magnificently.) While Ferrer would not publicly comment, Clooney would suggest that he wasn't cast because of lingering concerns about his stature in Hollywood.

When he was not dealing with his tangled personal and professional life, Ferrer was consumed with preparations for *The Shrike*. He would visit mental wards to gain insight both into the patients as well as the day-to-day activities of such a place. Ferrer would also collaborate with the writer Joseph Kramm; as he would in all his productions (he was also a producer here, investing at least $5,000 of his own money), Ferrer would insist on collaborating with the author to fine-tune the piece, especially during the out-of-town tour that would precede the Broadway opening.

Perhaps the biggest point of contention had to do with the play's ending, wherein the character of Jim is released into the care of Ann, but it's made clear that he has only exchanged one kind of confinement for another. According to Ferrer, everyone was encouraging him to cut the last scene; the prevailing attitude was that the final scene was anticlimactic and needlessly lengthened the play. Yet Ferrer felt moved by the last scene. Furthermore, if the last scene was cut, he wouldn't know how to turn the preceding scene into the "new" last scene. Up until the play's arrival in New York, both he and author Kramm agreed on this.

However, the night before they opened in New York, Kramm said to Ferrer that "maybe we ought to change the last scene." When Ferrer asked why, Kramm replied that, sitting out in the audience, he came to the conclusion that they ought to cut it. So Ferrer sat him down after the performance and also called the general manager to remain nearby in case they had to change the program. After some pointed questioning from Ferrer along the lines of "what precisely did you think," Kramm finally said "something that made sense. I said, 'Now *that* changes the picture,' and we cut the scene . . . the programs were done all over again and we opened that night without that last scene."

An essential aspect of Ferrer's skill as a director was being secure enough in his own abilities that he encouraged suggestions that would improve the work. As he said on many occasions, the suggestions would be theirs, but as director he would receive the credit: "I listen to anybody who has any sense at all . . . you never know where it's going to come from; you keep your ears and eyes open and if somebody says something that makes sense, you listen to it."

With its new last scene somewhat firmly in place, *The Shrike* opened to positive notices from the New York critics. Judith Evelyn was unanimously praised for her precise, subtle performance. Critic George Jean Nathan said that "she managed the evil wife with subtlety and uncommon intelligence in its depiction of rapacity and selfishness under the outer coating of solicitude and gentility." In 1967, after Judith Evelyn passed away, Ferrer would recall how "she drew on an apparently bottomless well of neurotic energy to charge that stage with relentless electricity. You remember her ovation during the calls."

Ferrer was applauded for both his staging as well as his quiet playing. The *New York Times* critic Brooks Atkinson felt that "since Mr. Ferrer has scrupulously cast the subordinate roles with an instinctive relish of good work in the theater, the scenes in the ward have the ring of plausibility and the various characters are vividly portrayed . . . whatever the precise quality of the play might be, Ferrer acts the part of the husband with complete and moving conviction. He does not fool around with it superficially. He draws a harrowing portrait of an intelligent man caught, trapped and broken by a system he cannot influence." Atkinson also pointed to Ferrer's skill in portraying a man in a constant state of flux while still being able to "develop a part through a series of exterior influences."

All too often, Ferrer would be accused of coasting on external effects, allowing the distinctive voice to carry the burden at the expense of projecting the character's inner life, but it appears that with *The Shrike* (and is apparent in the later film version) Ferrer has used the external forces at work to deepen his inner portrayal. In this case, the wheels don't show; it all seems natural, uncalculated, even spontaneous. He would also elaborate later on how, as an actor, he was able to maintain the intensity throughout the run of the play—and especially for the devastating final scene: "At one point I killed every single person that I loved—I saw them lying there on their deathbeds—to work myself up to the point where I was moved . . . because about the third or fourth month of eight times a week, I can't be as stimulated as I was the first month. . . . I killed my father and my daughter and my best friend . . . I ran over strangers." For Ferrer, he had to do anything and everything to ensure that the performance was the equal to opening night: "You have to give the audience their money's worth . . . and secretly you do terrible things to the people you love, if that's what you need. In a kind of shameful way, you use any tool at hand, and it isn't anything you mean, but you use anything that moves you to get it to move you again, too."

The accolades would continue at the Sixth Annual Antoinette Perry (Tony) Awards, held on March 30, 1952. Ferrer would win the Best Actor award for his performance in *The Shrike* and would also win Outstanding Director for both *The Shrike* and *The Fourposter*. Judith Evelyn, though nominated for Best Actress, lost to Julie Harris for her performance in *I Am a Camera*. Finally, *The Fourposter* would win the Outstanding Play honor. While playwright Joseph Kramm did not win a Tony for *The Shrike*, his play would have the distinction of receiving the coveted Pulitzer Prize in 1952.

Ferrer was not content to rest on his laurels, as there were other projects, past and present, that demanded his attention. *Anything Can Happen* would be released in the spring of 1952, but it had already received some notice during previews for its depiction of assimilation and its celebration of America as a land of opportunity for all Americans. One such reviewer felt that while he was sure it wasn't intended to be a piece of American propaganda, he wished "it could be shown in every city and hamlet behind the Iron Curtain." *Variety* called the film "a heartwarming comedy," but Bosley Crowther took issue with the film's story, contending that the tale was plausible twenty years earlier, but, given the current political climate, "the prospect of such a young fellow arriving today is nigh absurd." Following the film's release, Kim Hunter, who had also been named in *Red Channels*, would find himself blacklisted for nearly five years. There were some protests directed toward the film and Ferrer at other screenings, notably a screening in Baltimore; even though Ferrer had seemingly been cleared, he could not escape the cloud that emerged after his appearances before HUAC.

It's not that he didn't stop trying: Ferrer would take any opportunity to declare that communism should be outlawed and that he has always been a good American. One of the ways he chose to demonstrate that took a page out of James Cagney's book when it came to dealing with suspicions of being un-American: act in the life story of one of the most patriotic Americans ever to grace the stage, George M. Cohan. Ferrer probably had more in common with Cohan than Cagney had, being an accomplished director, producer, and performer. While Ferrer possessed Cagney's energy, he certainly lacked Cagney's musical-comedy prowess, but he had been dutifully taking singing and tapdancing lessons. And even though doing a straight remake of *Yankee Doodle Dandy* was out, writer-director Ferrer could not be dissuaded from working on *The Musical Comedy Man*, a new show about Cohan's life that would incorporate the familiar patriotic Cohan songs.

Ferrer, perhaps feeling that being represented on Broadway with three plays (*The Fourposter, The Shrike, Stalag 17*) didn't constitute enough of a presence, obtained the rights to yet another play, one that he would only produce and direct. It was *The Chase* by Horton Foote, a native Texan. His play was about a frustrated, decent Texas sheriff who wants to quit, and an escaped convict who returns home and complicates the sheriff's plans—namely, by intending to kill the sheriff. In addition to the three main characters, of the sheriff, his wife, and the convict, Foote also populated the play with deputies, townspeople, and other criminals. Foote, who would later attain fame for his screenplay adaptation of Harper Lee's *To Kill a Mockingbird*, originally sold the option for the play to Celeste Holm and John Haggott. They had envisioned getting a big star like Gary Cooper to play the lead. It was probably wishful thinking (or a publicity stunt) on their part, since Cooper had a little Western called *High Noon* that was about to reach the theaters. (In addition, acting onstage could pose a mighty challenge for a shy film star, as Spencer Tracy discovered in 1945 when he starred in Robert Sherwood's *The Rugged Path*. It lasted for eighty-one performances, and Tracy, feeling pressured every minute of it, never returned to the stage.) The rights eventually reverted to Foote, which were then acquired by a very interested Ferrer, who saw *The Chase* as an opportunity to depict something meaningful about justice and small-town tensions.

With Cooper remaining unavailable for the starring role of the sheriff, Ferrer found his lead from the ranks of available American leading men. John Hodiak was cast as the duty-bound sheriff in what would be his stage debut. Hodiak was a competent leading man who had done some fine early work at Twentieth Century-Fox in films such as *A Bell for Adano* and *Sunday Dinner for a Soldier*, but by 1948, he was labeled box-office poison by theater exhibitors. Hodiak was now an MGM contract player either lending support to star players like Robert Taylor in *The Bribe* and Spencer Tracy in *The People vs. O'Hara*, or he was the lead in shaky "A" vehicles like *A Lady Without Passport*, opposite Hedy Lamarr. For the part of Hodiak's wife, Ferrer cast his *Anything Can Happen* costar Kim Hunter, who could be relied upon to lend strong support to Hodiak, who was himself a Broadway neophyte.

The Chase, like Ferrer's still-running *The Shrike*, would have out-of-town previews in Philadelphia. However, director Ferrer was also performing most nights as the lead in *The Shrike*. Consequently, while *The Chase* was in Philadelphia, Ferrer developed a routine of finishing his performance every night, catching a train to Philadelphia, and working with the playwright Foote until 5:00 a.m. Then Ferrer would sleep a few hours, coach the cast until the late afternoon, then catch the train back to New York in order to make the evening performance of *The Shrike*. He would do this weekly, except for the two days that *The Shrike* had matinee performances.

When *The Chase* opened in April 1952 at the Playhouse Theater, a few critics noted Ferrer's quick planning, as it began rehearsing March 3 (or six weeks after *The Shrike* opened) for its April opening, but they mentioned this in the context of suggesting that perhaps the strain was starting to show. *The Chase* was Ferrer's fifth production since 1951; he would also have to take a night off from *The Shrike* to attend the premiere. Critic John Chapman, a Ferrer supporter, called the play "a vivid piece of theater," but he was in the minority. Most found the play dull and were surprised that Ferrer wanted to direct it. Ward Morehouse said that "Ferrer has put showmanship into the job, giving some of his players too much freedom . . . to carry on interminably." George Jean Nathan said that Ferrer's style of staging is "if the play is paced so slowly, it will acquire an appearance of immense depth and authority."

Hodiak and Hunter would fare relatively well with the critics, who seemed to find more fault with Foote's source material. Brooks Atkinson found that "the acting is excellent," that Hodiak has a "loose, leisurely sincerity that is thoroughly agreeable," and that Hodiak was lucky because he had Hunter playing his wife. However, Atkinson echoed others in his view that though Foote's story may be authentic, it gives "the impression of being imposed on the characters and the author." A crucial plot point in the play has to do with the sheriff's reaction upon finding that the killer is running loose in his town, with the sheriff determined to capture him alive. In the end, though, the sheriff is forced to kill him. Critics found that while Foote might have intended this to be dramatic, by this time, there wasn't much drama left to be had. Despite the overall criticism, a few observers praised Ferrer for maximizing what was viewed as a flawed, sprawling script and for bringing out textured performances by the two leads.

For a short time on Broadway, the Ferrer name would not only be associated with four Broadway plays, but also the film of *Anything Can Happen*. Three of these plays—*The Shrike*, *Stalag 17*, and *The Chase*—were all on Forty-eighth Street, east of Broadway, leading it to be dubbed Ferrer Lane for a time. On one or two occasions, the lucky pedestrian might have been surprised to see Ferrer, in costume for *The Shrike*, scurrying to *The Chase* to impart some last-minute thought or suggestion before scurrying back to his own performance. All these inspirations did little to prolong the run of *The Chase*, which closed after only thirty-one performances. It was a rare Ferrer stumble, but one he could take in stride, since he was still enjoying his success in *The Shrike* and was about to find himself back in front of the cameras.

CHAPTER 9

Film Star, City Center Savior, and Newlywed

IN JUNE 1952, FERRER BEGAN FILMING *MOULIN ROUGE* IN PARIS AND London, under John Huston's direction. *Moulin Rouge* was a fictionalized and romanticized biography of the impressionist painter Henri de Toulouse-Lautrec (1864–1901), who gained notoriety with his depictions of the bohemian Parisian nightlife of the late 1800s, particularly the dancers, prostitutes, and other colorful characters of the time. He also suffered from a genetic bone condition, and an early accident resulted in his growth being stunted, so that he was only four feet, eight inches tall. Filming would largely take place over that summer of 1952, but Ferrer became involved in the project long before that.

His involvement actually commenced in 1950, when he had spoken with the actress Hedy Lamarr at the Beverly Hills Hotel. Lamarr was a beautiful film star who was far more intelligent than most realized given that it was subsequently discovered that her scientific collaborations with the composer George Antheil would result in a frequency-hopping program that would be utilized by the United States government. It was not out of the realm of believability, then, for Lamarr to have asked Ferrer if he had read any good books lately. Lamarr then produced a copy of Pierre La Mure's book *Moulin Rouge* and suggested he read it. Ferrer did, and asked Lamarr to arrange a meeting with the author. He would then purchase not only the dramatic rights, but also a large share in the screen rights. For a time, he used his box-office power to try to get the work produced as a play, but he met with little success.

About two years after Ferrer secured the rights, writer/director John Huston, at the peak of his success with *The Treasure of the Sierra Madre*, *The Asphalt Jungle*, and *The African Queen*, was on the prowl for another subject. James Woolf, the co-owner of Huston's film company, Romulus Films, gave Huston a copy of the book. Almost immediately, Huston visualized the closing scene, in which a dying Lautrec, with his mother and father in attendance, would visualize the various subjects of his life's work. As Huston described in his autobiography, *An Open Book*, "He smiles and his eyes open. He is hallucinating. The shades from his beloved Moulin Rouge enter to bid farewell to their friend. The music of the can-can starts and Lautrec breathes his last. It would be a truly happy ending." Huston at once decided that the story of the tortured artist would make an ideal film.

Huston then contacted José Ferrer about making a picture of *Moulin Rouge*, telling the actor he intended to buy the rights to the project, whereupon Ferrer informed Huston that "you might as well talk to me about the rights. I own them." After negotiating with Ferrer, Huston realized he did not want to do another film with Sam Spiegel, after some tension during the making of *The African Queen*. In his search for financing and a distributor, Huston discovered that "nobody wants to finance a picture about a dwarf." Fortunately, he and Ferrer were able to acquire a distribution deal with United Artists, with the film co-financed by Moulin Productions and Great Britain's Romulus Films (co-owned by James and John Woolf).

Both Huston and Ferrer had to endure a lengthy and complex series of preparations before they were to commence filming. For Huston, the difficulties lay in both casting and the use of color. The movie's plot would have little to do with Lautrec's real life and instead conform to the standard biographical artist trope, meaning the artist would forever be unhappy in love, either spurning the affections of one, or enduring the rejection of another, with the artist only able to truly immerse himself in his art. The women in the artist's life—namely, the chanteuse, the prostitute, and the young woman of means—would be played by Zsa Zsa Gabor, Colette Marchand, and Suzanne Flon, respectively. Besides engaging the French actress Flon for her onscreen attributes, the married Huston also found time to indulge in an offscreen affair. This development would only serve to anger Flon's lover, who at one point during filming, accosted an unprepared Huston, who would retaliate later only to be confronted with the lover brandishing a gun—which, fortunately for Huston, misfired.

The biggest problem facing Huston though was how to reproduce not only Lautrec's work but the atmosphere of late 1800s-era Paris. He and cinematographer Oswald Morris experimented with color in order to create a more subtle effect than was possible using just plain Technicolor. The Technicolor process was a three-color process in which three different negatives, each individually sensitive to red, green, and blue, are run through a camera and printed together. What Huston and Morris did was to remove one of the color negatives and replace it with black-and-white to achieve a special texture. The artist Marcel Vertes was also hired to create paintings and sketches that would emulate Lautrec's style.

There would also be some problems with the Breen Office, centering on Huston and co-writer Anthony Veiller's screenplay. In a script that included all kinds of women, Breen insisted that all references to solicitation and prostitution were to be avoided. Huston and Veiller managed to appease both the strictures of the Breen Office while also suggesting the flavor of the time period, or as Huston put it, "within the limits of moral censorship."

For the five-foot ten-inch Ferrer, the technical problem lay in how to portray a man only four feet, eight inches tall. Researching Lautrec for months was the easy part; Ferrer and the filmmakers had to figure out how he could convincingly appear as a much shorter man. He would be fitted with a pair of short artificial legs that were strapped to his knees, with his own lower legs out behind him and out of camera range. The illusion would further be assisted by some carefully angled camerawork, and some long shots with a genuine dwarf, as well as some specially padded boots. (Ferrer would dub these "torture boots.") In order to tolerate the discomfort generated by these new "legs," Ferrer practiced yoga, spending weeks controlling his breathing and jackknifing his body into improbable postures. This provided Ferrer with the strength and endurance to wear the legs for a sustained period of time, since he was on call every day, excluding the can-can sequence. Besides playing Lautrec, Ferrer would play Lautrec's father, who leaves the family after his son's accident and subsequent affliction, which in the film is partly caused by a genetic bone condition that perhaps stemmed from his parents' status as first cousins.

Huston was nothing short of effusive regarding Ferrer and his work ethic, telling interviewers that he "never saw such an amazing guy, so many talents." Huston marveled at Ferrer's mastery of several languages. He knew about Ferrer's fluency in French and Spanish, until "one day Silvana Mangano [the Italian actress] visited the set; he spoke Italian fluently too." Huston also cited Ferrer's fearlessness and easy mastery of new skills, noting that when Ferrer learned Huston was planning to go to Ireland to do some riding, Ferrer joined him: "I don't think he'd ridden a horse since he was a kid . . . he came along and soon he was taking jumps as if he'd been riding all his life."

As for Ferrer's performance in the film, Huston believed that "in the picture he's perfect. One thing you'll notice is that in playing this dwarf, this grotesque, he never for one minute gives the character self-pity. It's a proud and whole character, which is what Lautrec should be." Viewing the film today, except for the occasional touch of self-pity, in the midst of drowning his sorrows after he has failed in love once again, Huston's take on Ferrer's performance is pretty accurate. Ferrer endows both roles with dignity, aloofness, and a smattering of vulnerability. Playing Lautrec Sr. in the scene when he renounces his own family (while young Lautrec listens in the shadows) is nicely judged, but, of course, it is as Lautrec the painter with which Ferrer acquitted himself most admirably. He is thoroughly convincing, both as gifted artist and tortured man. In his scenes with Colette Marchand's Marie, Ferrer brings a great deal of sensitivity and empathy; their scenes crackle with emotion, both in the early stages where he is trying to save her (and himself); later with his true love (Suzanne Flon), Ferrer endows Lautrec with a pride offset by a small degree of self-loathing, which renders him incapable of making a full human connection. Considering the potential for Lautrec to be insufferable, Ferrer manages to keep the character's humanity always present. However, as many critics agreed, the true highlights of *Moulin Rouge* are the scenes in the eponymous club and its environs, around which the viewer feels the energy and vitality of Paris, including the Parisian dancers, brawlers, artists, and gentlemen (and not-quite gentlemen) who populate the buoyant, dizzying Paris of the 1890s.

The filming of *Moulin Rouge* had been completed in September 1952; both Huston and Ferrer knew the result would surely be a critical success and hoped to get the film into theaters in time for Academy Award consideration. However, in late 1952, before the first previews, Ferrer still hadn't managed to escape the stigma left by the HUAC hearings. He had been denied a permit by the British Ministry of Labour to appear in the Old Vic's production of *The Seagull*. Ostensibly it was because the Old Vic was government-subsidized and created for British actors, but British Actors Equity also told the Labor Ministry that it did not approve of "foreigners" appearing in the national theater. More evidence of Ferrer's damaged standing was revealed in a confidential letter to Henry Rogers from Paul Kohner, in which Kohner stated that "there is considerable opposition to Ferrer in many circles, particularly among newspapers. There is an absolute ban against him in the *LA Times*." Henry Rogers, who was handling publicity for the film, would include Ferrer in the advertising to the extent that Ferrer's contract demanded but no more. Kohner would implore Huston to bring the print to the United States for the world premiere but to leave behind Ferrer, as Rogers was trying to have the advertising focus on Huston, fresh off his triumph in *The African Queen*.

One of the most fervent groups of picketers of the upcoming release was the American Legion; in particular, they brought up Ferrer's past association with Paul Robeson, since Robeson had recently accepted an honor from the Soviet Union. In response to the Legion's accusations, Ferrer assured them he was against communism: "It is my conviction that an artist cannot function under Communism. . . . I condemn Paul Robeson's acceptance of Stalin's so-called Peace Prize. Any American who accepts an award from the Soviet Union does a tremendous disservice not only to his own country, but in the cause of peace throughout the world." Ferrer would also contact Lewis Gough of the American Legion in a further attempt to ally himself with its mission: "Because as an artist I am unalterably opposed to any form of oppression, I am wholeheartedly in accord with the American Legion in their fight against Communism. I have made mistakes in the past, but they were of the head and not of the heart. I assure you they will not be repeated. I invite opportunities to join in the anti-Communist fight when and where, time permitting, my abilities can be effectively utilized."

The reaction of the Legion did not discourage other reviewers, who found Huston and Ferrer's collaboration to be a thing of beauty. The film was praised for its use of color, the recreation of bohemian life, and the energy which captures the Moulin Rouge (if perhaps slightly less for its emotional content). The *Hollywood Reporter* felt that "Ferrer turns in a masterful portrayal, playing with a dignity and saturnine wit that inspire sympathy, not pity." Otis Guernsey of the *Herald Tribune* would view the film as a sprawling panorama with a hero that is "more heroic than human . . . the film leaves one admiring but unmoved." *Moulin Rouge* did receive Academy Award nominations for Best Picture, Best Director (Huston), Best Actor (Ferrer), Best Supporting Actress (Marchand), Best Costume Design, Best Editing, and Best Art Direction, winning awards for Art Direction and Costume Design. Even though it had the benefit of what would be a large promotional campaign, with a gross of close to $5 million, the film still incurred a million-dollar loss, according to

Variety. Still, *Moulin Rouge* contains one of Ferrer's most accomplished performances and remains one of his best-known films. On more than one occasion, Ferrer would speculate that this portrayal, along with Cyrano and perhaps his work on the forthcoming *Caine Mutiny,* constituted his most recognizable roles.

As he was loath to let a minute go by without taking on a new project, the years of 1953 and 1954 would see Ferrer not only direct a new play on Broadway but also return to City Center for a series of two-week revivals, act in three films, adapt a French play as a vehicle for Olivia de Havilland—and, finally, get divorced and married (for the third time). As far as the public knew, Ferrer was still married to Phyllis Hill; while working on *The Shrike,* there were a few carefully placed articles designed to protect the sanctity of their union. These might have been done to convince the American public that, despite all the other critical articles dissecting Ferrer's testimony before HUAC, he was just a hardworking, ambitious, and energetic artist and devoted husband.

Nevertheless, Ferrer was very much involved with Rosemary Clooney, on both a personal and professional level. Mitch Miller, the powerful head of Columbia Records who prided himself on having his finger on the pulse of the public's taste, wanted Clooney to record a little ditty called "Come On-a My House." After hearing the music and what were, in her mind, the empty lyrics, she demurred. However, Ferrer told her that the song did have its roots in the Renaissance—and a Christopher Marlowe play at that. This convinced her to go ahead with what became one of her most identifiable recordings. In addition, Clooney's clandestine trip to visit him on location in *Moulin Rouge* did little to dampen her ardor. These published puff pieces were occasionally offset by stories of alleged dalliances with others. Indeed, Clooney confronted Ferrer when she heard rumors of a fling with another starlet. According to her memoir, Clooney had read that Ferrer was seen stepping out with a starry hopeful named Tempest Storm and demanded that this had to stop.

One can surmise that this confrontation would not be the last; while they were seeing each other and even after their eventual marriage, Ferrer (and others) would remind her that he's "a Latin man," the connotation being that as a Latin man, it would be considered a point of honor for him to have several conquests to his credit. Clooney would say that he would use this consistently as a rationalization for his extramarital endeavors. However, Ferrer must have grown more confident, either in the public's capacity to forget and forgive, or in the wavering resolve of the current Mrs. Ferrer, because he and Clooney allowed themselves to be seen in public together as a couple. For instance, the two attended the Academy Awards together in March 1953, with Clooney lending moral support for nominee Ferrer.

The Academy Awards took place about five days after Ferrer's latest directorial effort had opened on Broadway. It was the gentle, whimsical, and occasionally black comedy *My 3 Angels*. Written by Sam and Bella Spewack, it was based on a French comedy *La Cuisine de Anges* (or *Angels Cooking*) and is set in French Guiana on Christmas Eve. It is on this magical and eventful evening that three Devil's Island convicts endeavor to resolve the fiscal and romantic problems of hapless storekeeper Felix Ducotel and his bourgeois family; the storekeeper's lack of business acumen puts him in the crosshairs of his avaricious brother-in-law Henri Trochard, even as his daughter is in love with Trochard's vacuous nephew. Ferrer cast the veteran Austrian actor Walter Slezak as the lead convict; it was Slezak's first stage appearance in twelve years, as he had been accumulating a string of movie credits, mostly as witty villains or comic relief, in films as diverse as *Lifeboat* and *The Princess and the Pirate*. (Ferrer would also lease his house in Ossining to Slezak for the run of the play, since Ferrer would be filming nonstop in the coming months). The other two convicts were Darren McGavin (twenty years before his indelible Kolchak in *The Night Stalker*) and Jerome Cowan, a reliable character actor not seen on Broadway since *Boy Meets Girl*, which Ferrer had a small role in. Henry Daniell, another Hollywood veteran revered for his screen villainy, was cast as Trochard.

My 3 Angels did exceptional business and received good reviews during its preview run in Hartford, and when it opened in March, Ferrer was given a lot of credit for taking a play which consists of murder, theft, and forgery and converting it into an amusing night at the theater. Slezak in particular was praised by *Times* critic Brooks Atkinson for playing with "a wonderfully, light touch. . . . Slezak, Cowan and McGavin make the first act fresh and funny, and never literal." Critics found some fault with the character of Trochard—and the actor who portrayed him, Daniell—as both were found to be more of a real scoundrel than a comic figure. Critics also found that the play became a little duller after the character's entrance. (This was also a shortcoming of the 1955 film version *We're No Angels*, which bubbles along with convicts Humphrey Bogart, Peter Ustinov, and Aldo Ray, but then stumbles when Basil Rathbone's sneering Trochard enters the scene.) The critics' caveats aside, *My 3*

Angels was another Broadway success for Ferrer, as the play ran for 344 performances.

As usual, Ferrer had little time to revel in the applause; he was on his way to Hollywood, first to attend the Academy Awards—he would lose the Best Actor award to Gary Cooper for *High Noon*—and then to begin filming *Miss Sadie Thompson*, with Rita Hayworth, for Columbia Pictures. It wasn't a picture Ferrer was keen on doing, as he had several other projects in the pipeline, including reuniting with John Huston on a projected film version of *Richard III*, starring and directing in a stage production of *Hamlet*, and starring (as well as making his film directorial debut) in a film version of *The Shrike*. (Ferrer productions had also made their way across the Atlantic, as both *The Shrike* and *Stalag 17* were playing in London houses, with varying degrees of success.)

Columbia Pictures studio head Harry Cohn and executive producer Jerry Wald had high hopes for *Miss Sadie Thompson*, as Rita Hayworth had been off the screen for a few years (following her marriage to Prince Aly Khan) and had just enjoyed a commercial success with *Affair in Trinidad*. Ferrer had misgivings about this latest remake of W. Somerset Maugham's *Rain*, a tale of sin in the South Seas which had already been filmed in 1932 with Joan Crawford as Sadie and Walter Huston as a fanatical minister who is undone by his conflicting desires to save Sadie and have her for himself. Ferrer initially turned down the role; Milton Pickman, a studio executive, said that Ferrer "didn't want to do it from an artistic standpoint. He didn't think the original conception of the role would be believable to a modern-day audience." According to Pickman, Ferrer and Wald spoke over a number of days, with Ferrer making changes in the script and Wald becoming more and more convinced that Ferrer should have the role. Finally, Ferrer, after the changes, believed that this was now "a hell of a role, and accepted the part, for $125,000." Ferrer recalled it a little differently in talking with Hayworth biographer Barbara Leaming, suggesting that his acceptance of the role was on the advice of his agent: "I had been grilled and cross-examined by Ward Bond and other Hollywood 'heroes' who decided I was all right. But Hedda Hopper was still against me." So his agent believed that if Ferrer would agree to star with Columbia's very hot Rita in a picture produced by Harry Cohn, "it would dispel any lingering hesitation anyone else might have about hiring you. I accepted the job, on that crass, opportunistic basis."

Producer Jerry Wald, who had optioned the rights in 1952, was presenting a watered-down version of the venerable tale. In the original story, Sadie is a prostitute stranded on an island in the South Seas who

attracts the unwanted attentions of a fanatical minister determined to
save her—until he determines to have her for himself. The earlier versions (Gloria Swanson's silent version, as well as Crawford's 1932 portrayal) would earn their lead actresses kudos but also precipitated a temporary decline in their careers. Rita Hayworth's career was solidly on the
rise again, but Wald and Cohn hedged their bets in these somewhat mor-
alistic times by making Sadie more of a "good-time, happy-go-lucky gal"
who worked as a singer at a bawdy military base—and not the prostitute
she had been in the original. (There were several musical numbers, with
the non-singing Hayworth's voice dubbed by Jo Ann Greer.)

Columbia also planned to take advantage of the relatively new 3-D
format to make *Miss Sadie Thompson* a more visceral experience for moviegoers (as well as a profitable one for the studio). Moreover, Davidson
was no longer a missionary; instead he was the wealthy plantation owner
whose father had been the missionary. In this version, Davidson (a powerful, influential presence who is feared all over the South Seas) is motivated both by a desire to impose his unyielding sense of morality on the
natives—and by guilt, since he is plagued by never having been able to
save anyone. As Ferrer recalled, "The trouble with the script was that in
those days they didn't dare call a spade a spade. All the things in the story
thought to give offense were quietly eliminated." If Ferrer really made
the changes that Pickman credits him for, then despite his intentions, he
may well bear some responsibility for the uneven results that made their
way to the screens in February 1954.

Miss Sadie Thompson, under Curtis Bernhardt's direction, is fairly entertaining at times, especially when Rita Hayworth and Aldo Ray are sizing
up each other, brawling with each other (or other servicemen, including a young Charles Bronson), or playing out aspects of the contrived
romance (that ends happily in this version). Ferrer, however, gives one
of his least-invested major performances in this film. As the intolerant,
insufferable Davidson, Ferrer exudes not only these qualities in the extreme, but he also projects the distinct feeling that even he can't believe
in the platitudes and the moralizing that he is espousing—all the more
ironic considering Ferrer's presumed input. As conceived for this version,
Davidson's mania is so pronounced that it is inconceivable that people
would tolerate his presence for a minute, much less for a civilized meal.
An early cozy dinner scene is upended by Davidson's unpleasant pontificating, which his dinner mates forgive, since he has money and power.
There is little trace of humanity or modulation in Ferrer's portrayal of
Davidson; he is content to bellow and leave it at that. Later, when Ferrer's

Davidson tries to save Sadie—and then later attack her—Ferrer's playing is a little too detached and unpersuasive, making his transition (rushed as it already is) from potential savior to lecherous victimizer even more abrupt and unconvincing.

The film would not be the success Columbia heads had hoped for, especially not in 3-D, which had lost its novelty appeal by 1954. After an initial release in that format, *Miss Sadie Thompson* would be reissued strictly in traditional 2-D. In addition, Rita Hayworth incurred Harry Cohn's wrath by her growing attachment to the crooner Dick Haymes, who was having problems due to his immigration status (Haymes was Argentinian born). Hayworth received some of her best reviews for the film; *Variety* said that Hayworth "catches the feel of the title character well, even braving completely deglamorizing make-up, costuming and photography to fit her physical appearance to that of Sadie Thompson." *Cue* would say that "Hayworth steals the acting honors, while Ferrer practically sleepwalks through his role." In Ferrer's hands, Davidson was no longer a missionary bigot, but merely a narrow, evil man.

After filming was completed, Ferrer would remain very much on the Columbia radar, as he was also considering making his directorial debut on a proposed Jerry Wald project *Stretch on the River*. Internal studio memos between Milton Pickman and Jerry Wald reveal that Columbia wanted Ferrer as a director—even a first-time one—but Ferrer was reluctant to grant Columbia an option on future pictures. There are even talks of reuniting him with Hayworth on another melodrama called *Rough Company* and a light comedy called *The Half-Naked Truth*, despite the fact that Ferrer was hedging on both. On *Rough Company*, while Ferrer liked the premise of a broken-down theatrical company, he thought the film lacked "real excitement and a sense of danger"; as for *The Half-Naked Truth*, it was a remake, but Ferrer thought he and Hayworth deserved a little more than the "remake of an unimportant picture." He did, however, sign with Stanley Kramer (his films now released through Columbia Pictures) for a pivotal part as defense attorney Barney Greenwald in the upcoming film of Herman Wouk's *The Caine Mutiny*; simply going from film to film was not enough for the prolific Ferrer. Informed that his start date on *The Caine Mutiny* was August 1953 (the rest of the cast began filming in June), Ferrer filled the time between *Sadie* and *Caine* to tend to a few upcoming stage performances.

One was translating (Ferrer was fluent in French and four other languages) and working on an adaptation of an original French comedy *The Dazzling Hour*, by Anna Bonacci. Collaborating with the writer Kelli

Frings on the adaptation, the play centers on a composer of oratorios who wants his music to be heard. When he learns the minister of culture is visiting, he arranges for the minister to visit his home. However, the composer learns the minister has an eye for the ladies, and his respectable wife flees the scene, leaving the composer to hire a prostitute to take her place. If the premise seems familiar, it's because it would later be utilized in Billy Wilder's 1964 *Kiss Me, Stupid*, starring Ray Walston as an aspiring pop music composer (Peter Sellers had been first choice but suffered a heart attack during filming), Dean Martin as a lecherous musical star called Dino, and Felicia Farr and Kim Novak as the wife and prostitute, respectively.

For the play, which would be staged at La Jolla Playhouse (with an eye toward a Broadway run), Ferrer wooed and won Olivia de Havilland for the role of the respectable wife, while Kent Smith was the composer, John Emery the minister, and Mary Sinclair the prostitute. When *The Dazzling Hour* opened in late July, critics felt the play was flawed by too much talk and a slow, labored pace. As much as Ferrer wanted to direct de Havilland, he was unable to coax the proper comedic tone; she was criticized for her sheer lack of lightness and an inability to connect with the audience. Most doubted the play would make it to Broadway—and they were correct.

By late July, with *The Caine Mutiny* to come in August, Ferrer probably was not concerned about the fate of *Dazzling Hour*, for a number of reasons. In the midst of Ferrer's "downtime" between his completion of *Miss Sadie Thompson* and the August 8 start date for *The Caine Mutiny*, he had booked another show besides *The Dazzling Hour*. A Hollywood producer would say that "empty time is Joe's only phobia," so when Ferrer received an offer to appear in the singing-dancing lead role in *Kiss Me, Kate* at the State Fair Auditorium in Dallas in late July 1953, he quickly accepted, hoping that those fifteen years of voice lessons hadn't gone to waste. Ferrer would play Fred, an actor/director whose company was performing Shakespeare's *The Taming of the Shrew*, and as Fred was also playing Petruchio, Ferrer would have to brush up both on his Shakespeare *and* his singing.

While rehearsing both *The Dazzling Hour* and *Kiss Me Kate*, he and estranged wife Phyllis finalized their divorce, and a week later, on July 13, 1953, Ferrer and Clooney were married in a small ceremony in Durant, Oklahoma. Durant is a small town roughly ninety miles north of Dallas, and the couple eloped there because in Texas, a couple had to wait three days to get the results of their blood tests, but in Durant, a couple could get a blood test and just proceed to the courthouse to get married. Ferrer's agent and Clooney's manager were in attendance, as well as Louise Gentry, a deputy clerk at the Bryan County Courthouse. (The local medical clinic alerted her that the famous couple was on their way.) In an interview after Clooney passed away in 2002, Gentry recalled that "the wedding lasted but two minutes. The judge didn't know he was marrying a famous couple." Gentry also remembered that "they were in a hurry . . . they wanted to get back to Dallas for the evening performance."

Years later, Louise Gentry went to Hollywood to appear on the game show *About Faces*. She was a mystery guest that Ferrer finally identified as "playing an important part in his life." Later she received a family photo along with a note from Ferrer, on which he wrote "I thought you might like to see our family now." As for his performance in *Kiss Me, Kate*, although a Dallas critic found his voice to be "audible" and "awful," it meant little to Ferrer. He had a new, talented wife, and a strong role in a big-budget production—and the prospect of directing and starring in the film of *The Shrike*. To risk repeating a cliché, Ferrer's future did appear to be limitless.

CHAPTER 10

Life Is Rosie

"ROSIE, HE'S TERRIBLE." THIS WAS MITCH MILLER'S FIRST OF MANY PRO-
nouncements on José Ferrer, but it had nothing to do with his behavior
during the marriage, or on his honeymoon for that matter. (Ferrer and
Clooney's daughter Monsita, who loves her father, acknowledged that
"Mother told us he was philandering during the honeymoon.") What
Miller was referring to was a record by Clooney and Ferrer on which
they sang together on "You Make Me Feel So Young" and a song from
Clooney's 1954 Paramount film *Red Garters*. Clooney and Ferrer would
occasionally join musical forces during the course of their union, despite
Clooney's reservations about Ferrer's talents in this area. These charming
duets would present a smiling Clooney and Ferrer to the public, Hollywood's new golden couple. In some of these, notably their duet in the
MGM musical biography *Deep in My Heart*, they simply radiate goodwill,
mutual affection, and a genuine enjoyment of each other's company.

Clooney and Ferrer were determined that their mutually successful individual careers would not preclude a mutually satisfying sense of marital
bliss. Ferrer already owned an apartment in Manhattan and the country
house in Ossining; with Clooney, he purchased a home at 1019 Roxbury
Drive in Beverly Hills. The house belonged to Ginny Simms but had been
lived in by George Gershwin and crooner Russ Columbo, who had died
there in a freak accident. His neighbors would include Eddie Cantor,
Hedy Lamarr, Jack Benny, and his Princeton pal, Jimmy Stewart. Ferrer
was able to pay $150,000 in cash, thanks in large part to his *Moulin Rouge*
earnings. Clooney and Ferrer had an arrangement whereby Ferrer would
pay the bills on the New York residences, while Clooney paid the bills in
California. (She would soon find what a daunting task this would be.)

Professionally and personally, things couldn't be better. Clooney was not only a recording star with Columbia but was being groomed by Paramount Pictures to become a movie star (hence their concern over any potential lapses in morality). She would soon begin filming *White Christmas*, with Bing Crosby, Danny Kaye, and Vera-Ellen; the film became a huge hit at the time and turned into a perennial holiday staple. (Ferrer couldn't very well advise Clooney on performing, but he did suggest to her, "Always do your own make-up when you can.") Ferrer was beginning *The Caine Mutiny*, although he still harbored a desire to sing and dance. (Family friend Ian Bernard would tell him, "You are the worst singer in the history of the world.") To Clooney, "'Can't' was a four-letter word to him. There was nothing he felt he couldn't master with the proper training. He intended to sing opera one day." In spite of her reservations, Ferrer eventually would.

For now, opera, as well as a proper honeymoon had to wait since Ferrer was shooting *The Caine Mutiny*, and Kramer was pleased that Ferrer had agreed to come aboard. Producer Kramer had already lined up an all-star cast for this adaptation of Herman Wouk's tale of a fictitious mutiny in the United States Navy during World War II. This wasn't Wouk's first go at adapting his own book, as he had earlier reworked the novel into a two-act play called *The Caine Mutiny Court-Martial*, which debuted on Broadway in January 1954, starring Lloyd Nolan as Captain Queeg. Humphrey Bogart had been signed to play Captain Queeg (the actor was a few years older than the book's conception of Queeg, but Bogart was still very much the star in 1953). Popular MGM actor Van Johnson won the role of Maryk, the honorable yet torn officer who relieves Queeg of command; it was a chance for Johnson to deepen his screen image. (He would also allow the camera to catch the scars he suffered in a 1943 accident that almost cost him his career—and life.) Fred MacMurray, normally cast in light comedies (*Double Indemnity* being a notable exception), would be Keefer, a glib novelist who introduces Maryk to terms like "paranoid schizophrenic." In later interviews, Ferrer would be unstinting in his praise of MacMurray's work, feeling that the underrated actor gave the film's best performance. The unknown Robert Francis was given the role of young, impressionable Ensign Willie Keith, whose story *The Caine Mutiny* really is (and as critics would note later, thanks to Francis's earnest but stiff playing, this would prove to be a slight detriment).

Where does Ferrer fit in to this starry ensemble? Kramer thought a dynamic actor would be needed for Barney Greenwald, the lawyer who reluctantly defends the mutineers, so he looked for "a tour-de-force actor who could take over in a picture where there had already been a lot of taking over. I picked Joe because he was the best finale I could think of." In a letter to Ferrer dated April 9, 1953, Kramer might have sensed some trepidation on Ferrer's part: "It doesn't sound as romantic as Bergerac, nor as colorful as Lautrec, but I have the feeling that Greenwald can be the most dramatic of all."

The director Edward Dmytryk had some misgivings; it might have been because, like Ferrer, he too had appeared before HUAC. One of the famous "Hollywood Ten" who went to jail for contempt rather than answer charges, Dmytryk later relented and purged himself before the committee, naming a few friends and associates as communists—and forever earning the enmity of those like writer Dalton Trumbo who refused, at great cost to his career and health, to buckle under the pressure exerted by HUAC. Dmytryk's other concern was the so-called Ferrer temperament, the notion that actor Ferrer would not suffer fools (or indecisive directors) lightly and would be quick to throw his weight around. As it turned out, Dmytryk had little to worry about, as Ferrer's behavior on the set was said to be extremely ingratiating. On Ferrer's first day of shooting, which happened to be his entrance into the courtroom for the court-martial, Ferrer entered on his knees, whistled the theme from *Moulin Rouge*, and asked if anyone wanted to buy a painting. Dmytryk would later say of Ferrer, "He's a good director and knows the value of not interfering. For a man of his stamp, his position, Joe was extremely cooperative. He is sane, rational, pliable and susceptible to direction, although he doesn't need much." (As for the bandage on Ferrer's hand, according to film historians Richard Pena and Ken Bowser, it is in character; in the book, Greenwald had suffered burns on his hands during combat, and in the play, Greenwald also wears a bandage).

In reality, producer Kramer and director Dmytryk would face far greater difficulties in bringing *The Caine Mutiny* to the screen. For both Kramer and Dmytryk, there was plenty at stake, since the $2,400,000 budget Columbia afforded the color, widescreen movie was by far the largest Kramer and Dmytryk had at their disposal. (For Dmytryk, this would be his entrée into big-budget films since he rarely returned to his earlier, more modest fare like *Crossfire* and *The Juggler*.) There was the matter of condensing the 560-page novel; writer Stanley Roberts provided a 190-page script, which the studio demanded be cut to about 150 pages. Wouk himself was a nuisance, saying repeatedly, "This isn't the way I wrote the navy." As Kramer viewed the story structure, he saw each protagonist as having his own act: "What's significant is Willie Keith's growth from the time he comes aboard, but each (of the five principals) has his act. Bogart strides on board as a Captain Bligh. Keefer incites the mutiny through Maryk. Maryk takes over the ship. Then we fade in on Greenwald—who takes over the entire finale." Neither Dmytryk nor Kramer were happy with Columbia's insistence that the movie run no longer than two hours; Dmytryk insisted that the movie would work best as a three-hour film, but Columbia was just as adamant about adhering to its edict of two hours, and no longer. According to Dmytryk, screenwriter Roberts left because of Columbia's edict, while writer Michael Blankfort trimmed an additional fifty pages from the script to get it to its 125-minute running time.

There was also the technical issue of the typhoon, during which an indecisive, frightened Queeg is relieved of command by the more level-headed Maryk and, to a lesser extent, Keith. Kramer believed that "the typhoon had to be of such fury that it would stand up under the scrutiny of a court-martial . . . even after I saw [production designer] Rudolph Sternad's sketches, I kept asking special-effects man Larry Butler, 'Are we going to see this on the screen?' I think we've managed it." To the modern viewer, though, the typhoon itself, shot on several stages in a studio tank, is one of the least convincing aspects of the film; it's not the intensity of the acting that lets the scene down but the constant cutaways to what seems to be a toy boat rocking back and forth at sea.

These misbegotten effects did not require the cooperation of the United States Navy, but other elements did. For the exterior shots concerning naval actions, two actual destroyers doubled for the *Caine*: the *Thompson* in San Francisco and the *Doyle* in Hawaii. The problem for Kramer was to get coverage without interrupting naval operations "and still use destroyers, minesweepers, carriers, tugboats and 'copters." Dmytryk was relieved at how cooperative the navy was for these exteriors, though by now the most important battles Kramer fought with the navy had already been decided.

These battles focused on how the navy was to be portrayed in the movie. Kramer representative George Glass would say that the navy was concerned about only two things, that Keith should "grow up" in the service, and that the movie would make clear, "as the novel had, the Navy's justification of its system." Kramer himself would elaborate, admitting that "Captain Queeg and the *Caine* are not exactly exemplary of the Navy. But the book says that despite the man and this ship, the Navy is the greatest organization of its kind in the world—*the line of defense*." However, the Navy's objections ran deeper than that, beginning with the film's title. The navy wanted the title changed from *The Caine Mutiny* to something like *The Caine Incident*. In order to preserve the title, and get the film produced, Kramer had to make two major concessions. First, he had to include the opening statement, which begins, "There has never been a mutiny in a ship of the United States Navy." The other major concession came in Greenwald/Ferrer's final speech where he drunkenly berates the officers of the *Caine* in the wake of winning an acquittal for Maryk. The screenwriter had to insert some remarks wherein Greenwald chastises the officers for their failure to make allowances for Queeg's illness. Kramer acquiesced, even though the film clearly shows the officers had been making allowances every day. By December 1952, the navy bestowed its approval on the script and assigned a technical advisor to assist in the production and ensure that the film presented the navy in a flattering light.

Indeed, viewing *The Caine Mutiny* today, the most problematic elements involve the film's fidelity to the novel's presentation of Ensign Keith as the protagonist. As Kramer stated, it's Keith's story, and the viewer dutifully follows him at length as he delves into an idyllic romance with singer May Wynn (played by actress May Wynn, who was in real life called Donna Hickey but took her new stage name from the character she played), which is interrupted by a harridan of a mother, and finally joins the tired crew of the *Caine*. The scenes focusing on Keith, off the ship and not bolstered by his veteran costars, are so tiresome they leave the viewer longing for Keith to cut his leave short and get back onboard. (Even beyond the four stars, the crew includes such impressive newcomers as Lee Marvin, Claude Akins, Jerry Paris, James Edwards, Whit Bissell—and Keith's first captain, nominated for a Best Supporting Actor no less, is veteran Tom Tully.)

The major strength of the film lies in the strong portrayals of the four major players. Bogart is a superb Queeg, whether lashing out at his officers or subordinates, rolling his steel balls, or uttering evasions in the courtroom—or even simply trying to explain himself to Keith after an earlier outburst. Van Johnson, leaving his earlier "pretty boy" image behind and letting his scars show, gives a terrific portrayal of an anguished officer whose loyalty to his ship's welfare supersedes his adherence to the chain of command. When his Maryk challenges Queeg, Johnson convinces the viewer that it is only because he truly believes that he has exhausted all the other possibilities (including an aborted attempt at reporting Queeg, when Keefer makes it clear true evidence is lacking). As noted earlier, Ferrer felt that MacMurray steals the film, and this writer concurs. MacMurray's Keefer is all glib patter and outward support for relieving Queeg, even introducing Maryk to the psychological jargon essential to "diagnosing" Queeg—but, when the chips are down, Keefer does everything to distance himself. Keefer's appearance at the court-martial (under questioning by the prosecutor, played by E. G. Marshall) where he professes little knowledge of Maryk's plans and proclaims himself as "flabbergasted" by Maryk's actions, suggest both a talent for self-preservation and a latent disgust with his own behavior.

As for Ferrer, he is most persuasive as Greenwald, especially in the courtroom scenes when he is sizing up "the mutineers" and Keefer, assessing the situation ("Frankly, I'd rather prosecute"), or quietly and systematically breaking down Queeg's defenses to reveal the character's mania and incompetence. It's true that Ferrer's drunken speech at the victory dinner, including his defense of Queeg and denunciation of Keefer, is a tour de force showcasing the actor's timing, delivery, and ability to infuse the tirade with nuance and shadings. However, as satisfying as Ferrer's bravura performance is, along with the now-famous hurling of the drink in MacMurray's face (who appears mortally wounded), the viewer has seen what Greenwald's character hasn't—a ship being run by an obsessive, delusional, paranoid, petty, frightened man who doesn't deserve to be in command of a sailboat, much less a ship in the US Navy. When the book presented Greenwald's apologia for Queeg at greater length and depth, the reader by then had been presented with events that could have been open to interpretation. The movie leaves no such possibility so that Greenwald's speech, effective as it is, rings a little hollow.

By the time *The Caine Mutiny* was released in September 1954, the play *The Caine Mutiny Court-Martial* had become a hit on Broadway, directed by Charles Laughton with the aforementioned Lloyd Nolan as Queeg, a now-seasoned John Hodiak as Maryk, and Henry Fonda as Greenwald. While this might have been viewed as positive publicity for the forthcoming film, Columbia pushed back the release date, claiming it had too many releases in early 1954. The movie proved to be a substantial commercial success and earned several laudatory notices, not only for being "one of the most exciting maritime adventures committed to film" but for the casting and performances. *The Caine Mutiny* received a number of Academy Award nominations, including Best Picture, Best Editing, Best Writing, and Best Music. Of the principals, Bogart received a nomination for Best Actor (he would lose to Marlon Brando for *On the Waterfront*), but Johnson, MacMurray, and Ferrer were all somehow neglected. (Tom Tully's Best Supporting Actor nomination—incredibly—was the only other acting nod.) Ferrer himself would rate it as one of his better performances, and certainly one of the roles for which he is best remembered.

Immediately after he completed filming *The Caine Mutiny*, Ferrer was back in New York City, this time to use his celebrity to assist the non-profit City Center, which had again found itself in difficult financial straits. By chance, he had seen Jean Dalrymple at a fund raiser and was told there would not be enough money to open the fall season. Dalrymple asked for a contribution, but he replied, "I'd like to do more." Ferrer said he would be happy to produce and act in a series of plays for the benefit of City Center. He and Dalrymple polled the subscribers and the three shows that initially emerged were *Cyrano de Bergerac* (Nov. 11–22), *The Shrike* (Nov. 25–Dec. 6, and a play that Ferrer was happy to revive since his departure to film *Moulin Rouge* effectively ended that show's run), and Shakespeare's *Richard III* (Dec. 9–20). He also decided to add *Charley's Aunt* for the holiday season—and "because the Center had the open time."

Ferrer let it be known that this endeavor was far from a one-man show, and that all the principals involved, Ferrer included, would be getting (as in the earlier City Center engagement) far less than their usual salaries—in the neighborhood of $90 per week. And Ferrer was able to attract some major talent, including Vincent Price, Margaret Wycherly (James Cagney/Cody Jarrett's Ma in *White Heat*), Jessie Royce Landis, and Maureen Stapleton. He was able to lure back many of the players from his *Cyrano* and would also borrow Arlene Dahl from MGM to play Roxane (he had wanted Dahl for the movie). Ferrer was also able to use Judith Evelyn and several other actors from *The Shrike*, and he and author Joe Kramm felt "we could scarcely do better." Before the shows opened, Hollywood star Ferrer would say that "it's good to be back on Broadway. I never want to stay away from the theater for any considerable length of time. But still I want to go on making pictures. My picture career is attractive to me financially as well as artistically."

Ferrer's choices proved to be generally sound ones, both with regard to artistic merit and audience potential. His production of *Cyrano de Bergerac* received good notices—not only for his eloquent, exuberant portrayal but the energy and panache of his staging. *The Shrike* also earned raves, especially for Judith Evelyn's return as the title character. And *Charley's Aunt* was viewed as a delightful throwback, a fast-paced romp in which the 1953 Ferrer impressed with all the verve he had displayed in his 1940 version.

Richard III, however, was another matter—and the only play he had not previously starred in. It was staged by his *Othello* director Margaret Webster (if she had any criticism of Ferrer's performance before HUAC, she apparently kept it to herself, as the two worked harmoniously together throughout). Ferrer also was intrigued by the character of Richard, especially the emptiness the king felt when he achieved his ambitions: "Richard is bold, ruthless, witty, ambitious and all the other things dictators . . . more or less have to be. But the thing that fascinated me most was the fact that once he ascended the throne . . . he was suddenly deprived of horizons. Suddenly he had nothing more to desire, and this man . . . found himself spiritually and morally bankrupt, unsure, superstitious and afraid." While Margaret Webster's staging was seen as a fresh creation, Ferrer's performance was viewed as lacking force, eloquence, and stature. On this occasion, his once-vaunted energy flagged, leaving behind a surface characterization. As Brooks Atkinson would say, while Ferrer deserved credit for all he has done for City Center, "this is an undistinguished *Richard III*. That has to be said, also."

When Ferrer ended his City Center engagement, he was finally able to have a proper honeymoon with Rosemary Clooney. They would spend a total of ten weeks in Europe, visiting Great Britain, Ireland, France, and Spain. In London, Ferrer introduced Clooney to Laurence Olivier and Vivien Leigh; they visited director John Huston at his home in Dublin; they spent some time in France and were able to see *Fourposter* playwright Jan de Hartog. While in France, Clooney would overhear a conversation between Ferrer and de Hartog. According to Clooney, she overheard Ferrer treating de Hartog with details of various sexual escapades in New York. When she later confronted Ferrer, he offered to arrange for her to return home. After some soul-searching, she decided to stay.

Both Ferrer and Clooney wanted a large family, though it might be more accurate to say that Ferrer desired a big family, and Clooney wanted more than anything else to please him. The family started small, as it was Clooney's half-sister Gail who came to live with them. This was after Clooney's mother announced she would be going on tour with Rosemary's sister Betty, who was still performing as a singer (though without sister Rosemary's nationwide success). Within a matter of months, Rosemary would find out she was pregnant while husband José was acting in his next film, a lush MGM production.

In April 1954, Ferrer would begin work on *Deep in My Heart* for MGM, a biography of composer Sigmund Romberg. The project had been in development for a few years, at a time when musical biographies were somewhat the rage in Hollywood: George Gershwin, Cole Porter, Al Jolson, Rodgers and Hart, Jerome Kern—all had their lives heavily fictionalized for the screen. If the subject's life lacked sufficient drama, then drama was invented. If there was too much drama, then events and characters would be compressed. Regardless of the subject's love life, quite often there was no place for fidelity to facts (as in the very fictional love interests in the Cole Porter biopic *Night and Day* and the George M. Cohan rouser *Yankee Doodle Dandy*). Regardless of the structure, there would always be ample time to include signature songs, usually by performers from the studio stable. On rare occasions, such as with *The Jolson Story*, the subject of the film was still alive (and, in Jolson's case, would contribute his own vocals and even appear in a long shot).

In the case of *Deep in My Heart*, Sigmund Romberg was among the living when MGM announced plans to film his life story. It would be called *The Romberg Story* and would tell the story of how Hungarian-born, Vienna-educated composer Romberg arrived in America in 1909 and proceeded to compose 2000 songs and seventy-nine operettas. Some of these operettas, like *Maytime*, *New Moon*, and *The Girl of the Golden West*, would be immortalized on film via the dulcet tones of Jeannette MacDonald and Nelson Eddy. Producer Arthur Freed, who had become synonymous with high-quality MGM musicals (such as *The Wizard of Oz* and *Meet Me in St. Louis*), allowed composer/arranger/associate producer Roger Edens to handle the property. There was some talk of Romberg playing himself, but while different writers labored over a treatment, Romberg died in 1951. The difficulty of presenting Romberg's life on film had to do with his life being pretty successful, almost from the time Romberg arrived in America. MGM utilized Elliot Arnold's book as source material, but even that worked more as historical fiction, and Leonard Spigelglass's treatment was even more fanciful. The Romberg of the script would be influenced by no less than three rather formidable women, including the attractive (if fictional) blonde he would eventually marry—and there would be plenty of screen time for an assortment of musical interludes.

There was still the necessity of casting Romberg. Early press releases stated that Kurt Kasznar (from *Anything Can Happen*) would play Romberg. Stanley Donen, the film's director, (he had already co-directed *On the Town* with Gene Kelly and had recently completed *Singin' in the Rain*) was a very hot commodity—and he desired someone with equal power to carry the film. He was already friends with both Ferrer and Clooney; Clooney would suggest in her autobiography that it was Donen who revived Ferrer's career after his difficulties with HUAC, but history (and

Ferrer's casting in *Miss Sadie Thompson* and *The Caine Mutiny*) belies this claim. In fact, Ferrer was at a career peak and he balked when first offered *Deep in My Heart*. Ferrer believed that "all he does is introduce a string of vaudeville acts. Then they offered to read the script for me . . . after an hour and a half, I found myself completely entertained. I liked it. It's not art, but it accomplishes what it sets out to do and, of its kind, it's quite good." Donen was happy to land Ferrer, believing that Ferrer was "the hottest thing going at that time. Roger and I thought we'd burst when we got him." The casting would puzzle Ferrer since he "never knew Romberg, but people tell me he and I were not at all alike. What we are trying to capture is the spirit of his life and I think the script does that admirably."

Joining Ferrer in *Deep in My Heart* was Metropolitan Opera star Helen Traubel, a larger-than-life dramatic soprano who would play the fictitious Anna Mueller, a fellow émigré and mother figure for Romberg. Traubel would have equal screen time with Ferrer, and be given several musical numbers, both solo and in tandem with a willing Ferrer. (As Donen would recall, "Ferrer loved doing it. He studied singing all his life.") Merle Oberon, in her first American movie in five years (having spent that time starring in British and French films), and Doe Avedon were cast as the two romantic interests, with Ferrer's Romberg finally choosing the young, decorative blonde (Avedon) over the more platonic but affectionate friendship he enjoys with Oberon's real-life actress/lyricist Dorothy Donnelly. (Many critics speculated that Ferrer's Romberg should have ended up with Oberon's elegant Donnelly, a Romberg collaborator who died too young in 1927.) Walter Pidgeon and Paul Henreid were also prominently featured, while Romberg melodies were performed by a star-studded array of MGM musical stars: Cyd Charisse, Ann Miller, Howard Keel, Jane Powell, Tony Martin, and Gene Kelly (who would join his dancing brother Fred in their only screen appearance together). Rosemary Clooney also appeared in a duet with husband José; their performance of "Mr. and Mrs." resulted in one of the film's highlights. The viewer can see their evident joy at performing together—Ferrer is mostly able to keep up with Clooney in the singing department, and the two execute a lively soft-shoe. It's a moment that captures the duo not only at the peak of their careers but in their personal lives.

Ferrer was featured in a number of other musical performances, including duets with Helen Traubel (notably "Leg of Mutton") and a final solo of Romberg's haunting "When I Grow Too Old to Dream." The performance that occupied most of his time was a seven-minute solo that he "spontaneously" performs in a cabin (where he is working on his next show) for his hoped-for bride and her critical mother. Known by either "Jazza-a-doo," "Jazza-Dazza-Doo," or "Bombo," Ferrer rehearsed the tour de force not only at the studio but also at Hollywood parties: "I did it at Cole Porter's last night. All they have to do is ask me—sometimes that isn't even necessary. By doing the number privately I can see what parts are good and what needs trimming. It's just like a tryout in the legitimate theater." Under any name, the number is entirely Ferrer's as he sings, dances, cavorts, mugs, moves back and forth, and assumes different characters, usually in exaggerated snippets of dialogue and finishing in blackface with a Jolson impersonation. It was the first time Ferrer had been encouraged to engage in antics that would make a vaudevillian proud. (He had previously indulged himself onstage in *Let's Face It* and *Charley's Aunt*, but this was a glossy MGM musical that was almost preordained for commercial success.)

Some critics would be dazzled by Ferrer's breathless performance, and this writer feels, after seeing it a number of times, that it is one of Ferrer's finest (if most atypical) moments on film. *Los Angeles Times* critic Philip Scheuer would admit "there is little that Ferrer cannot do—drama, dialect, comedy, singing, dancing." Scheuer though did not feel this assessment extended to "Jazz-a-doo": "To me, the low point in hot-cha José's exhibition was a one-man show 'Jazz-a-doo' which ran for three acts—or seemed to. Yet others will applaud it as devastatingly clever." Ruth Waterbury in the *Los Angeles Examiner* reserved her vitriol for Miss Traubel, believing "the prima-donna was all wrong for the screen: too tall, too weighty, too non-young." Most praised Roger Edens and Stanley Donen for the other musical performances, including a sumptuous pas de deux by Cyd Charisse and James Mitchell (from *The Desert Song*) and Gene Kelly and brother Fred teaming on "I Love to Go Swimmin' with Women." *Deep in My Heart* was a substantial hit for MGM and supplied even more proof that there was nothing the indefatigable José Ferrer couldn't achieve if he tried. This would be tested by his simultaneous excursions into both film directing and married life.

CHAPTER 11

He Directs Movies, Too

DESPITE HIS PERSONAL TRIUMPH WITH THE 1954 RELEASE OF *DEEP IN My Heart*, the long-gestating feature-film version of *The Shrike* continued to consume Ferrer's professional attention. After some preliminary negotiations with Columbia fell through, there was the possibility of costarring with Ida Lupino at RKO, but nothing came of it. Some progress was finally made on *The Shrike* when Ferrer signed with Universal-International Pictures to both star and direct, and Joseph Kramm's Pulitzer Prize winning play would be adapted by Ketti Frings. Perhaps the biggest news was to be Ferrer's choice for the shrewish wife, June Allyson. Many people were surprised at this somewhat atypical casting, for Allyson was best known for her sweet and sincere roles opposite the likes of Van Johnson, Peter Lawford, and Humphrey Bogart; she was also the wife of star-turned-director Dick Powell.

A number of Allyson's friends advised her against taking the role, as did husband Powell (oddly, since he was known to radically depart from his wholesome crooner image to become a screen tough guy), but the actress stood firm, believing the role to be a welcome change of pace from the sympathetic spouses that had dominated her screen output. Screenwriter Frings also believed Allyson was a fine actress, especially after viewing Allyson's work as the adoring, pragmatic wife to Jimmy Stewart's Glenn Miller in the hit *The Glenn Miller Story*. Ferrer concurred and told interviewers she would do an exceptional job in the challenging title role. Yet the wife that Allyson portrayed was not exactly the part as written and performed in the original production. The part was softened somewhat; as Ferrer would admit around the film's release: "We enlarged

134

on the stage play. We show the wife as a really nice girl who changes because of her husband."

Why would Ferrer agree to change a play that had achieved such success on Broadway with its stark, uncompromising subject matter? One has to consider both the commercial and creative aspects. *The Shrike* would not only be his directorial debut; he would also have a significant financial stake in the production, adding up to approximately 50 percent. Casting Allyson would be good box-office insurance, but Ferrer was also privy to his own advisors who felt the source material was too downbeat for the moviegoers. Ferrer himself also felt that for films to succeed, they needed to appeal to a cross-section of the public; he could be elitist in his taste, but he always believed that art and commercial success need not be mutually exclusive.

The Shrike began filming on location in New York City in September 1954 and finished shooting in early November. A number of scenes were filmed in the Times Square area, and the hospital sequences were filmed at Bellevue Hospital. Many of the play's original actors appeared in the film, including Edward Platt, later of *Get Smart* fame and a Ferrer "regular." For Ferrer in his role as first-time movie director, filming *The Shrike* would be a collaborative process. He hired one-time actor Leon Charles to be the dialogue director, and his alter ego. On the challenges posed by directing himself, he would say, "The actor in me said one thing, the director sometimes quite another. . . . I tried to let the director win." Ferrer also enlisted the cooperation and input of his various technicians, whom he acknowledged knew more about films than he did. Perhaps, because some of Ferrer's own money was at stake, the shooting proceeded smoothly and under-budget.

The finished product is an assured film belying his own inexperience behind the camera, but as Ferrer would say about directing (as well as anything else he would attempt), anyone can learn anything with the proper amount of time. It's true he was quite familiar with the piece, but the film both opens up the play while maintaining a tight grip on its flawed protagonists—particularly the husband.

As the film opens, we see Ferrer's Jim Downs on a stretcher in a city psychiatric hospital, after having attempted suicide by swallowing an overdose of pills. His wife, Anne (June Allyson), arrives, but we learn that the name emerging from Jim's delirium is not his wife's but that of another woman. After he revives somewhat, Jim makes it known he would like to be released, especially since there is the possibility of a theatrical job. The doctors inform him that he can only be released into

Ann's custody, and although outwardly solicitous, Ann has no intention of facilitating Jim's release, and has also blocked the woman (Charlotte, played by Joy Page) from visiting. These early scenes in the hospital, including Jim's meeting his fellow patients in Ward F (as opposed to the dreaded Ward 7, for violent patients), effectively reflect Jim's isolation and disorientation. Ferrer the director allows the other actors, whether patients or administrators, to have their moments; indeed, it might seem that Ferrer has even relegated his own character to the sidelines, but this only serves to emphasize the character's ineffectuality and powerlessness.

It is only when Ferrer is interviewed by a sympathetic doctor that the viewer sees firsthand (if one is to trust the flashbacks) the living hell that Jim and Anne's marriage has become. At first their relationship seems idyllic as stage manager Jim and ambitious but encouraging actress Ann find love and happiness, especially after Jim successfully becomes a director, with Ann in his cast. They marry—but now director Jim has started, out of commercial necessity, to utilize bigger-name actresses for the parts that Ann desires. Ann's jealousy begins to emerge, leading to confrontations at casting sessions and further unhappiness when Jim can't provide her with adequate roles. There is a glimmer of happiness when Ann becomes pregnant, but she suffers a miscarriage and thereafter begins to cling to Jim, attending rehearsals and offering unsolicited advice. Gradually, Jim's career begins to decline. Even more damaging are the insinuations that not only is Jim losing his touch, but that Ann has been inserting herself into the creative decisions. One flop is followed by another, and the downward spiral continues, with Jim losing confidence in his abilities, and Ann questioning his desire and competence—even suggesting that he quit the theater and work for her father's company. It is only when Jim meets with Charlotte, an actress in his latest flop, that he has any moments of happiness. (In later flashbacks, it becomes clear that Jim fell in love with Charlotte *after* leaving Ann, and that his suicide attempt happened after he realized he had come to the end of his tether and could no longer afford to make any one happy—let alone himself.)

After hearing Jim's tale thus far, his doctor, though sensitive, doesn't believe Jim is ready for release, which costs Jim his chance at a rare theatrical offer. (We discover later it is for a stage manager's job, which for Jim, would be a comedown.) It becomes clear to Jim, through conversations with the nurse, and some unfortunate visits from Ann, that the only way of being released is to assure Ann and the doctors that he is a different man—namely, one who will not leave his wife's jurisdiction for another woman—no matter that Charlotte (appealingly played by Page) might be more of a soulmate than Ann has any hope of being.

It is a visit from Jim's brother Larry—wherein Jim recounts his interlude with Charlotte—that sets Jim on the road to release. Larry advises Jim to swallow what is left of his pride and tell the doctors and Ann what they want to hear: that he is indeed contrite and willing to renounce Charlotte and begin life anew with Ann. As portrayed by Ferrer, Jim's final interview with the doctors is a masterwork of despair and self-loathing—both for his past and in his current angst-ridden state of one struggling for the right words to say in order to be "free." It is one of Ferrer's best moments on film and a ready answer to those who dismiss him as nothing but a cold and foreboding film presence, devoid of any vulnerability. If only the film ended on this abject note; it does conclude shortly thereafter, but it's with a different ending than the creative forces would have wanted.

Not that the dissatisfaction was unanticipated. Before filming and during the editing, Ferrer made no pretenses about being completely faithful to the source material. He told interviewers that Allyson's character would be softened, that she would begin as a nice girl, but slowly become jealous and clinging. Ferrer would say it "was enlarging the stage play," but the changes, including the new flashbacks, dilute some of the film's power. According to Allyson, however, there was something akin to the playwright's intent in the film's original ending. Yet preview audiences hated it, and the studio forced Ferrer to shoot the compromised ending, in which a chastened Allyson admits that she needs help, that she has indeed been rather shrewish (or akin to "the shrike"), and that she will give Ferrer his freedom; for his part, Ferrer admits he was lying but concedes (unconvincingly) that you have to work for your happiness. The film ends with Ferrer and Allyson walking towards an implied hopeful future. The ending doesn't work—it's too sudden, dismissive in its treatment of the compassionate Charlotte, and unrealistic. In fact, it undermines all we have seen before. Allyson was unhappy with the reshoot and implored Ferrer to keep the original, but Ferrer's response was: "What can you do? You can't fight City Hall."

In his bid to be both artistic and commercial, Ferrer wound up disappointing himself, the critics, and the public. Yet reviewers found much to praise in *The Shrike*, especially in Ferrer's performance and the realistic settings; they centered their criticism on the weakened ending and an overall diminution of Allyson's character from, as *Los Angeles Times* critic Philip Scheuer would say, "a pouncing bird of the title . . . to a nagger."

It's doubtful the critical nitpicking caused Ferrer to lose any sleep since, at any given time, he would have a number of pressing engagements. Foremost among them was his renewed standing as a father and would-be family man. Ferrer had become a father for the second time (his first with Clooney) with the birth of Miguel José in the early morning of February 7, 1955. The night before Ferrer had been playing chess at home with Stanley Donen, who remained a good friend of the Ferrers since *Deep in My Heart*. Clooney remembers telling her husband, "I think it's time to go the hospital, Joe." Ferrer said "right" but did not move. It's only after Clooney repeated it that he jumped from his seat, gathered the chessboard and a few books, and leaped into their Jaguar—followed by a virtual motorcade accompanying them to St. John's Hospital. With the birth of Miguel followed by the birth of Maria on August 9, 1956, it seemed the Ferrers would make good on their intention of having a sizable brood. Ferrer and Clooney would have three more children together, as Gabriel would arrive on August 1, 1957, followed by Monsita on October 13, 1958, and Rafael on March 23, 1960. Besides their own children, Rosemary's nine-year-old half-sister, Gail, came to live with them, after Clooney's mother announced that she wanted to sing with Rosemary's sister Betty. The children generally stayed in the couple's California home; when Ferrer was in California, his routine would consist of getting up at 6:30 in the morning, playing tennis, and having breakfast with Miguel. Clooney would say that one of Miguel's first words was "dennis."

However, Ferrer couldn't simply be there in the role of father; he had to pursue other interests besides the wife and children. In addition to the tennis, there were the singing lessons and the fencing lessons, and his love of sports in general. The family had a huge swimming pool and often had friends over on warm afternoons. On one occasion, Ferrer beckoned his wife to join him for a swim; she demurred, claiming she had her hostess duties to attend to. Clooney would soon reveal that she couldn't swim, leading him to hire a swim coach. Clooney would find that Ferrer "hated chronic ignorance, that anyone can learn *anything*." Clooney would let on that "it's tough to be married to a man like Joe. I can't keep up with all his interests, but I think I'm a good audience for him." Quite often being a good audience meant listening to husband Ferrer read poetry or speak one of the several languages he was fluent in—or even accompanying Ferrer in the kitchen, where he demonstrated that he was an accomplished chef.

One interest that Clooney found it difficult to comes to terms with was Ferrer's interest in other women. In her autobiography, Clooney recounts stories of young ladies who would call even when she was at home and demand to "speak to Joe." When she would speak to Ferrer about these calls, he would both try to mollify her and contend that this was the way he was used to living—and that faithfulness wasn't all it was cracked up to be. Said Clooney in 1992: "Fidelity wasn't important to him. It wasn't important in his life, but it was important to me." Publicly she continued to be the good wife, but privately her doubts about Ferrer were festering, especially since her husband made no attempt to curtail his professional (or personal) pursuits, even those that took him out of the country.

After filming *The Shrike*, he ironed out a deal with Columbia Pictures and Warwick Productions (producers Irving Allen and Albert "Cubby" Broccoli) to direct and star in *The Cockleshell Heroes*, a fact-based World War II drama depicting Operation Frankton, wherein ten Royal Marines agreed to undergo intensive training for a special mission to navigate their way through heavily mined waters to blow up German shipping in the Bordeaux Harbour—by using small two-man boats, the Cockleshells of the title. Only two survived: Colonel H. G. (Blonde) Hasler, the leader of the operation, and Major Donald Sparks. Both were retained to serve as technical advisors on the film.

To help promote the film, as well as assist in Ferrer's preparation, Hasler went to Hollywood and met with Ferrer, who would be playing the leader of the commandos in the film's fictionalized version of the events. Hasler was intrigued by Ferrer's ability to assume his mannerisms, habits, and even his voice. In the film, the Hasler character would be renamed Stringer, and the film would recount the idealistic, unconventional Stringer's difficulties in training his men and in commanding their respect—notably that of the somewhat more conventional Captain Thompson.

Ferrer and his producers needed someone of equal stature for Thompson—early drafts of the screenplay by Bryan Forbes had suggested the evolving relationship between Stringer and Thompson but still needed to be more sufficiently developed. The solution, so far as finding a strong Thompson, presented itself when Ferrer and producer Allen asked Trevor Howard to take the part. Howard had been one of Britain's most popular and critically acclaimed actors, with *Brief Encounter*, *The Third Man*, and *The Heart of the Matter* among his credits. Ferrer had wanted Howard from the beginning, and Howard, whose career was in the relative doldrums in early 1955, was delighted to make his first Hollywood movie and have the opportunity of gaining international stardom.

Unfortunately, the screenplay was not enjoying the same forward momentum as the casting. Forbes's draft was criticized by Ferrer and others as being too generic, with not enough attention being paid to the special nature of the mission or the esprit de corps of the Royal Marines. Richard Maibaum, who would gain fame in the early 1960s as the screenwriter of the early James Bond films, was hired to do a rewrite; Ferrer would express many of the same reservations to producers Allen and Broccoli, adding stilted dialogue and a lack of humor to his overall critique. Evidently a number of criticisms of Maibaum's work made their way to Forbes, who was willing to work on the film, even without being under contract.

In addition to the machinations regarding the script, Ferrer was concerned over the logistics involved in the existing screenplay, this being a more expansive undertaking than his debut film, *The Shrike*. He hired an assistant director to break down the first fifty-one pages into sets, locations, and cast; at the same time, concerns over Rosemary's health since the birth of Miguel almost caused him to delay his arrival in England.

Eventually, the producers and Ferrer arrived at what they considered a workable script which would shoot at both Shepperton Studios and in Portugal for the exterior locations, a locale that was chosen because of the generally favorable weather conditions. In addition, according to Christopher Lee (who played a submarine commander in the film), the unit was able to utilize the submarines of the Portuguese Navy, which possessed the antiquated look the filmmakers needed; in addition, most of the action scenes would be filmed along the River Tagus in Lisbon. Before filming began, Ferrer and his fellow "commandos" (including Anthony Newley as Marine Clarke, the film's surrogate for Sparks) endured some rigorous training with the Royal Marines in order to handle canoes.

The use of the Lisbon location in the warmth of May was not without its drawbacks. Because the mission occurred in December, the actors' onscreen attire had to conform to what winter conditions would demand—namely, waterproof battle dress with thick sweaters and socks and boots—and, under these circumstances, the short-sleeved crew members were more fortunate. Life could be even more precarious at sea, as Trevor Howard and David Lodge nearly lost their lives when their canoe capsized on the River Tagus; Lodge, who was wearing a frogman's suit, nearly suffocated before two Royal Marines taking part in the film rescued the two men. Hasler was still in his role as technical adviser, but

he was growing a little more disenchanted each day with the film's fictitious elements; he would leave the production earlier than the producers
would have liked (Sparks remained) and would later collaborate on a
memoir of his wartime experiences, largely to dispel the fanciful way he
believed the dangerous mission was being covered.

Disillusionment would not be limited to Hasler, though, as other
somewhat conflicting events unfolded late in the filming, culminating
in Ferrer's abrupt departure from the film in late July 1955. There was
the occasional disagreement between Ferrer and the producers. One letter from Broccoli requests that in order to have the picture "playable,"
director Ferrer should eliminate the strong British accents (especially the
Cockney ones) that might eventually necessitate redubbing. Ferrer, as
the director/artist, wanted to retain the "British feel" (especially since this
was a British mission), but, as a businessman who had a 20 percent stake
in the film, he did what he could to placate the producer and preserve
his own financial stake.

Yet it came as a surprise when Ferrer's contract was terminated in late
July, followed by Columbia's buying out Ferrer's interest in the picture.
As Irving Allen would say to any news agency that asked him, Ferrer
left of his own accord, leaving the production in disarray: "When Ferrer
finished the film, we found he had made a tour-de-force for Joe Ferrer.
But he seems to have forgotten the rest of the cast . . . so I've been busy
doing close-ups of Trevor Howard that Joe forgot to do when he was busy
doing close-ups of himself." Allen also claimed that Ferrer neglected to
complete some action sequences that his character did not figure in, like
blowing up some German ships. When asked about these allegations,
Ferrer replied, "Let him live in his world and I'll live in mine." Before
the film's premiere, however, producer Broccoli sent a conciliatory letter
to Ferrer, alluding to certain unfortunate events and extending Ferrer an
olive branch in the form of an invitation to attend the premiere of the
film, which many believed would be a great success.

In many ways, *The Cockleshell Heroes* helped form the template for a
kind of war film that has never gone out of style: the top-secret commando raid by a few select men, with scenes devoted to illustrating
the mission, choosing the men, the training and conflicts among the
participants (and occasionally with the military brass), and finally the
mission itself, usually carried out in a taut, suspenseful manner—along
with the inevitable toll in terms of heroic lives lost. Although there had
been others, such as 1944's *The Way Ahead*, *The Cockleshell Heroes*, with its
secret mission, six-month training period, treacherous journey through

mine-laden waters, and successful completion, along with the remaining heroes' struggle to return to England and safety, heralded the return of the action-packed, flag-waving World War II-era adventure.

In the finished film, Ferrer's Major Stringer (based on Hasler) has devised a plan to lead a special unit of volunteer marines to commandeer canoes up the Gironde River and into the Bordeaux Harbour, in order to blow up German blockade-running ships that were docked there. After a series of exercises and maneuvers meant to test the marines' mettle, Stringer whittles down the original volunteers to a group of ten men (in reality, the group consisted of twelve) to undertake the mission, with two men per canoe. Therein follows a series of training scenes, some rather comedic in nature; these sessions result in tension between Ferrer's Stringer and Trevor Howard's Major Thompson. Stringer resists the need to have the men undergo conventional drilling, while Thompson maintains that without intensity in the training, the men will be all too lax in discipline. When a test mission fails dismally, Stringer comes to understand that a strict regimen is in order and allows Thompson a greater input in the training, while Stringer instructs the men on how to handle both the canoes and the explosives.

The scenes with both Ferrer and Howard are among the film's highlights, from their first meeting—with Howard studying Ferrer and barely disguising his disdain—through Howard's eloquent but semi-drunken recounting of his own military failures. Some of these might have been among the scenes later reshot, but if one looks at them, there are a number of two-shots, which seem to refute Allen's claim that Ferrer "forgot there were others in the picture." Another highlight is a sequence (sans Ferrer—could this have been what producer Allen was referring to?) spotlighting Howard and his costar David Lodge wherein Major Thompson helps the marine Ruddock (Lodge) cope with his wife's new lover, by way of allowing Ruddock to throttle the wife's admirer.

But, in an intended crowd-pleaser for king and country (mainly for the Brits since this was an entirely British mission in real life, Ferrer's American Stringer notwithstanding), the mission is the most important thing, and the scenes recounting the journey down the river are fairly suspenseful, with the men facing the turbulent waters, choppy seas, and crushing waves (the River Tagus was certainly admirably standing in for the Gironde) even before they even reach their destination. A few canoes overturn and some of the marines are captured by the Germans (to be executed later) before they reach their targets, but the two remaining canoes, manned by Stringer and Marine Clarke (Anthony Newley), along with Thompson and Rubbock, reach the German ships, wherein the intrepid commandos dive into the water, attach the explosives to the hulls, and attempt to head home. Thompson and Rubbock, however, are captured by the Germans and executed when they refuse to divulge their mission. Stringer and Clarke emerge as the only survivors, arriving in England shortly thereafter as heroes.

When *The Cockleshell Heroes* was released by Columbia (late 1955 in England, with the US premiere in April 1956), the reviews were favorable, and it would be one of Columbia's most profitable films of the year. It would also prove to be the only critical and commercial success in Ferrer's directorial career, but there were those who took exception to the film. The discontent came from some unexpected areas. Whereas Christopher Lee was pleased to be taking suggestions from Ferrer the director, helping to cement a friendship that began with *Moulin Rouge*, Howard was less than satisfied: "The best thing about *The Cockleshell Heroes* was filming in Portugal . . . when I was there I ended up doing the commentary for a documentary about the country which won more awards than the film ever did . . . as for the film—well." Hasler and Sparks were not happy with the final results; although Sparks remained with the production after Hasler departed, both would later collaborate with historians to tell the true story of Operation Frankton (neither was pleased with it being redubbed Operation Cockleshell for the movie).

The critics would point to Ferrer's increasing assurance behind the camera. On the other hand, there were reviewers like C. A. Lejeune, who opined that "Ferrer seems out of place . . . the climax is untrue to history and subtly false to British sentiment." Another reviewer took aim at those somewhat fanciful scenes constructed for the story: "What a pity fictitious incidents had to be introduced in terms of light relief that is pushed too hard." In terms of the climax, Lejeune had a point; in the film, the mission is a success and within five minutes of screen time, the men are safe, and they proceed apace to England with smiles on their faces. The reality was much different and could have made for a film on its own, as Hasler and Sparks evaded capture with the help of the French Resistance and only made it back to England five months after the mission. The hurried conclusion had always been a concern of Ferrer's; in letters to the producers, he had hoped to have an ending that contained more of an acknowledgment of the human cost, but his requests were ignored.

The other criticism, regarding those comic hijinks, turns out to have played a substantial role in the circumstances that precipitated Ferrer's abrupt departure. Allen and Broccoli had agreed that the film lacked sufficient comedy, so they had asked Forbes to rewrite Maibaum's revision, without telling Ferrer. Forbes then was engaged to reshoot some scenes on an adjacent lot, also done without Ferrer's knowledge. When Ferrer became aware of these actions, he left the picture, thus bringing some of Allen's earlier claims into question. The actions of Allen and Broccoli would also add to Ferrer's increasing ill will toward producers in general, as he would later say that any difficulties he had in making films was solely due to his differences with producers over content and artistic merit. (Ferrer would also have plenty to say about the editors who were all too willing to sacrifice subtext for time constraints.)

Even though Ferrer was making film his major creative outlet, he did find the time to revisit his signature role in a 1955 television production of *Cyrano de Bergerac* on *Producers' Showcase*. He assisted in the staging and starred in the telecast, along with Claire Bloom's Roxane and Christopher Plummer's Christian. (Plummer would later perform the title role both on television and on Broadway—in his memoir, Plummer would credit director Ferrer for "giving Christian back his 'balls.'") While he was hesitant at first, several factors contributed to his decision to once again assume what had emerged as his signature role. Ferrer could never resist a challenge, whether it was taking up singing, directing for stage and film, or directing and acting on live television. For another, more people would see him on television in the ninety-minute production than had seen the movie or the stage version. In addition, his friends also helped persuade him, in particular Humphrey Bogart (they remained friends after *The Caine Mutiny*). According to Ferrer, "Bogey had just finished 'Petrified Forest' [a live television broadcast in 1955] and was glowing when I talked to him. He told me I'd have a lot of fun working for the electronic cameras and he was right."

As he had with *The Shrike*, Ferrer allowed there were several on set who had far more knowledge than he: "We have tremendous people working on this production. I don't know much about this medium but whatever I didn't know there was someone at my beck and call to explain it to me. I'll be disappointed if it doesn't come over on television as good as it did on the stage or in the movies." Ferrer was toying with the notion of dispensing with Cyrano's oversize nose, but, thinking that it might not play well with audiences of any age (including those who were familiar with *Cyrano* in the classroom), he decided to keep the famous nose. In the end, he enlisted the services of make-up expert Richard

Smith to come up with a foam-latex, Cyrano-worthy nose—one that would take two hours to apply.

The subsequent broadcast earned raves from the critics, and Ferrer would also be nominated for an Emmy for Best Actor, making him the first actor to have been up for the three major acting awards—the Oscar, Tony, and Emmy—for the same role. (Ironically, Ferrer lost to Lloyd Nolan's Captain Queeg in the *Ford Star Jubilee* presentation of *The Caine Mutiny Court-Martial*.) The success of his widely seen performance would lead Ferrer to continue to concentrate on the more accessible mediums of film and television. After the broadcast, Ferrer said that he could no longer afford the time to live with a play for a year: "I have only ten years in which to learn. I don't want to devote so much time to one play." For the foreseeable future, he would forego committing to acting onstage (although he was open to directing) for the more profitable pursuits of film and television, as long as producers and audiences desired his services. Ferrer would also make every effort to curb his "Latin" temperament and remain a good father and faithful husband, at least for a time.

CHAPTER 12

The Great Man and Married Life

IN ADDITION TO THE SEVERAL PROJECTS THAT FERRER INITIATED THAT were subsequently realized, there were a number of projects in the 1950s that never reached fruition. For instance, Ferrer, in his desire to solidify the sobriquet "song and dance man" to his list of creative feats (having enjoyed "loosening up" in *Deep in My Heart*, as well as onstage in *Kiss Me, Kate*), had tried to come to Broadway with *The Musical Comedy Man*, a new musical based on the life of George M. Cohan. He had optioned the property and worked on the book in the aftermath of the HUAC hearings, but it never saw the light of day. Eventually, there would be a stage musical inspired by Cohan's life, *George M!*, starring a post-*Cabaret* Joel Grey as the prodigiously talented and patriotic entertainer/songwriter/producer.

Perhaps the biggest project that occupied Ferrer's time—with no finished product to show for it, was his quest to make a film of Barnaby Conrad's novel *Matador*. Bullfighting films held plenty of appeal in the early 1950s for filmmakers, if not necessarily audiences, with the 1951 release of Budd Boetticher's *The Bullfighter and the Lady* and Robert Rossen's 1952 *The Brave Bulls*, starring that Mel—the *other* Ferrer. José Ferrer became interested in a film adaptation of *Matador* when he was making *Moulin Rouge* with John Huston; they were interested in doing the film jointly, with Huston directing and with Ferrer starring (and collaborating with Huston and Conrad on the adaptation). Huston eventually opted out of directing, having decided to do *Moby Dick* instead, but Ferrer was still interested in buying out Huston's share.

Complicating matters were others' perceptions of Ferrer in the aftermath of the investigations into Ferrer's political beliefs and background (inquiries that had earlier threatened to sabotage the premiere of *Moulin Rouge*). Author Barnaby Conrad initially didn't want Ferrer involved in any part of the production; a letter from Paul Kohner relayed Conrad's concerns, including his belief that Ferrer was a "controversial personality" and that Ferrer's "recent Paramount picture was an awful bust that had been boycotted in theaters." (Kohner was referring to *Anything Can Happen*.) Kohner proceeded to tell Ferrer that if Ferrer was indeed in the clear, neither he nor Conrad had to worry too much—he also suggested that Huston should buy the book himself and reach a joint deal afterwards.

As negotiations for *Matador* proceeded, Ferrer outwardly removed his name from consideration for the lead role, and actors such as Tyrone Power, Gregory Peck, Richard Conte, and even a young John Cassavetes expressed interest in portraying the lead role. For his part, Huston told some reporters that "José Ferrer has already been booked to play the role," and since they got on during *Moulin Rouge*, the director thought they would make "quite a picture." Conrad would also be mollified somewhat, telling friends and reporters that he had always envisioned Ferrer in the title role. Other actors then tried to join the film, as there were key supporting parts, actors such as Akim Tamiroff and Ricardo Montalban (who had a chance for a leading role in a Budd Boetticher-directed bullfighting picture called *Number One* but said he would rather take a supporting role in a Huston-Ferrer collaboration). Huston, though, was sticking to his plan to have a real matador play the pivotal role.

Besides the interest from fellow actors John Wayne and Bob Fellows, who had their own production company Wayne-Fellows (*The High and the Mighty* is perhaps their best-known venture), both liked *Matador* and offered to buy it. Ferrer said he would sell his share of the rights if Huston would sell, but Huston did not relinquish his share. There was also interest of another kind from the British censors, who said they would not allow "shots of spears on bulls' backs," or any shots of a dead bull. The Humane Association also weighed in with their trepidation over any film associated with bullfighting. This increased attention, however, did nothing to change the fact that *Matador* was far from being ready to begin filming, even after three years. Ferrer would tell Paul Ruiz, a production hopeful that "there's nothing doing on *Matador*." By the end of 1955, Ferrer had tired of pursuing the project, and by 1956, his interest, financial and otherwise, expired.

If Ferrer was encountering the occasional career obstacle, spouse Rosemary Clooney still had a successful recording career, as well as constant bookings in nightclubs and on television. Yet their respective careers did result in more than a little friction. One person who was emphatically not a Ferrer fan was her boss and mentor at Columbia, Mitch Miller. An off-the-cuff comment from Miller about Clooney since her marriage to Ferrer ("All of a sudden she's reading books") resulted in Ferrer demanding that Clooney leave Miller, claiming, "You're wasting your time with this joker." Clooney told Ferrer that quitting was out of the question and doubled down by informing Ferrer that Miller knew Uta Hagen and had warned Clooney she should have property in her own name: "He told me you blackmailed Uta." In any case, Clooney would certainly not leave Miller, who was providing her with hit tunes and an opportunity to stay in the public eye, since she had to decline a number of star roles for Paramount because of her pregnancies. In addition, when she could not go to New York to cut some recordings, Miller flew out to California to enable her to make the recordings locally. In spite of Ferrer's acrimony towards Miller, Clooney was not about to let her career collapse—especially since husband Joe made no attempt to curtail his pursuits.

In addition to frustrations for Ferrer in terms of realizing certain projects, there were mounting problems at home, too. Clooney's success was both a source of pride to Ferrer and a bone of contention. She had sacrificed her film career so that she could have more children. Having a big family was important to them both—only Ferrer wanted the family as quickly as possible, and as Clooney pointed out in her autobiography, she willingly complied—even if part of the motivating factor was to encourage an occasionally straying Ferrer to remain closer to home.

What bolstered Ferrer's self-esteem is the high regard that Universal held for him; even though *The Shrike* was not a financial success upon its 1955 release, the reviews had been favorable, so Universal-International—and producer Aaron Rosenberg in particular—began scouting properties for Ferrer to direct. Rosenberg and Ferrer agreed that they would adapt *The Great Man*, a best-selling debut novel by radio and television veteran Al Morgan.

The Great Man would immerse Ferrer in the world of radio and television, and the power of celebrity, in recounting the tale of the untimely death of a famous radio/television star—and the news reporter (Ferrer) who is tasked with coming up with a suitable memorial broadcast. What follows is both a searing look at television and fame as well as the corrupting power of celebrity. Fictitious celebrity Herb Fuller proves to be anything but worthy of celebration, and Ferrer's reporter has to make the decision whether to lionize him or present him as he really was, egregious flaws and all.

Although Fuller is deceased at the film's outset, it was speculated that Al Morgan based this beloved celebrity on several possible candidates. One was Arthur Godfrey, who was in the midst of a successful television career; in addition, Morgan had worked for Godfrey for eleven years prior to penning the novel. Two others were the extremely popular comedians (and variety show hosts) Jackie Gleason and Milton Berle. Berle, in particular, was convinced that the story was based on him and even confronted author Morgan, claiming, "You're the so-and-so who wrote that no-good story about me. But you didn't even scratch the surface. I could give you plenty more." What Morgan left out was whether Berle communicated any sense of pride during this encounter.

As happened on Ferrer's previous film, the filmmaker and his writer (Morgan, who had been signed as co-screenwriter) collaborated closely on the adaptation. Several changes had to be made, including eliminating a few characters and telescoping the narrative from five days to four. Ferrer himself was quite impressed with the original material and allowed many of the novel's key speeches to make it into the film verbatim. The narrative structure would be altered, however, as the book begins with the broadcaster considering whether to go on the air with the material he has uncovered, leading to the novel's extended flashback. One unique aspect of the film is its complete absence of flashbacks, as Fuller himself is never seen; instead, we learn about him through the people who knew him at his best (or worst).

Ferrer was able to assemble quite a cast for *The Great Man*. Some of his choices were not unconventional: Oscar-winner Dean Jagger (for *Twelve O'Clock High*), presently enjoying a string of sterling supporting performances in such solid hits as *Executive Suite* and *White Christmas*, was hired for the role of the network president; Jim Backus (who appeared in *Deep in My Heart* and subsequently become a close friend of Ferrer's, acting with him in future Ferrer-directed films) was cast as Fuller's press agent; and veteran character actor Keenan Wynn was engaged to play the owner of a New York station and the fellow who discovered the Great Man himself.

There were, however, several unusual casting choices that did elicit attention. Ferrer hired several actors in important roles who were more familiar to the public as singers or musicians. Bandleader Russ Morgan was cast as Fuller's musical conductor and perhaps his only real friend.

Singer Joanie Gilbert, who was carving out a career on the supper club circuit, made her dramatic debut as Ferrer's secretary—a straight role and one that both she and Ferrer hoped would lead to a more substantial acting career. Their hope was only intermittently realized, though Gilbert did earn a great deal of respect from director Ferrer—not to mention a featured role in Ferrer's *The High Cost of Loving*.

For the pivotal role of a singer on Fuller's show, pursued and exploited by the late Fuller, Ferrer lured the sultry Julie London (who recently scored a big hit with her record of "Cry Me a River") away from a very successful performing and recording career. She was tasked with playing a challenging, emotional role that did not require any onscreen singing (although her character is heard singing a song). Indeed, London's character, and the ruthless exploitation she had been subjected to by Fuller, to the extent that she had turned to drink to escape him, epitomizes the degradation that women faced in the working world, regardless of whether their employers were in the entertainment field or not.

Perhaps the most unusual choice was for the character of Mr. Beasley, who appears midway through the film. Mr. Beasley is the small-town radio station owner who had given Fuller his start. The character provides Ferrer's news reporter with a crystal-clear picture of what the Great Man was really like, via a well-developed, uninterrupted monologue. Ferrer had hoped to engage either Burgess Meredith or his friend and *Fourposter* collaborator Hume Cronyn, but neither actor was available. Kurt Frings, who was both Ferrer's friend and cast member Keenan Wynn's agent, suggested Keenan's father, Ed Wynn, for this key part. Wynn was a beloved comedian whose career was currently in eclipse, and though Ferrer was intrigued, he was unsure whether Wynn could handle the distinctly non-comic demands of the role.

According to Keenan Wynn, Ferrer called and posed the question: "Do you think your father could play the part?" Initially, Keenan thought his father would never consider doing anything like this and that "it would be ridiculous to ask him." But Ferrer persisted: "Do you think he *could* do it?" Keenan would encourage his father to try it, especially since it wasn't a big part. Ferrer came to see Wynn to persuade him himself, bringing the script along. Ferrer read Beasley's monologue aloud in a dramatic fashion; Wynn read it in more of a comic manner. Afterward, Ferrer said he wanted the finished scene to be something between the two readings. Heartened by this experience, and by Ferrer's patience, Wynn agreed to participate in the film in his first dramatic role in a career which had spanned over fifty years. Wynn was seventy, but he felt the timing was right to take the part: "I've preached against comics trying to turn into tragedians but at this point I was desperate and said all right, I'd try anything." As a footnote, although both father and son were in *The Great Man*, they shared no scenes together. That would come when they costarred in the live-television drama, Rod Serling's classic *Requiem for a Heavyweight*, with the elder and junior Wynn as trainer and manager, respectively, for the over-the-hill boxer played by Jack Palance.

Shooting began on April 6, 1956, and continued through May 15, 1956, with some retakes done in August. Consistent with Ferrer's directorial method, particularly when it came to directing scenes in which he prominently figured, Broadway actor Leon Charles was again hired (he had worked previously on *The Shrike*) to portray Ferrer during rehearsals while Ferrer and the cinematographer Harold Lipstein would set up the various camera angles. In addition to his capacity as Ferrer stand-in, Charles also served as the dialogue director. While most of the picture was filmed on a Universal soundstage, Ferrer and a post-production crew were sent to New York to photograph some exteriors.

To extract certain results from his actors, Ferrer resorted to some unusual, perhaps debatable methods. The big moment for London's character was a drunk scene; the prevailing wisdom was that for any kind of scene, even a drunk scene, the actor should remain in full control of his or her faculties—in other words, you've got to be *straight* to play *drunk*. Conversely, Fred Astaire, in the classic *Holiday Inn*, played his big drunk scene (and ensuing dance) with a fair amount of alcohol in his system, and while the scene does play well, Astaire said he would "never do that again." Choosing to fly in the face of conventional wisdom, London decided to have a few drinks prior to filming the scene. As London would recall, "That was no imitation. That was real. There's nothing worse than someone pretending to be drunk when they're not. I told the director how I felt, and he said why don't you try a couple of slugs and see if you can remember your lines too. When I'd reached the point of where I wanted to be, it was a case of holding it or sobering up and losing it." The filming proceeded with London managing to both hold her liquor and deliver a sensitive performance. After the film's release, she let it be known that she wanted to concentrate primarily on acting, which resulted in roles in films such as Anthony Mann's *Man of the West, Saddle the Wind*, and, much later, a regular role on the successful Jack Webb-produced series *Emergency*.

A different kind of challenge emerged with Ferrer's handling of Ed Wynn. Ferrer had allotted three days to shoot Wynn's eight-minute scene. Wynn was acting in public for the first time without his clown shoes and funny hats in order to portray the pious owner of the radio station that provided Fuller with his first big break—before Fuller left, having exhibited signs of the insensitivity and arrogance that was to come. Ferrer wanted to stage the scene, especially Wynn's monologue, in one unbroken take. After some laborious rehearsals, during which Ferrer and Wynn endeavored to arrive at the right blend of comedy and drama, Ferrer suggested they start filming. As the scene began, Wynn momentarily faltered, then, as Ferrer tells it, "It was one of the really moving moments of my life. You could feel yourself cringe for the old man and feel the effort of that polished steel brain as he reached from his memory for the words he had lost. Then his real class as a performer showed." Wynn didn't exactly deliver the words as written; instead, he delivered a well-articulated monologue that seamlessly combined the essence of the speech with Ferrer and Morgan's words—and with director Ferrer's tacit approval. As Ferrer remembered, "He ad libbed the sense of his speech and that was more moving than the words he couldn't remember. Then suddenly his memory started to click again, and he slid back to the lines as written." Wynn would be proud of his achievement: "I didn't think I could do it . . . when I saw myself in the rushes, I was amazed at how I looked. I had never seen myself as I really am. But here was an old guy with a bald head and an ugly kisser." He added, "No wonder I had marriage problems."

Appearances aside, Wynn is indeed excellent in the finished film, and *The Great Man* stands as Ferrer's most successful, completely realized achievement as director/writer/actor. (Some might be partial to Ferrer's later *I Accuse!*, which boasts arguably his best cast.) Ferrer was also proud of his directorial efforts on the film, even though when he would refer to it later, it was with a twinge of regret, and symptomatic of his troubled relationship with studio executives. "On *The Great Man*," Ferrer pointed out, "I was given complete autonomy and the only place that I ran into any trouble was that I felt the cutting was much too sharp: the producer and the head of the studio took out one or two scenes that I thought were fairly valuable. I don't know that the picture was enormously damaged, but in each case texture had gone."

Although Ferrer mentioned "one or two scenes," the reality is that the first cut, especially in light of Morgan and Ferrer's streamlining of characters and incident from the novel, ran a little under three hours. After the aforementioned cuts were made, *The Great Man* had a running time of a little over ninety minutes. More than sixty years after it was made, *The Great Man* still has something relevant to say, not only about the destructive elements inherent in the pursuit of fame but also about greed, redemption, the abuse of power, and the personal cost of integrity. Moreover, the insights into the business side of television are just as timely as ever.

What remains in the final cut is observant, sharp, well-paced, and well-played—all due in no small part, to director Ferrer's skill in eliciting fine work from his entire cast, and that includes himself. The screenplay is a series of incisive encounters, as Ferrer's Joe Harris meets a group of characters who have something to say about the revered Herb Fuller's upcoming memorial, from Dean Jagger's executive Carleton, who wants it to be respectful and ornate, to Keenan Wynn as Fuller's manager, who seeks to be the power behind the "new" Fuller (which he hopes will be Ferrer's Harris). And then there are those who might rain on the Fuller parade, such as Ed Wynn's small-town station owner, Julie London's disillusioned, alcoholic cast-off, Harris's secretary (Joanie Gilbert), who reveals how Fuller propositioned her. Even Fuller's manager (Keenan Wynn) reveals how certain career-making Fuller broadcasts were enhanced in the editing room.

Ferrer's directing doesn't draw attention to itself; if anything, it is self-effacing and generous, allowing the capable actors to dominate their respective scenes. The pacing is spot-on, the screenplay is deliberately paced, and the revelations distinctly spaced in getting across the rot at the heart of the late, lamented Herb Fuller. Ferrer and Morgan are also realistic (and prescient) in terms of what will succeed on television and what studio executives will support. At the end of the film, Ferrer's Harris is *this* close to delivering the memorial that his contract demands, but at the last minute decides to proceed with everything he has learned about Fuller, the bad as well as the good. (The book's conclusion is a little more equivocal and open-ended.) The powers that be (represented by Dean Jagger) might be momentarily displeased, but they recognize that the integrity displayed by Ferrer means greater respect for the studio, higher ratings, and, in turn greater profits, when one factors in that success in television is usually measured in ratings and advertising revenue.

Ferrer also excels onscreen, with a subtle, often underplayed performance as the conflicted announcer. Ferrer's Joe Harris would like nothing better than to have the broadcast catapult him back into the limelight. He is patient and even condescending with certain individuals (such as the characters played by the Wynns). Because the other characters have most of the lines, Ferrer has to achieve many of his effects with gestures, reactions, and looks—and much of the time, he is effective without having to resort to his booming baritone. Even in his key speeches, Ferrer's voice and overall demeanor convincingly evoke wariness, disappointment, and the growing inner conflict within a man who is increasingly uncomfortable with perpetuating a lie from coast to coast.

When *The Great Man* was released in January 1957, many critics were in competition for who could communicate the most enthusiasm for Ferrer's results. The *New York Times* raved that the film was "a smashingly brutal and generally absorbing expose," while the *New York Herald Tribune* let it be known that "Ferrer directed the movie thoughtfully, using dialogue as his cutting edge instead of flashbacks" and went on to praise most of the cast, including actor Ferrer, who "plays the role with attractive restraint," and the "biggest surprise and pleasure of the film, Ed Wynn." The *New York Post* felt the film "gives a few swift kicks where it hurts . . . it is all quite realistic." The same review also cited Ferrer who "again proves his striking versatility." Despite its excellent cast and all the critical approbation, *The Great Man* still disappointed at the box office (and today is still lacking a proper DVD release—oddly enough, only *Return to Peyton Place* and *State Fair*, Ferrer's two non-starring directorial efforts, have been granted a suitable afterlife on video). While Ferrer's film cannot compete with the histrionics found in the more well-known, roughly concurrent media expose *A Face in the Crowd*, starring Andy Griffith and directed by Elia Kazan, the subtlety and craft of the performances, screenplay, and direction in *The Great Man* continue to gain admirers, especially through repeated, prime-time showings on Turner Classic Movies.

For now, Ferrer could not only congratulate himself on a job well done but also about the fact that there remained studios desirous of a José Ferrer film—and with Ferrer in his expected capacity as star, director, and, occasionally, credited co-writer. This time, it was Metro-Goldwyn-Mayer that would grant Ferrer a larger budget than usual (when compared to the relatively modest expenditures from Columbia and Universal), as well as a fairly prestigious cast for a picture that presented one of the most shameful examples of injustice—military and otherwise—from the turn of the century.

CHAPTER 13

Dark and Light, in Theater and Film

IT WAS CLEAR FROM JOSÉ FERRER'S EARLIER STAGE CAREER THAT HE was not content to produce and direct what were considered to be "mere entertainments." When the opportunity presented itself, he was happy to write and direct more challenging, socially conscious fare, including *Strange Fruit*; therefore, in 1957, when MGM offered him the chance to star and direct in *Captain Dreyfus* (the working title for what would eventually become *I Accuse!*), Ferrer quickly accepted.

The real-life story of the French Jewish officer, Captain Alfred Dreyfus (1859–1935), as well as the injustices suffered by him and his family, was well-known to American audiences because of the success of the 1937 Warner Bros. drama *The Life of Emile Zola*, starring Paul Muni as the journalist Zola and Joséph Schildkraut as Dreyfus. A significant portion of that film revolved around the famed writer's efforts to secure justice for Dreyfus, who had been wrongly convicted of treason in 1896—partly because he was a Jewish officer in the anti-Semitic French military. The French Army had been aware that there was a traitor in their midst, and the aloof and very Jewish Dreyfus provided a convenient scapegoat when he was arrested, convicted, and imprisoned on Devil's Island. His conviction came about because of damning letters he had allegedly written, as well as a series of articles in the French press virulently condemning the man. When famed writer Emile Zola came to Dreyfus's defense and demanded a new trial (especially in light of some new, possibly exculpating evidence), the war minister declared he had absolute proof and demanded that Dreyfus's former superior, Picquart (the only officer loyal to Dreyfus), and Zola be brought up on charges themselves. Zola's famous article helped gain support for Dreyfus, but it would take several years and the combined efforts of Zola, Picquart, and Dreyfus's wife to obtain a formal pardon for Dreyfus (a deal Dreyfus accepted only reluctantly, since it did not acknowledge his innocence). In 1906, twelve years after Dreyfus had been arrested, he was finally cleared and reinstated in the army to the rank of major. (In the film, it is because the real traitor, Major Esterhazy, needed money and published his true confessions; in real life, the process was more circuitous, with the publication of the papers of German attaché Schwarzkoppen that showed Esterhazy's duplicity. These papers were not released until 1931, hence the need for dramatic license.)

Ferrer and MGM wanted to utilize French locations for the film, but the French government refused to grant permission to shoot exteriors in Paris. Fifty years after the events that were to be depicted, France was still a little sensitive about the subject; up until 1957, Muni's *Zola* film had never played in France. Ferrer tried to convince the bureaucrats that he had no wish to show France in a bad light. He said, "We only presented the facts as it actually happened. The fact that France cleaned house and reinstated Dreyfus is clearly indicated in the picture." In retrospect, it appears that Ferrer was employing the same tactics to win over France as Stanley Kramer was when trying to convince the navy to support *The Caine Mutiny*: Ferrer presented the argument that France finally did the right thing and therefore should not be judged by the actions of a few. Ferrer tried to bolster his case with his assertion that it's a healthy nation that feels secure enough to show its own shortcomings in dramatic form, believing that it's better to be self-critical than to have somebody else do the criticizing. Ferrer's arguments were not successful, so MGM shifted the locations to Brussels, with the interiors to be filmed at MGM's Elstree Studios in London.

Ferrer succeeded in attracting what was the best cast he would ever direct on screen. While Ferrer himself would star as Dreyfus, Viveca Lindfors would costar as his patient, resourceful wife; the charismatic Anton Walbrook, shown to great advantage in the Michael Powell/Emeric Pressburger films such as *The Red Shoes*, would have the opportunity to steal many a scene here as the suavely villainous Esterhazy. David Farrar, also a Powell/Pressburger favorite, lent stalwart support as Dreyfus's brother, while Leo Genn displayed dignity and nobility as Dreyfus's sympathetic superior, Picquart. There were also Herbert Lom and Harry Andrews as two of Dreyfus's official persecutors, and playwright/actor Emlyn Williams as Zola. Further down the credits one can see other stage and screen veterans like Felix Aylmer, George Coulouris, Laurence Nai-smith, Michael Hordern, and Charles Gray. Ferrer told interviewers that there was no flexing of egos among this formidable cast. On the contrary, Ferrer recalled that "once the picture started, they realized that I, like they, was only doing my best for the story. We were really one big family. I never had a more talented or understanding cast with which to work."

Shooting for *I Accuse!* would take place from April through early June 1957, and Ferrer was confident that he was up to the challenge of both starring opposite and directing the theatrical luminaries in his cast. "I like taking on both jobs because they afford two different, though re-lated types of creative stimulation and excitement," he said. On occasion Ferrer the director had to remove certain scenes of Ferrer the actor, ac-knowledging that "it's hard on the ego . . . if it's a fight between Ferrer the director and Ferrer the actor, the director always wins." Perhaps his biggest challenge as director was how best to utilize the black-and-white CinemaScope format. For Ferrer, CinemaScope presented a problem (as it would for other directors accustomed to filming intimate, character-driven stories). Ferrer acknowledged the difficulty when speaking with Hy Hollinger of *Variety*: "This is a picture about people, and it requires a lot of close-ups. I had to find a way to get around what seemed an un-natural shape."

The finished product is a polished, well-intentioned, unsentimental yet occasionally deeply felt drama with fine work from Ferrer both in front of and behind the camera. Ferrer portrays Dreyfus the way he discov-ered him to be in his research: somewhat cold and aloof, but an efficient bureaucrat. Yet, when this rigid façade crumbles under the accumulated weight of the supposed evidence, Ferrer does a good job of portraying degrees of outrage and helplessness. Yes, Ferrer does underplay (for him), but it is quite an effective contrast to the scenery-chewing of Lom and Andrews as co-conspirators and Walbrook's unctuous, eternally schem-ing Esterhazy. And while it's true that this approach doesn't lend one to easily sympathize with Ferrer's Dreyfus, it's clear that Ferrer would like the viewer to understand Dreyfus the way he is, without sentimental overtones. He could have easily played the martyr throughout, but in-stead Ferrer plays his part with a sense of disbelief toward the charges and incredulity at the system. He knows he's done nothing wrong as an officer; his only offense lies in being Jewish during a time when anti-Semitism was on the rise in France (and, regrettably, elsewhere).

The film gathers force and power as the injustices and betrayals begin to wear on Dreyfus. Yet Dreyfus himself is absent during several key sequences, and Ferrer the director is content to let the veteran cast carry the proceedings. There is little conventional directorial flair of the kind that calls attention to itself; as he did in *The Great Man*, Ferrer lets the other actors contribute the pyrotechnics. There are a number of powerful scenes, including the courtroom scenes when Dreyfus is disgraced; scenes showing him in his solitary cell on Devil's Island, close to a breakdown; his defiant comment, "I am innocent, long live France"; and, of course, the scene in which Zola gives his famous "I accuse" speech, delivered with force by Emlyn Williams.

Upon the film's release in 1958, critics took note of Ferrer's restrained approach to the Dreyfus incident; while they praised the performances, some thought Ferrer's handling of the events was too subdued. The *New York Times* critic Bosley Crowther wrote that "Mr. Ferrer, who directed and plays the leading role, is to be commended for trying to put in focus the essential nature of the affair. But unfortunately, this achieved intention does not make for a very dramatic, exciting film." Fellow critic Philip Scheuer agreed, stating that "director Ferrer might well have given us a more positive, imaginative filmic treatment. . . . As always in a Ferrer film, the acting, starting with the star himself, is exemplary."

When the film was completed in early June 1957, MGM offered Ferrer another opportunity to both direct and star in a movie. Throughout shooting and into post-production, the movie was going to be released under the title *Bay the Moon*. Ferrer starred as an ordinary fellow, a married purchasing manager who believes, after an oversight and some later misunderstandings, that he is about to be fired. A number of Ferrer veterans were cast in the film, including Edward Platt as a sympathetic executive, Jim Backus as an executive at another firm, and Joanie Gilbert (from *The Great Man*) as a family friend. Gena Rowlands, who was making a name for herself both as a star on Broadway (in *Middle of the Night*) and as the new wife of actor John Cassavetes, was cast as Ferrer's wife who discovers she is pregnant on the day that Ferrer has (erroneously) thought he would be fired.

Rowlands had recently been signed to a contract at MGM, and in interviews during filming, she let her feelings be known about the intended title: "It's a comedy and I think it's going to be funny, but I loathe the title, *Bay the Moon*." After being informed of the Shakespearean origins (Brutus in *Julius Caesar* says, "I'd rather be a dog and bay the moon than be such a Roman"), Rowlands added, "I can't figure what it has to do with the story. It's not pertinent and doesn't sound like comedy. This story is about people building up trouble that is nonexistent. The husband has not been invited to a business luncheon when a big group comes to buy out the concern he is in. So he assumes he is being sacked. My character is going to have a baby. He doesn't want to tell me his worries because he's afraid of annoying me and I don't want to tell him mine." MGM must have worried about the title, because it was changed in mid-December from *Bay the Moon* to *The High Cost of Loving*.

The part of a middle-class clerk with career insecurity had some elements that Ferrer could identify with, especially the fear that he might soon be put out to pasture. Also, the plot device of the wife's pregnancy was something that Ferrer understood completely, since he enjoyed entertaining little Miguel and his new sister Maria when he wasn't at the studio. One thing Ferrer found it difficult to relate to was the kind of home his character would live in—especially since Ferrer was living in a Beverly Hills mansion in which, as daughter Maria recalled, "We had a trampoline, a sparring bag, dance floor, really a ballet floor in the three-car garage, complete with those dance bars."

Since Ferrer and Rowlands were playing a young, average, middle-income couple, director Ferrer wanted their home and furnishings to look real. Robert Relyea, the assistant director (who also fielded several phone calls from young women who either already knew, or wished to contact, the still-married Ferrer), recalled that the art director and designer had dressed an MGM soundstage to look like the interior of an average American home, but Ferrer didn't think it was accurate: "I don't believe any of us know what a typical American home looks like, so how can we create such a set?" Relyea called Bruce Greenland, a teacher friend of his who lived in the suburbs with his wife and children. Relyea asked if he and Ferrer could visit, and an excited Greenland said yes. The trip was an eye-opener for Ferrer, but not for Relyea, who already had known that "the average home doesn't have fancy items adorning an elegant mantle or nifty trinkets on a coffee table that's perfectly matched to a couch and loveseat. The average home, circa 1958, was sparsely decorated, not very detailed, and not very interesting to a ticket-buying audience. . . . on the ride back to the studio, Ferrer could only shrug his shoulders, shake his head and say, repeatedly, 'Real doesn't work.'"

Even though "real doesn't work" when it came to sets, Ferrer attempted to bring a light but realistic touch to the proceedings. The opening ten minutes of *The High Cost of Loving* came in for particular praise, as it consisted entirely of the young couple's daily morning routine, shown without dialogue. It's an exquisitely timed sequence, with the marrieds seamlessly entering and exiting kitchens and bathrooms, having coffee—and all with the intimacy and comfort of a real couple. Ferrer rarely played an ordinary fellow; he is very restrained here yet working hard to make the average man interesting. Ferrer's Jim is your typical hardworking functionary who tries to work within the system but does not suffer fools, or those who would belittle him, gladly. Jim has spent fifteen years establishing his worth, and when his company is going through a transition, he deeply resents it when he believes (falsely, as it turns out) that the company is proceeding without him.

Jim's assumption that he will be fired leads him to seek out other employment, so he pays a visit to an executive friend (Jim Backus) who had always thought highly of him. The resulting scene, which begins with Backus praising Ferrer and then letting him down gently because of the latter man's age, struck a chord at the time and is even more relevant now, with corporate takeovers resulting in the widespread firing of older employees. Ageism, job security (or insecurity), career frustrations, the fragility of the American Dream—these are all weighty themes that are incorporated into what should be a light, romantic comedy with serious undertones. However, due to Ferrer's restrained staging and acting, *The High Cost of Loving* plays more like a drama with light undertones, with the wife's pregnancy treated more like a comic device alongside the husband's mounting despair over his presumed termination, including an impulsive decision that nearly results in career suicide. The tone is more serious and the situation a little too uncomfortable for the film to succeed as a comedy. Indeed, upon its 1958 release, the *World-Telegram* noted: "At times Ferrer seems as though he were still playing Dreyfus." Paul Beckley of the *Herald Tribune* acknowledged that "the intention is laudable enough, but the unfortunate fact is that a mere misunderstanding is too weak to support a full-length film." For her part, Wanda Hale of the *New York Daily News* felt otherwise, writing, "It's not a big picture, but it's a lovely picture, heartwarming and humorous."

After Ferrer completed filming, he would have some time before his next project, a musical version of *The Captain's Paradise*. Whenever Ferrer found himself idle, he could not remain still—there was too much to do, and Ferrer was a lifelong learner. As his daughter Monsita recalled, "My father wanted to be a great chess player. When we were little, Bobby Fischer [the US chess champion] came and stayed a week. He wanted to excel in tennis, so Pancho Gonzalez and Pancho Segura would come and play tennis every morning." He also was a stylish (though not very good) golfer. As Monsita remembers, "He was very well turned out . . . when he hit the golf ball, he had the most outrageous outfits. He was a terrible golfer, but he loved golf. He would say to me, 'Sooty (my nickname), I've found the secret. My game is *transformed*!'"

Ferrer would never lose his love for learning; according to Monsita, her father learned to windsurf while he and son Miguel were doing *Hawaii Five-0*; he would take dance lessons though they seemed to have no discernible effect. Monsita said, "He loved to embarrass me—he'd dance, and I'd cry 'Stop!'" Maria remembered when her father took a class in African music and worked to feel the rhythms. According to Maria, her father "didn't want to be left out; he participated in everything he saw as new and interesting. He wanted to be a part of it."

Ferrer not only maintained his love of learning, but he also passed this quality on to his children. The shelves at home were adorned with books, as were the floors in the study. Although the children were privileged, their parents tried to downplay their own status as celebrities. Monsita would recall that they had neighbors like Mitzi Gaynor and Agnes Moorehead, and went to school with the children of such stars as Dean Martin and Debbie Reynolds, yet they didn't realize their parents were "stars" until one day when they were out with their mother and some people came up to her to ask for an autograph. Of course, being the child of a celebrity had its advantages. Ferrer's son Rafael would recall his father taking him to see a production of *Medea* in Greek—in Greece. When the children were older, Ferrer would take them to operas, musicals, ballet, dramas, and comedies, both good and bad. He would tell Rafael, "If I only took you to things that were good, you would never know what was bad." In the 1970s, when Ferrer was living in New York and Monsita was attending Skidmore College in upstate New York, he would purchase two sets of schoolbooks for her so that she wouldn't have to lug the books each time she visited.

Ferrer never lost the desire to learn and explore new areas of interest. His son Rafael recalls his father taking him to see a magician from Argentina. According to Rafael, "The final act was cutting his daughter in half—he was going to use a circular saw. 'Anyone who has a weak stomach, please leave.' My father *loved* this. Afterwards, he said, 'I want to be a magician. I want to learn card tricks.' He wanted us to learn together. He had a thirst for knowledge like no one I ever knew." As Ferrer had done with his children, he passed not only this curiosity but his vast expanse of knowledge onto others. For actor/dancer Tim Jerome, who would be Ferrer's understudy on *Man of La Mancha*, it would be in the form of acquiring Ferrer's knowledge of the graphic arts through accompanying Ferrer on frequent trips to museums so that toward the end of the tour, Jerome began collecting art himself, eventually amassing a sizable and valuable collection. Ferrer's nephew, Carlos Campo, recalled how he would call his uncle about literature, and whether it was from a Victorian novel or contemporary poetry, "it was as though he had just studied it the night before. He could quote passages, make specific references, and display his erudition without being arrogant."

Ferrer could be somewhat of a disciplinarian at home, particularly if anyone dared to use profanity around the house since he maintained a strict "no profanity" policy. His son Rafael would say that Ferrer believed that a gentleman didn't engage in the use of such language, particularly around women. Ferrer would tell his children that "if you use swear words, it shows you don't have a large vocabulary." He would backpedal somewhat as the children became older—and after his meeting with the Puerto Rican poet and playwright Pedro Pietri.

Pietri was one of the founders of the Nuyorican Movement, which was a cultural and literary movement that began in the mid-1960s involving Puerto Rican writers, poets, musicians, and artists who resided in and around New York. Their work would largely draw attention to those in the Puerto Rican community who had become marginalized. Ferrer would serve as a mentor to Pietri and produce and direct a few of his plays. While Pietri's work was powerful, it also liberally employed the use of the "f-word." Maria would apprise her father of this, but he would insist "those words in the circumstance had purpose." Ferrer didn't entirely soften his stance against such language. Rafael would recall (with a bit of awe) that Ferrer, in his seventies, got into a heated argument with a cab driver that escalated into something more physical after the cab driver used some ill-judged terms around Ferrer and his daughters.

Ferrer enjoyed being a father; he also enjoyed being home and entertaining. The family's friends and neighbors in Beverly Hills included Humphrey Bogart and Lauren Bacall, George Burns and Gracie Allen, and Bob Hope. The Ferrers would host dinner parties on Monday or Tuesday nights, since they were usually the quietest nights of the week. Son Gabriel said in a recent interview, "There were a lot of parties. Once I snuck downstairs and sat with Nat King Cole and he played the piano. To us, it was just another Tuesday." Since Ferrer was a self-taught chef, he would prepare or supply the recipes for the menu. When they weren't dining in style at home, the Ferrers could be seen in the hottest, most glittering nightspots in Hollywood; places like the Coconut Grove, Chasen's and Romanoff's all counted the Ferrers and their friends among their loyal clientele. Composer friend Ian Bernard would say that "he ruled the roost."

José Ferrer from the 1933 Princeton University Yearbook, the *Nassau Herald*. Courtesy Seeley G. Mudd Manuscript Library, Princeton University.

Another photo of Ferrer from the *Nassau Herald*. Courtesy Seeley G. Mudd Manuscript Library, Princeton University.

Othello: Ferrer's Iago and Paul Robeson's Othello in one of many intense moments. Library of Congress, Prints & Photographs Division, FSA/OWI Collection, LC-USW33-054941-ZC.

Happier times: Uta Hagen, Paul Robeson, and Ferrer cheer on teammates at a softball game in Central Park, New York, in 1943. Library of Congress, Prints & Photographs Division, FSA/OWI Collection, LC-USW33-054933-ZC

Ferrer's film debut in *Joan of Arc,* with Ingrid Bergman and Gene Lockhart.

Ferrer with second wife, Phyllis.

Ferrer as the dying dictator
Farrago in *Crisis*.

As *Cyrano de Bergerac*,
with Mala Powers as
Roxanne.

Ferrer with Rosemary Clooney at the Twenty-third Academy Awards presentation ceremony in New York City (held in conjunction with the Hollywood ceremony).

Moulin Rouge: Ferrer as painter Toulouse-Lautrec, with Colette Marchand.

Portrait of Ferrer, circa 1950.

Anything Can Happen:
Kim Hunter and Ferrer.

Miss Sadie Thompson: Ferrer
going over a scene with
dialogue director William
Anderson.

The Caine Mutiny: "Here's to you, Mr. Keefer": Ferrer's Greenwald hurls his champagne at Fred MacMurray's Keefer while Arthur Franz and Herbert Anderson look on.

Ferrer in repose and reviewing lines.

Sigmund Romberg (Jose Ferrer) and the girl (Doe Avedon) whose love was the inspiration for his glorious songs.

M-G-M's "DEEP IN MY HEART" In COLOR

Copyright 1954 Loew's Incorporated   COUNTRY OF ORIGIN U.S.A.   Property of National Screen Service Corp. Licensed for display only in connection with

Ferrer (as composer Sigmund Romberg) and Doe Avedon in *Deep in My Heart*.

The Shrike: a posed shot with June Allyson and Ferrer.

The Great Man: Dean Jagger's network president tells Ferrer's commentator what should be in the memorial.

I Accuse: Ferrer's Captain Dreyfus before his ordeal, with Harry Andrews and Anton Walbrook.

I Accuse: Ferrer's Dreyfus suffers public disgrace.

The High Cost of Loving:
Ferrer and Nancy Kulp.

The Marcus-Nelson Murders: Ferrer with Gene Woodbury.

Portrait of Ferrer, circa 1973.
Ray Fisher / Contributor /
Getty Image

Forever Young, Forever Free:
Ferrer as the compassionate
Father Alberto.

Voyage of the Damned:
Ferrer as the corrupt
Cuban immigrations
official.

The Return of Captain Nemo: Ferrer with Burr DeBenning and Tom Hallick in a would-be television epic.

Fedora: As the mysterious Dr. Vando, with Gottfried John and a forcibly restrained William Holden.

Ferrer with his daughter Monsita. Courtesy Monsita Ferrer.

Ferrer accepting the Florida Prize for his work in the performing arts in 1990. Also pictured: Charles Stout, Governor Robert Martinez, and Stella Ferrer. Photograph by Mark T. Foley, State Archives of Florida, Florida Memory.

Grandpa Ferrer with former wife Rosemary Clooney, Monsita, and grandchild. Courtesy Monsita Ferrer.

Family photo: Daughters Maria and Monsita, with proud Papa (and Grandpapa) Ferrer. Courtesy Monsita Ferrer.

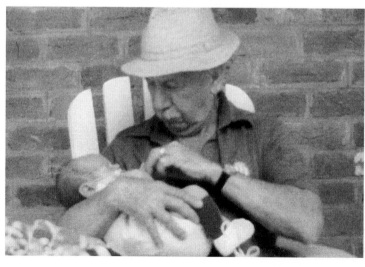

Doting grandfather. Courtesy Monsita Ferrer.

Although Ferrer would have to return to New York to begin serious preparations for *Oh Captain!* (as the show was finally called), Clooney couldn't travel with him because she was involved in a project of her own, *The Rosemary Clooney Show*, a series of live half-hour television programs. The broadcasts also showcased the talents of composer/arranger Nelson Riddle and his orchestra. Riddle had orchestrated some of Frank Sinatra's finest Capitol recordings (such as *Songs for Swingin' Lovers*), and this would mark the beginning of a highly satisfying professional—and, later, more personal—collaboration with Clooney. Ferrer was the guest star on the November 28, 1957, program. She would recall that "Joe was supportive, but he was also envious. He constantly took singing lessons because he marveled at the ease with which I sang, and he wanted to be able to do the same thing." The broadcasts were Monday through Thursday, so quite often she would fly out to join Ferrer on the weekends, especially when he was actively rehearsing the show.

Oh Captain! was an adaptation of the 1953 Alec Guinness comedy *The Captain's Paradise*, about a British sea captain who has a proper British wife in England and a fiery mistress in Paris. Of course, he assumes the two will never meet . . . but that wouldn't make for an interesting show. The music and lyrics were by Jay Livingston and Ray Evans. Ferrer collaborated on the libretto with Al Morgan, author of *The Great Man*, since they had enjoyed a congenial working relationship.

For the role of the captain, Ferrer chose Tony Randall, who had recently achieved some success on Broadway (1955's *Inherit the Wind*), television (*Mr. Peepers*), and film, with strong roles in *Will Success Spoil Rock Hunter* (1956) and *No Down Payment* (1957). He had also been up for what later became the Dean Martin role in *The Young Lions*. (Martin starred along with Marlon Brando and Montgomery Clift when the World War II epic was released by Twentieth Century-Fox in 1958.) Though Randall admitted that not getting that part was a "big disappointment," he allowed that if he had done that film, "I probably wouldn't have got *Oh Captain!*" Randall, like Ferrer, had taken singing lessons for years to strengthen his speaking voice. When he previously tried out for another musical, "producers gave me the old fish eye . . . so I forgot about musicals until José Ferrer discovered that I could sing a little."

Despite the combined efforts of Ferrer and Randall, not to mention a cast that included Abbe Lane, Jacquelyn McKeever, and Ferrer mainstay Edward Platt, *Oh Captain!* made little impression on critics when it opened in February 1958. Ferrer supporter Brooks Atkinson of the *New York Times* said that "the billing on the first page of the program looks like

a casting agent's directory. But the quality does not fulfill expectations."
While he found Randall amusing as the glum Captain, Atkinson felt Ferrer's writing and direction to be lackluster: "As co-author and director,
Mr. Ferrer has substituted leers for wit and generally debased the style
to the level of an old-fashioned varsity show. Mr. Ferrer has been away
from Broadway too long. New York is a big town now." In an attempt
to generate more interest for the show, Ferrer recorded the entire score
from the show, from March 14 to 17, 1958. *Billboard* noted that "Ferrer
sings with charmed persuasiveness." Despite Ferrer's efforts, *Oh Captain!*
ran just over four months, closing on July 19, 1958.

At least *Oh Captain!* managed to have some staying power on Broadway. The same could not be said of Ferrer's next theatrical foray, Milton
Geiger's *Edwin Booth*. For this production, Ferrer would again be involved
as actor, director, and co-producer (along with the Playwrights Company)
in presenting this biographical drama covering the last forty-two years in
the life of the famous tragedian, who was forever linked to his brother,
John Wilkes Booth—better known as the assassin of President Abraham
Lincoln. After Booth retired from the stage, he would go on to found the
Players Club, a social club designed to bring actors into contact with writers, businessmen, and other artists. Twentieth Century-Fox had already
produced *Prince of Players*, a 1955 film version of Booth's life starring Richard Burton as Edwin and John Derek as his infamous brother, John.

Edwin Booth would be Ferrer's first stage appearance since his run of
plays with City Center in 1953. It was also important for him to do Booth
justice; Ferrer was not only a great admirer of Booth's, but he had been
a member of the Players Club since 1935 and would later become the
president of the club from 1982 until shortly before his death. When
asked about the role of Booth, Ferrer said, "When I read it, I was very
moved. I knew it was a play that deserved a hearing." Geiger's play called
for a single set with three levels and a cast of nine to enact the three-act drama. Lorne Greene would play a drama critic friend of Booth's
who would function as the play's narrator. The play would cover most
of the important events in Booth's life, including his brother's assassination of Lincoln (which is handled offstage—but the ramifications are
felt onstage, as Edwin Booth prematurely began his long retirement).
Edwin Booth would also afford Ferrer several opportunities to recreate the
Shakespearean roles that Booth had become famous for.

Edwin Booth had its world premiere at La Jolla Playhouse before moving on to the Huntington Hartford; it would undergo some changes between the two venues. In La Jolla, critic Philip Scheuer noted that the play started late, lasted over three hours, and that Ferrer was overextending himself playing both Booth and his father. In addition, he permitted himself so many Shakespearean orations that Scheuer felt Geiger should have granted the Bard a co-writing credit. After the play went to the Huntington Hartford, Scheuer saw significant improvement; Ferrer had given up the role of the elder Booth and permitted himself fewer dramatic recreations.

The main fault of the play, as Scheuer saw it, is that "though we are assured Edwin Booth was born to a shower of stars, the Booth we see never lives up to this mystique, this intimation of supernatural godliness." As for the staging, it was rather straightforward. As he had done with *I Accuse!*, Ferrer took a historical subject and treated it in a way that did not inspire gasps or cheers; instead, he gave it a basic integrity that generated respect and resulted in a generally absorbing drama. Even though the reviews were only fair to middling, Ferrer persisted in bringing the show to New York. In terms of the critics and lackluster audience turnout thus far (*Auntie Mame* and *The Music Man* were also playing—tough competition), Ferrer said only this: "LA is a lousy town for drama—everybody goes home to his ranch or the suburbs for the night."

If the West Coast reviews of *Edwin Booth* were lukewarm, the New York notices when it opened in late November were positively frosty. One of the major criticisms had to do with the episodic approach which reviewers felt prevented the show from achieving any real emotional depth. The *New York Times* reviewer Brooks Atkinson, while acknowledging Ferrer's genius and past accomplishments, found his work unexceptional as both director and actor: "*Edwin Booth* is like an old-fashioned stereopticon lecture presenting the life of an actor in thirty easy lessons. Everything we know about Booth suggests he was a man of perception and grandeur—neither Geiger nor Ferrer works with that level of distinction." Perhaps his harshest words were for Ferrer the actor: "His acting is broad, heavy, obtuse. There is no life inside the characters."

For Ferrer, the New York reviews were a devastating blow—perhaps Ferrer the director allowed Ferrer the actor to indulge too much, and he considered closing the show immediately. Nonetheless, the audiences had thus far proven enthusiastic, and Ferrer was also heartened by some encouraging words from non-New York critics. To keep the show running, he invested some more of his own funds, appealed to theater groups, and ladies' clubs, but all to no avail. *Edwin Booth* closed on December 13, 1958, after only twenty-four performances. Ferrer would later refer to it as "a longhair play which every longhair hated."

If this setback had occurred the previous year, Ferrer would have been ready to begin another project—in all likelihood a film. This time there was no project in the offing, with both *I Accuse!* and *The High Cost of Loving* having completed their theatrical runs and no film offers forthcoming when 1959 began. Another opportunity would soon materialize, courtesy of some changes that occurred during previews of the musical *Juno*, based on Irish playwright Sean O'Casey's classic *Juno and the Paycock*. O'Casey's original drama was set in the Dublin slums of the early 1920s, during Ireland's civil war. The main characters are Captain Jack Boyle, the strutting paycock who has never seen the sea and prefers liquor to water, and Juno, his hustling, respectable wife. O'Casey's original play, which starred Barry Fitzgerald and Sara Allgood, was reputedly the greatest success in the Abbey Theater when it opened in 1924. Over thirty years later, librettist Joseph Stein decided the play should become a musical: "I thought it had all the vital elements of a musical treatment. The characters are larger than life. A powerful story. Rich and lusty humor. The kind of language that sings . . ."

Stein had called on the playwright in England, and even though O'Casey was unsure as to what an American musical was, he agreed to let Stein work on the adaptation. Stein then called on Marc Blitzstein (*The Cradle Will Rock*). The Playwrights Company agreed to produce, and Agnes de Mille was engaged to do the choreography. Shirley Booth, best-known for *Come Back Little Sheba* (this was before television's *Hazel*), and Melvyn Douglas were signed for the leading roles. Douglas, who had been a reliable MGM leading man and was now concentrating on the stage, had never done a musical, was assured by Blitzstein: "I'll worry about the song end of the business." The original director was the veteran Vincent J. Donehue, whose Broadway resume boasted such credits as *The Trip to Bountiful* and *Sunrise at Campobello*.

Juno, as the show was now called, began performances for two weeks at the National Theater in Washington in advance of its Broadway premiere. There was some praise for de Mille's dances and Blitzstein's music and lyrics, but the book and Donehue's staging came under fire. The first act ran long at over 100 minutes, and several critics pointed out that Donehue and Stein hadn't done an adequate job of integrating the songs and dances into the story.

After the disastrous Washington engagement, *Juno* headed to Boston. There, the production team decided to delay the New York starting date from February 26 to March 5. An extra week would be added to the Boston run, which was slated to begin on February 4. Some of de Mille's dances were dropped, then reappeared. Klein, who claimed he had the blessings of O'Casey (who "tied no strings to the play"), shifted the single living room set of the play and moved the action to the street, the pub, and a public square. By the end of the first week of the Boston previews, Donehue withdrew from the show, claiming he left because the writer and producer were not incorporating his suggestions.

Following Donehue's departure, the Playwrights Company contacted Ferrer, who agreed to take over the troubled show during the Boston run. This would be Ferrer's fourth production with Playwrights, following *Key Largo, The Fourposter,* and *Edwin Booth.* Ferrer set about incorporating Stein's changes, providing new bits of business (both comic and dramatic) for the seasoned leads, and trying to bring a sense of cohesion to the company and the show. Boston critics couldn't decide whether the show was too faithful to the O'Casey original or not faithful enough.

The storm clouds that lingered over *Juno* would not disperse after its New York opening in March 1959. Ferrer was generally spared by the critics, who were more concerned with Stein and Blitzstein's contributions. Critic Richard Watts contributed perhaps the most positive notice, remarking that "*Juno* is lively, reasonably tuneful, and tells its story simply and straightforwardly . . . it is helped by Ferrer's staging, a competent piece of work. But it hardly suffices." The *Daily News* said that "Ferrer has directed the production with a good eye for drama—my wish is that O'Casey could have written the book, music and lyrics." Brooks Atkinson believed that director Ferrer had rebounded after the *Booth* fiasco, but still felt that "this *Juno* alternates between vigorous scenes and commonplaceness . . . every scene connected with the troubles in Dublin retain O'Casey's fiery spirit but the comedy scenes are only derived from O'Casey . . . it does not quite hang together." The Playwrights Company, having recently suffered a loss with *Edwin Booth,* announced that *Juno* would be closing on March 21, after sixteen performances and an estimated loss of $300,000.

Ferrer then made a rare television dramatic appearance on a 1959 episode of *General Electric Theater.* It was called "Survival," and the title was certainly apt with regard to his attitude towards his somewhat diminished status in both theater and film. Ferrer's last two films had been worthy efforts but were commercially unsuccessful, while his most recent stage productions received, at best, lukewarm responses, or were, at worst, immediate flops. If Ferrer the director was spared for *Juno,* it was because he was viewed as someone who had entered the fray after the outcome had already been decided. Ferrer's lack of employment, which took its toll on both him and his family (particularly in contrast to his spouse's continued success), was no doubt a deciding factor in doing the television show.

Of course, it wasn't Ferrer's first foray into television, and he had recently made appearances on both variety and game shows, occasionally in the company of Clooney. Besides previously being in demand elsewhere, Ferrer had his reasons for avoiding television: "In those early days of TV, everything was hit and miss, and too damned hurried . . . the day of the broadcast we were up at 8:00 AM, blocking out movements, working out camera cues, worked straight through to airtime. Needless to say, I was completely pooped by then." He also acknowledged that, by November 1959 (when the show was broadcast), television had changed but there was still too much red tape cluttering the medium, in the form of producers, sponsors, and network executives.

Ferrer let it be known that he was open to doing more television but was now in rehearsals for his fourth Broadway play in two years. It would be Saul Levitt's *The Andersonville Trial*, another real-life courtroom drama, this time set after the end of the Civil War. The defendant is Henry Wirz, who was commander at a Confederate prison camp in Andersonville, under whose watch over 10,000 Union prisoners died. Wirz's defense was that he should not be held personally accountable for the wretched conditions, since he was just following orders. But the play poses the same question that was raised during the post-World War II Nuremburg trials: does an officer have the moral duty to disobey orders he regards as inhuman?

Originally Ferrer was supposed to portray Baker, the defense attorney for Wirz, but he landed the director's chair in July 1959 and gave up the role. Albert Dekker (*Dr. Cyclops*, among many other film credits) would play Baker, but there were many other meaty roles to fill, including Wirz and the Judge Advocate (or the equivalent of the prosecutor). George C. Scott would be cast as the Judge Advocate, and it would be a difficult experience for the actor, both during rehearsals and later when performing. The actor felt waves of hatred coming from the audience, as they appeared to be sympathizing more with the accused than the prosecutor's quest for justice. According to Scott, Ferrer wrote him a letter during the run: "He wrote me a wonderful letter . . . he said you must continue to do what you're doing because you're doing it very well and you must not allow their feeling to stop the kind of work you're doing."

For the part of the defendant Wirz, Ferrer cast Herbert Berghof, influential Actors Studio teacher/director and current husband of Uta Hagen.

Berghof had acted in films and stage, but was more renowned for his work on behalf of both the Actors Studio and HB Studios, which he co-founded in 1947, and which wife Uta would later join as his partner. Upon hearing Berghof got the role, director Vincent Donehue asked jokingly, "Who gets custody of Uta?"

The Andersonville Trial would call for one set, four scenes, and many actors—all of whom, except the lawyers, enter for their one scene, and then, according to Ferrer, "have nothing to do the rest of the evening." The play had its initial tryout in Philadelphia, and though the reviews were generally encouraging, there was the need for cutting. When asked about how he approached the material, Ferrer said, "You can't direct Shakespeare as you do *The Andersonville Trial*, but it's my job to represent the author as faithfully as I can in either case. When we go into rehearsal, I know two things. I have read a script which has excited me and about which I understand what is wanted. I also know there'll be hard work . . . there are elaborate preparations for the result on the audience, not elaborate chalk lines for the actors."

The Andersonville Trial opened on December 29, 1959, to mixed reviews. While there was no mystery about the resolution (especially if audiences knew their history), critic Jack Gaver thought that "the playwright and his director, stage star José Ferrer, manage to stir up a nice theatrical storm for most of the two acts." The *New York Herald Tribune* critic Walter Kerr was even more expansive, calling the play "a walloping piece of showmanship round a beady-eyed search for a moral principle . . . each of these vignettes, under Ferrer's superlative direction, is coaxed and carved to perfection." John Chapman of the *Daily News* lauded the actors' contributions: "Berghof draws an astonishingly touching portrait of Wirz . . . his prosecutor is most remarkably played by Scott . . . it is the best courtroom play since *The Caine Mutiny*."

It's left for the *Times'* Brooks Atkinson to add a minor caveat; while he felt the play came to life in the second half when it probed the moral issues, and that Scott and Berghof acted their scenes with force, Atkinson believed "there was something hollow about the conclusion—actors confronting one another, not men caught up in the mysteries of a debate about morals." In spite of the absence of unanimous praise, *Andersonville* was a serious, thought-provoking courtroom drama and, with a high-powered cast, it went on to have a modestly successful Broadway run of 179 performances. About a month after the opening, Ferrer admitted that while he would like to continue to alternate between theater and film, it was a remote possibility at best: "I enjoy making pictures, but since I'm not allowed to function there today, I accept it with regret. I have no snobbishness about Hollywood. A lot of theater people look down their noses at Hollywood, just as picture people look down on television. What they should realize is that all are part of the same game." In other words, survival was the order of the day.

CHAPTER 14

Taking the Jobs and Keeping Up Appearances

BY 1960, FERRER HADN'T ACTED ON THE SCREEN FOR ROUGHLY TWO years, and even his most recent acting roles from 1958 were in his own self-directed properties. Ferrer would be the first to say that without a project to look forward to, he would become restless, which would feed his insecurity; Rosemary Clooney would reflect that "if a week or ten days went by after he finished a project, he'd feel rejected." He would spend his time at home as productively as he could: reading, painting, indulging his passion for languages and cooking, taking singing lessons, collecting art, and accumulating recording equipment—even being a good father. In terms of finances, he and Clooney—who was still maintaining her successful performing career on records (1960 would see the release of one of her best albums, teaming with Nelson Riddle on *Rosie Solves the Swingin' Riddle*), radio, and television, and effectively paying most of the bills—agreed to avoid the subject of money.

During this lean period, Ferrer and Clooney presented the outward appearance of contentment to various popular journals. Clooney would tell interviewers how Ferrer would allow her to sleep in, while he not only changed diapers but also made breakfast for their burgeoning brood, which would include five children, four dogs, one mother-in-law, as well as several servants. (Apparently there was a revolving door at the Ferrer household. One would comment as he was leaving that "the Ferrers may be able to live with each other, but I cannot live with them"). Their Beverly Hills house was adorned with Picassos, six antique chess sets made of porcelain, ivory, and wood, a grand piano, $14,000 worth of recording equipment in the living room (where Clooney would record parts of her daily radio show with Crosby), masterpieces of modern art, as well as Miguel's electric train table, which shared pride of place with his father's collection of pre-Columbian artifacts.

Ferrer would tell interviewers that he "feels strangely fulfilled, mostly because of his wife and children," but even he would say that "the first year was agonizing." Part of it might have stemmed from the need to keep proving himself, not only as a husband and a man, but as a proud Puerto Rican. He was conscious of his Latino heritage but sometimes would treat it lightly; he was fond of saying that he was "just a leetle Puerto Rican boy who made good." This desire to prove himself may have extended to other areas as well; Clooney would say that during this period, Ferrer was far from the model of fidelity and that he still received calls at home from female admirers. When she confided her concerns to her good friend Kathryn Crosby, she would gently remind her, "You have to be realistic. You have to realize you married a Latin man."

Of course, Ferrer wasn't entirely inactive, courtesy of his several Broadway ventures. But the lack of true success—and, in the case of *Edwin Booth*, one outright flop—continued to gnaw at him. He did several guest shots on television, making several appearances on several popular shows from the period. One such appearance was on "Marriage—Handle with Care" for the *U.S. Steel Hour* in December 1959. In the sketch called "Marriage de Fausto," Ferrer starred opposite famed television comedian Sid Caesar in an operatic satire with Caesar as Faust and Ferrer as Mephistopheles. Pianist-composer Earl Wild had composed the score, and after the broadcast, suggested that Ferrer join him the following summer for the Santa Fe Opera's production of Puccini's *Gianni Schicchi*. Ferrer would play the title role in this rollicking opera as part of a double bill with Igor Stravinsky, who would be conducting his *Oedipus Rex*. Ferrer conceded that he was "scared to death," but later admitted that opera "had been a secret ambition of mine for many, many years, but I never thought it would be realized. About three years ago, I started to study seriously and began to get the real rudiments of voice."

Ferrer received some favorable notices for his excursion into opera. *Newsweek* noted that, in his green tunic, salmon tights, knee-length cloak and flaming red wig, "he looked and acted every conniving inch the shrewd but flamboyant peasant . . . in his big aria, he even convinced most of the capacity audience that he sang it to the manner born." Ferrer's appearance in *Gianni Schicchi* speaks volumes about his insatiable desire to challenge himself, in this case with the exacting demands (not to mention the inherent pressures) of opera. There are some, notably spouse Rosemary Clooney, who felt that he was never entirely comfortable with singing and that it was a challenge he would never successfully meet. Ferrer was filled with trepidations, his first inclination being to question composer Wild's sincerity: "I thought he was kidding, but a month later he called me back. I asked him, 'Are you serious?' and he assured me he was. I figured if it was a disaster, it wouldn't mean too much to me—I could always go back to acting. So I told him: 'If you have that kind of guts, so have I.'"

Even though Ferrer declared he could go back to acting, there were still no screen offers forthcoming. It came as a surprise, then, when Jerry Wald—formerly with Columbia Pictures and now with Twentieth Century-Fox—called with an offer to direct *Return to Peyton Place*. A few years earlier, Fox had a smash with *Peyton Place*, the film adaptation of Grace Metalious's bestseller about a New England small town with a carefully scrubbed veneer that masked all kinds of prejudices, hypocrisy, and salacious behavior. The book itself sold ten million copies, while the film grossed approximately twice that. Producer Wald apparently prevailed upon the reluctant author to devise a sequel to her wildly successful novel and she finally did, though she would say that the resulting book was more like "a Hollywood treatment. It was never intended to be anything else."

Even after securing the film rights to Metalious's sequel, Wald found himself encountering other difficulties, namely, that none of the original stars would be available for the proposed sequel. Lana Turner, who created the role of Constance McKenzie in *Peyton Place*, was unavailable or too expensive, her asking price having gone up considerably after the success of the first film. Hope Lange, who played the troubled Selena, decided she didn't want to revisit her role, while Diane Varsi, the original Allison, had decided to retire from the screen. In addition to casting woes, the writers' strike proved to be a formidable obstacle, and a series of writers, including Walter Reisch and Harry Brown, toiled unsuccessfully on the adaptation.

Ferrer was grateful for the opportunity, especially since he felt that his other films' lack of commercial success (only *Cockleshell Heroes* could be considered a financial success and that was primarily due to the British box office) made the studio heads "scared of letting me direct anything." The project was not something he initiated, and though he perceived that it was "offered to me as a last resort," he felt he could do something with the material and perhaps find his way back to a position of prominence as a director, which he professed to be his preferred mode of artistic expression.

Whatever feelings of humility Ferrer might have felt when accepting the project would soon fade. After the succession of failed attempts to devise a workable treatment of Metalious's book, Ferrer engaged the services of writer Ronald Alexander for the final script. Buoyed by his and Alexander's contributions (Ferrer would always work closely with the writer in every film he directed, save for perhaps his final directorial effort, *State Fair*), Ferrer took a firm stance early on when he and producer Wald did not see eye to eye. After arguing with Wald on some matter, Ferrer leaned across his producer's desk and said, "Jerry, you're buying Joe Ferrer. Maybe you bought the wrong man, but you bought him, and you'll do it my way, or you'll do it without me.'"

Together, Wald, Ferrer, and Alexander were able to find ways to continue a narrative despite certain important characters from the original either having been killed (as was the case with the characters played by Betty Field and Arthur Kennedy) or dropped entirely (such as Lloyd Nolan's Dr. Swain). A decent cast was assembled, partly because of certain conflicts, partly because of budgetary constraints. *Return to Peyton Place* was filming in the shadow of Fox's *Cleopatra*; there were colossal expenditures already for that production, which caused Fox executives to rein in other projects. Consequently, the budget was nowhere near as expansive as the first film; there would be more studio backlot shooting, and stars of more limited luster. Therefore, after efforts to sign notables like Gene Tierney (for Constance MacKenzie) and Joan Crawford (for the town's pillar of hypocrisy and bigotry, Mrs. Carter) fell through, Wald and Ferrer managed to secure the services of Eleanor Parker and Mary Astor for the roles of Constance and Mrs. Carter, respectively. Carol Lynley, whose star was on the rise after *Blue Denim*, was cast in the lead role of Allison MacKenzie, Peyton Place resident and budding author, whose debut novel scandalizes the town and unearths dormant hostilities. Tuesday Weld was now Selena, trying to live down her troubled past (which included killing her drunken, abusive stepfather). Jeff Chandler was the smooth yet sincere (and married) New York publisher who serves both as a mentor and potential love interest for Allison. Ferrer himself would not act onscreen—however, you can hear him in a scene where Allison is being interviewed about her novel. The interview shown in the film isn't Ferrer, but the voice is clearly that distinct Ferrer baritone.

Even though all of the principal acting talent from the original *Peyton Place* did not participate in the sequel, one important contributor made the return engagement: composer Franz Waxman, whose lush score did much to enhance the original film. Director Ferrer was able to convince spouse Rosemary Clooney to contribute her own formidable talents to the theme song for *Return to Peyton Place*, "Season of Love," by Waxman and Paul Francis Webster.

According to actress Carol Lynley, Ferrer presided over "a professional, very calm set. Joe was very good at conducting business and keeping things moving." Part of keeping things moving had to do with Lynley's love life; as she was leaving the set, Lynley told director Ferrer she was getting married at 8:30 the following morning. Ferrer said, "How nice for you . . . your first scene is scheduled for 11:30. Be here." When he wasn't tending to the actors, Ferrer was making a favorable impression on the writer Ron Alexander: "He fills you with his love of life. I have worked with him for 15 hours on a script problem and gone home recharged instead of drained. He gives to you; he doesn't take from you."

There were several plot strands to contend with, including Allison's emergence as an author and her return to the town she has immortalized (and scandalized) in print; Selena's desire to move on and possibly find happiness with a ski instructor; and the machinations of Mrs. Roberta Carter, who simultaneously plans to wreck her son's new marriage to "that foreign woman" (Luciana Paluzzi) while ensuring that Allison's book is banned from the local library and using her power with the town council to fire the virtuous high school principal, who is not-so-coincidentally Allison's stepfather. Several earlier drafts had run afoul of the Production Code; while the basic story was acceptable for those moral standard bearers, they did take issue with the adulterous affair between Allison and her publisher (which, as filmed, consists of one tentative kiss and the assurance that "nothing happened"). Selena's description of what happened to her had to be toned down. The lovemaking scenes were generally deemed to be a little "too passionate," while certain words were to be avoided altogether, such as "hell," damn," and "raped"—though "attacked" was acceptable.

Considering the melodramatic nature of the material, *Return to Peyton Place* emerges as an entertaining, fairly restrained film. Ferrer's direction is tasteful and perceptive throughout. While Lynley delivers mainly a one-note performance, other actors do some good work here. For example, Tuesday Weld lends a touching vulnerability to Selena, Eleanor

Parker finds the right notes as the troubled if well-intentioned mother (whose relationship with Allison seems to have regressed since the first novel/film), and veterans like Jeff Chandler and Robert Sterling manage to transcend their limitations and give convincing portrayals. Mary Astor steals the film as the bigoted, scheming Mrs. Carter, whether feigning concern for Selena, driving a wedge between her son and her new, unwanted daughter-in-law, or exuding an iron grip over the town council—and, in effect, the town. Astor's performance reaches its peak during the climactic town meeting, which is well-paced and acted, particularly by Astor and Weld.

This concluding town hall sequence was so well-executed that it probably caused the filmmakers to do away with another section of the scenario. In the book, the seething Mrs. Carter returns home to attempt to kill her incapacitated daughter-in-law by way of setting the house on fire, losing her own life in the resulting inferno. It was probably shot; though studio records don't make mention of it, one can see some fire footage in the trailers for the film. One can only surmise that the creative heads decided that anything following the scene would be anticlimactic and that the footage was discarded. As it stands, Mary Astor's understated, quietly defiant exit is among her finest moments on screen, and a tribute to Ferrer's ability with actors (Miss Lynley notwithstanding).

The notices for *Return to Peyton Place* were largely favorable, with critics noting Astor's towering portrayal, the tasteful sets depicting a picture-perfect New England (within the confines of the studio lot), Alexander's screenplay, and Ferrer's deliberate, capable handling of the material. If the sequel didn't become the monumental success of its predecessor, *Return to Peyton Place* proved to be a moneymaker for Twentieth Century-Fox when it was released in May 1961. It also temporarily helped Ferrer on the way toward being a bankable director.

Ferrer's screen success was mitigated by the gradual dissolution of his marriage. Clooney had been able to withstand Ferrer's failings, notably when it came to upholding the sanctity of the marital vows, but it was a different matter when the children became affected. One evening while Clooney was doing a show in England, the care of the children was entrusted to husband Ferrer (and the hired help). Ferrer did not remain home, however, as he was out with "a friend" (as Clooney recounts), and in their absence, daughter Maria had to be taken to the hospital. After Ferrer came home, he tried to keep Clooney from finding out about both Maria's illness and his own absence. Clooney discovered what had happened from her son Miguel, after which she decided to kick Ferrer out.

According to Clooney, Ferrer replied, "You knew before you married me the kind of man that I am—I can't change." Despite several close calls in the past, the Ferrers had managed to keep their marriage intact, but now Clooney was particularly intent on dissolving their union.

Fortunately for Ferrer, Twentieth Century-Fox was anxious to work with both him and Ron Alexander. Producer Darryl F. Zanuck secured the screen rights to Irving Wallace's controversial novel *The Chapman Report*, a fictional tale concerning the experiences of some women involved in a Kinsey Report-like survey. Advance word was so enthusiastic that Zanuck bought the rights while the book was still in galley proofs, paying $175,000 for the privilege, outbidding three other major studios. It subsequently became the bestseller all had hoped for, retaining third place on the bestseller lists for seven straight months.

Naturally, before filming was to commence on a controversial bestseller like *The Chapman Report*, there were the usual complications. Zanuck himself addressed the pitfalls of adapting this racy bestseller, taking pains to assure cinemagoers and censors that "we are not making pictures for adults only" and tried to assure the public that "the picture will speak for itself on its own dramatic value." The current script was also problematic, as the adaptation by Don Mankiewicz was turned down by the Production Code. When Ferrer was hired in early 1961, he brought along writer Ron Alexander to create a version more palatable to the censors and the public. Ferrer addressed some of the indelicate aspects of the storyline, which includes vivid descriptions of sexual activity. Ferrer said these would be deleted, but the screenplay would remain essentially faithful to the novel.

Ferrer compared the making of *Chapman* to the filming of the original *Peyton Place*, which he felt proved that a difficult property can be put on the screen effectively and with good taste. He added that "we had almost no trouble in filming *Return to Peyton Place*." (He neglected to mention the censorship problems plaguing *Return*, but in all fairness, these occurred before his participation in the film.) Ferrer and Alexander labored on the script for a number of months, hoping to overcome what Zanuck deemed the pre-censorship that was condemning their film. Their efforts were not proving satisfactory to either Richard or Darryl Zanuck, and so at the end of May, both Ferrer and Alexander withdrew from *The Chapman Report*, citing "unresolved differences." The film would subsequently be made at Warner Bros. under the direction of George Cukor, who did not regard it as a highlight of his career.

Ferrer's unsatisfying experience with *The Chapman Affair* notwithstanding, he was once again engaged by Twentieth Century-Fox to come to the rescue of another troubled production. Like his previous directorial effort *Return to Peyton Place*, this new endeavor would be another slice of Americana, albeit the next one would be far less lurid. He was hired to direct Twentieth Century-Fox's remake of the 1945 Rodgers and Hammerstein movie musical *State Fair*—itself a remake of the Will Rogers 1933 classic (sans songs). Ferrer was a late arrival to the project, which had been in various forms of development. Originally contract directors like Harry Keller and Walter Lang were attached to the project, and Lang was the most recent hire, until he fell ill. Even though Ferrer had no prior experience with film musicals, he had directed *Oh Captain!* on Broadway, so it was felt that he could deliver the proper blend of humor, sentiment, and homespun charm. Ferrer had a big supporter at Fox in Jerry Wald, but on this project, Charles Brackett (former Billy Wilder collaborator on projects like *The Lost Weekend* and a skilled scenarist in his own right) was to be on the hands-on producer, with a script from Richard Breen.

Certain creative choices for *State Fair* had been made prior to Ferrer's arrival. Originally the story of a rural family's visit to the Iowa State Fair, the setting was now changed to the Texas State Fair, where the two impressionable adult siblings find love and/or disillusionment, while the mother and father each try to win various contests, such as the "Prize Hog" competition for the father and the pie-eating contest for the mother. Rodgers and Hammerstein had created the songs for the original and were asked to contribute a few new songs; Oscar Hammerstein died in 1960, but Rodgers proceeded to write the words and music for five new songs.

There were several actors who had been considered, with filming to begin in 1960, but the movie was shelved (again, partly due to the overwhelming costs for Fox's runaway production of *Cleopatra*, followed by the projected costs for the all-star D-Day epic, Zanuck's *The Longest Day*). Spencer Tracy, Gary Cooper, Bing Crosby, and even Arthur Godfrey were considered for the role of the father; Shirley Booth and Irene Dunne were under consideration for the mother; Carol Lynley, Pamela Tiffin, and even Darla Hood (of *Our Gang*) looked to take part in what was deemed a sure-fire success.

In the end, Alice Faye came out of retirement to play the role of the mother. (Rodgers had added a number for her role as Mrs. Frake.) Faye had famously left Fox about seventeen years earlier, after Darryl Zanuck and director Otto Preminger cut some of her scenes from her non-singing role in the film noir *Fallen Angel*. Her casting led to speculation that Faye's former Fox screen partner, Don Ameche, would be cast as the father.

However, it was another former Fox player, Tom Ewell, who "returned" to Fox to play the father—Ewell's contract with Fox had only just expired after the ill-fated adaptation of the F. Scott Fitzgerald novel *Tender Is the Night* (starring Jason Robards and Jennifer Jones), but Fox played up his return. For the small but crucial part of the judge of the pie contest, Art Carney (Richard Rodgers's choice) was considered, but the plum part instead went to Wally Cox.

As for the younger set, Pat Boone was signed to play Wayne, now an avid race car driver but still an innocent at heart, while Pamela Tiffin was cast as the wistful Margy. Ann-Margret, who had just made her screen debut as Bette Davis's daughter in Frank Capra's *Pocketful of Miracles*, was to play Emily, a colorful showgirl. Bobby Darin, then at the height of his popularity as a recording star, was making inroads into films and secured the key role of Pat, a newscaster who falls for the impressionable Margy. He also got to sing one of his own compositions (Darin had abundant talent, but his career and life were cut short by his health problems).

Ferrer was handed a budget of $3 million and a forty-four-day shooting schedule; the studio hoped this would provide enough time for a holiday release. Shooting would begin in Texas in August (to accommodate Pat Boone's concert schedule) and move to Oklahoma for the race car scenes. Ferrer was quick to admit there would be differences between this version and the others. For one thing, "This Frake family is a group of 1961 hep people who go to the movies, watch TV . . . in spite of the fact they live on a farm, they are not strictly bucolic. . . . Our treatment is so new, I don't believe there is any chance for comparison with a memory, for mere nostalgia. Also, we have a younger, more up-to-date vital cast— the youngest cast ever used in *State Fair*."

Ferrer worked hard to get good results out of this young cast. With Pamela Tiffin, he advised her to sing the Rodgers and Hammerstein classic "It Might as Well Be Spring" as a song of awakening, along with the fear of leaving girlhood behind. Ferrer also made the decision to have Ann-Margret, cast as the "bad girl" Emily, dye her hair orange. As the actress later recalled, "They felt it matched my character and captured the attention of the naïve farm boy [Boone]." Boone himself felt that, even though Ferrer hadn't directed a movie musical, he was quite helpful to the younger players; he credits Ferrer for coaxing what he felt was some of his best onscreen work. The only cast member Ferrer had some difficulties with was the mercurial Darin, which slowed the pace of filming.

Another challenge had to do with the sheer scope of the production. As Ferrer admitted around the time of the film's release, "I had never done a picture with such big scenes on location. I had to learn a great deal about handling large masses of people on location. We didn't do any day for night stuff in color, we shot everything night for night. It was an education to learn first-hand what had to be done to make this possible." In one sense, Ferrer and Fox were fortunate in that the city of Dallas agreed to start their preparations for their State Fair early in order to accommodate the shooting schedule.

Some problems had to do with the censors, who had to be appeased since *State Fair* was to be a huge Christmas release, a picture for the entire family. For example, in "Willing and Eager," the duet between Ann-Margret's Emily and Pat Boone's Wayne, the lyrics had to be cleaned up so as not to suggest an illicit affair. There were suggestions on how to handle both Emily and Margy, specifically concerning various states of dress and undress. There was special concern over Richard Rodgers's new number that Alice Faye sings to daughter Pamela Tiffin, "Never Say No." Geoffrey Shurlock from the Production Code didn't want it to seem that "the mother was encouraging her daughter to submit sexually to a man in an illicit way."

Perhaps the biggest challenge that Ferrer had to face was his deteriorating relationship with producer Charles Brackett. In interviews, Ferrer would not mention Brackett by name, but would say that "the only difficulty I had in *State Fair* was a complete and total disagreement from beginning to end with the producer. It was a nightmare relationship." This seems to have begun when Brackett viewed some of the rushes. Studio records reveal Brackett grudgingly complimenting Ferrer on some farmyard footage, which, he said, was "more imaginatively shot than previous stuff." In another memo from Brackett in early October, Brackett criticized the change of a certain word (from "metabolism" to "digestive"), which eliminated a possible laugh; Brackett proceeds to chastise Ferrer for neglecting this even though Brackett had brought it up in the first read-through. Brackett then insisted that several scenes had to be reshot, while he criticized others. Some other Brackett missives: "The scene with Red Hoerter is a wretched piece of film; scene with Burdick is pretty bad, to have omitted Jerry's final line is appalling; the flow of the scene is clumsy at the beginning; the use of this longer phrase is an injury to the movement of the scene." It became so tense between Brackett and Ferrer that Peter Levathes, a Fox executive, advised Brackett to stay away from the set: "If you have anything to say, say it through me." Although Ferrer had the support of Jerry Wald, he definitely did not have the backing of associate producer Curtis Harrington, who believed that Ferrer wasn't very good as a director.

In mid-December, more changes were being made and sought, and Brackett and Breen were sending Ferrer new pages. One pivotal scene in question had to do with the family's return after the life-altering events at the fair. Fox executive John Healy shared his disappointment with the scene, specifically that "as shot, it lacks a moving and nostalgic quality." While Ferrer balked, this scene appears to have been redone (though the finished version still lacks the maximum emotional impact).

By the time of the film's release in the spring of 1962, Brackett and Ferrer seemed to have reached some sort of tentative rapprochement. After seeing a March preview, Brackett noted that "the picture went well, some trims were made, none you'd object to. I'm writing to commend its many virtues. I think you've given the studio a real moneymaker." Ferrer (who was off on location) responded, "Thank you for the kind letter. I'm happy there's hope for this picture." Fox did plenty to promote the film, not only exploiting the nascent star power of Darin and Boone, but also the explosive star quality of Ann-Margret, who was also featured in several syndicated columns, courtesy of Hedda Hopper.

Upon its release, as Ferrer would note, "the film was murdered by the New York critics." In addition to these negative reviews, *State Fair* suffered in comparison with another recent release: *West Side Story*, with music by Leonard Bernstein, words by Stephen Sondheim, and choreography by Jerome Robbins, was credited with revitalizing the movie musical. By contrast, Ferrer's direction was looked on as uninspired, and the remake itself was considered unnecessary. Rodgers's new songs were received only tepidly, and none of them acquired a shelf life after the movie's release. Perhaps discouraged by the vehemence of such criticism, audiences did not turn out in droves, and the movie didn't come close to recouping Fox's investment of more than $3 million. The apparent failure of the film did not deter the studio from testing the property in the future, as Twentieth Century-Fox produced a 1976 television version of *State Fair*, directed by David Lowell Rich, with the intention of a possible series spinoff.

Is *State Fair* the movie the outright failure that the critics would have you believe? Having viewed the film a few times recently, it is certainly not a dismal affair. Some of the performers fare rather well, including Wally Fox's tipsy judge, Bobby Darin's smooth womanizing announcer, Ann-Margret's sultry Emily, and even Pat Boone and Tom Ewell, who share a touching father-son scene that Boone credits as his best onscreen moment. This is in the aftermath of Boone's character's split with Ann-Margret's Emily; there had been rumors of an offscreen romance between the two, which might have added to their onscreen fireworks. However, Alice Faye as the mother doesn't get much to do, and her new song by Rodgers is pretty forgettable. And though Ewell is good most of the time, even Bing Crosby could not have made the character's love song to his hog any less laughable. Tiffin is adequate as Margy, but in her big solo, "It Might as Well Be Spring," Ferrer the director undercuts her plaintive delivery by shooting her in long shot, overwhelmed by the vast expanse of Texas; whether it was for the sake of CinemaScope or not, this disrupts not only the intimacy of the song but also the viewer's connection with the character. And even though the ending was reshot, there is still plenty to detract from the emotional impact—namely, Boone's rapid (and unconvincing) transition from an alcohol-sodden, emotional wreck to the idealistic and hopeful young man as seen in the beginning. As written and directed, this transformation comes out of nowhere, and the rushed nature of the conclusion does little to disguise this.

State Fair was the last major Hollywood film that Ferrer directed; however, this was not immediately apparent, as he was planning to do another big-budget film for Fox, *The Long Ships*, which would involve lengthy location shooting in Yugoslavia. He held no illusions about his two most recent directorial endeavors. With *Return to Peyton Place*, Ferrer felt he was offered it as a last resort, and as for *State Fair*, he felt "it had a certain old-fashioned easy going entertainment quality. . . . I cannot say in all honesty that either of the pictures . . . are subjects I would have chosen for myself. But on the other hand, since I am not master of my fate, I try to create success for myself by doing films that perhaps would not be my first choice, but hoping to attain the position where I can do the pictures that would be my first choice." Ultimately, Ferrer would not direct *The Long Ships* once shooting was postponed; Jack Cardiff would be the director, and he and his stars, Richard Widmark and Sidney Poitier, would spend six months in Yugoslavia, toiling away on a film that upon its release in 1964 would prove to be an even bigger financial fiasco than *State Fair*. As to why Ferrer couldn't get another major directorial assignment, perhaps he knew best when he theorized that "if it [*State Fair*] does badly at the box office, then it's going to be tougher for me."

As if this professional setback weren't enough, he still had to go through the heated emotions brought on by the end of his marriage to Rosemary Clooney. The entire affair figured prominently in the tabloids, surfacing with regularity while Ferrer was filming in Dallas. Before the court proceedings began, Clooney painted Ferrer as a "charming individual who was only interested in himself." She expressed surprise at discovering that Ferrer's family was wealthy, and that he himself had millions in assets in Puerto Rico. "He never told me anything about his affairs, business or otherwise. . . . I thought the way to hold him was to have a lot of children and I did—one right after the other," she told the powerful columnist Louella Parsons. Clooney would maintain before the divorce trial began that there were no extramarital affairs involved in the divorce—on either side. Ferrer himself would not comment during the lengthy pre-trial period, even shutting off his phone in Dallas to avoid speaking to reporters.

When Clooney took the witness stand in May 1962, she spoke—under oath—as to why she was proceeding with the divorce: "He engaged in a series of affairs with other women since the beginning of our marriage." When she confronted him about his infidelity, Ferrer would either dismiss her, or as Clooney would say about the last time they spoke of this matter: "It was about his conduct . . . he said he couldn't change." She also alleged that Ferrer demonstrated "violent shows of temper both at home and in public which made me very upset."

Clooney also expressed outrage over how her husband handled the earlier incident concerning their daughter Maria, while she had been away doing a concert: "Without my knowledge, my daughter Maria was taken to the hospital. My mother asked that I be called but Joe said he didn't want me to worry even though I had told him I always wanted to be informed about my children." As Clooney was seeking financial support for her and the children, she said she had gotten an ulcer from her marital troubles and claimed that her main means of support was $1,000 per week from her radio show. Complicating (and possibly thwarting) Clooney's attempts at financial restitution was the fact that she and Ferrer had signed a prenuptial agreement (Clooney alleged that Ferrer forced the papers on her and that she signed without having read them) which basically said: "What's yours is yours and what's mine is mine."

Though she testified that she wouldn't have signed had she known what was in the papers, the judge ruled that this testimony was inadmissible.

Ferrer testified that his own financial situation was precarious, as he told the court that his primary source of income for 1962 consisted of $35,000 compensation for one week's work in the forthcoming *Lawrence of Arabia*. (Ferrer was not being entirely truthful here, as will be described later.) He also provided a vivid account of how actors go broke living beyond their means: "It costs me $6,000 a month just to run our Beverly Hills home, with its eight servants. I thought it a bit excessive, but then I'm no housekeeper."

Clooney and Ferrer became officially divorced on May 9, 1962. Clooney had sought $8,180 monthly in alimony and child support, but Ferrer maintained he was insolvent. Ultimately, Clooney would receive one dollar a month in token alimony, plus $300 a month for each of the children. Ferrer also agreed to allow Clooney and the children to live rent-free in their $150,000 home in Beverly Hills. The settlement also stipulated that "there is no community property" belonging to the couple and that the prenuptial agreement signed by each prior to their marriage is "a valid and binding agreement." They also agreed to divide several personal items, including their numerous paintings and furniture. For example, a piano was awarded to Rosemary, but a $10,000 hi-fi set went to Ferrer—though it had to remain in the house so that the children could use it. Despite their divorce, Ferrer admitted, "I want to come home if she'll have me." Clooney retorted that "there was no chance for reconciliation." Even then, there was always room in Hollywood for a sequel, and since both were denizens of show business, their pas de deux was far from over.

CHAPTER 15

Once More into the Breach

AMIDST THE PERSONAL AND PROFESSIONAL TURMOIL OF 1961–62, IT came as a relief for Ferrer when he found himself in demand as an actor again in two major films. Ferrer accepted a cameo role in David Lean's sweeping historical epic *Lawrence of Arabia*; he was also offered a strong, featured role in Mark Robson's *Nine Hours to Rama*, a fictionalized version of the events leading up to Mahatma Gandhi's assassination in 1948. Ferrer's work on Robson's movie would be completed first, but it would be released after Lean's film. Lean had long been intrigued by T. E. Lawrence, who had been present for the birth of Arab nationalism and had fought alongside the guerillas to victory against the Ottoman Turks. Lean had wanted to make the film as early as 1952, and screenwriter Robert Bolt produced a screenplay that sought to simultaneously illuminate and preserve the enigma that was Lawrence.

Lean gathered an all-star cast for his film, which was his first since *The Bridge on the River Kwai*. In addition to Peter O'Toole, who was signed for Lawrence (thanks to Lean having seen his work in the little-known *The Day They Robbed the Bank of England*), veteran Lean players joined the cast, including Alec Guinness (a bit too old as Prince Faisal), Claude Rains (who previously starred in Lean's *Passionate Friends*, now playing a devious official named Dryden), and Jack Hawkins as Allenby (Lean had originally wanted Cary Grant). In addition, there were Lean newcomers such as Arthur Kennedy as a reporter, Omar Sharif, Anthony Quinn (as the Arab pirate), and Ferrer, who was offered the part of the Turkish Bey. He was initially unhappy with the size of his part; Ferrer would later remark that when his agent presented him the script, the agent told him it was 300 pages long and that the actor was in three of them. To ease his discontent, Ferrer naturally asked for more money. His subsequent $35,000 salary (as he would later testify in his divorce trial) was more than the salaries of O'Toole and Sharif combined.

Bolt's version of Lawrence's life does touch on Lawrence's sexuality and his craving for pain. One of the pivotal scenes in the film is Lawrence's capture by the Turkish garrison in 1917 by men who didn't know who he was. He had foolishly gone alone on a reconnaissance mission; after being captured, some of the men made salacious advances. He rebuffed one of these advances with a knee to the groin and afterward, he was savagely lashed and beaten. Lawrence would recount this episode in his *Seven Pillars*: "I remembered a delicious warmth, probably sexual, was swelling through me." Ferrer is only on screen for five minutes as the sadistic Bey but later would reflect that his work was one of the highlights of his career. (This powerful, suggestive scene was condensed in the original 1962 release, with some of the footage restored for the 1989 reissue.) In this brief but vital interlude, Ferrer is able to communicate the Bey's arrogance, intelligence, and as his sexual ambivalence and self-loathing. The Bey examines Lawrence as if he were a combination of prisoner and prize; after Lawrence impulsively strikes the Bey, he orders a prolonged beating (which seems to last from night till dawn), after which the battered Lawrence is hurled into the alley. Parenthetically, O'Toole would ad lib, after the Hawkins character asked him what happened in Deras: "I was fucked by some Turk!" Hawkins replied, "What a pity." This ad libbed, amusing interlude set off the painstaking, meticulous Lean, who was said to be quite angry with their "disgraceful behavior." O'Toole would also say that watching Ferrer work in this scene was akin to a master class in acting. Ferrer himself took a great deal of pride in his performance. In 1983, when historian David Del Valle (with whom he worked on the PBS documentary *The Horror of it All*) told Ferrer that his favorite performance of his was in *Lawrence of Arabia*, Ferrer replied, "Interesting you say that, since for me, it's my finest screen performance."

In contrast with his small but significant role in *Lawrence of Arabia*, Ferrer took a major part in Mark Robson's *Nine Hours to Rama*, a story about the assassination of Mahatma Gandhi (1869–1948), filmed on location in India. He would not be Gandhi—that part would be played, and memorably at that, by writer and actor J. S. Casshyap. Instead, Ferrer was to be the police superintendent who uncovers a plot to kill Gandhi who must try to either locate the assassin or convince Gandhi to forego his public appearances until the assassin has been apprehended.

Based on a novel by Stanley Wolpert, Robson and his collaborator had to "telescope and eliminate a lot of material from the novel" in order to hone in on the main flow of the story—the inevitable clash between the force of violence and the force of nonviolence, as the storyline incorporates flashbacks at it weaves together a tale of a determined assassin (Horst Buchholz) who sees Gandhi and his philosophy as a betrayal of India; the equally determined police official (Ferrer) who suspects an assassination attempt will be made by sundown; and the gentle intransigence of Gandhi, who is equally determined to spread his nonviolent philosophy and is equally resistant to any form of violence to stop the attempt.

Robson, accompanied by the film's screenwriter Nelson Gidding (who remained on location throughout the entire filming), bore witness to some unique occurrences during the lengthy shooting. For instance, Robson had the rather fortunate problem of trying to "photograph and capture the world of material that you find in India . . . shooting on the streets was made difficult by the crowds that would gather. In India if you simply took out your wristwatch and look at it for 20 to 30 seconds, you would draw hundreds of other people who would look at your watch with you." Another challenge for both writer and director was to see that the film communicated the spirit of Gandhi. For this, they not only went back to the novel, but also to what Gandhi said during his lifetime; the goal, according to Robson, was that "everything he says in the film he said in life."

Ferrer found his part of the police superintendent in *Nine Hours to Rama* interesting for a number of reasons: "Philosophically he represents a man who is torn between two duties. He is a policeman, entrusted with looking after the people's well-being. On the other hand, he has a very strong feeling for Gandhi and what Gandhi stands for . . . also Gandhi stands for nonviolence, and there are times when to create safety you have to resort to violence." The challenge for Ferrer was how to keep his role from becoming monotonous, since in all his scenes, his police chief is "basically always saying the same thing: How can I save Gandhi's life?" Ferrer believed that Gidding and Robson devised "not obvious but nevertheless very clear means of playing variations on what could be called the same theme."

Ferrer's observations were accurate; the strongest sections of the film have to do with the superintendent's attempt to locate the assassin, gather any official cooperation he can, and try to convince Gandhi to remain out of harm's way. Perhaps the best scene in the film is the police official's lengthy dialogue with Gandhi. Casshyap's portrayal of Gandhi is nicely etched through his dialogue, make-up, and warm, quietly impassioned delivery; it is almost as if actor and character have been fused into one beatific presence. Ferrer's performance is also imbued with not only passion but also sincerity and understatement; in Ferrer's eyes, this represented some of his best acting work, and it would be difficult to disagree.

The film falters with the character of the assassin and his "story." Buchholz has some of the fire, but there is little shading in his portrayal, and his backstory (and various encounters with women who will either help or hinder his quest) tends to dilute the tension that might easily have propelled the film. However, the last fifteen minutes, as police superintendent, assassin, and Gandhi converge in the fateful (and climactic) moments, have urgency and suspense, regardless of any previous knowledge regarding the outcome. While the film was not commercially successful on its release in 1963, the film garnered some good notices, especially for the work of Ferrer and Casshyap.

In the meantime, the success of *Lawrence of Arabia* is well-known: multiple Oscars, including Best Picture (although none for O'Toole, who would lose to Gregory Peck's Atticus Finch from *To Kill a Mockingbird*). For Ferrer, this success (albeit in a role that was barely more than a cameo) led to an intriguing offer—and it came at the London premiere of the film. Producer Herman Levin, flushed with the triumph of his *My Fair Lady*, the Lerner-Loewe musical based on George Bernard Shaw's *Pygmalion*, was now looking for other properties that could be transposed into musicals. He decided that Terence Rattigan's play *The Sleeping Prince*, which had starred Michael Redgrave and opened on Broadway in November 1956, would be that property. (*The Sleeping Prince* was not a notable success, either on the stage—it closed in December 1956—or in the subsequent film adaptation starring Laurence Olivier and Marilyn Monroe.) Levin engaged Hollywood screenwriter Harry Kurnitz to write the book (which was still under its original title) and Noël Coward to do the music and lyrics.

For the role of the prince, who is humbled by a simpler, younger woman, Levin had sought Rex Harrison (his Henry Higgins), thinking that Harrison wouldn't hesitate. This time, however, Harrison declined, so the search continued. Next to be considered was Christopher Plummer, and both Levin and Coward were quite keen on Plummer—however, Plummer told them that he had already committed verbally to Jules Styne's musical adaptation of *The Ghost Goes West* (which never made it East). Which brings us to the London premiere of *Lawrence*: Ferrer saw producer Levin and casually inquired what the producer was up to. Levin told Ferrer about the show and Coward's involvement; Ferrer then asked whether they needed a director. Levin told Ferrer they had already engaged the services of Joe Layton, and the two men left it at that. A few months later, Levin called and offered him the part of the prince.

Several factors contributed to Ferrer's accepting the role. This was the first time he would be cast as a leading man in a Broadway-bound musical. With Coward doing the music and lyrics, accomplished pro Layton at the directorial helm, Kurnitz's skill for witty dialogue, and the formula of cultured, stuffy older man confounded and enthralled by the likes of a simple young woman not having reached its saturation point yet, all systems seemed "go" for another big Broadway hit. Ferrer also needed a success in which he had the indisputable leading role; his more recent starring role, in his 1958 Broadway production *Edwin Booth*, had flopped, and his lead in *Nine Hours to Rama* was in service to a film that was more successful critically than commercially.

Finally, he was in the process of reconciling with Rosemary Clooney. They had never really been apart; since the divorce trial, Ferrer had regularly visited the children and spent a great deal of quality time with them—indeed, perhaps even more than when they were married. In addition to seeing the children, Ferrer was attempting to convince Clooney that he was capable of change, and that if she were to take him back, he would be more like the responsible husband and father she wanted him to be. Before the final decree was granted, the two did officially reconcile and remarried in 1964.

Looking back at this period, it seems unusual that the two did reconcile. By the early 1960s, Rosemary Clooney and Nelson Riddle's harmonious professional collaboration (including the hit albums *Rosie Solves a Swingin' Riddle* and *Love*) had developed into a personal, more intimate relationship. Clooney's daughters Monsita and Maria acknowledged this; Monsita said that Riddle and her mother "really connected with each other" and were "head over heels in love." Maria added that "Nelson was kind and sensitive. A musician and a singer—it was a match made in heaven, but it could be hell on earth." What might be in question is when the love affair commenced. Nelson Riddle's biographer Peter Levinson writes that the affair began in the late 1950s (at a time when Clooney was busy both with producing recordings and having children), and that Riddle's wife (of twenty years) Doreen had discovered the affair and issued an ultimatum. However, Monsita contends the affair did not begin until the early 1960s, after divorce proceedings had commenced. One might choose to believe a little of both versions, since it is possible that the affair—and Doreen's discovery—happened after the divorce. In any case, before their reconciliation, it seemed that Ferrer and Clooney had "moved on." (Riddle was continuing to see Clooney, even if, according to Levinson, he assured Doreen he wouldn't.)

It also seems likely that Ferrer did not discover the affair until after their divorce. (One need only remember Ferrer's actions during his and Uta Hagen's marriage to reach that conclusion—had Ferrer known about Clooney and Riddle, Riddle would have been among the witnesses at the trial.) After the divorce had been granted in May 1962, Riddle was in London scoring Stanley Kubrick's *Lolita*, and Clooney would write to the busy composer—only she wouldn't send the letters directly to Riddle but instead she would send them to the secretary who was assigned to him at the time, Stella Magee. While others (such as Levinson) contend it was "coincidence" that Ferrer and Magee would later marry, Monsita told me that, according to her mother, "Stella showed my father the letter[s] between my mother and Nelson." While it is uncertain when this occurred, what is undoubtedly true (as documented as part of a later legal skirmish between Ferrer and the Internal Revenue Service) is that Stella would accompany Ferrer throughout Europe in late 1962 as Ferrer's personal secretary. They also (according to Monsita) began their romantic relationship during the time period between her parents' divorce and their reconciliation.

Amidst all these romantic complications, Ferrer went to audition for Coward in January 1963, after hearing Coward play the score. According to Coward, "He sang perfectly charmingly . . . perfect stage authority. He is ugly but he is also curiously attractive . . . and a good name." Coward added, "There was no doubt in any of our minds, except with a small teeny one in mine." Rehearsals would begin in September 1963, which would leave Ferrer time to work on some other professional commitments.

In January 1963, Ferrer went to audition for Coward, after hearing Coward play the score. According to Coward, "He sang perfectly charmingly . . . perfect stage authority. He is ugly but he is also curiously attractive . . . and a good name." Coward added, "There was no doubt in any of our minds, except with a small teeny one in mine." Rehearsals would begin in September 1963, which would leave Ferrer time to work on some other professional commitments.

Perhaps the most unexpected of these appearances was Ferrer's decision to accept an offer from the Royal Poinciana Playhouse in Palm

Beach, Florida, to dance the part of the doctor in the ballet *Coppelia*. It is the story of a doctor who creates a mechanical doll so lifelike that he falls in love with her. According to reporter Jim Bishop, who saw the opening night of the one-week engagement, Ferrer came onstage with black satin breeches and "when he went into his first-time step, the applause was thunderous." Ferrer had never done a ballet before, but he allowed himself to be persuaded by producers Jo Anna Kneeland and her husband, Ted Kneeland. Ferrer intimated to Bishop that he accepted because it was an offer when none were forthcoming: "I'm a distinguished has-been. They won't put me in a picture because they think I'm an egomaniac."

Ferrer would give several interviews throughout the 1960s attesting to his "employability" or lack thereof. For all his frankness and self-deprecation, he was still being offered film roles. A key example was his participation in director George Stevens's next project. Stevens had completed *The Diary of Anne Frank* and had spent a number of years preparing *The Greatest Story Ever Told*, about the life and martyrdom of Jesus Christ, based on the 1949 novel by Fulton Oursler. While other directors had been attached previously, Stevens persevered, acquiring the rights to the novel for George Stevens Productions (for United Artists) and visiting Jerusalem for a number of weeks to scout locations—although the filming would actually be completed domestically in places like Arizona, Nevada, Utah, and Death Valley.

It was not the choice of locales that engendered controversy for Stevens; rather, it was the all-star cast that he had assembled. The players included Max von Sydow as Jesus. Von Sydow was a star because of his films for director Ingmar Bergman but was largely unknown to American audiences. Therefore, to buttress the box-office appeal, Stevens proceeded to cast box-office insurance, including John Wayne as a Roman centurion, Sidney Poitier as Simon of Cyrene, Charlton Heston as John the Baptist, Dorothy McGuire, Van Heflin, Telly Savalas, Ed Wynn (still enjoying offers for dramatic roles seven years after Ferrer's *The Great Man*), Claude Rains as Herod, and José Ferrer as his son. When shooting had finally begun in October 1962 in Arizona, Stevens neither had a completed cast nor finished script; Stevens would also film at his customary unhurried pace. Michael Anderson (James the Younger) later recalled, "We all thought, okay we're going to work, and we sat there for three weeks . . . we rehearsed this scene a little, and that . . . we all realized we're not going to knock this movie off." Snow also postponed shooting and some filming had to be done on the backlot of Desilu Studios. Finally, Stevens allowed other directors to lend a hand; Jean Negulesco (a veteran studio director for Warner Bros and Twentieth Century-Fox with credits including the 1953 version of *Titanic*) assisted with the Jerusalem street scenes and David Lean filmed the Herod scenes with Rains and Ferrer.

By the time *The Greatest Story Ever Told* was released in 1965, after re-shoots and cast additions, the budget had ballooned to nearly $20 million (from an initial estimate of between $3 and $9 million). Audiences had grown weary of spectacles in the wake of the release of Twentieth Century-Fox's bloated *Cleopatra*. The critics also were critical of the "all-star" approach, believing that audiences were more inclined to play "spot the stars" rather than become engaged in the story. While Max von Sydow earned most of the praise that was offered (and Wayne's Centurion much of the derision), Ferrer acquitted himself well as Herod Antipas, the son of Rains's Herod the Great. When Herod expires early in the film, Ferrer's son of Herod assumes the task of locating the savior and would-be threat to his power. He shares most of his scenes with an unusually animated and fiery Heston as John the Baptist. Although few reviewers mentioned it, their scenes crackle with tension; the actors are well-matched, as Heston's bloodied, doomed but swaggering John the Baptist causes Ferrer's insecure Herod to doubt himself even more and assert his own power to compensate. When Herod calls for John the Baptist's death, Ferrer suggests that John the Baptist has struck more of a chord than he is willing to admit. It is a well-conceived performance that was unfortunately submerged beneath the excessive star voltage that Stevens thought would be the film's salvation.

During this busy year of 1963, Ferrer also took another stab at his signature role: director Abel Gance (of *Napoleon* fame) offered him the chance to play Cyrano de Bergerac opposite Jean-Pierre Cassel's D'Artagnan in the none-too-imaginatively named *Cyrano et D'Artagnan*. In this adventure tale, which has nothing to do with Rostand's play, Cyrano and D'Artagnan meet, travel to France, and try to keep from their country from being embroiled in a revolution. The cast also featured Sylva Koscina as the woman who comes between the two swordsmen. This would be a French-Italian co-production, and just about the only similarity this *Cyrano* had to the earlier film (other than the well-staged sword fights) was how difficult it was for Ferrer to secure his paycheck. In this case, Ferrer had been promised $50,000, but only received $45,000. Against the advice of his representatives, the actor continued to do work on the movie. Later, one of his representatives, Bill Joseph, noted that late payments were the norm for Italian films.

Ferrer would also become involved in another European production, *Stop Train 349*, again with star status, albeit in a showy but nonetheless distinctively supporting role. The film, written by Victor Vicas and directed by Rolf Haedrich, was inspired by a real-life incident that happened at the East/West German border. *Stop Train 349*, filmed on location in Berlin, is mainly set aboard a sealed American train that transports US soldiers and their dependents from East Germany to Frankfurt in West Germany. The premise is that a German refugee has escaped and boarded the train, which has been stopped at the border of East and West Germany. Sean Flynn (son of famed swashbuckling star Errol Flynn) has the lead role, that of a young American officer in charge of the train who initially does not know of the refugee's presence and refuses Germany's demands to search the train. When Flynn discovers the refugee is aboard, he plans to protect the escapee, even though it would be a violation of duty, as the Americans have pledged to not allow the trains to be used for aiding refugees.

Ferrer is a hard-boiled reporter who bulldozes his way aboard the train, loudly declaiming his desire to reach his destination, until he gets wind of the refugee's presence and tries to get the proverbial scoop. He is the stereotypical brash newspaperman, and Ferrer's playing is akin to what theater critics would accuse him of in later endeavors—being all bark, no bite, with nothing to show beneath a loud surface. The much-vaunted Ferrer baritone is very much in evidence, but the cadences are absent, and mostly what remains is monotony delivered at a high volume. The only respite from the braying comes in his climactic scene with the conflicted Flynn, when he quietly (for a change) reminds Flynn of his duty: "The courage to obey is one of the things that separate the men from the boys." Surprisingly, Ferrer garnered some decent notices for this performance, with one critic writing that the actor "gives a sharp, definitive performance." Flynn himself also received some good reviews for his earnest portrayal, but most of the praise was reserved for Hans-Joachim Schmiedel's touching performance as the tired, embattled refugee.

Upon Ferrer's return to America, he still had some time before beginning rehearsals for *The Girl Who Came to Supper* (the new title for the upcoming Noël Coward musical, previously called *The Sleeping Prince*), and he used it to further explore the medium of television. Ferrer was the uncredited narrator for the pilot episode of the popular situation comedy *Bewitched*, establishing the premise in a mock-documentary style. Ferrer would also appear as an escape artist in ABC's *The Greatest Show on Earth*, and later be the special guest star on Danny Kaye's CBS variety show, where his appearance was so well-received that he would again appear on Kaye's hit program in 1964. Ferrer also had been in negotiations with MGM's television department to produce and star in a series based on Agatha Christie's Belgian detective, Hercule Poirot. The show never came to fruition and Ferrer later expressed his disappointment and frustration: "I don't know what happened to it, really. We never got to shoot the pilot film. Everything in TV seems to be done through committee, and I don't know how to work with twelve people."

Fortunately for the restless Ferrer, rehearsals for *The Girl Who Came to Supper* finally began in September. The first week of rehearsals went rather well, according to Coward, who thought "Joe Ferrer charming to work with." By now, Florence Henderson had been cast in the role of "The Girl" of the title. She would say in her memoir that "it was clear that singing in a musical comedy was outside his comfort zone." Clooney herself thought that Ferrer was overreaching and that he did not possess the voice or technique to sufficiently impress in a singing role; yet Ferrer didn't go into this venture completely unprepared. In his efforts to master everything he could, Ferrer had never stopped taking vocal lessons, performed in musical works as diverse as *Kiss Me, Kate* and *Gianni Schicchi*, and was throwing himself into the role with his customary verve.

From Coward's journals it would appear that during rehearsals, Ferrer was either good or frightful, depending on the rehearsal, performance, or Coward's mood of the moment. Coward had been having his own issues with director Joe Layton, particularly with what he perceived to be Layton's over-direction ("too much movement, too many props and everybody overacting like mad and trying to be funny"). Early on, Coward thought that Ferrer was vulgar. By the opening in Boston, however, Coward felt that Ferrer had improved, both in his vocals and his overall charm. Coward also felt that Layton had cleaned out the extraneous business, so when the show moved on to Philadelphia in November, there was hope for success, especially on the heels of good notices in Boston. Yet one could see that Coward was still on the fence about Ferrer: "He has all the signs of being a good comedian, but those evil fairies at his Puerto Rican christening bestowed on him short legs, a too large nose . . . a toneless singing voice and a defective sense of timing. It is extraordinary to me that an actor of his years . . . should still misjudge his effects and walk through laughs." It was during the Philadelphia engagement that Coward began filling in for director Layton, who had been hospitalized with infectious hepatitis.

Despite the good reviews and the occasional friction onstage (and off-stage), nothing could have prepared Ferrer, Coward, and company for the devastating events of November 22, 1963. President John F. Kennedy had been assassinated, and as Coward put in his journals, "the whole country is in a state of deep shock." As the nation began a period of prolonged mourning, it was not the ideal time to convince audiences they should venture out to the theater for an evening of musical mirth and merriment—particularly when one of Ferrer's numbers, "Long Live the King," had everything to do with assassination. Coward had to write another song to substitute for this unfortunately timed song, and the show moved on to New York for its early December opening.

Coward had taken over the direction full-time, since Layton was still in the hospital (though he made an appearance in New York to wish the company luck). Opening night went smoothly, as Coward wrote in his journals that Ferrer was "better than he has ever been hitherto . . . he made a great success and nearly stopped the show with 'Middle Age.'" The first notices were also favorable, except for those in the *Herald Tribune* and *New York Times*. Walter Kerr thought very little of the book, though he did like Ferrer and Coward's music and lyrics. Other reviews began to appear, and they were hardly raving; in fact, *Time*, *Newsweek*, and the *New Yorker* all panned the show, with even Coward's music and lyrics coming under fire.

By January 1964, if the notices, middling business, and poor weather weren't enough to raise concerns, Ferrer himself exacerbated tensions within the company. He elected to fly down to Puerto Rico to attend Rosemary Clooney's opening night and was stranded there while a raging snowstorm persisted in the Northeast. His understudy, David Brooks, gamely tried to make the performance from his home in New Jersey but arrived late to the theater—and too late to see that the performance had been canceled. Producer Levin was angered since Ferrer hadn't asked permission; he even wanted Ferrer to pay the costs for that canceled performance. Coward too was outraged, and Ferrer's wasn't the only unprofessional behavior on display. Florence Henderson had decided, prior to the show's opening, that she wasn't up for a particular Saturday matinee performance and didn't inform the company until ninety minutes before curtain. After her understudy gave a sensational performance (and following a tongue-lashing from Coward), Henderson was back onstage, but according to Coward, she "had lost the respect of the company." It is no wonder that Coward would write on January 13 that "I am in revolt against José Ferrer, *The Girl* . . . and everyone connected with it."

By mid-March 1964, *The Girl Who Came to Supper* had its closing night, after a run of 112 performances. It was far from the success that any of its creators had hoped for. In the eyes of many, Ferrer had impressed with his singing and comic timing. If critics weren't enthused, peers as illustrious as John Gielgud said that "Ferrer put over his numbers surprisingly well" (though Gielgud added that he wished Coward himself had played the role). Coward placed a large portion of the blame not on his own contribution, but on the book, the state of the Broadway theater, and on Ferrer himself: "I tried to wishful-think myself into believing that José would be good, but I knew in my heart from the very beginning that he was miscast." It also seemed to confirm Clooney's long-held opinion that Ferrer couldn't cut it as a singer, although there continues to be proof, on television and in films, that Ferrer could do more than just carry a tune. He had shown a light touch on several occasions, and on a few of these, as in the underseen *Anything Can Happen*, he even successfully incorporated warmth and vulnerability into his persona.

This vulnerability would not be evident at all in his next film, Stanley Kramer's *Ship of Fools* (1965), written by Abby Mann from the bestseller by Katherine Ann Porter. Porter's novel is about the passengers and crew of the *Vera*, a German passenger freighter headed from Vera Cruz, Mexico, to Bremerhaven in 1933. Mann (who had scripted Kramer's *Judgment at Nuremberg*) freely admitted his adaptation differs from the original: "To make the picture, I didn't feel I had to be true to anything about the novel except its theme and its intention . . . unless I made these changes, nobody would look at the movie. It would be too long, too many people, too little action."

Even with Mann's streamlining, this version of *Ship of Fools* boasts an impressive cast enacting the interwoven tales of love, misplaced hope, disillusionment, and destiny. Kramer's cast, consisting of twenty-five principal characters, included Simone Signoret as a fallen countess, Oskar Werner as the idealistic ship doctor, Vivien Leigh as a disillusioned American divorcee, Lee Marvin as a vulgar ballplayer, Elizabeth Ashley and George Segal as a young American couple, Michael Dunn as a sardonic, philosophical dwarf, and German actor Heinz Ruehmann as a German Jew who remains loyal to his fatherland, even as it is threatens to destroy him.

Kramer selected Ferrer for the part of a loud-mouthed publisher, the kind of man with a wife at home and a mistress onboard, the latter played Nicole Courcel, who had been with Ferrer in *Stop Train 349* (it was he who suggested she be cast for this film). He is the embodiment of the anti-Semitic German who welcomed Hitler's advance to power, a dangerous buffoon who professes "some of my best friends are Jews" while scheming to ostracize the Jewish passengers onboard the ship. As Kramer recalled, the part is "a German who professes to have no prejudice, but he preaches racist nonsense in stentorian tones." Kramer cast Ferrer thinking the role would be a sharp contrast to his Iago or the wise Cyrano. According to Kramer, Ferrer's role was "a thoughtless bigot, the kind who paved the way for Hitler's rise in Germany." He believed Ferrer would be ideal for the part because he believed that "Ferrer had the range, power, and simplicity to convey why Hitler's message found an enthusiastic reception among the German people."

Ferrer is effective in the early going, commandeering the captain's table, proclaiming his pride in Germany, flaunting his mistress, and scheming to get the proud, dignified Jew (Ruehmann) moved to another table. He also shares an amusing scene with Ruehmann as his unwilling roommate, grudgingly listening to Ruehmann's attempts to be civil and then attempting to sleep despite Ruehmann's snoring. The problem with Ferrer's portrayal is that, as with *Stop Train 349*, he relies on volume and bombast, and the accumulated effect is wearying, and needlessly transparent. If the viewers aren't taken in by his proclamations, why are these seemingly intelligent passengers? As in *Stop Train 349*, it's all style and little substance. There are some surface effects, but the character is painted with strokes too broad to be entirely effective. Nevertheless, Ferrer did come in for his share of praise when the film was released in 1965, with the *Hollywood Reporter* calling him "indelibly vulgar" and saying that he gave "a superior performance."

Oddly enough, Ferrer's role in *Ship of Fools* contributed to his desire to do more in the light entertainment side of show business, specifically comedy and music. He would remind people that his first Broadway play was a comedy (*Spring Dance*), that his first hit (*Brother Rat*) was a comedy, and that even his role in *Ship of Fools* was a comic one ("even though I play an SOB Nazi"). Ferrer signed on to do another guest spot in Danny Kaye's hit show and he would tell reporters that his true motivation was "to establish myself as a song and dance sort of performer . . . why? For several reasons . . . obviously it would increase my employability and I can use the dough. Secondly, I just happen to love to sing." Monsita Ferrer recalled that her father "loved music. He would say 'you can't do a musical and not be happy.' He would find himself in such a depression after a serious film, like *I Accuse*." Could it be that he wanted to compete with his more obviously talented spouse, or maybe even seek to have her collaborate with him in his musical endeavors? While Ferrer didn't address the former (this writer believes that was part of his motivation, even if he didn't acknowledge it), he played down the possibility of teaming with his relatively recently reconciled Rosemary. "No, she doesn't need me," he would tell entertainment columnist Hal Humphrey. "She sells what she does best—great singing. She's a solo star. We're relaxed about our careers because we're relaxed about our basic talents. I want to stand on my own two feet as a music attraction." It's possible that Ferrer was counting on television to do this; according to Monsita, "My father would forever be looking for ways to reinvent himself."

Ferrer would have another opportunity to prove his mettle in musical comedy and show that he was more than a "highbrow," courtesy of Melodyland Theater, which was presenting *A Funny Thing Happened on the Way to the Forum*, with music and lyrics by Stephen Sondheim. The show was a success when it opened on Broadway in 1962, where it also benefited from a dynamic star performance from Zero Mostel. The madcap musical comedy, set in ancient Rome amongst some very lusty Roman households, centers on Pseudolus, a Roman slave trying to buy his freedom by finding a virgin for his master, Hero. Many complications ensue.

Ferrer was cast in Mostel's role, the resourceful Pseudolus who begins the show with a rouser that has become a comic anthem, "Comedy Tonight." Carrying the show was a challenge that Ferrer relished, especially since he loved musicals and wanted to disprove those who thought he lacked the common touch: "I love good vaudeville, good burlesque, slapstick. . . . As a performer I have rarely had a play that lifts me up unto my toes, leaves me exhilarated. This damn show picks you up every time you play it." At the same time, he was sanguine (for him) about the possibility of directing more movies, as neither *The Chapman Report* nor *The Long Ships* had panned out for him: "You slit your wrists and pour your blood into directing a picture, and then some resident genius who has never created anything, takes your work and hacks it into something you can't recognize."

Ferrer would earn good notices from his limited *Forum* engagement. Cecil Smith found that the "great classical actor is right at home in these wild and bawdy and often uproariously funny proceedings," singling out the work of Ferrer, Iggie Wolfington, Ben Lessy, and Paul Jayson for their handling of both the double entendre lyrics of "Everybody Ought to Have a Maid" and the accompanying soft-shoe, "a number that brings down the house."

After the two-week run was over in July 1965, Ferrer had more time to spend at home, and though he would always be good with the kids, things would become strained between him and Clooney. According to Clooney, one of the problems was her increasing dependency on drugs, especially "downers," a problem Ferrer addressed in a roundabout way since the two were rarely communicating by that time. As for Ferrer, Clooney would recall that "Joe was still waiting for the phone to ring, insisting we eat dinners on trays in the den so he wouldn't miss a call." When he lashed out, it would be at things; one day, son Miguel's drum set bore the brunt of Ferrer's wrath, another time it was the children's bikes. On one occasion when Clooney tried to tell Ferrer his break would come, he mimicked her and told her that things always came easy for her. When she replied it wasn't true, Ferrer said, "I have to work for everything we have," leading Clooney to retort with: "Hey, I'm the one who works damn hard. It's my work that pays the bills!" Clooney would write that after Ferrer replied, "This is what you call work?" he proceeded to smash several of her records against the wall.

In April 1966, Ferrer and Clooney separated, and on August 17, she again filed for divorce, citing extreme cruelty. During this period, Ferrer left their Beverly Hills home, having lined up a few projects. Actor Edward G. Robinson was about to start filming *Cervantes, the Magnificent Fool* (it would undergo numerous title changes) in Spain with Alain Delon, under Hollywood veteran Vincent Sherman's direction. However, Robinson was injured in a car accident and had to drop out; the delay (and some salary demands) led to Delon leaving the film, and when shooting began in July 1966, Ferrer and Horst Buchholz (as Cervantes) would lead the cast. The film would cover Cervantes's early life, including his time in Algeria and being taken prisoner by the Turks. Louis Jourdan and Gina Lollobrigida were also in the cast, but director Sherman's hopes for success were thwarted by the chaotic filming, the international cast (nobody understood each other), lack of financing, and finally, the decision to re-edit the film to resemble an action movie. Sherman tried but failed to remove his name from the credits. *Cervantes, the Young Rebel* would barely receive an American release, though it did well in Europe.

Besides *Cervantes*, Ferrer received a rare chance to costar in a film comedy when he finally accepted a role in Carl Reiner's directorial debut, *Enter Laughing*. Reiner also co-wrote the script, which was adapted from his own "autobiographical" novel (and subsequent play by Joseph Stein). *Enter Laughing* had run for over a year on Broadway when it was produced in 1962, starring Alan Arkin as an aspiring Jewish actor (based on Reiner) in the 1930s who joins a shoestring theater company run by an aging, alcoholic would-be impresario. For the film, Reiner cast the young Reni Santoni (having seen Santoni's appearances on *The Merv Griffin Show*) as the brash young lead, Shelley Winters and David Opatoshu as his parents, Jack Gilford as his skeptical but understanding employer, and Ferrer as the producer/director/actor.

Initially, Ferrer said no but Reiner persisted, telling Ferrer how much he loved his piano playing and storytelling at the Stage Door Canteen. After some more flattery, Ferrer finally relented, and the result is one of his better later performances. Ferrer's Harrison B. Marlowe is a pleasure to watch, whether patiently enduring Santoni's audition, coping with his sex-starved daughter (Elaine May) who wants the singularly untalented Santoni in the play, or directing the dense Santoni while armed with both a hidden flask and a knotted kerchief on the head (Monsita would say that it was her own father's kerchief, knotted in four corners the way the elder Ferrer had). Critic Charles Champlin found Ferrer "splendidly hammy" while *Film Daily* thought that Ferrer "bellows and bounces about in grand style."

While filming *Enter Laughing*, Ferrer was also engaged in what he believed would be the final stages of adapting Thomas Mann's *Death in Venice* for the screen. Mann's original novella would have been a daring work for any filmmaker, as it deals with an author suffering from writer's block who is liberated by the stunning youth he meets while in Venice. Ferrer had acquired the rights in 1963 with the intention of both acting and directing, but there were early problems with the script. Ferrer, who felt it had too much voiceover, would collaborate on an outline with Harry Craig. Besides the problems of making an adaptation, contract difficulties with Mann's widow, Katia, would lead to further delays, as there were disputes over copyright.

Even though Ferrer had intended to play the lead of the obsessed writer, Laurence Olivier expressed an interest in playing the part, though he did not firmly commit. Later, Max von Sydow would also be interested in the role, but he wanted some creative control over the script (though he agreed with Ferrer that there should be less voiceover). A budget was drawn up, with Ferrer to receive $100,000 for directing and $25,000 for producing, plus an undisclosed sum for co-writing. Von Sydow then announced that should the film proceed he would require $250,000 for his services. This demand swiftly made von Sydow into a former cast member. Ferrer then sent John Gielgud the script, which the actor returned.

Months would pass, with Ferrer waiting for some pages from Craig. After he received a working script from Craig (who had been abroad), Ferrer sent a copy to several actors, including Burt Lancaster; again, they all returned the script and politely declined. By early 1967, director Luchino Visconti told Ferrer he would like to purchase the option; after some protracted negotiations, Ferrer settled for a lump sum of $37,000 and Visconti proceeded to make the film starring Dirk Bogarde. It was yet another example of how Ferrer would invest himself in a prospective project only to be thwarted by the demands and caprice of others. It did not deter Ferrer from initiating other projects and continuing to collaborate with fellow writers in an attempt to navigate the minefields of modern-day filmmaking.

Ferrer's next creative endeavor would find him on Broadway again, with yet another lead in a musical. *Man of La Mancha*. starring Richard Kiley as Cervantes/Don Quixote, had been playing Broadway to huge grosses since it opened in 1965, and the producers were planning to cast the road company version. In addition, Kiley would be going on a two-week vacation and they needed someone with star power and a commanding presence to replace him. It might have come as a surprise for Ferrer to be considered, especially with the lukewarm *The Girl Who Came to Supper* still in people's memories. Ferrer was asked to audition to see if he could deliver the goods, since the part of Don Quixote was a much more dramatically and musically demanding one than the relatively lightweight Prince. Rafael would recall that the producers made his father audition five times: "They didn't trust my father's singing, but he really, really wanted the part." Although he had to endure a period of waiting, Ferrer finally got the role and proceeded to play the part not only on Broadway but in the subsequent touring company for almost a year. A return Broadway engagement took place in 1969. (Together with his work on the film *Cervantes* in Europe, the author was very much a part of Ferrer's life during this time.)

Ferrer's understudy during the run was a young actor named Tim Jerome, who went on to be nominated for a Tony for his performance in *Me and My Girl*. Jerome, who was twenty-four at the time, played Dr. Carrasco when he wasn't going on for Ferrer. As Jerome recalled, "I only went on for him *once*—and that was because his son was graduating. I'll tell you about José. He called the entire company for a rehearsal with *me* in the role and directed that rehearsal. He didn't have to do that, but he did it for me." According to Jerome, it was a very happy company, and Ferrer was fortunate to have Tony Martinez as his Sancho, since they were good friends and had known each other from Puerto Rico. Jerome remembered that Ferrer was incredible to work with onstage: "He looked you in the eye . . . totally consumed in the character, but with some humor behind the eyes." Jerome explained that what he derived from Ferrer was the nature of the onstage connection between two people at the same time: "You're yourself the actor and you're the character. The 'you' that you are is hidden—you want the audience to suspend their disbelief. You want the audience to think something *real* is going on. Theater is a ritual: actor and character, but you don't see the actor."

Actress and singer Jana Robbins, who joined the road company straight out of college as an understudy for Maura K. Wedge as Aldonza/Dulcinea, also had much to say about working with the formidable Ferrer. She attested to his acting expertise: "You saw a *performance*—he delivered every night. Joe never walked through anything. He was consistent on stage—he couldn't sing. He would talk-sing 'The Impossible Dream.' He acted it extremely well."

However, this would not be the first impression Robbins had of her future costar. A few days after joining the company in Dallas, Texas, and before going onstage with Ferrer for the first time, Ferrer invited Robbins to a dinner party honoring him. "He picked me up in a big car—me, the driver, and José. The dinner was in a private room, maybe forty to fifty people, and he never talked to me. On the ride home, we're seated in the backseat, and all of a sudden, he lunged at me and kissed me! I pushed him away and said, 'I'm shocked! I need you to know I'm engaged!' 'I'll get out here.' You know, if he was interested, he could have talked to me, flirted with me . . . there are so many things he might have done. There was no finesse . . . he just lunged!" A few days later, Robbins made her first appearance onstage with Ferrer. "I got through the performance, and there's this beautiful last scene, and I have to walk past Ferrer, whose character was on the floor dying. After the show, the stage manager knocks on the door with a note from José, which read: 'Please don't step on my feet.'" When one hears about these incidents, one is disappointed and disturbed on various levels. Perhaps Ferrer had done this before. It is possible that he acted this way because he just expected actresses would be consenting partners all too willing to succumb to the power of celebrity and his presumed charm? Yet to hear others tell it (like Robert Relyea from *High Cost of Loving*), there were several women who called the set looking for Ferrer. Would someone like Ferrer be able to survive in our current era, in light of the wave of female empowerment that has taken a long time to arrive?

It is remarkable that, in spite of Ferrer's initial boorish advances, Robbins got to know the actor mainly through social outings with him and Stella—and after she got married to her college sweetheart. Robbins, who remains active both as a performer and producer, now feels that she came out of the entire experience "feeling great. That he let it go and respected me." Robbins also got to know Stella, who was officially Ferrer's secretary (but, according to both Robbins and Jerome, "everyone knew they were together"). Having spent many evenings with Ferrer and Stella, Robbins saw Stella as "elegant, efficient, soft-spoken but firm. She was respectful and respected, as was he—when he wasn't misbehaving!"

For someone whose confidence had suffered a jolt with the premature closing of his previous Broadway musical outing, Ferrer's success as Don Quixote/Cervantes, both musically and dramatically, was an extremely gratifying interlude for the actor whose talents in this area had been downplayed and even denigrated by many, including his soon-to-be former spouse, Rosemary Clooney. In late 1967, Clooney's divorce from Ferrer would become final. Maria would recall that day at the Santa Monica courthouse: "I remember my father and mother coming out separate doors at the courthouse; I was devastated."

Despite this being their second divorce, with all of its apparent finality, the story didn't really end for Clooney and Ferrer—and not just because of their devotion to the kids. Monsita said, "For my mom and dad, they were the love of each other's lives. I never knew Mom to act the way she did around Daddy. Their love affair continued even after their second divorce. . . . A gift my Mom gave was the way she loved Dad. Mom always said unequivocally that 'what happened is between us. Your dad loves you—don't forget that. He loves you; he is an amazing dad.' All of us had a fantastic relationship with my Dad."

Ferrer was adrift both personally and professionally, and for the fifty-three-year-old Ferrer, the next twenty-five years would find him struggling to find his footing in an industry that was intent on keeping the accent on youth and forgetting those who had previously scaled the heights and were now descending to earth.

CHAPTER 16

Paying the Bills—the Movies, 1967–92

IN THE AFTERMATH OF THE DIVORCE, AND WITH HIS *LA MANCHA* COM-mitment winding down in 1967, the fifty-four-year-old Ferrer had no immediate film or television prospects, and for a man of Ferrer's work ethic, sitting idle was impossible—for him, as well as for those around him. He was also faced with a whopping tax bill because of some questionable claims and deductions that were made in 1962. Ferrer had gone to Europe to film *Nine Hours to Rama*, *Lawrence of Arabia*, and *Cyrano et d'Artagnan*, with taxable income amounting to over $225,000. However, Ferrer claimed this income was exempt because he was a bona fide resident overseas—and not a resident of the United States at this time. He also filed for certain deductions, including the cost of his personal secretary, Stella Magee. At first, the Internal Revenue Service concurred, but later it reversed its findings. The IRS found that while Ferrer was in Europe and India, he was staying in a series of hotels and temporary accommodations, in no way making him a "bona fide resident." Many of Ferrer's deductions were disallowed (though he was granted the secretarial expense for Miss Magee), and the final tax bill amounted to $122,000.

Ferrer presumably had holdings in Puerto Rico, but it might have been the combination of this unforeseen financial calamity—and the lack of promising offers—that would lead Ferrer to make some curious choices over the years, both in film and television. In interviews, Ferrer admitted that he had made some bad artistic and personal decisions, alienated some he had not been in the position to alienate, and refused to curry favor with those in power (much like Cyrano). He also felt, not without justification, that older actors in America were not treated with the same level of respect as older actors in England. Ferrer believed that, as an actor, he still had plenty left to give. As far as the movies were concerned, what they would offer Ferrer was the occasional strong, featured role in a major film, one or two leads in minor fare, and many parts that were little more than cameos. Ferrer knew he could and should have been offered better parts, but he said, "I don't bear resentment. I was fifty when I made *Lawrence of Arabia*. In the years that followed, I should have been doing things that taxed my ability as an actor. I didn't get them. Instead, I played bankers and doctors and corrupt businessmen and did guest shots on TV. Actors in Europe are more fortunate. Richardson and Gielgud go on doing fine work. Pinter writes plays for them. Here, the older actor is refuse. If I could afford it, I'd never act again. . . . I'm only doing things that pay the bills."

As Ferrer was officially divorced from Clooney, he was now openly seeing Stella Magee, who was British-born and had been Ferrer's secretary when he was filming in Europe. There is not much on record about his actual courtship of Stella, and Ferrer was content for it to remain that way. Ferrer's marriage to Clooney had kept them both in the spotlight and in the tabloids; he was happy not to be hounded in his personal life. Before they married in 1977, Ferrer would refer to Stella in print as his lady friend. Later, he would say that he was happily married to "an English girl. She's a wife. She spends 24 hours a day worrying how to make me happy. She's so caring and so solicitous that she brings tears to my eyes because I don't think I deserve it. But I've got it and I appreciate it." Rafael observed the relationship and believes "she loved him . . . they loved each other."

One persistent newsworthy item (as far as the tabloids were concerned) about their evolving relationship pertained to the earring that Ferrer began wearing in the mid-1970s. Ferrer would tell interviewers that he had grown bored by listening to his lady friend talking so much about getting her ears pierced that he decided to get his done also. In reality, according to his son Rafael, Stella was afraid to get her ears pierced, so helpful husband José accompanied her and in a show of solidarity, got his own ear pierced. As Ferrer would say, "It's more masculine. Now, she doesn't say a word, and everybody talks about *my* ear." Ferrer would often incorporate an earring into a television or film role, including his appearances in *Fedora*, *Paco*, and *The Fifth Musketeer*.

One can peruse the Ferrer filmography from the late 1960s through the late 1980s and easily find several candidates for the "What is *José*

Ferrer Doing Here?" Award. At a cursory glance, one might think the winner to be *Zoltan, Hound of Dracula,* or as it was better known on its 1978 release, *Dracula's Dog.* The casual reader might glimpse the title and ask, "What is *Ferrer* doing here?" but having finally seen the film recently, I was pleasantly surprised. It's actually an enjoyable horror tale. The premise is that Dracula's dog, Zoltan, has been sent to America to bite Michael Pataki, who plays Dracula's last living descendant. Ferrer gives an assured, restrained performance as Transylvanian Inspector Branco, a dignified, persistent Van Helsing-type on hand to hunt the dog and protect Pataki and his family. Director Albert Band manages to achieve a good sense of atmosphere, a couple of jolts, and a tense scene with Ferrer and Pataki trapped in a cabin holding off an attack of killer dogs.

Albert Band's son, Charles, had directed Ferrer in the 1976 film *Crash,* which had a wilder premise than *Dracula's Dog.* In *Crash,* Ferrer was a supposedly invalid husband, intent on killing his wife (Sue Lyon) whom he believes is trying to kill him. He may not be wrong, since during the course of the film, it's revealed she does have certain occult powers—one of which involves a car that's tearing up the streets of Los Angeles. The cast includes veterans who had seen better days, among them Lyon (*Lolita*), Leslie Parrish (*The Manchurian Candidate*), and John Ericson (whom Ferrer had directed in *Stalag 17*), and all provide as much conviction as the material will allow. Ferrer is in good form, feigning helplessness while planning to rid himself of his wife; he gives the lines with more weight and bite than they warrant. While Ferrer can't quite make the character's climactic choices believable (it is when the car takes control at the end that the movie loses its edge), no one could accuse him of phoning it in.

Which brings one to what may be his true cinematic nadir—not only for Ferrer but for costar James Earl Jones, too. It's a turgid, would-be horror film/travelogue called *Blood Tide,* written and produced by Nico Mastorakis, and directed by recent film-school graduate Richard Jeffries. Filmed in Greece in 1980, it revolves around a treasure hunter (Jones) who unleashes a monster after explosions he has set. Martin Kove and Mary Louise Weller were the leads, while Ferrer played a glum villager. The amount of waste in the $2 million film is staggering. It fails as a travelogue, it conjures no shocks, and it criminally misuses two of the major classical actors of the century. It's dispiriting to watch Ferrer and Jones share a scene, and not have one credible, noteworthy thing to say. There are several moments where Jones's character spouts snippets of Shakespearean verse, mainly because producer Mastorakis thought it would be a good idea. The only amusing line to emerge from this dreck is when

Jones's girlfriend comments that "he once played Othello in college and never got over it." The only possible answer for Ferrer's presence would be the free Grecian getaway—but even then, the cost was too high.

There would also be many Ferrer cameos throughout this period, some barely reaching two minutes in length. Some of these appearances were in the horror genre, such as 1980's *The Sentinel*, about a beautiful model (Cristina Raines) who moves into a New York brownstone where things begin to go bump in the night. Director Michael Winner had several stars putting in brief but showy appearances, including Ava Gardner as a real estate agent, Martin Balsam as a professor, Burgess Meredith as a neighbor, and the priestly trio of John Carradine (blind and sinister), Arthur Kennedy (a concerned cleric), and finally, Ferrer, whose major function is to do some solemn intonations at the beginning and at various points in the narrative. He would make similarly fleeting appearances in other genre pictures, including *Bloody Birthday* (1981) and *The Being* (1983).

The billing was larger for Larry Cohen's long-delayed *The Private Files of J. Edgar Hoover*, but the screen time was about the same. The project was first announced in 1976 with a 1977 release date, but it did not reach theaters until 1978. Writer/director Cohen initially wanted Charles Durning to play the older Hoover in an episodic story that would follow Hoover from the days of Dillinger through his involvement in the Red Scare. His personal life with lifelong companion Clyde Tolson (to whom Hoover left his estate) would also be examined. The film would purport to show the real Hoover, who was always helping presidents violate the law and then use that knowledge against them. José Ferrer was one of the first names announced in a cast that would include Jack Cassidy (in his last role), Celeste Holm, Lloyd Nolan, Dan Dailey (as Tolson), with James Wainwright and Broderick Crawford as the younger and older Hoover, respectively. Ferrer played Lionel McCoy, the associate director of the FBI and most of his very limited screen time consisted of briefing certain agents in hallways or defending the agency's actions. J. Hoberman of the *Village Voice* called it "pulp of the highest order," but much of the critical discourse had to do with the disparity in appearance between Wainwright and Crawford.

Ferrer was involved with several all-star projects in the late 1970s and early '80s, with producers paying well for distinguished actors to round out casts and contribute an aura of sophistication and expertise that would both elevate the written word and attract audiences to the theaters. There would be battles over billing, which were largely settled with the main star (or two) sharing the top spot and everyone else relegated to alphabetical order. When a third or fourth star was too big for either the top slots or be crammed into the alphabetically decided cast, there would be the credit "and so-and-so distinguished star."

One such epic that seemed promising was a loose remake of the Alexandre Dumas swashbuckler *The Man in the Iron Mask*. This version, initially called *Beyond the Iron Mask*, began filming in 1976. It was later retitled *The Fifth Musketeer* upon its release in 1979, and featured an aging D'Artagnan and his three musketeers springing into action to protect their protégé Phillippe from the evil machinations of twin brother King Louis XIV and his scheming minister Fouquet—namely, their plan to permanently lock Philippe in the Bastille in the dreaded iron mask. Cornel Wilde would star as loyal D'Artagnan while Beau Bridges had the dual roles of Louis and Philippe. Ian McShane was Fouquet, Rex Harrison the chief minister, Ursula Andress and Sylvia Kristel the mistress and fiancé of Louis, respectively (apparently the king was a busy fellow). There was also a "special" appearance by Olivia de Havilland as the queen. Ferrer portrayed Athos, with the other musketeers played by Alan Hale (whose father saw his share of action with Errol Flynn) and Lloyd Bridges (father of Beau). For Ferrer, the prospect of engaging in swordplay and swashbuckling, as well as the location shooting in Vienna, was enough to brighten his spirits (one can see these four aging but antic musketeers cavorting on the 1976 television special *Perry Como Christmas in Austria*, shot in Vienna when the film was still called *Beyond the Iron Mask*).

It's a shame that the resulting film, *The Fifth Musketeer*, lacks the verve and panache of its predecessors. The action is uninspired (save for some moments at the climax) and the script by David Ambrose is pedestrian, but the biggest disappointment is the lack of characterization afforded the musketeers. They're "all for one, and one for all," but there is little interaction among Athos, Porthos, and Aramis, and little effort given to differentiate them. Why assemble all these fine actors and give them relatively little worthwhile to say; the scenarist saved the best lines for McShane's Fouquet, at the expense of the other characters.

One of the more prestigious later projects for Ferrer was his participation in *Voyage of the Damned*, directed by Stuart Rosenberg (*Cool Hand Luke*) and produced by Lord Lew Grade. Sir Grade was known for his big-budget, all-star productions of the late 1970s and early '80s (though some of the quality led to his sobriquet "Lord Low Grade"). *Voyage of the Damned*, from 1976, was his first production and one of his most ambitious efforts. Reminiscent of *Ship of Fools* in terms of the time period and its shipboard of disparate characters, this *Voyage* was different in that it was based on a regrettable historical event. In 1939, the German government had allowed approximately 900 German Jews to buy passage on a Cuba-bound passenger ship sailing from Hamburg—however, Germany did not inform the steamship that Cuba had denied their landing permit before the ship had even sailed. It would become clear that Germany was using the voyage to see if other countries would allow the Jewish passengers entry.

The star-studded cast of passengers, shipboard officials, and various politicians and diplomats included Max von Sydow as the humane captain, Faye Dunaway and Oskar Werner (from *Ship of Fools*) as a prominent lecturer and his wife, James Mason as a sympathetic Cuban official, Orson Welles as a Cuban industrialist, Luther Adler and Wendy Hiller as a dying professor and his wife, in addition to Julie Harris, Nehemiah Persoff, Sam Wanamaker, and Maria Schell as other weary, desperate passengers. Ferrer plays a corrupt Cuban official, only too happy to profit from some of the more desperate and solvent passengers when the ship is docked in Cuba. The movie alternates between scenes of great depth and other scenes awash in sentimentality, but the scenes showcasing Ferrer's venal bureaucrat parrying with other officials show the actor to be in fine fettle. It's a small part that benefits from Ferrer's controlled playing. As critic Rex Reed noted, the film's strength was in the acting, singling out "José Ferrer's stupid yet conniving smirk as the corrupt Cuban immigration officer who holds many trump cards in his slippery fingers."

One role that Ferrer had never gotten around to playing was that of an emperor, but innovative, visionary director David Lynch (*Eraserhead*) rectified this when he cast Ferrer in his ambitious 1984 adaptation/condensation of Frank Herbert's seminal fantasy novel *Dune*. Ferrer would be Shaddam IV, the malevolent Padisham, Emperor of the Universe. Shaddam IV was similar in spirit to his King Herod in *The Greatest Story Ever Told* in that, like Herod, the emperor is obsessed with scouring the universe to locate the Chosen One. In this case, it was a young Kyle MacLachlan as the hero and Sean Young as his staunch ally and eventual love interest. The young MacLachlan was cast in the title role soon after graduating from college, and he would enjoy working with the veteran Ferrer: "It was wonderful. José was a lovely guy. Would always come to work wearing golf pants. And he would go off when we finished and play golf."

Director Lynch came in for his share of praise from Ferrer, even though the actor disclosed, not for the first time, that if he could afford to stop acting, he would do so. Despite his feelings about show business in general, Ferrer insisted that *"Dune* was very good for me and Lynch was interesting to work with. He works very quietly and very privately. He's very explicit about what he wants; he could tell me in three words and that was it."

While there was room in Lynch's reimagining of *Dune* to allow for some effective (and exaggerated) histrionics, notably from Kenneth Mc-Millan and Sting, most of the other performers, Ferrer included, had little opportunity to make more than a slight impression. The critics found *Dune* to be a disappointment (though its author Frank Herbert would be one of its biggest champions), and this was echoed in director Lynch's frank assessment: "I started selling out in *Dune*. I probably shouldn't have done the picture, but I saw tons of possibilities. There was so much room to create a world . . . but I got strong indications from [producers] Raf-faella and Dino De Laurentis about what kind of film they expected, and I knew I didn't have final cut . . . little by little, every decision was made with them in mind." Lynch's words echo the situation that director Fer-rer found himself immersed in during the late 1950s, as he battled and compromised with producers who held fast to the bottom line, whether financial, creative, or both.

Perhaps Ferrer's most ludicrous appearance in a major film occurred in the 1978 production of Irwin Allen's *The Swarm*. One cannot really ask "What is Ferrer Doing Here?" because it was pretty obvious. It was the chance to get a nice paycheck and make an impression in an all-star film among such sterling company as Henry Fonda, Michael Caine, Katharine Ross, Richard Widmark, Richard Chamberlain, Fred MacMur-ray, Ben Johnson, and Olivia de Havilland (the last three engaged in an unfortunate later-in-life onscreen triangle). The premise had to do with a swarm of killer bees wreaking havoc on the populace, and the efforts of scientists (Caine, Fonda, Ross) and a military official (Widmark) to subdue the threat.

The fact that the disaster movie genre popularized by producers like Irwin Allen had been already played out was of little concern to the il-lustrious talent. Ferrer has one scene, which he was able to complete in one day by crossing from one Universal soundstage (he was filming the TV miniseries *Return of Captain Nemo*) to another. Yet the scene was one of the most ludicrous any major actor was ever involved in—here, Ferrer plays the head of one of those high-tech laboratories, and when informed about "the swarm," he loudly informs his scene partner Richard Chamberlain that "there are no bees here, this is a secure installation, there could never be any bees here." And, of course, cue the invading bees for the deadly punch line, complete with a slow-motion close-up of Ferrer agonizingly engulfed by the little buzzers. It's brief, ridiculous, and memorable for all the wrong reasons—one can only hope that Ferrer was well-compensated.

Somewhat more interesting was his brief turn in the 1984 Charles Bronson action film *The Evil that Men Do*. Bronson is a retired assassin living on an island paradise and Ferrer is a humanitarian doctor who visits Bronson to persuade him to come out of retirement and assassinate Joseph Maher's evil, influential doctor (a Mengele in everything but name). Ferrer's doctor is strictly a functional character as he is somewhat of a "Basil Exposition" here, detailing Maher's atrocities and encouraging Bronson to "do the right thing." This involves not only eliminating Maher but also several corrupt government officials and unlucky henchmen. Even with the limited screen time (Ferrer's doctor disappears after the first fifteen minutes), the actor exudes compassion and some barbed wit amid the stream of exposition he provides; his presence even seems to energize Bronson, and the two play well off each other. However, Ferrer's real role is to goad Bronson into action—and, once he does, it's Bronson's film (with Theresa Saldana along as aide and love interest).

Ferrer also returned to his native Puerto Rico for a small role in the little-known 1979 release *A Life of Sin*. The film received attention at the time as the first movie produced in Puerto Rico with a budget in excess of $1 million; the movie also attracted some criticism since these investors insisted that the actors deliver their lines in English. The film starred Puerto Rican actress Miriam Colon as Isabel la Negra, a woman who becomes a famed Caribbean madam and philanthropist, and Raul Julia as Pablo, her partner and eventual betrayer. Ferrer was cast as a bishop who accepts Isabel's money while proceeding to damn her from the pulpit for her presumed wickedness after she is killed.

As was the case when Ferrer had been in his prime, there were the efforts that never made it to the screen. A huge disappointment for Ferrer occurred with the collapse of the Lina Wertmuller film, *Tuetre D'Agreste*, in which he was supposed to star with Sophia Loren. He had initially been enthused about the film, which was to be filmed in Italy: "I went in good faith. Why not? After all it was a film with Sophia Loren and Lina Wertmuller. But apparently there was trouble with the financing. From what I've read, she had good reason for backing out." Ferrer had spent a week in Rome on his own dime, since his travel money had never come through: "I was in Rome waiting to start. Then they told me Sophia wasn't doing the film . . . so I flew home. I wound up paying for my own trip here." It was experiences like this that would cause the actor to question his own worth, wondering whether there was something about his personality on the screen that is not particularly satisfying to an audience. As for continuing to act, he would say, "What's the point? I'm not doing anything that satisfies the soul—I'm only doing things that pay the bills." While Ferrer continually expressed gratitude for all his good, former roles (especially *Cyrano* and *Moulin Rouge*), the now sixty-plus actor also pointed out that "I can't say I wake up these mornings eager to get to work."

Among Ferrer's confidants was the actor Alexander Knox, who would appear with Ferrer in "Truman at Potsdam" as part of for television's *Hallmark Hall of Fame*. In a letter to Knox from around 1974, Ferrer would refer to projects that didn't develop: "David Susskind wanted to work with me on a project—then silence. I also contacted Ed Flanders and John Huston—there was more silence." In a later letter to Knox in 1987, after completing work on another less-than-stellar assignment, Ferrer wrote, "I may retire after this one. I'm not sure I want to continue putting myself through this agony."

Hidden among the plethora of all-star, occasionally bloated melodramas of the 1970s and '80s are a few relatively obscure entries in the Ferrer filmography. These were small-to-medium-budget efforts in films that might be classified now as simple, gentle family films. Ferrer received top billing in these films, though the leading roles were actually played by talented juvenile actors. Ferrer was on hand in both as the wise older gentleman, offering advice or refuge (or both) to the impressionable young leads. In both films, Ferrer appeared in his low-key but expressive mode, lending nuance to characters that easily could become overly sentimental.

Forever Young, Forever Free, from 1975, was the more accomplished effort, and more personally rewarding to Ferrer. A poignant drama filmed in both New York and Africa, Ferrer took the role, in part, for the opportunity to visit South Africa, "a place I might never get to on my own." He was also accompanied by four of his children, including Maria, who was also serving as the third assistant director. When he wasn't filming, Ferrer and family took several excursions, including trips to Cape Town and Johannesburg. He would be especially impressed with the Mala Mala Game Preserve, with its magnificent wildlife, which he found "a bit unnerving when viewed through an open land rover." He was also able to meet with famed *Cry, the Beloved Country* author Alan Paton, one of Ferrer's favorite authors.

Forever Young, Forever Free was the first joint production of Ely Landau and the Film Trust Group, written and directed by Ashley Lazarus from a story by Andre Pieterse (chairman of Film Trust). In addition to Ferrer, television star Karen Valentine would make her film debut, but the real stars would be the two child actors Norman Knox and Muntu Ndebele. The film centers on an Italian priest (Ferrer) and a Peace Corps volunteer (Valentine) who oversee the relationship between a white orphan boy (Knox) brought up in a Lesotho mission and the black herd boy (Ndebele) who becomes his faithful friend. The original title was *E Lollipop*, which was a reference to Ndebele's cry of delight. Ferrer viewed the project as a Walt Disney film made with sociopolitical overtones, and much was made of the contrast between life in rural Africa and the streets of New York, where the boys need to travel at one point in order to get the best medical attention. The two young leads are both exceptional, as they overcome some syrupy music (courtesy of Lee Holdridge) to establish the warmth of their bond.

Besides eliciting fine work from the two young leads, director/co-screenwriter Andrew Lazarus also took some unflinching looks at the harsh living conditions in Lesotho, and the difficulty for some (like the Valentine character) in observing that certain beliefs exist for a reason. Ferrer plays the priest as a dignified, devout, compassionate, and re-sourceful spiritual guide, whether he is trying to find the means to get to New York or alternately disciplining and playing mentor to the children, who remain devoted to each other despite some unexpected hurdles. *Forever Young, Forever Free* is a touching, underrated, underseen film that deserves a wider audience.

Less noteworthy was the 1976 *Paco*, directed by Robert Vincent O'Neill and costarring Pernell Roberts (still struggling to re-establish himself professionally after leaving the hit television series *Bonanza* in the early 1960s) and quirky character actor Allen Garfield. Filmed on location in Colombia, *Paco* tells the story of a young child (Panchito Gomez) who is trying to locate his uncle, who turns out to be a later-day Fagin running a gang of young thieves (and masquerading as an old, blind man to boot) but with a little more inner concern for his young charges. About a third of the way through the film, after establishing a gentle rapport between Ferrer's uncle and Paco, the film is then taken over by a planned heist by a film star blackmailed by a not-so-holy cleric Pernell Roberts. This star's hesitation to execute the daring heist gives way to a bit of bloodthirsty behavior when he realizes Paco can implicate him in the theft. It's left for Ferrer (who re-enters in the last twenty minutes) to assemble his young band of thieves to thwart the forces of evil and save Paco's life. Ferrer's performance earned some praise from the few who saw it in its initial release. One critic noted: "Ferrer, in prominent part and perky style, which keeps pacing lively and never permits it to descend into maudlin fare."

Ferrer later registered strongly in another low budget, but distinctively more adult work. *Natural Enemies*, written and directed by Jeff Kanew (his directorial debut) and based on a book by Julius Horowitz, is a downbeat but absorbing drama which received a very limited theatrical run in 1980. The premise concerns a successful, married publisher (Hal Holbrook) who wakes up one day and decides to kill his wife (Louise Fletcher) and children. Ferrer was cast as a family friend, a Holocaust survivor and author who has seen the horrors of the camps and consequently values, above all, the sanctity of human life. Ferrer makes the most of his two scenes with Holbrook, both of them understated without sacrificing intensity and emotional urgency. When he speaks about his experiences in the camps or suggests to Holbrook that he knows of Holbrook's intentions, Ferrer's penetrating eyes and expressive voice, coupled with Holbrook's mesmerizing performance, show that a "couple of guys sitting around talking" can make for a most compelling drama.

As Kanew would later recount, *Natural Enemies* was not the easiest experience for a neophyte director. Kanew acknowledged that the grim subject matter made it a strange choice, but he felt the need to do it; in fact, he produced it himself and subsequently lost all of his money: "People told me I'd get outside investors but the money never came in—I still feel good about it, even thought it was a learning experience and I didn't make a nickel." Another major obstacle was the on-set behavior of star Hal Holbrook: "He was testing me all the time. It was a complex script. He asked if I could handle it. I said, 'I'm pretty sure I can.' He was pretty insecure." When Kanew wanted to alter the book's dark ending to something perhaps a little more hopeful, Holbrook was adamant in retaining the bleak conclusion. "Holbrook told me, 'I don't want it to end this way. . . . I'm not doing it.'" Kanew grudgingly acquiesced, though when watching the film, and considering the events preceding, the director does manage to leave slight room for interpretation.

Ferrer was a different matter for Kanew; the actor was the writer/ director's first choice for the role as Kanew revered the older actor, especially his performance in *Crisis*. Ferrer and the other actors (including Holbrook and Fletcher) were willing to work for little or no money: "The reason I got him (Ferrer) was that he knew the producers . . . he didn't have to work too long, two hours one day, two hours another day."

Kanew was pleased with Ferrer's work and demeanor: "I was a novice. He was a pro. He was easy. The choices he made . . . he totally understood what he was doing. It was exactly the performance I wanted."

Apart from his appearance in *Natural Enemies*, Ferrer's best work in the late 1970s and early '80s would consist of three performances under the creative guidance of some major players in the fields of wit and humor: Billy Wilder, Mel Brooks, and Woody Allen. None of these films would be included among the major works in the filmmakers' respective canons, but in each film, Ferrer makes a notable contribution in roles both villainous and sympathetic.

Ferrer was finally able to work with Billy Wilder in the 1979 release *Fedora*, a movie which harkened back to the writer/director's earlier triumph with *Sunset Boulevard* in that the current film was also about a reclusive aging movie star, only this time she is pursued by a down-and-out producer (William Holden, solidifying the *Sunset* connection) to star in what would constitute a comeback feature for both of them. His efforts would inadvertently set in motion a chain of events that would lead to some unforeseen consequences and unexpected revelations.

A film about the fleeting nature of fame, as well as what some people will do to avoid the ravages of age and secure eternal youth, *Fedora* was not an easy film for the aging one-time wunderkind Wilder. Time (and the box office) had not been so kind to his recent films, among them *Avanti!* and *The Front Page*. Universal had hired Wilder to write an adaptation of Tom Tryon's novel *Crowned Heads*, but when they saw the script, the studio put the project in turnaround. (This may have been influenced by the failure of another Universal "inside Hollywood" release, 1976's *W. C. Fields and Me*, starring Rod Steiger as Fields and Valerie Perrine as his mistress, Carlotta Monti.) Wilder then had to scrounge around for some financing; he found some European investors and was able to shoot on location in Corfu and in German and French studios. Eventually, United Artists picked up the film for distribution (after the previous distributor, Allied Artists, dropped out).

William Holden appeared as the glib, desperate producer Barry "Dutch" Detweiler—a quarter-century after Holden's glib, desperate screenwriter Joe Gillis (and the ravages of time are etched into every orifice). Wilder also needed to cast an actress who projected both beauty and intelligence, as well as an aura of mystery. There were certain A-list names Wilder would have loved to use, such as Marlene Dietrich, who had been featured so memorably for the director in *A Foreign Affair* and *Witness for the Prosecution*. In the end, he had to settle for Marthe Keller, a Swiss-born actress who had just starred in *Marathon Man* and *Bobby Deerfield*. For the important role of the Countess, Wilder cast Hildegard Knef. Henry Fonda was also in the film, briefly, playing himself as the president of the Academy of Motion Picture Arts and Sciences.

As for Ferrer, he was cast as the mysterious Dr. Vando, confidant to the Countess and a plastic surgeon whose major function seems to be protecting Fedora from doing damage to herself and presenting the wrong image in public. As *Fedora* progresses, the viewer (and Dutch) learn much more about Dr. Vando, and his part in Fedora's enforced isolation from the world. It's a role that Ferrer plays with some relish, as it affords him the opportunity to deliver some biting lines and share a nicely charged scene with Holden in which each sizes up the other over some drinks in a rundown tavern. Ferrer also manages to endow the doctor with a degree of sympathy and humility not necessarily found in either the lines themselves or the developing storyline.

Upon its limited release in 1979, many reviewers compared *Fedora* unfavorably to Wilde's other films, especially *Sunset Boulevard*. There were those who differed and found much to admire in *Fedora*, such as Vincent Canby of the *New York Times*, who wrote that the film was "vintage Wilder, a seasoned, elegantly funny film." *New York* agreed with Canby and found that "Ferrer gives one of his liveliest performances as the debauched Dr. Vando." The biggest criticism had to do with the actress at the center; many believed Keller simply lacked the charisma necessary for the lead role. Wilder himself agreed with this consensus: "Casting was very difficult, but you get carried away and hope for the best. On *Sunset*, I was lucky enough to get Swanson . . . here it was more problematic. Looking back now, I have reservations about whether I should have undertaken it. Perhaps it was uncastable."

Ferrer would appear as a doctor of another kind in *To Be or Not to Be*, a 1983 remake of the 1942 Ernst Lubitsch classic starring Jack Benny and Carole Lombard. This new version of *To Be or Not to Be* was a Mel Brooks film in everything but the final credits. The production would be done under his newly formed Brooksfilms and would star Brooks alongside his wife, Anne Bancroft. Brooks had wanted to do the remake for a long time, but he was adamant that he not direct. The original *To Be or Not to Be*, as directed by Lubitsch, was a seamless blend of comedy and melodrama. It was set in Nazi-occupied Poland and depicted a Polish theatrical troupe that becomes involved with an American flyer and his attempts to thwart a traitor's plot to divulge the identities of those in the Polish Resistance movement. Perhaps Brooks didn't want the remake, which he hoped would be "more emotional, dig a little deeper," to be perceived as another madcap, "vulgar" Mel Brooks romp. Or maybe taking on the lead role, performing opposite wife Bancroft, singing, and dancing (the remake's theatrical company would be more of a vaudeville troupe) would be too much of a challenge for the seemingly inexhaustible Brooks if he also directed. In any case, Brooks eventually convinced longtime Brooks choreographer and associate Alan Johnson to direct, even after Johnson had repeatedly said no.

In the original as well as the remake, the traitor is Professor Siletski, a beloved Polish scholar who has secretly sold out to the Nazis. It is this role that Ferrer would undertake (played in the original by Stanley Ridges). According to Ferrer: "Siletski is a man only out for himself, he would sell his country and his mother down the river. Unfortunately, the world was and will always be filled with Siletskis." The role offered several opportunities for Ferrer to make an impression, all of which he capitalized on. In an early scene among patriotic Polish fighters, he feigns loyalty while managing to extract pertinent info, all of which proves damning for these soldiers' families. Later, in two exquisitely timed scenes with Bancroft (who knows of Siletski's deceit and has "joined" the cause), Ferrer's Siletski ascertains (or so he thinks) the nature of Bancroft's commitment to her husband and attempts to become her latest conquest—even if it means using his authority within the Nazi Party to compel her appearance. Later, when Bancroft arrives for their assignation, he masterfully conveys the peeved petulance of a frustrated "lover" (Ferrer makes it clear "love" is the last thing on Siletski's mind).

Professor Silestski's meeting with Brooks (who is impersonating Charles Durning's Nazi commandant Erhardt) is another highlight, particularly Brooks's actor struggling to come up with the right lines while trying (and failing) to keep his jealousy in check. Ferrer's work is impeccable and even manages to continue after his character's death—although the director does shortchange the character's onstage demise by keeping the camera at a distance. Siletski's villainy deserves a theatrical comeuppance, not one where the viewer is kept away. All the same, that is the only shortcoming (and not one of Ferrer's choosing) in what is a well-judged comic performance, one that deserves greater credit. *To Be or Not to Be*, though generally not considered to be the equal of the original, nevertheless has plenty of entertainment value of its own, including the Brooks/Bancroft musical numbers and the inspired efforts of a good supporting cast (including Ferrer, Durning, and Christopher Lloyd).

Ferrer portrayed yet another professor in what was perhaps his most textured performance of his latter period Dr. Leopold in Woody Allen's *A Midsummer Night's Sex Comedy*. This 1982 release also included Mia Farrow (Allen's then real-life romantic interest, several years before their acrimonious break-up and resultant scandal), good friend Tony Roberts (both in real life and in the film), Julie Hagerty, Mary Steenburgen, and Allen himself in what is essentially a six-character chamber piece—and a loose remake of Ingmar Bergman's 1955 romantic comedy (for him), *Smiles of a Summer Night*. This gentle, whimsical comedy, set in turn-of-the-century upstate New York, presents Allen as Andrew, a stockbroker and inventor, who together with his wife, Adrian (Steenburgen), hosts her cousin, Professor Leopold (Ferrer), his fiancée, Ariel (Farrow), their friend Maxwell (Roberts), and his date, Dulcy (Hagerty). Naturally, the glorious summer weekend at this country estate inspires all sorts of romantic inclinations—and not especially with one's partners, as Andrew and Maxwell are both enamored of Ariel (who has a history with Andrew), while the stuffy Leopold considers a last fling before marriage with the younger, more sexually liberated Dulcy.

Ferrer's Professor Leopold is a pompous, judgmental, and blunt academic whose presumed expertise also extends into the realm of singing, a prospect which no doubt pleased Ferrer as it called for a few solos—some of which are played for comic effect. Ferrer's wealth of musical knowledge impressed Allen: "We were lucky that José knew these songs [Schumann's 'Ich grolle nicht']. You know, I wrote the part and I was all set to say to him, 'Now listen, don't get upset, but you're going to have to learn some Schubert lieder, but he already knew them and could sing them. It was just one of those miraculous pieces of good fortune."

Besides Ferrer's talents in music, Allen was pleased with Ferrer the actor: "I had a wonderful time with him. I thought he was a delight in every way." Although, according to Allen, one line presented a slight problem. Ferrer had to say the line, "these are not my teeth," a line which depends on some nuance. Allen was not satisfied with the first few readings and had Ferrer redo it about thirty times. Finally, Ferrer said, "Now I can't, you've turned me into a mass of terrors!" Upon viewing the finished film, Ferrer seems to have delivered the line the way Allen wanted, because in the context, it's an amusing line indeed. One of the big knocks against Ferrer is he seemingly had "no talent for comedy," but on numerous occasions, this film being one of them, he exhibited a flair for comedy while also incorporating a delicacy of feeling. Ferrer's Leopold can be a little peremptory, but he also has his vulnerable side, recognizing the limitations of age and expressing nervousness about his impending nuptials to the much-desired Ariel. The highlight of his performance is his tender assignation with Hagerty's Dulcy, where his pomposity and formality take a back seat to both deference and diffidence in his almost bashful overtures to the knowing Dulcy.

A Midsummer Night's Sex Comedy was released in the summer of 1982, with the distributor Orion believing that the light, frothy film would be seen by audiences as an antidote to the special effects, hardware-driven movies. While the film did not live up to Orion's hopes at the box office and is generally recognized as second-tier Woody Allen, the clever writing, deft performances, and the enchanting setting (beautifully photographed by Gordon Willis) combine to make a charming entertainment. Critics would be mixed as to Allen's change-of-pace, with Pauline Kael lamenting "there is no depth in the lunacy . . . the women are all of the same type; there are three Annie Halls." However, Janet Maslin found that "all the actors are very good, particularly Hagerty and Ferrer, whose buffoonish Leopold has more depth and charm than might be expected."

Though this was perhaps Ferrer's best latter-day performance, he still had a number of films to go (*Dune, To Be or Not to Be*), including some cameos (as in a return engagement with Nico Mastorakis, *Hired to Kill*), but most of his work in the last ten years would be centered on television. He did have one last starring role on film: 1991's *Old Explorers*. Written and directed by Bill Pohlad for River Road Productions, the film is a poignant, occasionally perceptive and bittersweet look that examines aging, loneliness, and friendship. In *Old Explorers*, Ferrer stars opposite another respected thespian, James Whitmore. The two men play a pair of retirees who assume characters as world-famous explorers; in fact, these are elderly men fighting desolation and isolation by creating imaginary escapades. Since *Old Explorers* was adapted from a two-character play, the film opens up the action and includes new characters, with some location shooting done in Yuma. When their weekly adventures end, Whitmore is faced with the prospect of returning to his empty apartment, while widower Ferrer stays in his son's home—where he senses that he is not altogether welcome by either his son or his daughter-in-law.

Many of these explorers' adventures have to do with dangerous missions and assorted derring-do, and oddly enough, they usually end in the heroes' death. They are glorious, self-sacrificing deaths, to be sure, but triumph is usually not part of the results. However, when Whitmore's character suffers a stroke, Ferrer decides it is time for the explorers to engage in a real-life adventure. The two old pros work beautifully opposite each other, and their playing strives to minimize the maudlin nature of the proceedings. Ferrer does some controlled, quiet, and expressive work here as a man trying not to be relegated to the margins of society.

When *Old Explorers* was released in 1991, a year before Ferrer's death, the critics recognized how this minor but engaging film shed some light on the plight of the aged in society, especially the isolation, neglect, and lack of respect accorded the elderly. Nevertheless, this appreciation did not necessarily extend to the film's characterizations (aside from Whitmore and Ferrer). The *Los Angeles Times* felt that "the added characters seem contrived, one-dimensional, particularly the son and daughter-in-law." Tom Jacob of the *Daily News* echoed the *Times* in his belief that "the characters are too thinly sketched," though he found the film on the whole to be "mildly touching, thanks mainly to Ferrer's and Whitmore's engaging performances."

Ferrer's film work in the last part of his life was certainly not lacking in merit. Indeed, he gave some of his better, more richly nuanced performances during this period. If Ferrer wasn't the dominating force of yesteryear, he nevertheless seemed to be a good team player who generally conveyed the intentions of both the writers and directors, gaining their respect in the process. However, it's true that there were too many less-than-noteworthy efforts and too many appearances where the major motivation was the paycheck. This would extend into his television work as well, but there were also many chances yet remaining to show that he was still an actor of some value.

CHAPTER 17

Cashing the Checks—Television, 1967–92

IN SEVERAL INTERVIEWS THROUGHOUT THE 1970S AND '80S, FERRER ruminated at length over what he concluded was a relatively unsatisfying later career. He was frustrated with the lack of challenging roles that were offered him, as well as the plethora of cameos that came his way with alarming frequency. Upon reflecting on his television efforts, he frequently concluded that he had been confined to "guest shots on TV where I was usually the villain." It's true that he wasn't offered much that would challenge him, but there were certainly some juicy roles for Ferrer during this period, even in television. He would perform in a number of Emmy-nominated dramas (including *The Marcus-Nelson Murders* and *Gideon's Trumpet*), and work with some talented artists in what would turn out to be some meaningful work.

Perhaps what blinded Ferrer to the value of his later television career is the sheer amount of work that he took on just for the paycheck. As with his films throughout the last twenty-five years, there are so many parts that Ferrer accepted that led one to wonder: "Did he need the money that badly?" Again, this writer believes that Ferrer didn't *need* the work—he *needed* to work. Ferrer was comfortable enough (his 1967 tax bill notwithstanding) that he didn't have to take on *any* assignment that came his way, but sitting idle—even after he had gotten married to Stella (who would be his last wife) and was apparently content with his new bride—did not come easy for him. He was always ready to prove himself anew, to show that he still had worth as an actor, and to test himself—even if the material wasn't worthy.

221

If one were to explore Ferrer's television work during this period, one would see Ferrer making all kinds of appearances, several of which only relied on his sonorous voice. Two of these were in animated works where the distinctive Ferrer baritone was heard to good advantage. He reprised the role of Cyrano in 1974 for an ABC *Afterschool Special* that managed to capture the essence of *Cyrano de Bergerac* in an hour. The other was the classic stop-motion animated Rankin/Bass Christmas special, *The Little Drummer Boy*, first broadcast in 1968. Ferrer is in fine form as the scheming Ben Haramed, leader of a theatrical troupe who tries to have his players perform for the Magi.

Besides his participation in these animated ventures, Ferrer's vocal talents were employed in several documentaries. In one noteworthy effort, Ferrer helped shed some light on a fellow Puerto Rican luminary when he narrated *Roberto Clemente: A Touch of Royalty*, a short documentary about legendary baseball player and humanitarian Roberto Clemente. The Puerto Rican-born Clemente died in a plane crash while attempting to deliver supplies to his homeland; like Ferrer, he was a source of inspiration to his fellow Latinos, and Ferrer's impassioned narration helps make this moving documentary a fitting tribute.

Among several other efforts, Ferrer lent his vocal talents to 1983's *The Horror of It All*, with his narration enhancing an informative overview of the horror genre. Ferrer was a last-minute choice, as Orson Welles was originally supposed to narrate but "kept everything and everyone up in the air," according to historian David Del Valle, whose first documentary this was. Luckily for the creative team, the same agency that represented Welles also represented Ferrer. For Del Valle, this proved to be a blessing since "Ferrer gave the script an air of authority and grace." Ferrer was also a big fan of classic horror films, and for Del Valle, "this helped enormously with his reading of the material."

Besides his voiceover assignments, Ferrer's television appearances encompassed all manner of genres. He made guest appearances in shows like *Name of the Game*, *Great Mysteries*, *Starsky and Hutch* (as Crazy Joey Fortune), *Hotel*, *Matlock* (playing a criminal kingpin in an episode entitled "The Don"), *Fantasy Island* (what former big star didn't?), among others. Ferrer made some stabs at comedy in a couple of *Love Boat* episodes. One stars Ferrer as a formidable collector of artifacts whom the hapless ship's purser Gopher (Fred Grandy) runs afoul of; the laugh track thought it all terribly funny. Ferrer also appeared as a hypnotist (and murder victim) in a potentially intriguing *Murder, She Wrote* episode that rid itself of its promise when Ferrer's charismatic Cagliostro is murdered. The ensuing investigation by Angela Lansbury as the astute mystery novelist/amateur criminologist Jessica Fletcher results in many dialogue scenes but hardly a flashback to Ferrer pre-demise. Ferrer would even make a few appearances on the daytime soap opera *Another World*.

Two of Ferrer's most significant guest-star appearances from this period would be on two different popular crime series. On a 1981 *Magnum, P.I.* episode, "Lest We Forget," Ferrer plays a nominee for the Supreme Court who hires private eye Magnum to find a woman out of his past, specifically forty years, around the time of Pearl Harbor. When Magnum does find her, she happens to be June Lockhart, and their reunion scenes are marked by tenderness and a warm rapport. Nevertheless, what makes the episode somewhat special is that it marks the first time José and son Miguel appeared in the same show. Miguel would play the younger judge in the flashbacks, as his character falls for a younger Lockhart (also played by her daughter) in the days before Pearl Harbor. Of course, one can immediately see the resemblance between the two, and Miguel gives an assured performance as the love-struck serviceman.

In the 1974 *Columbo* episode, "Mind Over Mayhem," Ferrer was cast as the murderer, in this case, a proud, possessive father who presides over a "think tank" complete with a "Robby the Robot" type with all kinds of capabilities. Ferrer also has a celebrated, troubled scientist son (Robert Walker) who is about to be exposed as a plagiarist by colleague Lew Ayres. Naturally, Ferrer can't let that happen, as he kills Ayres and makes him look like an unfortunate victim of "a dope-crazed fiend." Naturally, by the first commercial break, Peter Falk's rumpled but perceptive Lieutenant Columbo suspects Ferrer, quickly dispensing with the "addict" theory. (It's not the only time on *Columbo* that a murder would be made to appear the work of a desperate addict.) Ferrer delivers a rich performance, with equal touches of arrogance, intelligence, and paternal pride, not just towards Walker but also the young Lee Harcourt Montgomery, playing a prodigy named Steven Spielberg (an inside joke, as Spielberg had directed the first *Columbo* episode, "Murder by the Book.") Montgomery said that he "liked working with Ferrer. I was a kid, but he treated me with respect," reflecting the characters' relationship in the episode. The final scene, in which Falk's Columbo tests just how much "the father loves his son," is delicately played by both Ferrer and Falk, and results in an unusually poignant denouement for the series.

Perhaps his most successfully sustained stint on episodic TV were his appearances on the popular 1980s sitcom *Newhart*. Bob Newhart's second successful situation comedy for CBS had him starring as a Vermont innkeeper, with Peter Scolari and Julia Duffy among the regulars: Duffy's Stephanie was a valued (though not terribly competent) employee and Scolari was Michael, Stephanie's adoring young swain. Ferrer portrayed Stephanie's somewhat stuffy and very wealthy father Arthur Vanderkellen in six episodes between 1985 and 1987. His best opportunity came in the episode "Lock, Stock and Noodlehead," in which Ferrer's Arthur suddenly comes to visit during a Colonial Day celebration, leading Stephanie to think there is trouble in paradise (namely, that her inheritance is gone). She is mistaken as to the cause, as Arthur's real problem is being retired and feeling that he is worthless. There are some funny lines, and Ferrer is both amusing and touching as the outwardly poised but occasionally befuddled Arthur, especially the scene where he and Newhart's Dick find themselves in the sticks (courtesy of Stephanie's attempt to reconcile her parents). The episode has a good payoff, and all of Ferrer's appearances on *Newhart* help put to rest the notion that he lacked any sense of comic timing.

It is quite possible that Ferrer's appearances on the CBS sitcom *Newhart* led to his being cast as part of the ensemble of the short-lived drama *Bridges to Cross* for the same network. The series starred Suzanne Pleshette and Nicolas Surovy as Tracy and Peter, two top reporters for a weekly newsmagazine. They are also divorced (from each other), and one of the series' conceits was to have them address the camera and recall their marriage. José Ferrer was cast as the magazine's editor, Morris Kane, with Roddy McDowall and Eva Gabor serving to round out the ensemble. In spite of all the talent in front of the camera, the writing (by William Blinn) and direction were seen as limp and uninspired, while John J. O'Connor of the *New York Times* decreed that "whether snarling, winking, or cooing at each other, Tracy and Peter end up being merely tiresome." *Bridges to Cross* premiered in April 1986, but the lethal combination of negative reviews and negligible ratings led to the show's early demise by mid-June 1986.

In addition to Ferrer's work in episodic television, he would make several appearances in television movies and miniseries, both of which were becoming increasingly popular in the 1970s and '80s. Some of these barely qualify as cameos, such as his fleeting appearances in *The French-Atlantic Affair* (1979), where ship captain Louis Jourdan tries to save his ship from an unstable and dangerous Telly Savalas. Throughout the four-hour miniseries, Ferrer is stuck on shore, on the phone and pretty ineffectual. There were the minor roles in costume dramas and would-be epics, such as his appearances in the remake of *Samson and Delilah* (Victor

Mature, star of the 1949 *Samson and Delilah*, would also appear as Samson's father), *George Washington*, in which he appears early to persuade a young Washington (Barry Bostwick) to undertake a secret mission, and *Peter and Paul*. Then there were the small roles in such ephemera as *Pleasure Palace* (starring Omar Sharif, with Ferrer as a character named Pokey), *Exo-Man* (as the corporate villain), *Crosscurrent*, *The Missing are Deadly*, *The Art of Crime*, and *This Gun for Hire* (a moody, unnecessary remake of the 1942 Alan Ladd film noir starring Robert Wagner).

There were even two abortive attempts in the 1970s to launch Ferrer as a television star. *Good Heavens* was a situation comedy whose premise involved Mr. Angel, a heavenly emissary who would come to earth and reward people for their good deeds. Ferrer was cast as Mr. Angel in the pilot under the direction of Carl Reiner, who had just finished directing the hit film *Oh, God!* He also had fond memories of Ferrer from their association on 1967's *Enter Laughing*. As Reiner recalled later in an interview with the Television Academy, when the pilot was shown to the producers, they felt that Ferrer came across as diabolical. The producers also suggested that Reiner take the role of Mr. Angel himself. Reiner thought this would constitute somewhat of a betrayal and for the moment declined; he then went to see Ferrer and told him the producers thought Ferrer's Angel could do with a little more charm. According to Reiner, Ferrer said, "That's as fucking charming as I can get." Ferrer did suggest (much to Reiner's relief) that Reiner assume the role himself. Reiner thought this to be a very generous gesture and agreed to play Mr. Angel. *Good Heavens* premiered in February 1976, and though the show ranked sixteenth in the ratings for the 1975–76 season, it did not return for a second season.

Ferrer's other flirtation with television series stardom came about because of producer Irwin Allen. Allen had some success with television shows like *Voyage to the Bottom of the Sea* and his cinematic disaster films like *The Poseidon Adventure* (1972) and *The Towering Inferno* (1974). In 1977, Allen was producing a three-part miniseries *The Return of Captain Nemo* in which Captain Nemo (who has been in suspended animation) is revived in time to help save the world from a dangerous madman (Burgess Meredith) who has a nuclear weapon and is quite intent on ending the world if his financial demands are not met. An interesting side note is that while Nemo acknowledges that the world sees him as a fictional character (because of Jules Verne's 1870 novel *20,000 Leagues Under the Sea* as well as the popular 1954 Disney film adaptation), the captain suggests that Verne based the story on real life.

While trying to thwart Meredith's deranged Professor Cunningham, Ferrer's Nemo must also contend with villainous Mel Ferrer as a shady Dr. Cook and help Horst Buchholz (as the ruler of Atlantis) preserve his kingdom. There are some enjoyable moments in the serial-like escapades, as when the two Ferrers utilize makeshift swords (giving them both a belated chance to swash and buckle), in their duel to the death, and the scenes where Ferrer's righteous Nemo and Meredith's unhinged Cunningham elevate the routine written words given them to enact. And the now sixty-five-year-old Ferrer is quite good as Nemo—lively, engaged, good-natured (well, Nemo had plenty of rest), formidable, and even restrained when the role demands it.

It's a pity that everything else about *The Return of Captain Nemo* seems so cut-rate. The proposed young costars lack any kind of charisma or rapport; the plotting is both riddled with holes and anticlimactic (Ferrer's Nemo disposes of the threat posed by Meredith's Cunningham in the first episode, yet Meredith still lingers to try to drain Nemo's brain). Technically, the show is a marvel—in all the wrong ways; more convincing miniatures could be found in an Ed Wood film, but ironically enough, the show was nominated for an Emmy for its special effects. As for the teleplay, Robert Bloch (of *Psycho* fame), who was one of the writers (his main contribution was for the "Atlantis" episode), would later recall the haphazard nature of the series: "They assigned each individual episode to a different writer. You had four writers working, neither one of them knew what the others were doing, and they had a three-week deadline."

When *The Return of Captain Nemo* premiered as a three-part miniseries in March 1978, Ferrer received some good notices for his commanding Nemo, but the ratings proved to be pretty dismal. Consequently, there would be no call for any further episodes, and the series itself would be re-edited into a two-hour drama for overseas theatrical release, *The Amazing Captain Nemo*. As happens with movie serials when they are shoehorned into a feature-length format, the editing is sloppy and the transitions don't make sense, thus calling even more attention to the substandard nature of the writing. At least Ferrer was able to sneak away for an afternoon to shoot Allen's *The Swarm*, though, as mentioned earlier, the only reward must have been financial.

A few years later, when both José and Mel Ferrer appeared together (more fleetingly) in the romantic pseudo-noir *Seduced*, starring Gregory Harrison and Cybill Shepherd, CBS would try to stir up some publicity with a "joint centennial," since both Ferrers had begun acting professionally fifty years earlier. In *Seduced*, José Ferrer is a shadowy corporate head, and Mel is a prominent stockholder whose murder in the early going sets events in motion. Both Ferrers remarked that they would occasionally be confused for the other, with Mel commenting that "some people tell me they expected me to be shorter" (thinking he had played Lautrec). It's a shame their reunions could not be in ventures more worthy of their talents.

As with Ferrer's movie career in this last quarter-century or so, he did manage to have some rewarding roles in television, occasionally starring but generally providing strong supporting character work, often standing out amid a formidable ensemble. If the roles weren't Shakespearean or classical, they would at least furnish Ferrer with the chance to endow these characters with some depth and nuance. The 1968 drama *A Case of Libel*, from a successful 1963 Broadway play by Henry Denker (who would adapt his work for television), was the dramatization of a trial wherein a liberal news correspondent Quentin Reynolds had been smeared as a drunkard and communist sympathizer by ultra-conservative columnist Westbrook Pegler. The subsequent libel suit went to trial, with Reynolds defended by the wily Louis Nizer. The play and television version fictionalized the names and compressed certain events (for time and dramatic impact), and in both incarnations—as well as a more recent 1985 version—it would receive positive reviews. Lloyd Bridges played Corcoran (based on the plaintiff Reynolds), Van Heflin reprised his Broadway role as his lawyer Sloane (Nizer), and Ferrer had the role of Boyd Bendix (Pegler), among an ensemble that would also include E. G. Marshall, Angie Dickinson, and playwright Marc Connelly (of *The Green Pastures*) as the judge.

The previous year, Ferrer would get another chance to sing on television in ABC's ninety-minute version of the musical *Kismet*, playing the role of the Bagdad poet/beggar that had been played on Broadway and film by Alfred Drake and Howard Keel, respectively. Ferrer got the role after producer Norman Rosemont had seen him in the national company of *Man of La Mancha*. When Rosemont was asked why he didn't get a real singer, the producer replied, "José Ferrer brings something to the role of Hajj in *Kismet* besides his singing." With this and the following year's *A Case of Libel*, it seemed that Ferrer was getting more acclimated to television's long hours and crushing pace, resolving to go where the work was—which was not, by this point, on Broadway or in the movies: "My agent says, 'José, you're not hot.' I could have told him that. I feel sorry for the poor guy. Once a year I see him, so he has to make his money somewhere else."

In 1971, Ferrer starred in another television adaptation of a Broadway play, this time under the auspices of the vaunted *Hallmark Hall of Fame*. The production was Paddy Chayefsky's "Gideon," which had a modest run on Broadway in 1961. The premise was inspired by the story of Gideon in the Book of Judges, wherein Gideon, a simple farmer, is chosen by an Angel of the Lord to lead the Israelites against the Midianites. Gideon succeeds, and while some believe it to be a miracle, the Angel is not so convinced. Peter Ustinov portrayed Gideon, while Ferrer was the pompous, judgmental Angel. Much of the interest in "Gideon" stems from the dialogues between man and God's representative, as Chayefsky's Gideon is reluctant to follow God's orders if they involve killing some elders. Critic John O' Connor of the *New York Times* found much to admire about the ninety-minute program, including the performances and much of Chayefsky's witty dialogue. O'Connor acknowledged that the play isn't especially deep and viewed the production as "a modest achievement, but its modesty can be very charming . . . Mr. Schaefer's production kept matters in low-keyed perspective. The play and everyone else concerned couldn't have been better served."

Ferrer returned to the *Hallmark Hall of Fame* in 1976, again under the direction of George Schaefer, for the historical drama "Truman at Potsdam." Adapted by Sidney Carroll from Charles Mee's book *Meeting at Potsdam*, the production depicts the July 1945 conference at Potsdam, where President Truman (in his first international conference) met with Winston Churchill and Joseph Stalin to conduct negotiations surrounding what they hoped was the imminent end of the war (as the atomic bomb tests in New Mexico had strengthened Truman's resolve to drop the bomb on Japan). Truman also wanted to end the war before Russia and Stalin became involved and demanded their share of the peace.

Ferrer was cast as Stalin, with Ed Flanders portraying Truman and John Houseman taking on the role of Churchill. In addition, Alexander Knox was cast as Henry Stimson, who was in Potsdam in an unofficial capacity and in one prescient scene, laments the loss of finesse and good manners in diplomacy. However, most of the drama depicts the verbal sparring among Churchill, Truman, and Stalin, and these confrontations are crisply played with undercurrents of humor. Of the three actors, Houseman, sporting an uncertain Churchill impression, is the weakest, while Flanders and Ferrer both offer excellent portrayals. Flanders makes Truman both salty and reflective, whether parrying with Stalin or discussing the use of the atomic bomb among his chiefs of staff (who do not share his resolve). Ferrer is a masterful, imperious Stalin, seemingly agreeable (except when he is not). In discussing what to do with the defeated German fleet, Houseman's Churchill declares his intentions to sink those that remain. Ferrer's Stalin replies, "Let him sink his share, I won't sink mine." Many television critics thought this summit amounted to good, absorbing theater, with the *Los Angeles Times* critic Cecil Smith writing that "Ferrer was a splendid Stalin, powerful, commanding, and utterly unbending."

Ferrer was also supposed to take on another role as a political leader. He was cast as Egyptian president Anwar Sadat, opposite Ingrid Bergman's Golda Meir in *A Woman Called Golda*. However, just before filming started, Ferrer dropped out, citing safety concerns. His son Rafael said, "My father was going to do the part—and just before he was leaving, Sadat was assassinated. My father didn't want to travel to the Middle East—he knew it might be seen as breach of contract, but he feared for his life."

Ferrer took on a significant role in another World War II drama, this one set during the rise of the Third Reich and incorporating both fictional and historical characters. 1985's *Hitler's SS: Portrait in Evil*, written by Lukas Heller, was a miniseries set from 1932 to 1945 in which the Third Reich was depicted through the eyes of two brothers, Karl and Helmut (John Shea and Bill Nighy), who start as students in Germany and later become members of the Nazi Party. Although Karl joins willingly, he gradually becomes disillusioned, while Helmut overcomes an initial reluctance and becomes one of the more active participants, rising to power in the SS.

The four-hour drama would mainly portray the brothers' involvement in historical events, including the infamous Night of the Long Knives, but there were some substantial, even offbeat roles for character actors. For instance, Tony Randall (the captain in Ferrer's *Oh Captain!*) appeared as a nightclub performer whose regular comic gibes at the Nazi Party's expense earn him a brutal interrogation. Ferrer contributes a touching portrayal of a Jewish professor of literature who serves as a mentor of sorts to the brothers, particularly Helmut. Ferrer's persecuted character—he first loses his position, then his home, and finally his life—is meant to represent the hardships of formerly prosperous, respected Jews under the new Nazi regime. The drama periodically cuts back to the plight of Ferrer's Professor Rosenberg, who has grown closer to Shea's unhappy Karl.

Ferrer plays down the potentially maudlin aspects and chooses to accentuate the professor's dignity in response to the various degradations that befall him. The actor's most powerful moment comes in his final scene. Rosenberg has been compelled to board a train bound for the death camps when he is recognized by an officer who is a former student. This officer offers him a way out, to which Ferrer's professor can only shake his head and board the train, preferring to die than go on living under Nazi rule. While the scene is not entirely unexpected, the understated playing gives it depth and feeling. It is one of Ferrer's better moments—on any screen, big or small.

Even though Ferrer tended to disparage his television appearances, preferring to group his roles into villainous, one-note bankers and lawyers, the truth is several good television dramas would present Ferrer as a resourceful attorney, usually employed to help right an injustice. In fact, the courtroom milieu, as well as the theatrical pyrotechnics that courtroom dramas promise, was the ideal venue for Ferrer the actor, with that baritone voice and his stentorian flourishes. (It is possible his work as defense attorney Greenwald in *The Caine Mutiny* was not far from the minds of producers and directors.) Three of his most effective television performances would be in absorbing and occasionally significant dramas where the Ferrer character had to argue a case on behalf of the underdog.

The Marcus-Nelson Murders, a 1973 show scripted by Abby Mann (his first for television since 1959's *Judgment at Nuremburg*), would later become best known as the drama that introduced Telly Savalas's Lieutenant Kojak. At the time, though, it was seen primarily as a disturbing drama based on a real-life murder case involving two girls who are murdered in their apartment; months later a young black man named Humes is picked up on an unrelated sexual assault charge and is discovered to have a picture of the two girls in his pocket. After a lengthy session with the police, Humes confesses to the murders and is quickly convicted on the lesser rape charge. However, Kojak is unconvinced of the confession and does some further digging, also securing for Humes a leading trial lawyer, Jake Weinhaus (Ferrer). Ferrer's role gives him many chances to exhibit the vocal strength that is part of his stock and trade; he is also able to invest the lawyer with pragmatism, compassion, and integrity, whether he is pointing out that jury members deliberating Humes's conviction were prejudiced or acknowledging that on many occasions, "the truth doesn't count in the courtroom." Ferrer's portrayal is a vivid, persuasively acted component of a good, gritty crime drama.

Ferrer's next major courtroom appearance—as an actor—was in another made-for-TV movie depicting a real-life court case. This time, however, Ferrer's lawyer would be arguing in front of the US Supreme Court. "Gideon's Trumpet" (1980) stars Henry Fonda as Clarence Earl Gideon, who was arrested in the early 1960s for breaking into a pool hall in Florida. Gideon could not afford an attorney, so he represented himself and was later convicted. While in prison, Gideon petitioned the court with a handwritten plea. The eloquence of the letter so impressed the judges (led by John Houseman's Chief Justice, with Sam Jaffe and Dean Jagger among the other justices) that they assigned prominent lawyer Abe Fortas to handle the case. Ferrer was cast as Fortas, with whom the actor was well-acquainted since Fortas had represented Ferrer in 1951 before HUAC. It was also a unique case for dramatic purposes, since Fortas and Gideon (as well as Gideon and the Chief Justice) never met face to face.

The issues at hand in Fortas's appearance before the Supreme Court revolved around the rights of the accused—specifically, when is someone entitled to counsel and does the Constitution entitle a poor man to have a lawyer at his side? The state of Florida had previously ruled that the state should have the right to determine if the defendant is entitled to counsel, while Fortas's argument was that a person cannot have a fair trial in absence of counsel. As Ferrer's Fortas points out in his persuasive argument, even when celebrated lawyer Clarence Darrow was on trial for allegedly fixing a jury, "he realized he needed a lawyer." Fortas was arguing for the rights of the accused, even if it meant asking the Supreme Court to preempt Florida laws.

The scene in which Fortas argues before court exhibits Ferrer's flair in the courtroom setting. Displaying eloquence, cadence, and quiet intensity, the court listens rapt, as does the viewer. In the end, Fortas won Gideon, if not freedom, then the right to a new trial, complete with lawyer (Gideon would eventually be acquitted); more important, the Supreme Court ruled that everyone was entitled to counsel and that courts were required to appoint a lawyer for a defendant who could not afford one. "Gideon's Trumpet" received several Emmy nominations, including Best Drama and Best Actor (Fonda), and while Ferrer wasn't nominated, the drama did provide further evidence that television was the best setting for him to flex his theatrical muscles.

Ferrer's last major courtroom outing would be in *Blood and Orchids* (1986), another crime drama. The two-part miniseries was set in and around a naval base in Hawaii in the late 1930s. Adapted by Norman Katkov (from his own novel), the drama is based on the real-life Massie case, wherein Lieutenant Thomas Massie shot a man he presumed to have attacked his wife. This fictionalized version centers around Hester (Madeline Stowe), the pregnant young wife of Lieutenant Lloyd Murdoch (based on the real-life Massie), as well as the daughter of wealthy, socially conscious Doris (Jane Alexander). After Hester is attacked after a party, four Hawaiians bring her to the hospital. The imperious Doris demands that Hester bring charges against the men, even though Hester insists they didn't do it (the husband's friend did). The resulting case serves to exacerbate the racial tensions on the island. When Murdoch fatally shoots the lead defendant, Doris summons crafty legal legend Walter Bergmann (Ferrer, in a performance loosely based on famed defense attorney Clarence Darrow) who arrives complete with a lovely wife (Sean Young). Further complicating matters is the presence of Kris Kristofferson's police chief, who is not convinced of the Hawaiians' guilt, though he is soon persuaded of the charms of the attractive Young.

This was Young's second appearance with Ferrer, as they had previously been in 1984's *Dune*. On the set of *Dune*, Young had started off on the wrong foot with Ferrer (courtesy of her faux pas of asking Ferrer about the HUAC hearings), but by the time they worked together in *Blood and Orchids*, their relationship had become far more cordial. Young recalled, "When we were in Hawaii, he would come into the make-up and hair trailer and I'd tease him, 'We're not bothering your golf game, are we, José?' He was always out there playing golf." Young enjoyed her experience with Ferrer: "You're basically dealing with an old pro. Some actors are into their own process and keep you out of their space. That wasn't José. He was easygoing. We would talk about what was going on the world. It was a nice gig."

Blood and Orchids may be pulp with pretensions toward social significance, but it is pulp of a pretty high order. The characters are well-drawn, the performances convincing, and the story builds enough momentum and contains enough interesting turns to sustain the four-hour running time. Ferrer's Bergmann dominates the second half of the drama; his perceptive and cunning Bergmann immediately and accurately assesses the situation, as he advises Alexander's deceptive Doris: "I want your daughter looking tragic and wounded." Bergmann is also aware of his wife's clandestine affair; the scene in which Ferrer confronts Kristofferson is emotionally charged, with Ferrer's Bergmann suffering a convincing diabetic seizure.

It is perhaps fitting that two of Ferrer's last television appearances were in prestigious revivals from the American theater: as it happens, two plays by Eugene O'Neill. The lesser of the two was *Rope*, for the Arts and Entertainment Network (A&E), under the banner of *American Playwrights: The One-Acts*. *Rope* was an early O'Neill effort, set on a failing farm on the coast of New England. It's a variation on the tale of the prodigal son, with embittered father Ferrer leaving a noose in his barn should his son (Brad Davis) return. Producer Stuart Goodman had been the first cameraman when director Lela Swift was directing the television cult hit *Dark Shadows*, and he lured Swift out of semi-retirement to direct this broadcast. Unfortunately, Swift and Ferrer did not get along. As Goodman recalls, "It was Ferrer's first cable show. He wasn't the star. They fought constantly. He did not want to take her direction . . . it could have been my fault. She [Swift] might have been past her prime." When *Rope* aired in April 1989, the critics found fault mainly with the sketchy nature of the play itself. Director Swift, Ferrer, and the rest of the cast received positive notices for their contributions—regardless of the tensions on the set.

The other O'Neill play in which Ferrer starred was an ambitious staging of *Strange Interlude* for PBS in January 1988. The telecast was based on a 1985 stage version in which Glenda Jackson starred as Nina, and she reprised her role for this adaptation. The play spans many years and utilizes the technique of characters directly communicating their thoughts in spoken asides. It centers on the mournful, neurotic Nina, who lost her first love at the end of World War I and consequently pursues one affair after another. Ferrer plays her father, who had objected to her ill-fated affair. The *New York Times* critic John J. O'Connor considered the play "long and demanding," but he also concluded that "for anyone interested in serious theater, this is required viewing."

Television provided Ferrer with many opportunities to do fine, sometimes exceptional work during his self-proclaimed fallow period. Although they were not the roles of his choosing, and definitely lacked the stature Ferrer would have preferred, they did provide him with both a decent paycheck and the chance to deliver committed, distinguished performances in a medium that was still in the process of enhancing its own standing. While television and film were Ferrer's primary modes of creative (and financial) fulfillment, the theater would not lose its allure for him. There would be more acting and directorial stage efforts in his final decades, although the lights of New York City would not always be the final destination.

CHAPTER 18

Final Bows, 1967–92

IT REALLY COULDN'T BE SAID THAT JOSÉ FERRER WAS CONTENT TO merely work—although many of his latter-day film and television projects seem to disprove that notion. He was also constantly looking for ways to challenge himself, to change the public's perception about him, and even to change the perceptions of executives who may have underestimated his versatility and value. On the stage, an actor is usually seen in the able company of other performers, with the ensemble providing a safety net in front of the paying audience. What could be more challenging for the actor than to present a solo performance, depending on only himself, the guiding hand of the director, and the technical expertise of the stage manager, as well as the light and sound crew?

The fifty-six-year-old Ferrer ventured into the realm of the one-man show, only his inaugural effort would be in a 1968 nightclub act in which Ferrer would be singing, dancing, telling some tales, and building a rapport with the audience. This was not an entirely unexpected move on Ferrer's part; he had recently been touring with *Man of La Mancha* and experienced some success in television variety shows with performers like Danny Kaye, Phil Silvers, Rosemary Clooney, even Tennessee Ernie Ford. As for his storytelling abilities, actors such as Henry Fonda would attest to his expertise in that department. Fonda would tell of how Ferrer could take any situation and develop it far beyond where the listener thinks it would go, and still keep the interest.

Ferrer the performer would take a different approach to the stage than Ferrer the actor. As he would tell interviewers, Ferrer the actor "will try to be anything but myself. . . . I do anything to persuade the audience I

am not José Ferrer." On the other hand, Ferrer the performer had a decidedly different goal: "I try to be José Ferrer and to make the audience
feel they are in my living room, that they are my guests and that I am
there to entertain them and make sure they enjoy themselves." He made
his official debut for the press at the Diplomat Hotel in Miami Beach (after he had made some changes following an earlier, more loosely struc-
tured attempt). The show would involve some reminiscences with some
special material from *Cabaret*, as well as "Where is the Life that Late I
Led," a *Man of La Mancha* medley, and a variety of ballads and up-tempo
numbers. *Variety* believed that Ferrer did well in what was a foreign medium for him: "Ferrer is not a great singer, but he knows how to put
songs across . . . this is a new medium for him and with the rapid strides,
he'll continue to grow."

Ferrer would perform his cabaret act sporadically over the next few
years, sometimes expressing a twinge of regret at not having sought out
further engagements, since he seems to have enjoyed the experience. His
other one-man show was more along the lines of what one would expect
from an actor with experience in the classics; it would be called *The Art of
the Monologue*, which Ferrer would perform beginning in 1977 at various
halls and theaters, such as the Schoenberg Hall at UCLA. Ferrer would
tell interviewers that while the one-man show was indeed a daunting
proposition, "it was better than sitting at home waiting for the phone
to ring. It's something I've never done before and may never do again."

The Art of the Monologue was a program that featured reminiscences
about his various stage productions, notably his Iago from *Othello*. The
second half consisted of Ferrer presenting three monologues from the
works of Beckett, Chekhov, and Argentine writer Leopoldo Lugones; according to Ferrer, the Lugones selection was a complete short story, but
"really more of a monologue, it has great dramatic force." While introducing these segments, Ferrer would also share with the audience that
the greatest monologist was Ruth Draper, who could convince audiences
that "she was young or old, beautiful or ugly." In the view of theater critic
Sondra Lowell, it only served to show that "Ferrer does not have this
facility. Although his delivery is interesting, there is not much difference
between each character."

Although Ferrer would periodically return to the format, he would
satisfy his desire to do theater with more communal endeavors. Occasionally these pursuits would take him abroad, as with his periodic
work in England with the Chichester Festival. In 1975, Ferrer directed
a production of *Cyrano de Bergerac* starring artistic director (and former

Henry VIII) Keith Mitchell as Cyrano in a production that was extremely popular with the public, although the British critics greeted it tepidly. He would return in 1988 to act in the production of Jean Anouilh's *Ring Around the Moon*, part of a strong ensemble that included Googie Withers.

Ferrer even revisited the role *Cyrano* in a musical called *A Song for Cyrano*, with songs by Robert Craig Wright and George Forest (not to be confused with the Broadway musical adaptation *Cyrano*, starring Christopher Plummer and with songs by Anthony Burgess and Michael Lewis). Ferrer had hoped to take his show to Broadway but wound up playing in regional theaters like Corning, New York, and Fairfield, Connecticut. The consensus was that even though time had diminished the electricity he had brought to the role, he still made a good Cyrano; however, reviewers believed there was nothing memorable about the score. They also felt that while acting was still Ferrer's forte, singing was not—and even if it were, the forgettable tunes did him no service.

In addition to *Cyrano*, there were a number of other opportunities to act, produce, or direct, and though he would find himself on the New York City stage, the journey would sometimes begin elsewhere. In 1976, Ferrer could be found in Huntington, Long Island, to star in the PAF Playhouse's production of *White Pelicans*, a new play written and directed by Jay Broad. Ferrer had flown in from his home on Old San Juan, and admitted that while he had been turning increasingly to regional theaters to satisfy his soul, he acknowledged that "I can only afford to do so many of these things. . . . I don't want to live indigently, so I walk a tightrope between what pays off in my pocket and what pays off in my gut."

Ferrer had never met Mr. Broad, but a mutual friend brought them together and he agreed to read *White Pelicans*, which is a two-character drama about two prospectors who are among the last to go off to find some gold and return only to find there is nothing left of the boom town they had departed. Ferrer was taken with the play, as it was, in his estimation, not your average play: "It was so mysterious, so deep that I was excited. It gives the actor a chance to act unwritten and unspoken business as well as the written word." Despite years of performing in efforts often beneath his abilities, Ferrer still maintained his enthusiasm for acting—that is, when the material challenged him or gave him the chance "to translate on stage the experience I underwent when I read it."

Ferrer's original costar was to have been Cliff Gorman, who had impressed audiences and critics as comedian Lenny Bruce in the 1971 Broadway hit, *Lenny*. However, five days before opening, Gorman left the play and was replaced by Christopher Lloyd, then an off-

Broadway veteran, and a few years before his fame as Reverend Jim on TV's *Taxi*. Lloyd would later recall Ferrer as a mentor and a friend, and while he didn't have an ongoing interaction after the play, "I respected him and had a good experience. I liked the man." Two years later, *White Pelicans* would be mounted off-Broadway, though Lloyd now wasn't available, as he was now shooting *Taxi*. Morgan Freeman would be the new costar, and Ferrer would produce as well as star; playwright Broad would double as director. Their combined efforts could not win anything approaching a favorable review; critic William Glover said that the play about luckless fortune hunters "quickly reduces parallel spectators to a parallel state of misfortune."

White Pelicans would only have a short run at the Theater De Lys (which would later become the Lucille Lortel Theater); six years earlier, for his first play at the Theater De Lys, Ferrer had directed *The Web and the Rock*. Written by Dolores Sutton and based on a posthumously published work by Thomas Wolfe, the play also did not receive a good reception. Director Ferrer was thought to have staged the "unbelievable play as briskly as possible," with the harshest words reserved for the writing itself, which the critics would concur was "a failure." The play would close rather quickly, but it was another example that Ferrer would continue to passionately support the cause of young playwrights.

While Ferrer was directing *The Web and the Rock*, an actor in the cast brought to Ferrer's attention to another script, and a few years later, Ferrer would find himself in Pittsburgh performing *The Interview*. Written by a young playwright named Tom Thomas, *The Interview* was about a famous recluse who consents to an interview with a young reporter. The play would have a two-week run, but Ferrer would offer to commit to a longer stay "if greener pastures don't beckon—after all, there are bills to be paid."

There were the houses in New York and Puerto Rico, and there were also the five growing children by Clooney, each of whom was either entering college, still in college, or on the verge of seeking employment. While Ferrer continued to lend his presence to several fledgling playwrights' new works, he felt that critics, with the exception of George Jean Nathan, were usually unkind to the "fumbling, faulty steps of the young playwright"—he could not afford to be unavailable if a more lucrative television opportunity came his way.

Ferrer did contribute his artistic support to the Puerto Rican poet Pedro Pietri. He had found much to admire in Pietri's often biting social commentary on the social and economic hardships endured by those in the Puerto Rican community. In 1973, Pietri had been instrumental in organizing the Nuyorican Poets Café on the Lower East Side of Manhattan, helping in the development of a new generation of Puerto Rican writers. Ferrer felt a kinship with Pietri, both with his artistry as well as the man himself. When Pietri became a playwright, Ferrer wanted to assist the author in finding a larger audience. He directed two of Pietri's plays for the H. B. Playwrights Theater. Both were dark, absurdist looks at the human condition as 1973's *Lewlulu* was about a pair of star-crossed lovers, while 1978's *The Living Room* was an exploration of the dichotomy between sanity and mental illness. It wouldn't be the only time that Ferrer would use his talents and celebrity for his fellow Latinos; he would use his influence to support Latino boxers, writers, and even chefs, when the occasion presented itself.

In 1978, Ferrer succeeded Ellis Rabb in the off-Broadway hit *A Life in the Theatre*, David Mamet's two-character play about actors; in various costumes and props, the two actors (James McDonnell costarred) do bits from various plays and discuss matters large and small while "offstage." At the end, the older actor is told the theater is closing, and Ferrer stressed over how to deliver "thank you," his last line in the play: "I'm thanking him for the life we have lived. For listening to me. For fighting me . . . it's a most complicated thing. I have to sum up the entire play in two words." The play proved to be fulfilling for Ferrer, who had no qualms about being the "second actor"; he had done it before with Richard Kiley and *Man of La Mancha*, and certainly the drama which involved an aging actor and the "changing of the guard" must have held some significance for the sixty-five-year-old actor.

Despite Ferrer's feeling that he would not be involved in directing a major Broadway production, he would soon be making yet another run at a Broadway success—and another musical, at that. Lyricist Alan Jay Lerner and composer Burton Lane, who had last teamed in the 1960s for the stage and film versions of *On a Clear Day You Can See Forever*, were now combining their talents on *Carmelina*. The show was based on a story that was the source material for the 1968 movie *Buona Sera, Mrs. Campbell*, which, incidentally, was a film neither Lerner nor Lane cared for. However, the two liked the premise, which involves a woman in wartime Italy who has affairs with three soldiers, and later, when she has a child (and not knowing who the real father is), tells each of them he is the father so that they will send money. She also reinvents herself as a widow, complete with the name "Campbell" (from the soup maker).

Lerner and Lane both felt their version would improve upon the film since their show would focus on the widow—and the consequences of her having based her life on a lie—and make the three men (now married themselves) less lecherous and more sympathetic. Lerner said, "I hated it in the movie when they left their children to try to make it with her." Starring as Mrs. Campbell (the role played by Gina Lollobrigida in the movie) would be Georgia Brown, and Ferrer was hired to direct. This wasn't the first time Ferrer's services had been desired by Lerner, as he had been previously sought to replace the director of the Lerner and Loewe musical *Camelot* while he was busy preparing *Return to Peyton Place*.

What made this project similar to *Camelot* was the tense rehearsal period, notably stemming from disagreements between Lerner and Lane. Remembered Lerner's daughter, Jennifer, who was the production adviser: "Dad and Burton were fighting all the time. Dad was difficult and so was Burton Lane. Besides he really didn't get along with Ferrer." According to *Carmelina* producer Roger Stevens, during the tour, which included stops in Delaware and Washington, DC, critics liked the score and thought the show had potential. But Stevens felt "the trouble is that the creators [including librettist Joseph Stein] did no work whatsoever on the road, I don't know how they could have professionally worked together, since half the time they [Lerner and Lane] weren't speaking to each other."

After a turbulent few months on the road, *Carmelina* opened in April 1979; many New York theater critics thought the writing old-fashioned. Walter Kerr of the *New York Times* was one of the dissenters, not so much regarding the old-fashioned nature of it all, but in that he found these aspects endearing. For Kerr, it was also curious that "*Carmelina* does all the easiest things awkwardly and most of the difficult things with considerable charm. Part of it may be due to the fact that director José Ferrer isn't truly a musical-comedy man. His best effects, when they come, tend to be on the straight side." Kerr cited the scene in which Carmelina confronts the three soldiers, which has "a wry but real tension" and would have been more effective in a show that wasn't a musical. As far as producer Stevens was concerned, though, the overall lackluster reviews and weak advance were enough reasons to close the show. While composer Lane felt a strong marketing campaign might have saved the show, *Carmelina* folded on April 22 after only seventeen performances, effectively putting an end to Ferrer's Broadway directorial career.

However, Ferrer's career as a stage director would be far from finished; it's just that the work took him elsewhere. Later in 1979, Ferrer

would reunite with *White Pelicans* playwright Jay Broad for an exten-
sively revised version of his 1972 play *A Conflict of Interest*. The play is
about an idealistic elder Supreme Court justice and his associate who
are pitted against some less-than-scrupulous politicians, including the
president, over the balance between judicial and executive power; as it
was originally performed before Watergate had occurred, what might
have seemed prescient then was now perhaps anticlimactic, hence the
rewrites to keep pace with a changing political landscape. This revised
version would have its premiere at the PAF Playhouse in Huntington before playing the regional theater circuit, including a stop at the Stamford
Center for the Arts.

Prior to the Stamford engagement, Ferrer reflected on his more unfortunate recent theatrical choices: "When you guess wrong two or three
times in a row, suddenly from being successful frequently, you go to being
unsuccessful frequently. . . . I keep hoping there will be a renaissance."
He also felt his present *Conflict* to be "a good yarn." Critics would consider
A Conflict of Interest to be well-acted, with reviewer Alvin Klein writing
that "Ferrer's staging is taut and telling, with enough time out for a touch
of levity." He noted in particular the visual image of all the president's
men down on one knee, being led in prayer to guide them: "Mr. Ferrer's
directorial flourishes embellish the play with sardonic comments."

One of the activities that provided the most pleasure for Ferrer in the
1980s was his increased involvement with the renowned Players Club in
New York City. It had been founded by actor Edwin Booth in 1888 following his purchase of a mansion in Gramercy Park. Booth's intention
was to establish a social club that would bring actors in contact with other
creative artists. Ferrer had portrayed Booth on Broadway and had been
a member of the Players since 1935, along with a host of other notable
members including George M. Cohan, Alfred Lunt, John Barrymore,
George S. Kaufman, James Cagney, and Gregory Peck.

So, when Ferrer was offered the position of president of the Players
Club in 1982, Ferrer was only too happy to oblige. (There had been one
or two members who objected to Ferrer based on their perception of
Ferrer's appearance before HUAC, but they were in the minority.) Actor
Robert Lansing, who succeeded Ferrer in the fall of 1991, recalled Ferrer's selflessness in assuming the presidency, especially when Ferrer was
either working when he was now living in Florida or was working "all
over the world." Lansing believed that Ferrer's symbolic presence proved
to be a great asset to the club; he also noted that one of Ferrer's major
contributions was bringing young people into the tradition-laden club.

Richard Thomas, one of those "young people," had worked with Ferrer in the television film *Berlin Tunnel 21* and recalled spending a great deal of time at the Players in the company of Ferrer. Thomas recalls several occasions where Ferrer the storyteller would keep his audiences listening and laughing: "José was one of the funniest men I knew. I know you don't normally associate that with José, but he was such a gifted raconteur."

In the latter part of his life, when Ferrer wasn't working as regularly as he would have liked, he spent a great deal of time holding court at the Players Club. He also continued painting but would admit: "I paint badly. My painting is imitative because I'm not a professional." Ferrer also spent time on his writing, sometimes contributing literary criticism, occasionally offering thoughtful commentary on the changing times. As his daughter Monsita said, "My father was always reinventing himself into something purposeful."

By 1983, Ferrer had made Miami, Florida, his primary residence for several years: "When I was living in New York, I needed a place to get away. I wanted it to be warm and to see palm trees. Miami became very beguiling to me because it's like being in the United States and Puerto Rico at the same time. I speak almost as much Spanish as I do English so my two backgrounds co-exist there for me." In 1982, he had made his first South Florida appearance in over a decade, starring in *The Dresser* at the Players State Theater. He had also recently had some high-profile, financially rewarding appearances in *A Midsummer Night's Sex Comedy* and *To Be or Not to Be*, as well a slew of television roles, so it was with a great deal of satisfaction that Ferrer announced that he would become the new artistic advisor of the Coconut Grove Playhouse for a token salary of $1 per year.

As artistic director, Ferrer would assemble the season's plays, direct one or two, act in some, and when he wasn't performing, take the stage and welcome theatergoers to the Playhouse. For his inaugural season, Ferrer decided to do a series of classic American plays: "I decided to play it safe, and I know these plays will not fail me because they are architecturally sound." These would include Moss Hart's *Light Up the Sky*, *A Funny Thing Happened on the Way to the Forum*, *Cat on a Hot Tin Roof*, *Arsenic and Old Lace*, *Life With Father* (with Ferrer starring as Clarence Day Sr. opposite *Anything Can Happen* costar Kim Hunter), and *A Soldier's Play*. Rafael Ferrer, who had appeared in the Grove's production of *Destiny in Half-Moon Street*, would also appear in *Life with Father* as Clarence Day Jr. Rafael has fond memories of the play, recalling what made his father unique, in both his roles as actor and producer. In a memorable scene from the play, the irascible father presents his wife with a china pug-dog: "My father got the original pug-dog, I believe from Lindsay Crouse's daughter . . . every time it came out, I had to hand it to Kim Hunter and I thought, 'Oh shit, if I drop this, I'm screwed.' I never did."

Rafael also marvels at the electricity his father still brought to the stage: "The most amazing thing is there is a scene where Day Sr. talks to Day Jr. about girls and Day Jr. has to sit agog, while I was in my twenties and could hold my own . . . in one performance he had the audience in his hands, and I sat, not like an actor. . . . Here I thought I was even, but it's like driving a Volkswagen against a Ferrari. I became a *fan*. When he turns it on, it was the most amazing thing."

If things were smooth onstage for Ferrer, whether acting or directing, offstage it was a different matter. He received torrents of criticism during and after his first full season. Detractors complained that his choice of shows had been too safe; they cited both cronyism and nepotism in his use of both "names" and family members. In terms of the nepotism charge, Ferrer asserted that "I wouldn't use them [Miguel and Rafael] if they weren't the best choices for the job." As for his use of "names" to sell tickets, board members had hoped that Ferrer would be able to attract "stars," and were not exactly pleased at the "names" he was able to use. In response, Ferrer said, "Believe me, if I could get big stars, I'd get them. I have little to offer them, small salary, two months' work, no appreciable recognition outside this area. It's a catch-22 situation. If he gets stars, he's going commercial. If he doesn't get stars, why no stars?"

Then there were the financial concerns, as the Coconut Grove Playhouse would lose money in its first season under Ferrer's guidance. The Grove had lost so much money during the summer season (roughly $40,000) that Ferrer had to abruptly cancel the last show, *The Rainmaker* (which would have followed a tepidly received production of *Last of the Red Hot Lovers*). In the fall of 1984, going into Ferrer's second season, the Playhouse had sold only 6,200 subscriptions, as opposed to the total of 9,700 subscribers during his first season (the theater's sell-out point is 22,400). Ferrer would have much to do in his second season to turn things around.

Since the Grove was in a financial bind, Ferrer would have to be prudent in his choice of material. He pulled a scheduled *House of Flowers* from the schedule, citing its prohibitive cost at a time when "we ought to retrench financially." For now, the season would consist of *Sleuth* (costarring Ferrer and Patrick Macnee of TV's *The Avengers*), *The Glass Menagerie*,

Betrayal, Pump Boys and Dinettes, and *When You Comin' Back, Red Ryder?*
He also decided to revive the Grove's Hispanic project, this time with a
Spanish version of *The Glass Menagerie* to be performed at certain times
during the run of the Tennessee Williams original: *Mundo Del Cristal* (as
in the play's Spanish title) would have Cuban-born actress Rosa Felipe
as Amanda (Constance Cummings would star in the English-language
counterpart), with the rest of the roles performed by local actors. When
asked why undertake both an English and Spanish *Menagerie,* Ferrer said,
"I've always had the determination to include the Hispanic community as
much as possible in our efforts . . . the English-language version should
pay its way, and the extra expenses are small."

All of Ferrer's talent and innovations could not guarantee success during his tenure at the Playhouse, and amidst reports that the Playhouse
was seeking a new director, Ferrer resigned after two turbulent and only
intermittently successful years. In a press release, Ferrer admitted that he
had no real experience in regional theater and had questioned his own
ability to handle the job. Although he had "happy hopes of succeeding,"
Ferrer was resigning because of what he viewed as obvious reasons: "Attendance and subscriptions have not increased, and overall my work
has not met with approval from the press." While Ferrer did produce
(and direct) the occasional critical success (such as *Cat on a Hot Tin Roof*),
it's likely that he played it too safe, preferring to stage the "war horses."
Since regional companies were generally thought of as a place to develop
new playwrights and provide more stimulating fare, Ferrer was criticized
for his conventional choices, especially since they did not produce the
desired box-office magic. It's even more regrettable that Ferrer did not
use his leadership position to help cultivate new authors, especially as he
was willing, in his capacity as an actor, to star in works by untested playwrights. Had Ferrer done so, he may have enhanced his standing with
the Grove subscribers—provided the bottom line was met.

Ferrer still believed in the durability and relevance of the classic American drama, and in 1987, he flew to Los Angeles at the behest of producer
Martin Manulis to direct Gore Vidal's *The Best Man* at the Ahmanson
Theatre. The seventy-five-year-old Ferrer was directing another political
play (his last had been *A Conflict of Interest*) and was grateful to Manulis
for the opportunity. Ferrer told interviewer David Galligan, "In a way, I
think I'm starting all over again. . . . I've been sitting by the phone waiting to be called for a guest shot on a television series. For the last few
months I've said 'to hell with that' . . . I'm going to do things that fulfill

me." Unfortunately, the reviews for *The Best Man* were disappointing, with some critics remarking the production was reminiscent of summer theater, and not a polished, professional production.

Ferrer's resignation from the Coconut Grove Playhouse did not end his involvement with theater in Florida, especially since he and Stella would continue to call the state their home. In 1988, Ferrer directed *Who'll Save the Plowboy* for the Ensemble Theater of Florida, a thought-provoking drama about a veteran who saves a friend's life only to see that he is now living a less-than-complete life, leading the veteran to wonder if it was all for naught. Ensemble Theater was impressed enough, both by his work and by his celebrity, to ask Ferrer back the following season—not only to act but to help raise money for the theater. In October 1989, Ensemble would promote *An Evening with José Ferrer*, a fundraiser for those well-heeled few who would share Ferrer's company and enjoy his musicianship, since he incorporated some piano interludes into the evening. Ferrer would also direct and act in *Helping Arthur Out*, starring as a retired director-turned-critic who is trying to recapture his brilliance while coping with deteriorating health. Given Ferrer's age (he had turned seventy-six) and the fewer theatrical opportunities that came his way, the play must have seemed a little too close to Ferrer's real-life situation. Ferrer's performance earned favorable notices for being "honest and natural, without resorting to theatrical shortcuts," as William Mosley of *Florida Today* put it.

Two of Ferrer's final stage appearances would be in the realm of musical theater. In 1990, the seventy-eight-year-old actor again journeyed to Sussex, England, to star in the Chichester Festival Theatre's production of *Born Again*, a musical based on Eugene Ionesco's *Rhinoceros*. *Born Again* featured music by Jason Carr and a libretto by Julian Barry and Peter Hall (who also directed). Ferrer inherited yet another Zero Mostel role, since he had created the part in Ionesco's 1961 production (and had reprised for a misbegotten 1974 film). The setting of this update was now a modern-day shopping mall in Ranchero, California, and Ferrer's costar was Mandy Patinkin. Reviewers were not kind, with Matt Wolf of the *Chicago Tribune* remarking that "Ferrer struggles to keep his dignity, advising Martin [Patinkin] early on to write about 'the enormity of the conformity' and doing an eventual rhino bump and grind to Carr's eclectic, utterly impersonal score."

Ferrer's last appearance on an American stage was in the musical revival *Fanny* for the Paper Mill Playhouse. *Fanny*, with a book by S. N. Behrman and Joshua Logan and music and lyrics by Harold Rome, was a success on Broadway when it opened in 1954, playing 866 performances. While *Fanny* never achieved legendary status, its supporters view the show as being filled with honest emotion and well-developed characters. Ferrer played Cesar, the father of Marius (the young man who loves and leaves Fanny), engaged in a lifelong friendly rivalry with Panisse (George Irving), the gentleman who marries the pregnant Fanny. In his review, Alvin Klein noted that while Ferrer may rely on his classy presence, his performance does gain momentum, and "by the time Ferrer sings 'Love is a Very Light Thing' in the second act, one is able to witness the flowering of a true singing actor." While Cesar had been created on Broadway by famed opera singer Ezio Pinza (though he is perhaps better known to Broadway audiences for *South Pacific*), composer Harold Rome's wife, Florence, loved Ferrer's interpretation: "It was totally different from anything Pinza did. It was more literate, nothing flashy. He let the play take precedence over him."

In 1991, Ferrer was scheduled to return to Broadway, costarring opposite Judd Hirsch in Herb Gardner's *Conversations with My Father*. Ferrer was cast as Eddie, an embittered bartender and first-generation Russian immigrant, in a play that explored the volatile relationship between Eddie and his son, Charlie. The determined Ferrer began the arduous process of memorizing his lines, but as his daughter Monsita pointed out, "Learning lines came harder for him." In addition, he was experiencing some discomfort and after undergoing some medical tests, Ferrer dropped out of the play on the advice of his doctors, who felt that he would not be able to withstand the rigors of a Broadway run. Producer Jim Walsh remembered being surprised when Ferrer called him with the news since Ferrer had seemed "strong and robust" when meeting about the play over the summer: "He had lunch with Herb Gardner, Judd Hirsch, and me. He got up to show us some business and made us laugh."

Ferrer had been diagnosed with colon cancer. Daughters Monsita and Maria recalled that initially Ferrer's wife, Stella, wanted to maintain a degree of privacy and not say anything. Monsita said that the doctor had informed Ferrer this was hereditary, and the children needed to know. When Ferrer and Stella were in Los Angeles, Ferrer met with Monsita, Maria, Gabriel, and Miguel. According to Monsita, Ferrer told them that he had been diagnosed with colon cancer and that it has spread and to "please check—early detection is essential." As Monsita recalled, it would be a private moment that was marred by Stella's insistence on taping the conversation: "He's saying this, and we're staring at this stupid cassette recorder." Maria agreed, feeling "it was an invasion of a private moment."

Although Ferrer had been raised as a Catholic, he didn't exactly follow the dictates of the Church. He did possess a strong belief in the spiritual world and God. As daughter Maria would tell me: "He had a belief in a higher power . . . he wasn't anything, but he was *everything*." Ferrer's sister Elvira, with whom he would always remain close, was extremely Catholic. Monsita recalled that toward the end, Aunt Elvira cultivated a holy garden. When Monsita asked her father about it, he said, "It clearly makes her feel better—it shouldn't hurt, maybe it'll help."

Ferrer would undergo some treatments at Columbia Presbyterian Hospital, where he was staying on the same floor as Sunny von Bulow (wife of Claus von Bulow). Rafael recalls visiting him, and that Ferrer's mordant sense of humor was still intact. "My father, he had a colostomy bag, and he says to me, 'You like my bag?' I said, 'Aaaah . . .' and he says, 'I gotta get some shoes to match.'" In his final days, he would be in Miami; the colon cancer had spread to his stomach, but he was still playing the "gallant." Monsita remembers that "when he was dying, he was a cadaver—but he was so macho. He would say, 'Let me take your bag.' I told him, 'It weighs more than you do.'" When she wasn't in Florida, Monsita would talk to her father every day: "I'd tell him I was going to see a movie, like *Grand Canyon*, and he'd want to talk about it with me and my husband." Ferrer died on January 26, 1992, at Doctors Hospital in Coral Gables, Florida. Monsita recalls that last day: "Stella called me at two or three in the morning, 'Your father's not doing well.' I didn't take a suitcase—I had to change planes in Charlotte . . . he died before I could get there." José Ferrer would be interred in his native Puerto Rico, in Santa Maria Magdalena de Pazzis cemetery in Old San Juan.

When asked about the death of her former husband, Rosemary Clooney said: "I shared the most important part of my life with him. I miss him very much." Long after their divorce, they had remained on good terms, as their children have attested. After they divorced for the second time, Clooney had announced her retirement from performing, ostensibly to be there for her children, but partly because of an addiction to sleeping pills and the damage they had been inflicting on her vocal cords. In the mid-1970s, Clooney made a professional comeback, courtesy of her good friend Bing Crosby, who invited her to tour with him. Clooney also recorded a series of albums with Concord Records, gaining fame later in life as a renowned jazz singer. She also reunited with her former boyfriend Dante DiPaolo in 1973, and the two were finally married in 1997. They remained together until Clooney succumbed to lung cancer in 2002.

The various respectful obituaries that relayed the news of Ferrer's death made reference to his longevity, his versatility, and his intelligence. Bruce Lambert of the *New York Times* would also note that "while his skill and intellect were often praised, some critics regretted that he failed to project much warmth." Before he died, Ferrer had begun receiving several honors commemorating his contributions to the arts. He would be inducted into the American Theater Hall of Fame in 1981. This award was given to those who had been in the theater for over twenty-five years, with at least five major production credits. Among Ferrer's fellow recipients that year were Lee. J. Cobb, Gwen Verdon, as well as two with whom he had a shared history: Uta Hagen and Jed Harris. Ferrer was the first actor—and first Hispanic—to be honored with the National Medal of Arts when the awards began in 1985 under President Ronald Reagan. Created by the Congress in 1984, it was the highest honor bestowed on an individual artist. Ferrer was the only actor among such august company as dancer Martha Graham, writer Ralph Ellison, and painter Georgia O' Keefe. It would be another two years before another actor received the honor (Eva Le Gallienne in 1987).

José Ferrer and his Academy Award became newsworthy as recently as 2016, with the revelation that his Oscar, which he had donated to the University of Puerto Rico, had disappeared. In 2000, the University of Puerto Rico was renovating its theater when the statuette was misplaced, not to be seen again. There was speculation that it had been stolen; Ferrer's son Miguel put up a cash reward for its return, but the Oscar was never recovered. Miguel was further dismayed at the Academy's refusal to replace it, even after Miguel offered to pay for it. According to Miguel, the Academy's attitude was if it's lost or stolen and the honoree was alive, they would replace it, but, if the honoree was dead, "then it's too bad."

Ferrer would be the posthumous recipient of several awards and retrospectives. In 2003, the Directors Guild of America's Latino Committee presented "A Tribute to José Ferrer," and several prominent members of the Latino cultural community were effusive in their praise of Ferrer. Actress Liz Torres (*Gilmore Girls*) said, "This man carried his culture with him and raised it to a new level." She considered Ferrer to be "our hero, our leader, our icon." DGA member Ricardo Menendez Matta recalled watching the Ferrer-directed *I Accuse* with his father: "He told me it was performed and written by a Puerto Rican. At the time, nobody from Puerto Rico was in the movie business. I never knew one could do that. Now I live it." In 2005, the Hispanic Organization of Latino Actors (HOLA) would rename its Tepsis Award, now called the "José Ferrer

HOLA Tepsis Award." In 2012, Ferrer became the first Hispanic actor to be honored with a "Forever" stamp from the US Postal Service. The ceremony was held at the Players Club, where actor John Martello recalled Ferrer's sense of humor, often aimed at himself—as in the evening when Ferrer went on stage as Cyrano without the long nose, "and nobody noticed the difference." Luis Balzac, representing then-Governor Luis Fortuno of Puerto Rico, hailed Ferrer as a product of two cultures and a symbol of the New World.

Throughout the last period of his life, Ferrer could be found composing touching tributes to his late former colleagues. On the occasion of the death of his *Shrike* costar Judith Evelyn, Ferrer had written: "Miss Evelyn leaves no immediate survivors. Accurate but not true. She leaves many survivors: those of us who worked with her, those of us whose paths crossed hers, and above all, the millions who saw her act. They too remember." By contrast, Ferrer did have his immediate survivors, including his last wife, Stella, and his six children, as well as an extended family in Puerto Rico and the United States. However, there are the countless others whose paths crossed his or have seen him act and have been influenced by his achievements in theater, film, and television. Ferrer was both a proud son of Puerto Rico and an American—one who transcended both stereotypes and expectations to become a respected actor and director. He was a survivor in an industry not known for its longevity, and he contributed meaningful work until nearly the end of his life. Some colleagues might say Ferrer was a flawed individual but even they would admit there was much to cherish and admire about the man and the artist. With any luck, future generations will remember.

FILMOGRAPHY

1948   *Joan of Arc* as the Dauphin
1949   *Whirlpool* as David Korvo
1950   *The Secret Fury* (uncredited)
1950   *Crisis* as Raoul Farrago
1950   *Cyrano de Bergerac* as Cyrano
1952   *Anything Can Happen* as Giorgi Papashvily
1952   *Moulin Rouge* as Henri de Toulouse-Lautrec and Count Alphonse, his father
1953   *Miss Sadie Thompson* as Alfred Davidson
1954   *Deep in My Heart* as Sigmund Romberg
1954   *The Caine Mutiny* as Barney Greenwald
1955   *The Shrike* as Jim Downs—also director
1955   *The Cockleshell Heroes* as Major Stringer; also director
1956   *The Great Man* as Joe Harris; also director
1957   *Four Girls in Town*—director (uncredited)
1958   *I Accuse!* as Captain Alfred Dreyfus; also director
1958   *The High Cost of Loving* as Jim "Jimbo" Fry; also director
1961   *Return to Peyton Place* as the voice of Mark Steele (uncredited); also director
1962   *State Fair*—director
1962   *Lawrence of Arabia* as Turkish Bey
1963   *Nine Hours to Rama* as Supt. Gopal Das
1964   *Stop Train 349* as Cowan the Reporter
1964   *Cyrano et d'Artagnan* as Cyrano
1965   *The Greatest Story Ever Told* as Herod Antipas
1965   *Ship of Fools* as Siegfried Rieber
1967   *Enter Laughing* as Harrison B. Marlowe
1967   *The Young Rebel/Cervantes* as Hassan Bey
1975   *e'Lollipop/Forever Young, Forever Free* as Father Alberto

1976 *Paco* as Fermin Flores
1976 *Crash!* as Marc Denne
1977 *Who Has Seen the Wind* as the Ben
1977 *The Private Files of J. Edgar Hoover* as Lionel McCoy
1977 *The Sentinel* as Robed Figure
1978 *Dracula's Dog/Zoltan, Hound of Hell* as Inspector Branco
1978 *The Swarm* as Dr. Andrews
1979 *The Fifth Musketeer* as Athos
1979 *Natural Enemies* as Harry Rosenthal
1979 *A Life of Sin* as the Bishop
1980 *Battle Creek Brawl* as Dominici
1981 *Bloody Birthday* as the Doctor
1982 *A Midsummer Night's Sex Comedy* as Leopold
1982 *Blood Tide* as Nereus
1983 *The Being* as Mayor Gordon Lane
1983 *To Be or Not to Be* as Professor Siletski
1984 *The Evil That Men Do* as Hector Lomelin
1987 *The Sun and the Moon* as Don Fulhencio
1990 *Hired to Kill* as Rallis
1991 *Old Explorers* as Warner Watney
1992 *Arrest the Reckless*

BROADWAY CREDITS

Sept. 1935–Nov. 1935	*A Slight Case of Murder* as the 2nd Policeman
Nov. 1935–Dec. 1935	*Stick-in-the-Mud* as the Chauffeur
Aug. 1936–Sept. 1936	*Spring Dance* as the Lippincott
Dec. 1936–May 1938	*Brother Rat* as Dan Crawford
Oct. 1937	*In Clover* as Frederick Parsons
Feb. 1938	*How to Get Tough About It* as Vergez
Jan. 1939–May 1939	*Mamba's Daughters* as St. Julien Wentworth
Nov. 1939–Feb. 1940	*Key Largo* as Victor D'Alcala
Oct. 1940–May 1941	*Charley's Aunt* as Lord Babberly
Oct. 1941–March 1943	*Let's Face It* as Jerry Walker (replacing original cast member Danny Kaye from Feb. 22, 1943–March 1943)
Sept. 1942–Oct. 1942	*Vickie* as George Roberts; also director
Oct. 1943–July 1944	*Othello* as Iago
May 1945–June 1945	*Othello* as Iago
Nov. 1946–Jan. 1946	*Strange Fruit*—director and producer
Oct. 1946–March 1947	*Cyrano de Bergerac* as Cyrano; also director and producer
March 1947	*As We Forgive Our Debtors*—director and producer
Jan. 1948	*Volpone* as Volpone
Jan. 1948–Feb. 1948	*Angel Street* as Mr. Manningham
May 1948	*The Alchemist* as Jeremy, Face
May 1948	*S.S. Glencairn*—director
June 1948	*The Insect Comedy* as Felix; also director
Nov. 1948–May 1949	*The Silver Whistle* as Oliver Erwenter
Dec. 1950–June 1951	*Twentieth Century* as Oscar Jaffe—also director and producer
May 1951–June 1952	*Stalag 17*—director and producer
Oct. 1951–May 1953	*The Fourposter*—director

April 1952–May 1952   *The Chase*—director and producer
March 1954–Jan. 1954   *My Three Angels*—director
Nov. 1953   *Cyrano de Bergerac* as Cyrano; also director
Nov. 1953–Dec. 1953   *The Shrike* as Jim Downs; also director
Dec. 1953   *Richard III* as Richard III
Dec. 1953–Jan. 1954   *Charley's Aunt* as Lord Babberly; also director
Jan. 1955   *The Fourposter*—director
Feb. 1958–July 1958   *Oh Captain!*—director and writer
Nov. 1958–Dec. 1958   *Edwin Booth* as Edwin Booth—also director and
                         producer
March 1959   *Juno*—director
Dec. 1959–June 1960   *The Andersonville Trial*—director
Dec. 1963–March 1964   *The Girl Who Came to Supper* as Grand Duke
                         Charles
Nov. 1965–June 1971   *Man of La Mancha* as Don Quixote (replac-
                         ing Richard Kiley from May 28, 1966–June 9,
                         1966)
April 1979   *Carmelina*—director

TELEVISION CREDITS

José Ferrer made many television appearances from the late 1940s through 1991. Ferrer guest-starred as "himself" on a number of talk shows, game shows, and variety shows. In addition, he made guest dramatic appearances on television series, and appeared (or starred) in a number of television movies and miniseries. These miniseries or television movie credits are noted in parentheses after the title; most other shows are his guest-starring appearances on established series. When possible, the networks have also been identified: Columbia Broadcasting System (CBS), National Broadcasting Company (NBC), American Broadcasting Company (ABC), and the Arts and Entertainment Network (A&E)

1949	*The Philco Television Playhouse*	"What Makes Sammy Run?" as Sammy Glick	NBC
	The Philco Television Playhouse	"Cyrano de Bergerac" as Cyrano	NBC
	We the People	as himself	NBC
1950	*Penthouse Party* as	himself	ABC
	Your Show of Shows	as host	NBC
1951	*Four Star Revue*	as himself	NBC
1955	*Kraft Television Theatre*	"Mr. Candido" as Mr. Candido	NBC
	Person to Person	as himself	CBS
	What's My Line	mystery guest	CBS
	Producers' Showcase	"Cyrano de Bergerac" as Cyrano	NBC
1958	*Tennessee Ernie Ford Show*	as himself	NBC

1958	The Lux Show with Rosemary Clooney	as himself	NBC
	The Ed Sullivan Show	as himself and Edwin Booth	CBS
1959	General Electric Theater	"Survival" as Joe Garvey	CBS
	The Ed Sullivan Show	as himself	CBS
	The US Steel Hour	"Marriage—Handle with Care" as guest star	CBS
1960	The Dinah Shore Chevy Show	as himself	NBC
1963	The Greatest Show on Earth	as Harry Kyle	ABC
	Password	as himself	CBS
	The Danny Kaye Show	as himself (also appeared in 1964)	CBS
1964	Bewitched	as narrator for Episode 1	ABC
1966	Mike Douglas Show	as himself (also appeared in 1968)	Syndicated
1967	Merv Griffin Show	as himself	Syndicated
	Kismet	as Hajj	ABC
1968	A Case of Libel (TV movie)	as Boyd Bendix	ABC
1969	Joey Bishop Show	as himself	ABC
	Name of the Game	as Adrian Blake	CBS
1970	The David Frost Show as	as himself	
	This is Tom Jones	as himself	ABC
	The Aquarians (TV movie)	as Dr. Vreeland	
1971	Banyon (pilot episode)	as Lee Jennings	NBC
	Hallmark Hall of Fame	"Gideon" as Angel	NBC
1973	The Marcus-Nelson Murders	as Jake Weinhaus	CBS
1974	Columbo	"Mind Over Mayhem" as Dr. Cahill	NBC
	ABC Afterschool Special	"Cyrano de Bergerac" as Cyrano	ABC
1975	Mike Douglas Show	as co-host	Syndicated
	The Missing are Deadly (TV movie)	as Ed Warren	CBS

1975	*The Art of Crime* (TV movie)	as Beckwith Sloan	CBS
	Medical Story (pilot episode)		NBC
1976	*Hallmark Hall of Fame*	"Truman at Potsdam" as Joseph Stalin	NBC
	Starsky and Hutch	"Murder at Sea" as Crazy Joey Fortune	ABC
1977	*Exo-Man* (TV movie)	as Kermit Haas	NBC
	The Rhinemann Exchange (TV miniseries)	as Erich Rhinemann	ABC
1978	*The Return of Captain Nemo* (TV miniseries)	as Captain Nemo	CBS
	Hallmark Hall of Fame "Fame"	as Francesco	NBC
1979	*The French-Atlantic Affair* (TV miniseries)	as President Brouchard	ABC
	Tales of the Unexpected	"Man from the South" as Carlos	Syndicated
1980	*Hallmark Hall of Fame*	"Gideon's Trumpet" as Abe Fortas	CBS
	Dinah!	as Himself	CBS
1981	*The Love Boat*	as Deke	ABC
	The Dream Merchants (TV movie)	as George Pappas	
1982	*Evita Peron*	Agustin Magaldi	
	Berlin Tunnel 21 (TV movie)	as Komanski	NBC
	Quincy	"Ghost of a Chance" as Dr. Stanley Royce	CBS
1983	*Another World*	as Reuben Marino	NBC
	Fantasy Island	as Nikros Karavatos	ABC
1984	*George Washington* (TV miniseries)	as Governor Dinwiddie	ABC
	Hotel	"Passages" as Alex Huff	ABC
	Murder, She Wrote	"Death Casts a Spell" as Cagliostro	CBS
1984	*Samson and Delilah* (TV movie)	as the High Priest	ABC
1985	*Hitler's SS: Portrait in Evil* (TV movie)	as Professor Rosenberg	ABC

1985	*Seduced* (TV movie)	as James Killian	CBS
	Covenant (TV movie)	as Victor Noble	
	Newhart	as Arthur Vanderkellen (Ferrer was a recurring character on this series, appearing in five episodes from November 1985 to November 1987)	CBS
1986	*Bridges to Cross*	as Morris Kane (Ferrer was a regular cast member on this series, which ran for six episodes from April 1986 to June 1986)	CBS
	Matlock	"The Don" as Nicholas Baron	NBC
	Blood and Orchids (TV movie)	as Walter Bergman	CBS
1987	*Magical World of Disney* "Young Harry Houdini"	as Dr. Grimaldi	
1988	*American Playhouse*	"Strange Interlude" as Professor Leeds	PBS
	Sesame Street	as Tio José	PBS
1989	*American Playwrights Theater*	"Rope" as Abraham Bentley	A&E
	Mother's Day (TV movie)	as Judge Leatham	Family Channel
1991	*Maniac Mansion*	"The Celebrity Visitor" as himself	Family Channel

SELECTED NOTES

CHAPTER 1: THE MANY SIDES OF JOSÉ FERRER

For thoughts regarding vaudeville and other early items, Michael Buckley's "José Ferrer Remembered (1912–1992)" was a very valuable resource. Some valuable information pertaining to the marriage of Ferrer and Rosemary Clooney was gleaned from Clooney's memoir *By Myself*, Malcolm McFarlane's *Late Life Jazz*, and interviews with three of Ferrer's children with Rosemary Clooney: Rafael Ferrer, Monsita Ferrer, and Maria Ferrer. Garson Kanin and Marian Seldes's memories of Ferrer are from Howard Kissel's "Ferrer's Unflagging Energy."

Interview with H. M. Wynant, concerning Ferrer, circa 1949.

CHAPTER 2: FROM PUERTO RICO TO PRINCETON AND PERFORMANCE

The José Ferrer Archives at Boston University was a very valuable resource, containing clippings from the *New York Times*, *Herald Tribune*, and other publications as well as personal letters. Background about Rafael and Maria Ferrer, as well as Ferrer's days at Princeton, came from various sources, including "From San Juan to Cyrano"; "Fabulous Joe Ferrer"; "All the Stage is His World"; press releases; and interviews with Monsita, Maria, and Rafael. Joshua Logan's *Movie Stars, Real People and Me* was also helpful. The clipping file on José Ferrer at the New York Public Library of Performing Arts also proved quite useful, with assorted reviews from the *Times* and *Daily News*, among other publications. In addition, the Uta Hagen/Herbert Berghof Papers at the New York Performing Arts Library were valuable, providing information on early Hagen/Ferrer teamings, a significant number of letters between Hagen and Ferrer, Hagen's interview with author Martin Duberman, and Susan Spector's superb work, "Uta Hagen: The Early Years: 1919–1951."

CHAPTER 3: *OTHELLO*: PAUL, UTA, AND JOSÉ

For information on *Othello*, including the backstage squabbles, I consulted Milly Barranger's exceptional *Margaret Webster: A Life in the Theater*; the José Ferrer Archives; Martin Duberman's *Paul Robeson: A Biography*; Hagen's interview with Duberman; and assorted articles from the *New York Times*. Joshua Logan's *Movie Stars, Real People and Me*. provided insight into Ferrer's unflagging energy and invention. Ferrer was also interviewed many times; a number of quotations here are from "From San Juan to Cyrano." Ferrer and *The Lost Weekend* can be found in Gene D. Phillips's *Some Like it Wilder* and in Charles Brackett's journals.

CHAPTER 4: *STRANGE FRUIT*—THEN *CYRANO*

The José Ferrer Archive and various articles in the *New York Times* and *Daily News* furnished information and background material on *Strange Fruit* and *Cyrano*. Uta Hagen's papers, her book *Sources*, and her interviews with Duberman provided background about the end of the marriage. "From San Juan to Cyrano" and "All the World is His Stage" also provided information on his struggle to get it to the stage, as well as the financial hole he found himself in. The story with the Boston critics comes courtesy of son Rafael. Joshua Logan's memoir provided insight into the *Cyrano* directorial credit.

CHAPTER 5: SCREEN AND STAGE

Michael Sragow's *Victor Fleming: An American Movie Master* and Bosley Crowther's *New York Times* articles provided background for *Joan of Arc*, as did clippings from the *Hollywood Reporter*, *Box Office*, and *Variety*. The *New York Times*, as well as the clipping file in the José Ferrer Archives and New York Library of Performing Arts, gave useful information on Ferrer at City Center, *The Silver Whistle*, and potential Ferrer projects. Also useful was *Richard Barr: The Playwright's Producer*, about City Center and *Romeo and Juliet*. Correspondence between Ferrer and Hagen's lawyers can be found in Uta Hagen's papers. Foster Hirsch's *Otto Preminger: The Man Who Would be King* was helpful with Ferrer's experience on *Whirlpool*. The Richard Brooks biography, *The World of Entertainment* and the file on *Crisis* from the Arthur Freed Collection at University of Southern California's (USC) Cinematic Arts Library provided insight into the making of the movie.

CHAPTER 6: *CYRANO*—THE MOVIE

Stanley Kramer's memoir, *A Mad, Mad, Mad World*, and Donald Spoto's *Stanley Kramer, Filmmaker* were helpful with the filming of *Cyrano*, as were production notes in the collections at USC and the Margaret Herrick Library. In addition, Bosley Crowther's "'A' Movies on a 'B' Budget" and papers in the José Ferrer Archives at Boston University were helpful, as was Gilbert Millstein's profile "All the Stage is His World."

CHAPTER 7: LEFT, RIGHT, OSCAR, AND CLOONEY

Twentieth Century and the Oscar party: Gloria Swanson's memoir *Swanson on Swanson*; "From San Juan to Cyrano"; and "All the Stage is His World."

Ferrer's troubles with HUAC: papers in the Ferrer Archives at Boston University; articles in the *New York Times* and *Chicago Tribune*; *Communist Infiltration in Hollywood*, May 22, 25, 1951 sessions; Michael Munn's *James Stewart: The Truth Behind the Legend*; and Milly Barranger's *Margaret Webster: A Life in the Theater*.

Ferrer's acting abilities: "All the World is His Stage."

Background on Rosemary Clooney: *Girl Singer*; *Late Life Jazz*.

Ferrer in Puerto Rico: *New York Times*; *Los Angeles Times*.

Stalag 17: José Ferrer Archives; clippings from New York Public Library for the Performing Arts and Margaret Herrick Library; and David Galligan's "'Best Man' José Ferrer" (for information on how Ferrer became involved).

CHAPTER 8: HE'S EVERYWHERE

Anything Can Happen: production files at Margaret Herrick Library; George Seaton's "Polyergic Performer is Director's Delight"; and articles in the *Hollywood Reporter* and *Variety*.

The Fourposter: Hume Cronyn's charming memoir, *A Terrible Liar.*

The Shrike: articles and production clippings in the José Ferrer Archives; "'Best Man' José Ferrer" for his thoughts on directing and sticking to the play's original ending; and reviews from the *New York Times* and *Herald Tribune*.

Seeing Rosemary Clooney: *Girl Singer; Late Life Jazz.*

The Musical Comedy Man: articles in *New York Times, Los Angeles Times,* and the José Ferrer Archives.

The Chase: articles and clippings in Ferrer Archives and New York Library of Performing Arts

CHAPTER 9: FILM STAR, CITY CENTER SAVIOR, AND NEWLYWED

Moulin Rouge: An Open Book; John Huston: Courage and Art; John Huston: Interviews; "Fabulous Joe Ferrer"; and Al Hine's "Paris in the 90s."

Miss Sadie Thompson: "Fabulous Joe Ferrer"; two fine Rita Hayworth biographies, Barbara Leaming's *If This Was Happiness* and John Kobal's *The Time, the Place, and the Woman.*

Ferrer and a proposed Hayworth reteaming: Jerry Wald Collection at USC.

Wedding to Rosemary Clooney: *Late Life Jazz; Girl Singer.*

CHAPTER 10: LIFE IS ROSIE

Ferrer/Clooney marriage: *Late Life Jazz; Girl Singer;* "Fabulous Joe Ferrer"; and interviews with Monsita Ferrer, Maria Ferrer, and Rafael Ferrer.

Caine Mutiny: Stanley Kramer, Filmmaker; A Mad, Mad, Mad World; "Caine Mutiny Filmmakers Relate How it's Done"; "Hollywood Canvas"; clippings from the *Hollywood Reporter* and *Variety*; and production notes at Margaret Herrick Library.

Return to City Center: "Return to the Beehive"; clippings from the Ferrer Archives and the New York Library of the Performing Arts; and *Margaret Webster: A Life in the Theater.*

Deep in My Heart: The Arthur Freed Collection at USC Cinema Arts Library; *Dancing on the Ceiling: Stanley Donen and His Movies;* clippings from the Ferrer Archives and the Margaret Herrick Library; and Ferrer's letter to Kenneth McKenna.

CHAPTER 11: HE DIRECTS MOVIES, TOO

The Shrike film: June Allyson's memoir; articles and clippings from the Ferrer Archives; production notes and files at USC Cinema Arts Library; and "José Ferrer's Interests are Varied."

Married life: *Girl Singer*; *Late Life Jazz*; and "Fabulous Joe Ferrer."

The Cockleshell Heroes: included in the Ferrer Archives are heated letters between Ferrer and the producers, as well as clippings and articles on the production; "Daring Commando Aids Film of Exploits"; and *When Eagles Dared*, a comprehensive look at fact-based World War II films.

CHAPTER 12: THE GREAT MAN AND MARRIED LIFE

Travails on *Matador*: correspondence in the Ferrer Archives at Boston University and in the Margaret Herrick Library; and *John Huston: Courage and Art*.

Early problems in the Ferrer/Clooney marriage: *Late Life Jazz*; *Girl Singer*; and interviews with Monsita Ferrer, Maria Ferrer, and Rafael Ferrer.

The Great Man: production files and notes at USC; Gary Berman's *Perfect Fool*; Keenan Wynn's *Ed Wynn's Son*; and Jose Ferrer's "Cyrano and Others."

CHAPTER 13: DARK AND LIGHT, IN THEATER AND FILM

I Accuse: Hy Hollinger's "Ferrer on France's Dreyfus Phobia"; Lowell Redelings's "The Hollywood Scene"; informative reviews by Philip K. Scheuer and Bosley Crowther; and clippings in the Ferrer Archives.

The High Cost of Loving: clippings and production notes in the Margaret Herrick Library; Robert Relyea's *Not So Quiet on the Set* (thanks to Ned Comstock for this, among other finds); and "Silver Blonde—Golden Future."

The state of their marriage and Nelson Riddle's presence in their lives: *September in the Rain: The Life of Nelson Riddle*; *Girl Singer*; and interviews with Monsita Ferrer and Maria Ferrer.

Oh Captain: articles and clippings in the Ferrer Archives and New York Library of Performing Arts; "Versatile Actor" (about Tony Randall).

Edwin Booth: the Ferrer Archives; clippings from the New York Library of Performing Arts; "Ferrer Terms Booth Most Challenging Role"; and Philip Scheuer's article on the play's evolution, "Booth Tragedy Uses Ferrer's Many Talents."

Juno: production notes, clippings, and reviews, including from the *Daily News* and the *New York Times*, found in the New York Library of Performing Arts.

Ferrer on television: "Television is Great, But . . ."

The Andersonville Trial, *Rage*, and *Honor*: "Return of a Mellowed Enfant Terrible"; production notes and clippings in the Ferrer Archives and New York Library of Performing Arts.

CHAPTER 14: TAKING THE JOBS AND KEEPING UP APPEARANCES

Failing marriage: *Girl Singer*; *Late Life Jazz*; *September in the Rain: The Life of Nelson Riddle*; articles from the *Los Angeles Times* and *New York Times*; and interviews with Monsita, Maria, and Rafael Ferrer.

Gianni Schicchi: "Ferrer in Debut as Opera Singer"

State Fair and *Return to Peyton Place*: extensive Twentieth Century-Fox production files, clippings, and correspondence at the Margaret Herrick Library; interview with Carol Lynley; thoughts on producers in "Cyrano and Others"; and a lengthy and revealing Ferrer interview in *Films and Filming*.

CHAPTER 15: ONCE MORE INTO THE BREACH

Lawrence of Arabia: Kevin Brownlow's *David Lean*; articles in the *Hollywood Reporter* and *New York Times*; recollections by Ferrer in assorted publications including *Films and Filming*' John Soister's *Claude Rains*; and "The Resurrection of Lawrence of Arabia."

Nine Hours to Rama: production articles at Margaret Herrick Library; Ferrer's insights into his role in "Cyrano and Others."

The Girl Who Came for Supper: *The Noël Coward Diaries*; *The Letters of Noël Coward*; Florence Henderson's memoir, *Life Is Not a Stage*; articles and clippings in the Margaret Herrick Library and the Ferrer Archives; and *Girl Singer*.

The Greatest Story Ever Told: *Giant: George Stevens, A Life on Film*; Kevin Brownlow's *David Lean*; production notes in the *Hollywood Reporter* and *Variety*; files in the Margaret Herrick Library.

Stop Train 349: production files in the Margaret Herrick Library.

Television work: interviews with Hal Humphrey, including "José Ferrer—Television's Reluctant Ham."

Ship of Fools: Stanley Kramer's *A Mad, Mad, Mad World*; Donald Spoto's *Stanley Kramer, Filmmaker*; and "'Ship of Fools' Under Way with Kramer at the Helm."

Funny Thing . . . and thoughts on directing: "Ferrer: Unequaled in the Theater."

End of marriage: *Girl Singer*; *Late Life Jazz*; interviews with Monsita, Maria, and Rafael Ferrer; and assorted articles in the *New York Times* and *Los Angeles Herald-Examiner*.

Man of La Mancha: Interviews with Jana Robbins and Tim Jerome; audition tale from Rafael Ferrer, "Ferrer Takes Over Don Quixote Role."

CHAPTER 16: 1967–92: PAYING THE BILLS—THE MOVIES

Many of the production notes and files for the films were found at the Margaret Herrick Library.

In addition, these were useful resources:

Fedora: Gene D. Phillips's *Some Like It Wilder*; Ed Sikov's *On Sunset Boulevard*.

Enter Laughing: Carl Reiner's memoir, *I Remember Me*.

A Midsummer Night's Sex Comedy: Eric Lax's *Conversations with Woody Allen*; John Tibbetts's "An Interview with Woody Allen."

Ferrer's disappointment over the Lina Wertmuller/Sophia Loren film and the current state of his career can be found in Roderick Mann's "For Ferrer, Paying Bills is Just an Act."

For the making of *Blood Tide*: "'Red Tide': A Study in Filmmaking."

"Natural Enemies": interview with director Jeff Kanew.

CHAPTER 17: CASHING THE CHECKS—TELEVISION, 1967–92

As in the previous chapter, much of these production files and clippings can be found at the Margaret Herrick Library.

Lee Harcourt Montgomery and Richard Thomas spoke about their working relationship with Ferrer. Sean Young talked about Ferrer during the making of *Blood and Orchids*.

Useful articles include "Potsdam—A Rare Triumph," "Ustinov as Gideon," "Crawford will Play FBI Chief," "New York Actors Keep Busy with Moonlighting," and "Behind the Prison Walls in 'Gideon.'" Stuart Goodman was interviewed about Ferrer's experience on "Rope."

CHAPTER 18: FINAL BOWS, 1967–92

Ferrer's one-man shows: "José Ferrer Sets One-Man Show in SJ"; press releases; and "Night Club Reviews—José Ferrer."

White Pelicans: Barbara Delatiner's "New Lines, Old Trouper."

Experiences in new works: "José Ferrer a Friend to New Playwrights."

Ferrer's Coconut Grove experience: "Ferrer Stirring Things Up for Players State"; "An Actor's Tough New Role"; and "Playhouse to Launch Hispanic Production."

A Life in the Theater: Mary Campbell's "José Ferrer Still Working on How to Say 'Thank You.'"

Directing *The Best Man*: David Galligan's "'Best Man' José Ferrer."

Carmelina: Bernard Carragher's "The Musicals that Flopped—A Post-Mortem"; Dominic McHugh's *Alan Jay Lerner: A Lyricist's Letters*.

Ferrer's later-day pursuits, including art and writing: Johna Blinn's "Celebrity Cookbook."

Robert Lansing's reflections on José Ferrer and the Players Club: Howard Kissel's "Ferrer's Unflagging Energy."

José Ferrer tributes have been documented on various sites, including the Directors Guild of America's "Tribute to José Ferrer" and "Regent University Film Fest Honors Ferrer."

For information on Ferrer's final illness and death, there were various newspaper tributes in the *New York Times* and *Los Angeles Times*, as well as remembrances by Monsita, Maria, and Rafael Ferrer.

BIBLIOGRAPHY

Allyson, June. *June Allyson*. Putnam, 1982.

Aloma, Orlando. "Playhouse to Launch Hispanic Production." *Miami News*, November 9, 1984: 25.

Anderson, George. "José Ferrer a Friend to New Playwrights." *Pittsburgh Post-Gazette*, January 7, 1976.

Barranger, Milly. *Margaret Webster: A Life in the Theater*. University of Michigan Press, 2004.

Berman, Gary. *Perfect Fool*. BearManor Media, 2011.

Bishop, Jim. "Bowled Over by a Ballet." *Journal-American*, April 18, 1963.

Blinn, Johna. "Celebrity Cookbook." *Clarion-Ledger*, April 9, 1981.

Brownlow, Kevin. *David Lean*. St. Martin's Press, 1986.

Buck, Jerry. "Behind the Prison Walls in 'Gideon.'" *Los Angeles Herald Examiner*, April 27, 1980.

Buckley, Michael. "José Ferrer Remembered (1912–1992)." *Theater Week*, February 10, 1992.

Campbell, Mary. "José Ferrer Still Working on How to Say 'Thank You.'" *Poughkeepsie Journal*, June 18, 1978.

Carragher, Bernard. "The Musicals that Flopped—A Post-Mortem." *New York Times*, June 10, 1979.

Chicago Tribune. "New York Actors Keep Busy with Moonlighting." December 28, 1967.

Clooney, Rosemary. *Girl Singer: An Autobiography*. Doubleday, 1999.

Coe, Jonathan. *Jimmy Stewart: A Wonderful Life*. Arcade, 2003.

Crespy, David. *The Playwright's Producer*. Southern Illinois University Press, 2013.

Cronyn, Hume. *A Terrible Liar*. William Morrow and Company, 1991.

Day, Barry, ed. *The Noël Coward Reader*. Knopf, 2010.

Delatiner, Barbara. "New Lines, Old Trouper." *New York Times*, April 25, 1976.

Duberman, Martin. *Paul Robeson: A Biography*. Knopf, 1989.

Ferrer, José. "Cyrano and Others." *Films and Filming*, July 1962.

Ferrer, José. "Return to the Beehive." *New York Times*, November 1, 1953.

Frank, Stanley. "Broadway's New Matinee Idol." *Saturday Evening Post*, March 8, 1947.

Galligan, David. "'Best Man' José Ferrer." *Drama-Logue*, October 8, 1987.

Gansberg, Alan. *Little Caesar: A Biography of Edward G. Robinson*. Scarecrow Press, 2004.

Grant, Lee. "Crawford Will Play FBI Chief." *Los Angeles Times*, November 22, 1976.

Hagen, Uta. *Sources: A Memoir*. Performing Arts Journal, 1987.

Hale, Wanda. "Moulin Rouge Worth Four Oscars." *New York Daily News*, January 11, 1953.

Henderson, Florence. *Life is Not a Stage*. Center Street, 2011.

Hirsch, Foster. *Otto Preminger: The Man Who Would be King*. Knopf, 2007.

Hirschhorn, Clive. *The Universal Story*. Crown, 1987.

Hollinger, Hy. "Ferrer on France's Dreyfus Phobia." *Variety*, June 26, 1957.

Hopper, Hedda. "Silver Blonde—Golden Future." *Chicago Tribune*, 1958.

Hughes, Howard. *When Eagles Dared*. I. B. Tauris, 2012.

Humphrey, Hal. "José Ferrer—TV's Reluctant Ham." *Los Angeles Times*, August 11, 1963: D26.

Humphrey, Hal. "Son's Advice Led Ed Wynn to Success." *Sunday Bulletin*, February 1957.

Huston, John. *An Open Book*. Knopf, 1980.

Jimmy Stewart On the Air. June 18, 2015. www.jimmystewartiontheair.com (accessed March 17, 2018).

Kissel, Howard. "Ferrer's Unflagging Energy." *New York Daily News*, January 28, 1992.

Kobal, John. *Rita Hayworth: The Time, the Place, and the Woman*. Norton, 1978.

Koenig, Danny. *Danny Kaye—King of Jesters*. Bonaventure, 2011.

Kramer, Stanley. *A Mad, Mad, Mad World*. Harcourt, 1987.

Lax, Eric. *Bogart*. William Morrow and Company, 1997.

Lax, Eric. *Conversations with Woody Allen*. Knopf, 2007.

Lee, Christopher. *Lord of Mischief*. Orion, 2003.

Lee, Laura. "They're All Pals from Princeton." *Philadelphia Inquirer*, June 5, 1946.

Lerner, Alan Jay. *The Street Where I Live*. Norton, 1980.

Logan, Joshua. *Movie Stars, Real People and Me*. Delacorte Press, 1978.

Long, Robert Emmett, ed. *John Huston: Interviews* (Conversations with Filmmakers). University Press of Mississippi, 2001.

Lyons, Leonard. "The Actor." *Long Beach Independent*, October 27, 1955.

Mann, Roderick. "For Ferrer, Paying Bills Just an Act." *Los Angeles Times*, July 29, 1986.

Maurer, Bill von. "Ferrer Leaves Playhouse." *Miami News*, January 5, 1985: 13.

McFarlane, Malcolm. *Late Life Jazz: The Life and Career of Rosemary Clooney*. Oxford University Press, 2013.

McHugh, Dominic. *Alan Jay Lerner: A Lyricist's Letters*. Oxford Press, 2009.

McManus, Margaret. "Family Rosemary's Top Interest." *Post-Standard*, October 21, 1956.

Metlsir, Aljean. "The Happy Marriage of Rosemary Clooney and José Ferrer." *Coronet*, August 1961: 145–51.

Meyers, Jeffrey. *John Huston: Courage and Art*. Crown, 2011.

Mills, Nancy. "'Red Tide': A Study in Film Making." *Los Angeles Times*, August 17, 1980.

Millstein, Gilbert. "All the Stage is His World." *New York Times*, March 25, 1951.

Millstein, Gilbert. "Fabulous Joe Ferrer." *Collier's*, December 25, 1953.

Mosby, Aline. "The Great Man." *Star Journal*, February 7, 1957.

Mosby, Aline. "News Notes from Hollywood." *Times Standard*, August 17, 1954.

Moss, Marilyn. *Giant: George Stevens, A Life on Film*. University of Wisconsin Press, 2004.

Munn, Michael. *Trevor Howard*. Stein and Day, 1990.

New York Times. "José Ferrer Denies He is a Communist." May 22, 1951.

Newark Star-Ledger. "The Broadway Stage." December 7, 1941.

Newsweek. "José Ferrer Sings Out." July 25, 1960.

Nichols, Lewis. "Return of a Mellowed Enfant Terrible." *New York Times*, January 24, 1960.

O'Connor, John J. "Glenda Jackson in 'Strange Interlude.'" *New York Times*, January 18, 1988.

O'Connor, John J. "'Leo and Liz' and 'Bridges to Cross.'" *New York Times*, April 24, 1986.

Payn, Graham, ed. *The Noël Coward Diaries*. Little, Brown and Company, 1982.

Pett, Saul. "Ferrer Juggles Many Roles with Magnificent Calm." *Democrat and Chronicle*, May 4, 1952.

Petzold, Charles. "Ferrer Played, Jim Sang." *Courier-Post*, October 14, 1966.

Phillips, Gene D. *Some Like it Wilder: The Life and Controversial Films of Billy Wilder*. University Press of Kentucky, 2003.

Plummer, Christopher. *In Spite of Myself*. Knopf, 2008.

Pollock, Dale. "Tough José Ferrer Displays His Sharp Wit." *Santa Cruz Sentinel*, August 19, 1977: 17.

Pryor, Thomas. "Hollywood Canvas." *New York Times*, August 23, 1953.

Redelings, Lowell. "The Hollywood Scene." *Hollywood Citizen-News*, March 4, 1958.

Reilly, Bill O. "Palabras, Neighbors." *Puerto Rican Journal*, April 20, 1975.

Reiner, Carl. *I Remember Me*. AuthorHouse, 2013.

Reiner, Carl. Interview by Morrie Gelman. Television Academy Interviews, 1998.

Relyea, Robert E. *Not So Quiet on the Set*. iUniverse, 2008.

Rothman, Cliff. "The Resurrection of Lawrence of Arabia." *Los Angeles Times*, January 29, 1989.

Salmaggi, Bob. "Television is Great, But . . ." *New York Herald Tribune*, November 15, 1959.

Salzman, Eric. "Ferrer in Debut as Opera Singer." *Stage*, September 26, 1960.

Scheuer, Philip. "Caine Mutiny Filmmakers Relate How It's Done." *Los Angeles Times*, August 20, 1953.

Scheuer, Philip. "The Shrike, Altered as Film, Still Arrestingly Difficult." *Los Angeles Times*, September 2, 1955.

Scheuer, Philip. "'Ship of Fools' Under Way with Kramer at the Helm." *Los Angeles Times*, August 2, 1964.

Schumach, Murray. "Enter: O'Casey's Juno, Singing." *New York Times*, March 1, 1959.

Scott, John L. "Versatile Actor." *Los Angeles Times*, March 23, 1958.

Seaton, George. "Polyergic Performer Is Director's Delight." *New York Times*, November 30, 1952.

Shearer, Stephen Michael, and Jeanine Basinger. *Gloria Swanson: The Ultimate Star*. Thomas Dunne Books, 2013.

Sherman, Vincent. *Studio Affairs*. University Press of Kentucky, 1996.

Silverman, Stephen. *Dancing on the Ceiling: Stanley Donen and His Movies*. Knopf, 1996.

Smith, Cecil. "Ferrer: Unequaled in the Theater." *Los Angeles Times*, July 25, 1965.

Smith, Cecil. "Potsdam—A Rare Triumph." *Los Angeles Times*, January 10, 1976.

Spoto, Donald. *Stanley Kramer, Filmmaker*. Putnam, 1978.

Sragow, Michael. *Victor Fleming: American Movie Master*. Pantheon, 1998.

Steward, David. *Rage and Glory: The Volatile Life and Career of George C. Scott*. Applause Theatre and Cinema, 2003.

Stimson, Charles. "Booth Tragedy Uses Ferrer's Many Talents." *Los Angeles Times*, October 5, 1958.

Thomas, Bob. "Hollywood." *Santa Cruz Sentinel*, April 18, 1956.

Thornberg, Henry. "Daring Commando Aids Film of Exploits." *Long Beach Independent*, February 24, 1955.

Tibbett, John. "An Interview." *American Classic Screen*, September/October 1982.

Tineo, Mae. "José Ferrer's Interests are Varied." *Chicago Daily Tribune*, August 21, 1955.

Trussell, C. P. "José Ferrer Asks Reds be Outlawed." *New York Times*, May 23, 1952.

Variety. "Night Club Reviews—José Ferrer." May 15, 1968.

Vogel, Michelle. *Gene Tierney: A Biography*. McFarland, 2010.

Washington, Fredi. "Editorial." *People's Voice*, January 26, 1946.

Williams, Kathy. "José Ferrer—An Actor's Tough New Role." *Miami News*, October 21, 1983: 21.

Wolf, Matt. "Pity the Rhinos." *Chicago Tribune*, September 23, 1990.

Wynn, Keenan. *Ed Wynn's Son*. Doubleday, 1959.

Zisk, Jack. "Ferrer Stirring Things Up for Players State." *Fort Lauderdale News*, October 31, 1982: 113.

INDEX

ABOUT THE AUTHOR

Mike Peros is the English Department Chair at Bishop Loughlin High School. He is the author of *Dan Duryea: Heel with a Heart,* published by University Press of Mississippi. Mike also reviews films for NoHoartsdistrict.com.